AP U.S. History For D

MW00989350

Covering Your Bases on the Essays

Two types of essay questions appear on the AP: Document-Based Questions (DBQs) and regular essays. Keep these lists on hand to remind you how to tackle them both with finesse.

At the beginning of the exam's essay portion, you get 15 minutes to read the questions and documents and plan your essay. Devote this time to planning your DBQ — the regular essays can wait. When the writing portion begins, try to spend about 45 minutes on the DBQ. For the **DBQ**, follow this process (see Chapter 5 for more info):

1. **Read the question _twice_ and circle key words** (time period, location, event, and so on — basically, whatever the question is specifically asking you to address).

2. **Take a mental inventory of what you know about the question, and jot down every related event and theme you can think of off the top of your head.**

3. **Circle words or ideas within the documents that you may want to refer to in your essay.**

4. **Analyze the proof.** What are some points you want to make about the question, and how does the information you have support these points? Jot quick notes in the question book.

5. **Develop a _thesis_, a general statement of the philosophy and main arguments of your essay.**

6. **Outline your essay in the question book.**

7. **After the 15 minutes of planning time is over, write the essay (finally!).** Arrange your essay by analysis points. In each body paragraph, try to use three pieces of proof taken from a mix of outside information and document analysis.

8. **Underline the main points and key terms in your DBQ essay.**

Remember: Use the pink essay-writing booklet _only_ for your essays; make notes in the green question book!

If you spend 45 minutes on your DBQ, you'll have 70 minutes total to devote to your regular essays. The AP recommends that you spend 5 minutes planning and 30 minutes writing each regular essay — try to stay within those times as much as you can. For the **regular essays** (see Chapter 6), follow this process:

1. **Choose the question you know the most about.**

2. **As with the DBQ, read twice, make notes, circle key words, and outline before you write.** Make a list of the political, economic, and social topics you remember from this era.

3. **Compose your thesis and outline your essay.** Take a clear stand that you can easily and reasonably support with analysis and proof. Stick to a five-paragraph

format for the essay: The first paragraph introduces your thesis, the three body paragraphs detail your three main points, and the last paragraph reinforces and amplifies the thesis.

4. **Write your essay.** Begin your essay directly with the thesis sentence, capitalize your key terms, and underline your main points; these measures will help your grader quickly navigate your essay. Use generalities — don't guess incorrectly about a specific name or date.

Highlights of Early American History: Before the U.S. Came to Be

This list helps you keep straight some potentially confusing facts about early America.

- **Early Empires:** _Mesoamerica_ is a history term for "middle of the New World." Early American Indian empires included the Aztec (around 1300) in Mexico, the Maya (from 800) in Central America, and the Inca (1400) in South America, their first letters from north to south spell _AMI_. Spanish _Conquistadores_ conquered these empires; the _encomienda_ system enslaved them.

- **North American Colonies:** First permanent English colony was Jamestown (1607) in Virginia. New England got started under the Mayflower Compact (1620). White indentured servants worked early tobacco plantations in Maryland (1634). The Dutch established New Amsterdam (1623); the English took it over and renamed it New York in 1664. William Penn started tolerant Pennsylvania in 1681. The Dominion of New England (1686) was a royal attempt to dominate the colonies.

(continued)

AP U.S. History For Dummies®

Highlights of Early American History: Before the U.S. Came to Be (continued)

- **Early rebellions:** Pope's rebellion against the Spanish in New Mexico (1680); King Philip's War in New England (1675); Bacon's Rebellion in Virginia (1675); New York Slave Rebellion (1712); Pontiac's Rebellion (1763).

- **Colonial History:** The First Great Awakening (1734) brought new social connections and more emotion to religion. Peter Zenger (1734) won a case for freedom of the press. Population in 1750 was French Canada 60,000 settlers, English North America 1.25 million. The English won the French and Indian War (1755), and they got Canada.

A Quick Trip through U.S. History

The following list gives you a quick overview of the main attractions from each period of U.S. history. Refer to this list often while studying, especially when you need to brush up on the U.S. history facts covered in the AP.

- **Run up to Revolution:** Navigation Act (1660); Stamp Act (1765); Boston Massacre (1770); Boston Tea Party (1773); Intolerable Acts (1774); Continental Congress (1774); Concord and Lexington (1775); Declaration of Independence (1776).

- **Revolution:** Influenced by the Enlightenment (1760); Battle of Saratoga (1777) allows French to enter the war; Valley Forge (1778); Charleston defeat (1780); Yorktown victory (1781); Treaty of Paris (1783).

- **Early U.S.:** Republican motherhood (1780) raises patriots; Articles of Confederation (1777); Shay's Rebellion (1786); Northwest Ordinance (1787); Constitutional Convention (1787); Federalists (1788); Bill of Rights (1791); Alien and Sedition Acts (1798); Thomas Jefferson (1801); Louisiana Purchase (1803); Era of Good Feelings (1820).

- **U.S. grows:** John Marshall Supreme Court (1803–1835); *Marbury v. Madison* (1803), Supreme Court review; *McCulloch v. Maryland* (1819), implied powers; *Gibbons v. Ogden* (1824), interstate commerce; *Missouri Compromise* (1820) establishes Mason-Dixon line; Erie Canal (1825); Andrew Jackson's democracy (1828); Second Great Awakening (1830).

- **Pre-Civil War:** Frederick Douglass (1845); Texas joins U.S. (1845); Mexican War (1846); Seneca Falls women's convention (1848); railroads spread out (1850); cult of domesticity (1850); *Compromise of 1850,* Fugitive Slave Law; *Uncle Tom's Cabin* (1852); Kansas-Nebraska Act (1854); Dred Scott (1857); John Brown (1859).

- **Civil War:** Lincoln elected (1860); firing on Fort Sumter (1861); South wins Peninsula Campaign and Second Bull Run (1862); North wins Antietam (1862); Emancipation Proclamation (1863); South wins Fredericksburg (1862) and Chancellorsville (1863); North wins Gettysburg (1863); North wins Vicksburg (1863) and Sherman's March to the Sea (1864); North wins war, Lincoln assassinated (1865).

- **Late 1800s:** Reconstruction (1870); important amendments — Thirteen, no more slavery; Fourteen, citizenship; and Fifteen, universal male voting (1869); Transcontinental Railroad (1869); Labor unions organize (1872); telephone (1876); Hayes-Tilden Compromise (1877); electric light (1879); *The Adventures of Huckleberry Finn* (1884); Jim Crow Laws (1890); *Plessy v. Ferguson*, separate but equal (1896); Spanish-American War (1898).

- **Early 1900s:** Teddy Roosevelt (1904); muckrakers (1905); Progressives (1910); Federal Reserve Act (1913); Federal Trade Commission (1914); U.S. in World War I (1917); Wilson's 14 Points (1918); votes for women with Nineteenth Amendment (1920).

- **Depression and World War II:** Prohibition begins: Eighteenth Amendment (1919), ends: Twenty-first Amendment (1933); Roaring '20s; Scopes monkey trial (1925); Stock crash (1929); FDR's New Deal (1933); growth of unions (1938); Pearl Harbor (1941); Lend-Lease (1941); Midway and North Africa (1942); Italy (1943); D-Day (1944); Victory (1945).

- **Postwar:** GI Bill (1944); United Nations (1945); Marshall Plan (1947); NATO (1949); Korean War (1952); *Brown v. Board of Education* (1954); Martin Luther King Jr. (1960); Cuban Missile Crisis (1962); Vietnam War (1968); Environmental Protection Agency (1970); Reagan and neoconservatives (1985); end of Cold War (1989); European Union (1993); World Trade Organization (1994); War on Terror (2001); Internet economy (2002).

AP U.S. History

FOR

DUMMIES®

by Greg Velm

WILEY

Wiley Publishing, Inc.

AP U.S. History For Dummies®

Published by
Wiley Publishing, Inc.
111 River St.
Hoboken, NJ 07030-5774
www.wiley.com

Copyright © 2008 by Wiley Publishing, Inc., Indianapolis, Indiana

Published simultaneously in Canada

For general information on our other products and services, please contact our Customer Care Department within the U.S. at 800-762-2974, outside the U.S. at 317-572-3993, or fax 317-572-4002.

For technical support, please visit www.wiley.com/techsupport.

Wiley also publishes its books in a variety of electronic formats. Some content that appears in print may not be available in electronic books.

Library of Congress Control Number: 2008925785

ISBN: 978-0-470-24758-7

Manufactured in the United States of America

10 9 8 7 6 5 4 3 2 1

WILEY

About the Author

Greg Velm has been teaching college and graduate-school students for more than 25 years. Greg is the Chair of the History Commission in Sacramento and is the author of the rip-roaring book *True Gold: History and Adventure in the Gold Country from Indians to Arnold.* American Indians were around for thousands of years before Arnold Schwarzenegger made all of California his movie set, but Greg has studied just about every minute of history from there to here. If the dinosaurs had written books, Greg would probably read them.

By the time he got through his own graduate education at the University of California, Berkeley, Greg had puzzled through thousands of pretty fiendish multiple-choice questions and written miles of essays. As he struggled to survive the Exam Inquisitors, he usually reflected on two lofty thoughts: "Why didn't I study more?" and "How can I psych up enough to survive this test?" Therefore, with his own students, he emphasizes test-taking skills as well as history smarts. If you want to become rich and famous, it helps to pass the tests.

Greg thinks that history is an exciting adventure, so in addition to appearances on television and radio, he's an in-demand speaker. He's been in the *New York Times, Time, Youth,* and *Via Magazine.* Greg has lectured at Berkeley, the University of San Francisco, and St. Mary's College. Because he wants human history to have a future, Greg serves on the boards of two environmental organizations.

Greg lives with his beloved wife near the American River in northern California. He tries to make sure that his three grown sons have good jobs so that maybe someday they'll send money home. When he's not living in the past, Greg rides mountain bikes through the Sierra foothills and tries to outsurvive other old dudes in the shortest triathlons he can find.

Dedication

To my mother, Miriam Berry, for teaching me that I was worthy of an exciting life. To my father, Don Velm, for showing me the glowing spirit that shines throughout history.

Author's Acknowledgments

Nobody ever writes a book by himself; his work is held up by the dedication of great people who came before him. Historians who have made the past an enlightening adventure include Will and Ariel Durant, Allan Eckert, Kevin Starr, Winston Churchill, H. W. Brands, Howard Zinn, Robert Bucholz, David Kennedy, Lizabeth Cohen, Eric Foner, Barbara Tuchman, and Alton Pryor.

I get by with a little help from my friends and fellow thinkers Mike Tucker, George Rosenfeld, Albert Lowey-Ball, Bob Greeley, P. K. Agarwal, Kendall Meredith, Terry Taylor, Mary Ann McDonnell, John Azzaro, Irick Collins, Bodhi Garrett, Katherine Blank, Eric Warp, Stuart Bair, Craig Lovell, Dan Egerter, Rick Kraus, Noel Neuburger, Erich Ryll, and Terry and Mo Burton. Thanks to my dear wife Jeanette for encouraging me in my journeys into the past.

Nothing is as modern as history — it tracks the progress of all the other specialties and is constantly reinventing itself when new research and understanding offer a clearer view of the past. Never, from the ancient Library at Alexandria to the ivy towers of Oxford and Berkeley, has collaborative scholarship been so alive as it is right now with the growth of information on the World Wide Web. Thanks to the dedicated teachers who create beautiful history sites and to the thousands of anonymous contributors to the 2,000,000 articles that make up the ever-expanding and improving world of Wikipedia.

Thanks to Ken Umbach and to Matt Wagner of Fresh Books for helping guide me to this book and to my editors at Wiley: Natalie Harris, Stacy Kennedy, Megan Knoll, and Kathy Simpson.

Publisher's Acknowledgments

We're proud of this book; please send us your comments through our Dummies online registration form located at www.dummies.com/register/.

Some of the people who helped bring this book to market include the following:

Acquisitions, Editorial, and Media Development

Project Editors: Natalie Faye Harris, Kristin DeMint

Acquisitions Editor: Stacy Kennedy

Copy Editors: Megan Knoll, Kathy Simpson

Editorial Program Coordinator: Erin Calligan Mooney

Technical Editor: Steven Collier

Editorial Manager: Christine Meloy Beck

Editorial Assistants: Joe Niesen, David Lutton, Jennette ElNaggar

Cover Photo: © Eric Meola

Cartoons: Rich Tennant (www.the5thwave.com)

Composition Services

Project Coordinator: Katherine Key

Layout and Graphics: Carl Byers, Alissa D. Ellet, Laura Pence

Proofreaders: Caitie Kelly, Betty Kish

Indexer: Sherry Massey

Publishing and Editorial for Consumer Dummies

Diane Graves Steele, Vice President and Publisher, Consumer Dummies

Joyce Pepple, Acquisitions Director, Consumer Dummies

Kristin A. Cocks, Product Development Director, Consumer Dummies

Michael Spring, Vice President and Publisher, Travel

Kelly Regan, Editorial Director, Travel

Publishing for Technology Dummies

Andy Cummings, Vice President and Publisher, Dummies Technology/General User

Composition Services

Gerry Fahey, Vice President of Production Services

Debbie Stailey, Director of Composition Services

Contents at a Glance

Table of Contents

Introduction

On behalf of all the scholars who can see that history is a wonderful adventure, welcome to the world. School's out, and it's time to have some fun getting credit for what you know. While you're in the game, you can make sure you've got the right stuff to make it through the AP U.S. History exam. *AP U.S. History For Dummies* contains all the information you need to know to tackle the AP exam head-on and emerge triumphant.

Millions have made it through the AP U.S. History examination before; it's the most widely taken single-subject test in the Advanced Placement world. If you're holding this book with slightly shaky hands because you're not sure you know enough to get a good score on the Big AP, you've come to the right place. On the other hand, if you race through the past so quickly that you feel like you already know most of the important stuff, this is a good time to test your knowledge. If you hated history and had to slap yourself awake through every dull lecture, now is the time to see the past come alive.

Please accept the apologies of all good adventure historians for any harm that instructors who parade historic humans as if they were plaster saints have done you. You didn't deserve to be crammed full of names, dates, and places without being shown the rainbow bridge of history that makes what happened before you were born important to everything you are today. Remember, no one ever lived in the past. Everybody you read about in history was struggling in their present, just like you, with no idea how it would turn out. The decisions they made, whether trying to do the right thing or swept away by emotion, form the world in which all Americans will live until they too can change their little bit of history for the sake of their children and their children's kids.

The history of the United States IS important. The U.S. and the New World arrived on the global scene like sunshine through the clouds. The late 1700s saw an almost-religious belief in the power of human progress and reason. That belief was called Enlightenment. The founding of the United States became Enlightenment in action. The U.S. is far from perfect, and its growth has included the subjugation of Africans, American Indians, and other minorities. Without ducking that reality, the United States has also been a meeting place for people and ideas from all over the world — the most diverse and unified society that history has ever produced.

The human beings who make up the United States have been brave and sometimes selfish but are usually welcoming of newcomers and eager to share their ideals of freedom with the world. You read a lot about Manifest Destiny and American Exceptionalism in history, as if the U.S. had some sort of cosmic advantage. The United States doesn't have to be exceptional or manifest to be beautiful; in a way, it's better for being the product of human possibility. The story of the U.S. is a great example of people from all nations working together to promote tolerance and real democracy. The fate of the United States is very probably a window unto the future of the world. When the Enlightenment came to the New World, it was just an idea; now it's a nation.

About This Book

I've designed *AP U.S. History For Dummies* so that you know the particulars of the exam itself thanks to the first sections, have access to the important points of U.S. History in the middle sections, and have a good practice run thanks to the practice exams in a later section.

Like the Internet, the book is also set up so you can hit it and quit it. You can bounce around between practice tests (Part V) and exam strategies (Part II) or just spend a few moments mentally downloading a little knowledge about a specific time in the United States' past, like Jacksonian Democracy (Part III). The words in italics — like *Erie Canal* (1817) — are especially likely to show up on the Big AP test. You also want to pay attention to the review questions scattered throughout the history sections.

Sometimes you may like to just skim through the pages to pick up the Tips and Warnings. That's fine as far as it goes, but be advised: To really understand the game, you've got to watch the whole field, not just the play action. Read the sections around the Tips to see why the Tips are important.

Conventions Used in This Book

In this book, I used the following conventions:

- ✔ Where I mention a Web site, I use monofont to indicate the address.
- ✔ **Bold** text highlights key words in bulleted lists and the action parts of numbered steps.
- ✔ Important words are set in *italics* and followed closely by a definition.
- ✔ In the history sections, important names, events, and concepts also appear in *italics,* followed by a key date in parentheses. This date isn't the only important date for that topic; it's just a key year associated with the name and a quick reference to help you keep concepts in order. The AP U.S. History exam is too hip to ask you to remember a lot of dates, but you do need to know the general order of events and trends.

What You're Not to Read

If you're pressed for time and need to read through this book in a hurry, feel free to skip over the sidebars. They contain interesting information, but nothing you absolutely need to know in order to pass the test.

Foolish Assumptions

Because you've picked up this particular book, I assume certain things about you:

- ✔ You plan to take the AP U.S. History exam soon, and you want to be prepared.
- ✔ You want a good idea of exactly what's on the AP U.S. History test, particularly how the test is set up and just how much writing you'll need to do.
- ✔ You're a busy person who has no time for useless information or explanations.

✔ You've already read a lot of high-quality U.S. History in your classes, and you've done some essay-writing on the subject.

✔ You have a reasonable grasp of U.S. History but need a convenient refresher.

How This Book Is Organized

If you dropped by the Table of Contents on your way to this Introduction, you may have noticed that *AP U.S. History For Dummies* is divided into six nutritious dishes. You can consume these parts in any order you want, save some for later, or share them with a friend. Here's what you've got to help you through the big exam:

Part 1: College Credit, Here I Come!

In this section, you meet the powerful secret society that controls your Advanced Placement test destiny, the College Board. With the information you gain here, you can decide whether Advanced Placement is just another Establishment buzzkill or whether the whole process may somehow be for your own good. You discover how to use the PES dispenser tactic (political, economic, and social history) to pop your way through the big exam. What kind of score can you get on the Big AP test, and what's that going to mean for your college education? Part I is where you find out.

The College Board actually influences the way AP history is taught. This part tells you what the CB told your teacher and fills in any blanks that your dear instructor may have neglected. As you prepare, you want to keep your mind in mind. You can soak up some tips for psyching yourself up so you can prepare better and more quickly and pick up some mental test taking tools.

Part II: Answering the Questions: Three Kinds, Three Strategies

Multiple-Choice, Document-Based Question, and Regular Essay — they all show up at the AP Inquest. This part of the book shows you the right approach (actually, several alternate keys) to each of the question types. Each kind of question gets its own chapter; you can pick up a specialist technique for each situation, just like a rock climber approaches each face with a different look.

For multiple-choice, you discover how to maximize your chances for a hit when you're not sure of the right answer and how to avoid the Question Troll of losing points for wrong guesses. Using a little knowledge to pry apart the five choices can increase your odds. Almost nobody gets all the multiple choice questions right; you just want to nail timing and answer management to score as high as you can in the minutes you've got.

The Document-Based Question on every AP U.S. History test introduces a dilemma for many exam pilgrims. For once, the test is actually giving you some of the much-desired answer right before your eyes. You could, like, just write the essay on how cool all those eight to ten original pictures and documents really are. That's a mistake. Chapter 5 shows you how to handle documents like a professor, combining their meaning with outside knowledge in the proof, analysis, and thesis (PAT) method.

In Chapter 6, you figure out how to write essays that teachers feel good about praising in the short time they have to evaluate your hard-earned creativity. Discovering how to list your evidence and plan your thesis are two of the keys to writing clear, fast, and grader-friendly essays.

Part III: Early U.S. History: From Dinosaurs to the Civil War

As you move into actual history, you start with the most test-worthy parts of the 95 percent of the human past in North America from which few written records still exist. As you cruise through the history sections in Parts III and IV, you want to pay special attention to the words that show up in italics with a date like *Christopher Columbus* (1492). The Big AP seldom questions you on exact dates, but you need to keep the people, trends, and events in the right general chronological order so that you can keep the development of history straight. The date in parentheses helps you associate a time with each fact.

American Indians lived in the New World — including the area that would become the U.S. — for thousands of years; settlers have only been here for a few hundred. The colonies had a rocky beginning but soon developed a personality of their own that included good-to-know political, economic, and social differences. Because about 20 percent of the questions on the test will deal with the time before the Revolution, you need to jump on board before you get to George Washington.

The American Revolution was a watershed event in the history of the world and also the formal beginning of the United States. The new country faced rebellion, political repression, and the threat of foreign attack, and that was all before it was 20 years old. Having survived to be a strong young adult, the U.S. grew and matured but with a terrible problem at home: slavery. The solution began with brothers shooting each other in the Civil War. About 30 percent of the Big AP will cover the period between the Revolution and the Civil War, which this part covers.

Part IV: U.S. History from After the Civil War to the Days of the Internet

In this last half of U.S. history (to the present day, of course), you get a grasp on the facts that form a core part of 50 percent of your score on the AP Showdown. Reconstruction started with an impeachment hearing in the North and ended with a political deal in the South; you want to understand the background. Social and economic trends became increasingly important as ex-slaves, working people, and women fought for equal rights. As the 1800s drew to a close, the U.S. stepped on to the world stage with old Rebels and Yankees fighting on the same side in the Spanish-American War.

Teddy Roosevelt's Big Stick whacked the way toward the Progressive Era. You can come to terms with how the pace of reform ebbed and flowed through the 1900s. America's first European war, also known as World War I, was followed by the Great Depression and then World War II. As that war ended, the U.S. was front and center as a world leader — no more hiding behind the great oceans. This Part also covers the background of the Cold War and the beginning of the policy issues that still face the United States. Social and economic changes continued to roll as the U.S. sailed into the 2000s.

Part V: Practice Makes Perfect: Two Tests Plus the Answers

This is the part where you can test your skills. Either you take the tests first to find out what you need to study *or* you study first, take the tests, and then study some more on the parts where you need help.

These *For Dummies* practice tests are beyond realistic. The real test will be a confusing jumble of dates and question styles. Fortunately, you have to go though the actual AP only once. To allow you to reinforce the sections in your test armor that are a little thin, I've arranged the practice tests mostly in chronological order. That allows you to pick out any eras or topics in which you seem to need help. You'll see a few out-of-chronological-order questions just to let you know what the real test will feel like.

Part VI: The Part of Tens

In the final part of your *For Dummies* AP U.S. History tune-up, you get to experience fun with a purpose. First you review ten monster events AP wants you to know. In the monster events category: colony set-up, working colonies, Revolution, Confederation becomes Constitution, prequel to Civil War, Jacksonian democracy, the Civil War goes down, U.S. grows to big dog, the country adjusts to world power, and, finally, the evolution of government support. This list allows you to review your foundation of understanding and pick up a few fun facts.

The next top-ten list on the menu is ten trends that never go away. Read and remember as you review U.S. diversity, American identity, culture, demographics, economics, women, minorities, reform, internationalism, and spirituality.

The Supreme Court is the important third branch of the U.S. government, and its decisions both determine and reflect social trends. The final list follows the top ten hits of the Supreme Court as it has handed down decisions over the years.

Icons Used in This Book

AP U.S. History For Dummies contains several icons that alert you to interesting or important points. Here are descriptions of each type:

The Tip icon leads the way to some smart moves to improve your score and nail down important history happenings.

You want to avoid common stumbling blocks by reviewing the Warnings before they get you.

This icon points out information that may not seem vital but is important to keep in mind while reviewing your test material.

Although every AP test is different, these questions represent popular topics for College Board Test Masters. The questions appear in the Part II and Part III chapters, and I give you only the correct answers for them to help you with your studying. Don't worry — there are plenty of full-blown multiple choice questions for you in Chapters 22 and 24!

This icon points out interesting but unessential information. If you aren't really a history head, you can skip these paragraphs, but trivia buffs will eat them up.

Where to Go from Here

At some point, you have to stop adjusting your equipment and just jump into the adventure. Here are three basic approaches; you can mix and match in any way that makes sense to you. When test day comes, it's going to be all about *you*, what's in *your* head, and what *you* can do with it. So make your *For Dummies* equipment work for *your* style of studying — just get moving now.

The old front-to-back approach actually has a lot to recommend it. By starting at the beginning, you have the test elements and exam-taking strategy in mind when you read the history section. This method can be useful in putting the history happenings into possible questions as you read. The reason you bought this book was presumably to get insider info on answering AP exam questions, not just to review history.

The middle, front, back strategy lets you start with the history and gain some context and confidence before you plunge into the cross fire of possible exam questions and strategy. Plus, if for some unknown reason you don't actually have time for the strategy or practice sections, you've at least read the history and sample questions. **Warning:** If you don't have experience with Document-Based Questions (DBQ's), at least read Chapter 5 on this topic. Students who try to answer a DBQ for the first time on the big exam are speeding without a steering wheel.

If you're the kind of person who jumps into the lake to see how cold the water is and then decides which way to swim, you may just want to jump right into the practice tests and see how you do. **Warning:** Unless you ace both tests, don't get overconfident — each test covers only half of U.S. History. Be honest with yourself: don't peek at the answers. The real AP exam isn't a crossword puzzle.

Good luck, and may your placement be advanced.

Part I
College Credit, Here I Come!

The 5th Wave   By Rich Tennant

"I practiced for the AP U.S. History exam all day yesterday, so I'm as ready as Alexander Hamilton giving the Gettysburg Address at the Alamo."

In this part...

Part I is designed to put a determined smile on your face when you open that exam book and pick up your pencil. Before you play a game, you've got to check out the rules, so in this part, you scope out the Grand Inquisitor itself, the College Board. This fine institution may influence your college fate; here's where you discover how it works. Before you get into the kinds of questions you'll encounter on the AP U.S. History exam, Part I gives you the lowdown on who creates the questions and how college admissions personnel use the test results. You also get a handle on the *PES* secret to test success: political, economic, and social information.

To get the highest score you can, you need to understand the kind of answers the AP U.S. History exam likes to see. When you have an overview of the test territory you'll be navigating, take a deep breath and use a little psychology to make your studying (and test-taking) as effective as possible.

Chapter 1

Acing the Test for a College Credit Payday

In This Chapter

▶ Checking out the College Board

▶ Putting together a game plan for success

▶ Decoding your score (and what it can do for you)

U.S. History may be a grand pageant of determination and growth, but chances are good that right now you just want to make sure you score some college credit for that long year you spent busting your butt in AP History. You're not alone; some 350,000 AP students have this same U.S. History exam looming over them right now.

Of all the AP exams, U.S. History is the most often taken Advanced Placement test in the entire fiendish College Board repertoire. You could call it the most popular, if popular is the right word for a national test that makes you sweat for three hours to try to earn college credit for something you've already been tested on too many times in high school. It's tough, but if you don't pass the AP, you don't get paid that college credit. This book is designed to give you the tools you need to ace the AP U.S. History exam. In this chapter, I give you an overview of the test and what to expect so you can prepare yourself for what lies ahead.

School Learning versus Test Prep

This book isn't just about U.S. History, fun as that is. This book is about the Ultimate U.S. History Test and how you're going to score well on that test. As you read, you're going to be practicing Challenge Question and PES responses until they become second nature.

The difference between school and Challenge Question test prep is simple: In test prep, you turn a fact into a question and then answer the question the whole time you're reading history. Mixing in questions with history is what the Challenge Question technique is all about. Your history review in Parts III and IV will be full of questions, but you'll go even farther if you get into the habit of asking and answering questions on your own. And, this *AP U.S. History For Dummies* guide works even better when you combine it with your school AP text. You can pick up some more tips on using outside books in Chapter 2.

The Power of the College Board: What It Is and What It Does

So just who is this College Board, and why does it have such control over your future? Ever notice how the power structure (also known as the Man) seems to be all connected? The College Board (which I'll call CB) is the connection between your present (high school) and your future (college). The CB is a well-meaning, not-for-profit membership association whose official mission is to "connect students to college success and opportunity." Okay so far, but like all connections, it only works if you reach out and grab it.

Founded in 1900, the CB consists of thousands of schools, colleges, universities, and other educational organizations. Each year, the College Board works with some 7 million students and their parents, 23,000 high schools, and 3,500 colleges in college admissions, guidance, assessment, financial aid, and enrollment. Among its best-known and feared tests are the SAT, the PSAT/NMSQT, and your current favorite, the Advanced Placement program (AP). All of these tests are registered trademarks of the College Board; when it comes to using tests for college placement, the CB is the Man. This can be a good thing.

With what it garners from grading all those tests, the CB gives schools feedback to improve teaching. You may not like the power that CB tests hold over your future, but without them, colleges could just pick the people who are richest or tallest or cutest or something. College Board tests give you the chance to prove what you can do; the AP U.S. History test pays you for what you know with college credit.

Counting the Currency of College Credit

Getting college credit through the AP exam is like finding a rich uncle you didn't know you had. Thousands of universities and colleges in the United States and many other countries are standing by to offer you college credit for the AP U.S. History work you've done in high school. All you have to do is get at least a *3* on the AP U.S. History Exam. (See the section "Score! What does it mean?" later in the chapter.)

When it comes to actually granting college credit, your future university holds all the cards. Neither your high school nor even the benevolent College Board can grant you credit; that has to come from your future school. Be very careful to see your prospective alma mater's policy on awarding credit for high school AP work in print before you enlist in its intellectual army. Either get the written policy from the school or go to collegesearch.college board.com/apcreditpolicy/index.jsp to download it from the College Board site. More about college policy on AP credit is in Chapter 2.

You'll be happy to know that the College Board is concerned with your bank account as well as your brains. Its recent study of college costs shows that a year at a public or state university costs an average of almost $13,000 in tuition, fees, room, and board (and that's just for in-state students). Add some books, pizzas, transportation, phone, toothpaste, and occasional fun — before you know it, your inexpensive public education is running $20,000 a year.

If you're planning to seek knowledge within the ivy-covered walls of a private college, get ready for an even bigger sticker shock: Average costs are more than $30,000 for basic tuition, fees, room, and board. By the time you count all those extras, a private college education can easily run $40,000 a year.

Working now and playing later

What if Mom and Dad are paying? In that happy circumstance, do you even care about costs? Yes, you do (or at least should). You'll probably be racking up some student loans during those long years that, unlike the ten bucks you once borrowed from Uncle Milt, the college loan sharks will definitely make you pay back with interest. Also, you probably won't be making much money while you're going to school. The average college graduate earns almost $14,000 more per year than folks her age who don't send their brains for a higher-education tune-up. You want to get to the big money as soon as possible.

If you score high enough on the AP exam to earn six juicy college credits for AP U.S. History, you can subtract that from the time you'll have to spend in college classes. (See "Score! What does it mean?" later in this chapter

for more information.) Or you can use the extra time to study sand castle architecture in Hawaii. Pass enough AP exams and you can save half a year or more of undergraduate tuition-paying time — what you do with that time is up to you.

But if you skate past the Intro to U.S. History course in college, will you be able to keep up with the poor suckers who had to take the sit-down version of Intro in college? Yes. The always-researching College Board found that students who tested out of introductory courses actually did better in upper-division subjects than the people who took the intro classes. This number includes AP students who just squeaked by with a *3* on the AP exam. So it's worth some effort to earn a Get-Out-of-Intro-Jail-Free card.

But, you hope, you'll be paying that for only four years before you earn your prestigious diploma, right? Not so fast. The average public university student takes 6.2 years to earn a degree; the average private school undergraduate clocks in at 5.3 years. (See the sidebar "Working now and playing later" for info on how AP tests can help you shave time off that period.) The total average college expense is $124,000 for a public university and $212,000 for a private college. Maybe you should just skip college and use the money for a luxury car to impress people during your long fast-food career.

Putting Together Your AP Game Plan

A little concerned about what you know (or don't know) about U.S. history? Don't worry. If I didn't start you at the beginning and work you gently to the end, this wouldn't be a *For Dummies* guide. Although I can't promise to turn you into a Pulitzer-prize winning history guru overnight, you don't need that anyway. You just need a decent score on the AP U.S. History exam.

Taking in the test basics

To help make that happen, I start you out in Part I with some inside tips on how to maximize your score when the big test day is finally upon you.

In Part II, you get tuned up with a few sample questions before you dive into the actual U.S. history in Parts III and IV. That way, you can be thinking about how to extract potential questions from the condensed history in the middle sections of this book.

Moving on to actual history

In Parts III and IV, I give you the basics of U.S. history from American Indians to the Internet. This review covers key topics the Test Inquisitors like to keep in their secret libraries to surprise and shock you. College Board tests aren't actually written by mad professors in a castle torture lab but by nice, tweedy historians who just want to be sure you know some true stories. The College Board U.S. History Development Committee has standards, and before you get to exam day, it's in your best interest to know about them.

Think like the test writers to survive their clever question schemes. They're not going to feel right asking you something obscure (like the color of Abe Lincoln's dog), but they'd feel really smug by tripping you up with something like "Who issued the Monroe Doctrine?" (Hint: It wasn't Marilyn Monroe.) The Grand Inquisitors are going to ask about concepts they consider key to American history — the important issues highlighted in your school text (but not literally highlighted — it's only a rental, you know). When you see a highlighted topic, make up questions about it while you're reading. These are *Challenge Questions,* and when you make them up, you're thinking like the test writers do.

Testing, testing, 1-2-3!

In Part V, I show you the AP test. No, not the very test you'll see on the big day. If I did that, the only teaching I'd be doing would be in the prison cafeteria. You'll get as close as I can honestly take you to the test you're going to conquer. I give you two sample tests with questions that have appeared before and will eventually appear again on the AP. After you take the practice tests, I go over the answers with you, including some warning about places you could go wrong. By the time you're done, you'll be in U.S. History shape, ready to run, dodge, and score with the best of them.

The Political, Economic, and Social (PES) Answer Secret

What I, the test makers, and hopefully you have come to appreciate is that history isn't just facts; the meaning behind those facts is just as important. These meanings are *trends* or *themes.* When you've got the themes, you have a framework on which to remember the facts. Plus, the AP is really big on themes. The main themes are PES: political events and decisions, economic realities and incentives, and social trends and conditions. Connect these themes, and you'll connect to success on exam day.

Don't make exam essays all about you. Just because graders recognize social trends and economics as an important part of history doesn't mean you'll get a good grade for an emotional reaction to the Compromise of 1850. History is still about what happened, not your feelings about it. Save that for drama class.

Applying politics

The old school of white-men-go-to-meetings-and-fight-battles history that your parents had to learn began to open up when a new generation of historians noticed that the past has always been influenced by the beliefs and actions of ordinary people, not just by leaders. Now people also concentrate on economic and social factors when they study history. Political events do serve as landmarks in history, so it's still important to have a general chronological sense of these landmarks.

In this context, *political events* include presidents and other important leaders, laws, legal decisions of the Supreme Court, civil conflicts, international relations, and wars. As you're studying your way through U.S. History, ask yourself:

- ✔ How did the government react to events?
- ✔ How and when did the leadership change?
- ✔ How were U.S. relationships with foreign governments affected?

You need to be armed with a reasonable idea of events and people in Congress and the Supreme Court. I give you a list of the ten most important Supreme Court decisions in Chapter 27.

Understanding the impact of economy

So, if big-dog leaders weren't the historical be-all and end-all, what did shape the past? Ever go to work even when you didn't want to, just to make money? Ever run after a sale to save some bucks or pass up something you wanted because it cost too much? Thinking about economics helps explain human behavior.

Economics led to the settlement of most of the United States. The settlers didn't move inland from the Atlantic coast just so they could watch the birdies in the country. They needed rich land to farm so that they could make money and support their families. Many of them had left Europe because they were starving back home.

Before that, Britain's annoying economic taxes pushed the colonists toward revolution. In the decades before the Civil War, the South hung on to slaves because each slave was worth as much as $50,000 in modern money, and slaves picked cotton, which was the basis of the Southern economy. In the 1930s, the Great Depression changed the politics of the country.

Economics includes prosperity, recessions, depressions (sometimes called *panics* in the past), taxes, tariffs on imported goods, inflation, corporate expansion, and profit incentives. Questions to ask as you read include

- ✔ How did economic fear or greed influence national politics?
- ✔ How did the nation's economic health determine or shape historical events?
- ✔ How did sectional economic interests influence national decisions?

Social history

Social understanding has been the big winner in the new vision that influences modern history writing and (most important for us AP U.S. History fans) test design. The announced goal of the College Board is to make the big exam multiple-choice questions be

- ✔ 35 percent on political institutions and policy
- ✔ 40 percent on social history, including cultural developments
- ✔ 25 percent on economic and international relationships

This breakdown means that social history has taken over as the new focus of the AP U.S. History exam. *Social history* includes beliefs about religion, race, national origin, and the roles of men, women, and families. Social developments also include the influence of literature, science, art, and philosophy on events.

Questions to ask while you're reading include

- ✔ How did the social structure change during this era?
- ✔ How did the choices people made demonstrate their cultural beliefs?
- ✔ What specific examples can you cite to show social beliefs?
- ✔ What role did religion play in the development of government and society during this era?
- ✔ Who were the major religious leaders and trends?
- ✔ How did the literature and art of this period reflect what was going on and shape what was about to happen?

Here are a few examples of the strong social currents in American life:

- ✔ The first permanent settlements in Massachusetts consisted of Pilgrims and Puritans, groups who made the dangerous voyage to the unknown New World for presumably religious, not economic, reasons. In fact, the Pilgrims' original decision to leave Europe was as much social as religious: They had religious freedom in Holland, but they couldn't stand the idea that their children were growing up Dutch. (See Chapter 8.)
- ✔ Perhaps the greatest example of the power of literature and social thought was the best-selling novel of the 1800s: *Uncle Tom's Cabin.* The depictions of the evils of slavery in this book helped send hundreds of thousands of men off to fight and die in the Civil War. (See Chapter 13.)
- ✔ Sensationalized newspaper stories and pictures helped launch the U.S. into war with Spain in 1898. (See Chapter 15.)
- ✔ The Democratic Party's increasing support of civil rights helped lead both to the loss of its traditional political hold on the South and to the fact that the Democrats managed to elect only one two-term president in the last half of the 1900s. (See Chapter 20.)

PES-ing your way through multiple-choice and essays

Half the credit on the AP U.S. History test comes from 80 multiple-choice questions. Your score on this section depends on preparation and reasoning skill. You get preparation in Parts III and IV of this guide to back up the preparation you already have from your AP U.S. History course and/or study. You can beef up on your reasoning skills in Chapter 4.

The other half of the credit on the big test comes from just three essay questions. This section is where the CB separates the Jedi Masters from the guys who don't know where to plug in their light sabers. Anybody can memorize facts; leaders are the people who can use those facts successfully. That's where PES comes in.

No, PES isn't a cute hard-candy dispenser, as fun as that may be. *PES* is the way of combining political, economic, and social information on an essay question to make test graders dispense high grades. Every essay needs to contain each of the three magic PES ingredients. The good news is the same set of ideas that prepares you for multiple-choice glory can, if used wisely, set you up for essay success. You can find more about PES in Chapters 5 and 6.

How it all applies to the AP

Here's a rundown of what you need to know about the Ultimate History Exam. After you understand what's on the big test, you can use the Challenge Question and PES techniques to amp up your study sessions.

So, what can you find out about the test ahead of time? Every essay question the CB has ever asked is public knowledge, so your review can be informed by that comforting I-know-what-was-on-the-test-last-year feeling. You can find some of the questions that have been asked on multiple-choice sections over the years, but the CB has mostly kept that part of the test officially secret. No matter how you try to crack the big test, the College Board is a moving target — it changes questions every year. The best preparation is to set up in the direction the test is going and be prepared for a few surprise turns.

As you can see in the earlier section "Social history," the breakdown of the multiple-choice questions are about 35 percent on political institutions and events, 40 percent on social developments, and the remaining 25 percent on economics and international relationships. You can count on the fact that the three essay questions you answer will contain all of the PES ingredients.

The time periods covered by the multiple-choice questions include

- ✔ 20 percent from the period between the American Indians and the ratification of the Constitution in 1789
- ✔ 45 percent from the period between Washington's first government in 1790 and the outbreak of World War I in Europe in 1914
- ✔ 35 percent from the period between 1915 and the present.

Because the AP test writers know that most teachers don't get through the whole history book by May, they usually go easy on asking questions about events that happened after 1980.

How the Exam Is Graded

Reality check time. You're going to be taking the biggest single-subject test in the history of the CB in the not-so-distant future. The number of students taking AP tests increases every year; this year, about a third of a million students will take the AP U.S. History test.

Machines score the multiple-choice questions. No problem there; machines never make mistakes, unless of course the machine is your computer, crashing when you really need it. The essay questions, on the other hand, are hand-graded by History Readers. Each test contains three essays; 3 essays times ⅓ million test takers equals 1 million essays. Even if the CB manages to draft every teacher between here and Rattlesnake Junction as a History Reader, that still doesn't leave enough time in the few weeks between test day and grades day to slowly savor each essay.

Your essays are going to be scanned by a very busy teacher, who will very quickly decide your grade fate. To make grading work for you, you have to figure out how to write essays that show key political, economic, and social (PES) points so clearly that a grader couldn't miss them from a speeding train.

Plan from the beginning to make your essays look grader-friendly. Practice writing short papers of about five paragraphs by using easily spotted key terms. Never guess at dates. You won't lose points for using an approximate time period, but you'll be marked down for trying to nail an exact year and getting it wrong. Your AP History teacher in school may help give you feedback on your work. Study the examples in this book. Remember — less fluff and more key terms equals higher grades.

Score! What Does Your Grade Mean?

It'd be great if you became an Oxford Pro History Guru, dropping in for lunch at the White House and giving the Nobel prize committee a laugh with your droll history wit. Failing that, I want you to at least pass this darn test with a high enough score to get some college credit. AP U.S. History test results break down on the 5 point scale shown in Table 1-1.

Table 1-1	Average AP U.S. History Exam Scores	
Grade	**Meaning**	**% Earning this Grade**
5	Extremely well-qualified	9%
4	Well-qualified	20%
3	Qualified	22%
2	Possibly qualified	36%
1	No recommendation	13%

So what grade do you need to get college credit? The answer is usually a *3* (qualified), unless you want to go to a selective school; then the answer is a *4* (well-qualified). A *5* gets you credit and a pat on the back anywhere in the galaxy and won't hurt your chances of admission to a good school, either. Go to `collegesearch.collegeboard.com/apcredit policy/index.jsp` to find out what the magic score is at the college you crave.

Gee, look — just over half of the people who take this test are eligible for college credit at most schools. Of course they are; the CB curves the test every year to make it come out that way. So ask yourself, do you feel lucky? How many really smart kids are already into their sixth month of cramming for AP U.S. History, with Wilson's 14 Points pinned to their lapel? How many dumb kids are hanging around the parking lot planning to wait for the last minute to study so it can be fresh in their well-ventilated minds? Can you be sure you're above the middle of those packs?

How Much Time Do You Have to Prepare?

Okay, so the test is in May. That gives you several months to prepare, right? Oops — your time is a little shorter than that? No problem. Every day, after you finish your high-school courses, extracurricular activities, jobs, chores, exercise, and attempts to have a social life, just devote three hours to a rigorous review of everything that ever happened in North America. Oops, again. Not going to happen, is it?

You think you've got it hard?

Students working toward a college education in medieval Europe were called *bajan* and had to have the top of their head shaved. After studying for a whole year (with no guarantee of admission), they gave a speech to the college. If the speech was good enough to get them in, they were washed clean from head to foot and paraded through town on a donkey.

Figure out your optimal study strategy by dividing the material in this *AP U.S. History For Dummies* book by the number of days you have to study before the test. If the answer comes out to one chapter a day over about a month left before the big test, make do with that. The secret is that you're going beyond reading; you're going to Challenge Question your way through U.S. history. (See Chapter 2 for more on the Challenge Question technique.) The following list gives you some more suggestions on how to proceed based on how much time you have:

- ✔ **If you have more than a month,** spend extra time with your high-school AP U.S. History teacher. Ask him for copies of past AP U.S. History exams and practice taking them. Use the Challenge Question study technique on your own high-school textbook. Check out some other AP History texts from the school library and Challenge Question your way through them.

- ✔ **If you have less than a month** before the killer exam, do a sample test from Part V. After you pick up the kinds of questions that will be on the test, apply them to the history information in Part III and Part IV, using the Challenge Question method described in Chapter 2. Mark the sections you're weak on and go back and do the problems from those weak sections three times.

- ✔ **If you have less than a week** before the test, read the Cheat Sheet and pray. Concentrate the little time you have on reading about the most heavily tested period — 1800 to 1970. You'll have to skip studying the 20 percent of the questions that don't cover that period, but you may get lucky. You're doing emergency salvage studying, and sacrifices are inevitable.

- ✔ **If you're first reading this book on the way to the exam,** don't make any marks in it; you may be able to give it as a gift. Practice breathing steadily through panic, which I discuss in Chapter 3, and trust that the time you spent watching the History Channel will pull you through.

Chapter 2

Wringing the Highest Score out of What You Know

*O*f course you want to pass the AP U.S. History exam. To do that, you're going to take a look inside the AP's head. After you understand how the test makers think, you can begin to prepare for success on your big day with AP U.S. History. To set yourself up for success, first you have to get a clear shot at what a good grade on the AP looks like.

Grading the Way the AP Grades You

If the College Board (CB) got a grade from students on how well it runs its Advanced Placement tests, it would probably get an A- (see Chapter 1 for more on AP basics). The big exams are well-organized and contain interesting original thought, and you certainly have to give the CB props for grading 1 million U.S. History essays by hand in six weeks. But if you said A-, the CB wouldn't know what you were talking about, because the AP deals in numbers rather than letters. The following sections explain what this scoring means, how it affects your college credit, and what impact certain scores have.

Converting letters to numbers

The CB talks in numbers. Most people know the famous range from flunky 200 to perfect 800 on the College Board's SAT tests. For you nervous takers of the AP U.S. History exam, you can count the important numbers on one hand: The CB gives grades from *1* to *5*.

How do those relate to the working alphabet world of most students: *A, B, C, D,* and *F?* And, while I'm on the subject, how come nobody ever gets an *E?* By sneakily checking the grades past AP U.S. History exam takers actually get in college, the CB sets AP Exam grade boundaries so that exams earning an AP grade of *5* are roughly equivalent to the average AP exam score of students who go on to earn college *A*s. They get to peek, those crafty CBers! They then make sure the exam receiving an AP grade of *4* equals the average scores of those college students receiving *B*s, and the lowest score corresponding to an AP grade of *3* equates to the average score of college students receiving *C*s. About half of the students who take AP U.S. History exam get a grade of *3* or better.

So there you have it:

5 = college A

$4 = B$

$3 = C$

$2 = D$

$1 = F$

In general, you can never be too rich, too thin, or have too high an AP score. Besides actual college credit, an AP U.S. History score of 5 looks great on your college application. In most institutions, though, you can get college credit simply by doing as well on the AP exam as college students who get Cs in Intro U.S. History. And you won't have a C on your college record; just a nice, satisfying notation that college credit is in the bank.

Nailing down a college's credit policy

Colleges are big institutions with impressive buildings and really smart people. You may be surprised, therefore, to hear that identifying the Advanced Placement credit policies of your favorite prospective colleges can be a little. . .well, slippery. The CB has wisely thrown up its hands at the prospect of keeping the shifting AP policies of America's more than 4,000 colleges and universities all on one page. Although the CB stays out of the middle, it does help you look for the information yourself.

 Go to collegesearch.collegeboard.com/apcreditpolicy/index.jsp to search for your school(s) of choice. Because links can get broken, you can also use a general search engine (such as Google), using terms like *College Board* and *AP credit policy*. When you're on an AP Credit Policy search page, search by the names of the colleges you may attend. If you don't see your college on the list the site returns, click "Next" in the lower right hand side of the college listing box. When you see the school you want, click on it. The College Board search engine will attempt to send you to the very page on the institution's Web site that deals with AP credit.

The word "attempt" is appropriate because despite the valiant efforts of the good people at CB, some colleges have a hard time keeping links pointed to their AP credit policies. Some sites provide PDF files, which you must comb through to look for the AP needle in a regulation haystack. Some sites let you click around the bush, forcing you to guess which links they may be hiding AP information under. In one search I conducted, even Harvard greeted surfers with a hearty welcome to the incoming freshmen, without a word about the fate of these fine freshmen with AP Credit. (Here's a tip: Don't plan to major in Computer Science at any institution whose Web jump greets you with a "Page Expired" message!)

Perusing AP policies nationwide

Here are some college AP policies determined as of press time. Remember, these policies can change — your credit mileage may vary! The State University of New York (SUNY) gives credit for an AP Exam score of *3*. Yale requires a *4*, minimum. Although Notre Dame has subjects that require anywhere from *3* to *5* for credit, AP U.S. History requires a *4*. Most state schools require a *3* — even the famous University of California at Berkeley. Stanford doesn't give AP credit for every subject, and one of the subjects it disses is U.S. History. At Cornell, Syracuse, and the University of Arizona, U.S. History requires a *4*. Brigham Young calls for a *3*. U.S.C (*3* minimum) and Washington University (*4* minimum) have a special deal: Add one more point (to a *4* for U.S.C and a *5* for Wash U), and you get specific course credit. The University of Nevada at Las Vegas has a high-roller deal: You get three credits for a *3* and six credits for a *5*.

Advanced Placement in the year 0

Standardized testing for advancement in China started with the Han Dynasty, around the year 0. And, like an Oriental College Board, Chinese placement exams kept cranking out the grades for almost 2,000 years. Over the years, the tests included military strategy, civil law, revenue and taxation, agriculture and geography, and plenty of confusing Confucian religious classics. If you think the AP U.S. History test is hard, try taking it in Chinese characters!

Students studied for a year in tiny cells that contained two boards that they moved around to make either a bed or a desk. The actual tests took two days, but the 5 percent who passed each got great government jobs. Later, the Chinese standardized tests inspired Western nations, including the United States, to have civil service exams. One day in the 1900s, an education guy said, "Hey, we could invent the College Board and head whip students with Advance Placement tests!" Just be glad you don't have to move around boards to make a bed.

Even though it's cumbersome, the College Board policy of jumping to the colleges' Web sites to let them tell their AP credit stories is a good idea. If the CB tried to play nanny to all those sometimes-yes-but-maybe-no policies, everybody could get hurt. The person you for sure don't want to get hurt on the way to a higher education is you. Nail down the policies of the schools you may want to attend. If you surf patiently around the college sites, you can usually find their AP policies hiding somewhere. Many times, thankfully, a college's AP policy comes up right away in a nice, clear chart, the way the College Board dreamed it would.

If the high tech Internet doesn't work for you, call the admissions office of the schools you're interested in and ask them where you can find their AP policy in writing. You can get the phone numbers of your prospective colleges from your school advisor.

When you're in the right place on the Net, make print out policy. Beware the colleges that have no clear AP policy. Some backward schools seem to think AP stands for Aunt Polly. Only apply to schools that give you AP credit (see Chapter 1 to find out why). If you're in the final strokes of choosing between two colleges, double-check to make sure each college's AP policy covers U.S. History.

Scoping Out What's Going to Be on the Test

The AP U.S. History exam is a comprehensive monster composed of 80 multiple-choice questions and 3 essay questions. You have to face one big *Document-Based Question* (DBQ), where the CB shows you a bunch of original documents and you write about the sources plus the knowledge you (hopefully) possess about the events behind the sources. The other two essay questions come in two groups of two questions each; you get to choose one question from each group to answer. The exam is graded 50/50 between multiple-choice and essays.

Author and playwright Norman Mailer once said, "If I knew what inspiration was, I certainly wouldn't tell you." If I knew *exactly* what questions will be on your AP U.S. History test, I would have to be one of the six teachers on the AP U.S. History Development Committee — and even the teachers don't know until the last minute. Also, if I knew and told, I'd have to go to teacher jail, where they don't give recesses. And the CB Office of Testing Integrity — sort of like a testing FBI — would catch up with you and strip you of your crooked, unearned *5* score. You can't have that!

But I can have a look at past tests to see what subjects tend to come up again and again and give you an idea based on professional observations. I can judge the trends by seeing the direction the big test is moving. You can also look at the announced subject material and time-period proportions to help choose which baskets to put most of your studying eggs in. In the following sections, you get a look at AP U.S. History teaching priorities as outlined by the very folks who make up the test. In Chapter 3, I show you how to study the way the Test Masters recommend. You also discover how to find previous tests to help you prepare for this year's AP challenge.

Don't mess with AP Test security. These guys have a sense of humor comparable to Homeland Security when someone pops a balloon. Forbidden actions include discussing multiple-choice questions from the exam with anybody — even your AP teacher. You can talk about essay questions a day after the test (to make sure that test takers in all the time zones in the world are done writing). The CB doesn't let you talk about multiple-choice questions period because it may use the questions again.

Acing the facts that mean the most

You can get a good grade — even a 5 — without having to correctly answer all the multiple-choice questions presented to you. In fact, if you get only half the multiple-choice points and score big on the essays, you can walk away with the top grade. That said, you really need to stock up on knowledge about social trends and movements, which is particularly useful for tying together essay responses. The good news is that this information also helps you answer multiple-choice questions.

The AP U.S. History exam is center-loaded, with a bias toward post-colonial history between 1800 and 1950. That doesn't mean you should neglect the way-back and only-just-recently events; you have plenty of points to gain from these time periods as well. But as you review, put a special polish on the time periods with the most credit attached. According to the committee that designs the test, the questions break down as follows:

20 percent: Pre-Columbian era to 1789

45 percent: 1790 to 1914

35 percent: 1915 to the present

Historians have a natural aversion to recent events; when happenings are still news, many don't consider them history yet. Sorting out the importance of recent events is difficult. For instance, Paris Hilton gets a lot of media coverage, but does that mean she belongs in the history books? Besides, getting too near the present can step on some still-sensitive political toes. Also, the AP test occurs in early May, and school often runs into June. Your friends at the College Board are kind enough to not test you on material you haven't covered yet. So don't spend much time on last year's hot topics; the AP test probably doesn't know they exist yet.

Why do the 300 years of early American history get less coverage than the 200 plus years after the birth of the United States as a nation? Well, this is U.S. History, and the U.S. didn't exist before 1776. More important, history is what humans choose to save to tell us about themselves. Historians believe people can learn more about their present selves from studying, for example, the rise of democratic ideas in the 1800s than from analyzing cod-fishing stories from the 1600s. But don't give up on that 20 percent of credit from before the Constitution; it's not just fishing stories.

Syncing your mind with the big test

I'm sure you want to make a little visit inside the minds of the Exam Mavens — the people who make up the big AP test. But you'd probably get in trouble with the AP security goons, and the mind-melding machine isn't quite ready yet anyway. Fortunately, the AP test bosses are willing to identify how their thinking is balanced between continuous themes in U.S. History and time-ordered chronological event topics. Themes are social and economic trends that happen over time; events are political happenings like wars and elections that happen in one specific period.

Balance has been a big issue in the history field since the end of the bad old days of names-dates-and-places boring history. When the New History broke out of the egg in the 1960s, professors were so glad to be liberated that some of them went overboard; they stopped emphasizing event topics all together and just went in for social themes. This disparity led to students cheering when the rebels closed in on Lisbon in the Spanish Civil War, only to find out later that those were bad Fascist rebels. Names and dates came back, but they're now brought to life by human social themes.

Today, the test writers still stress the social and cultural trends that underlie political events, but now it's important to know how trends and events fit in time. Dates are the gallon-sized baggies that hold social trends and political events together. You don't have to remember specific years, but you should have an idea of the decade in which trends and events unfolded.

The 80 multiple-choice questions that make up 50 percent of your score on the Big AP are a natural hang-out space for questions about hard and fast political events. It's hard to fit the nuances of schools of painting into five-choice questions and relatively easy to ask multiple-choice questions about elections and wars. Even so, four out of ten multiple-choice questions will be about cultural trends rather than political events. (You can find more about multiple-choice questions in Chapter 4.)

The Document-Based Question (DBQ), worth 22.5 percent of your total score, is all about the social and economic trends illustrated by political events. You'll be analyzing actual letters, pictures, and reports from a historic period and bringing in your own outside information to explain the era of the documents given to you. (More about answering the Document-Based Question is in Chapter 5.)

Two regular essay questions are each worth 13.75 percent of your overall score on the AP. These questions each require about a five paragraph essay. If your essays make a good argument using social, political, and economic happenings, you're on your way to a high score. (You can discover more about creating teacher-friendly essays in Chapter 6.)

Don't get too stressed by the difference between themes and topics, or by the definition of what's social against what's political history. Teachers can't agree themselves, and you see a lot of overlap. If you get the names, meanings, and time periods down, you'll do fine.

Digging the themes

Themes are the melody that runs through U.S. history. In the form of social or cultural history, these themes show up in 40 percent of the multiple-choice questions on the AP exam. Additionally, themes are the lifeblood of the essays. You can improve your score on that section of the exam by referencing at least two themes in every essay answer. Here, in alphabetical order, is a list of what the AP U.S. History Development Committee considers to be important themes in American History:

- ✔ **American Diversity:** The roles of class, ethnicity, race, and gender in the history of America. Discuss different groups in the United States and the relationships between them; this theme is about how groups in the United States are different.

- ✔ **American Identity:** What it means to be an American, as seen in different parts of the United States and different periods in history. Just what is the American national character, and how are Americans different from other people in the world? This is what teachers call *American exceptionalism.* You may think of American Identity as how groups in the United States are the same.

- ✔ **Culture:** What was popular and earth-shaking in different periods of U.S. history? This category includes literature, art, philosophy, music, theater, television, and film. Culture is what you can tell about the real beliefs of the country from what people watch, read, and sing.

- ✔ **Demographic Changes:** The political, economic, and social effects of immigration and movements within the United States. It also covers the way marriage, birth, and death rates have changed. How many kids were in the average family? How long did people live? What was the overall population size and density? Counting people helps in understanding trends.

- ✔ **Economic Transformations:** The effects of business and personal financial incentives on the United States, including buying, selling, and the changes in business structure (from small store owners to big corporations). You can discuss the effects of labor unions and consumer movements. Basically, if you want to get a handle on why people do things, check out their bank accounts.

- ✔ **Environment:** How the expansion of the United States has affected the environment in different periods of history. What's the impact of more people, the expansion of cities and suburbs, pollution, and industrialization? Mother Nature has limits that affect human history.

- ✔ **Globalization:** The relation of the United States to the rest of the world, from the first colonies in the 1500s to the present. This topic includes global leadership and dominance, colonialism, mercantilism, imperialism, development of markets, and cultural exchange. The United States isn't an island, however much isolationists want to make it one.

- ✔ **Politics and Citizenship:** What Americans believe about their revolutionary past, the importance of democracy, and the development of the U.S. nation. What do citizenship and civil rights mean? Just what is the United States, and who really is an American?

- ✔ **Reform:** The movement for social change. U.S. history has seen issues like women's rights, civil rights, anti slavery, education, labor, public health, temperance, gay rights, war, and government. It's time for some changes; heck, it has always been time for some changes.

- ✔ **Religion:** The variety of religious experiences and practices in the United States, covering the time period from the American Indians to the Internet. What's the influence of religion on economics, politics, and society? The way you view your deity and your purpose influences everything you do.

- ✔ **Slavery and Its Legacies in North America:** The meaning of slavery and other forms of forced labor (such as indentured servitude) in different periods of the nation's development. Subthemes include the money behind slavery and its racial dimensions, movements of resistance, and the long-term political, economic, and social consequences of slavery. After all, many of the leaders who founded the United States had the time to talk about freedom because slaves were doing their work for them.

- ✔ **War and Diplomacy:** How armed fights changed the United States, from the time before Columbus to the early-21st century war on terrorism. Perhaps the United States is a peace-loving nation, but the fact remains that the nation has been involved in a war about once every 20 years.

Don't get so caught up in the story of certain themes that you forget the decades in which they happened. You don't have to know the exact years for themes, because most of them are continuous. However, you do need an idea of the development of trends, at least in ten-year periods. Abolition, for instance, was minor in the 1820s but huge in the 1850s. Also, it helps to root trend answers to the approximate year of key developments. For example, *The Liberator* was an important abolitionist newspaper founded by William Lloyd Garrison in 1831. This newspaper founding marks the beginning of the growth of abolition in the northern United States.

Calling out topics on the College Board

Although the melody of historical themes makes for interesting understanding, historical events and topics still pay the rent when it comes to your overall AP exam score. Here are the important chronological event topics specified by the College Board in its U.S. History Course Description:

1. **Pre-Columbian Societies:** The first people who lived in the Americas. American Indian empires in the Southwest, Mesoamerica, and the Mississippi Valley. American Indian cultures of North America before the explorers arrived. Before Columbus sailed the ocean blue, for thousands of years American Indians lived true.

2. **Transatlantic Encounters and Colonial Beginnings (1492–1690):** Explorers meet the American Indians. Spain's empire in North America. The English settle (perfect name) New England and most of the Mid-Atlantic and South regions, and the French set up in Canada. Settlers arrive, sometimes with hope and sometimes in chains, in the Chesapeake region. Religious diversity leads to different American colonies. Early revolts against colonial authority: the Glorious Revolution, Bacon's Rebellion, and the Pueblo Revolt. The colonists got off to a rocky start — fighting each other wasn't too smart.

3. **Colonial North America (1690–1754):** How the population expanded with more immigration. Trade made the port cities like Boston and New York grow while farming expanded in the country. The impact of the Enlightenment and the First Great Awakening. How British and other colonial governments affected North America. Don't forget, as much of American history passes before the Revolution as after it.

4. **The American Revolutionary Era (1754–1789):** The French and Indian War leads to the Imperial Crisis and fighting back against British rule. Next comes the U.S. Revolution, state constitutions and the Articles of Confederation, and the federal Constitution. Local freedom is going too slow; been great, Great Britain, but gotta go.

5. **The Early Republic (1789–1815):** Washington, Hamilton, and the building of a national government. Political parties begin with the Federalists and Republicans. The meaning of Republican Motherhood and education for women. Effects of Jefferson's presidency. The Second Great Awakening. Settlers move into the Appalachian West. The growth of slavery and free black communities. American Indians fight back. The causes and outcomes of the War of 1812. It's great to be free, but what will we be?

6. **Transformation of the Economy and Society in Antebellum America:** The United States settles down to raise a family. The start of industrialization and changes in social and class structures. How steamboats, trains, and canals created a national market economy. Immigration and reactions against it from nativists. Planters, independent farmers, and slaves in the South grow cotton.

7. **Transformation of Politics in Antebellum America:** The development of the second party system. Federal authority and the people who fought against it: judicial federalism, tariff controversy, the Bank of the U.S., and states' rights debates. Jacksonian democracy increases popular government but has limitations. So, besides getting ready for the Civil War, what else did you do?

8. **Religion, Reform, and Renaissance in Antebellum America:** Shaking up what people believe. Evangelical Protestant revivals, ideals of home life, and social reforms. Transcendentalism and utopian communities. American growth in literature and art.

9. **Territorial Expansion and Manifest Destiny:** Moving on West and stepping on some toes. Americans push American Indians across the Mississippi river to the West. The United States adds new territory, Western migration and cultural changes, and the beginning of U.S. imperialism and the Mexican War.

10. **The Crisis of the Union:** Oops, couldn't keep that slavery thing in the closet forever. Slaveholder-versus-antislavery arguments and conflicts, the Compromise of 1850 and popular sovereignty, and The Kansas-Nebraska Act. The emergence of the Republican Party, the election of 1860, Abraham Lincoln, and the South leaves the Union.

11. **Civil War:** Fighting for the soul of America. North–and–South societies are at war. Resources, mobilization, and internal disagreement. Military strategies and foreign diplomacy. The role of blacks in the war. Emancipation. The social, political, and economic effects of war in the North, South, and West.

12. **Reconstruction:** The Civil War was a serious operation; it took a while to recover. The plans of Lincoln and Andrew Johnson versus Radical Reconstruction. Southern state governments: goals, achievements, and shortcomings. The role of blacks in politics, education, and the economy. The outcome of Reconstruction. The end in the Compromise of 1877.

13. **The Origins of the New South:** Okay, no slavery; what's Plan B? Retooling Southern agriculture: sharecropping and crop-lien systems replace slavery. The expansion of manufacturing plants and business. The politics of segregation: race separation, Jim Crow, and disenfranchisement.

14. **Development of the West in the Late 19th Century:** Meanwhile, back on the ranch, the natives are restless. Rivals for the West: miners, homesteaders, ranchers, and American Indians. Building the Western railroads. Government policy toward American Indians. Men and women, race, and ethnicity in the far West. What Western settlement did to the environment.

15. **Industrial America in the Late 19th Century:** The money is talking, and people are walking into the future. How corporations took over industry. The effects of technology on the worker and workplace. National politics and the growing influence of corporate power. Labor and unions. Migration and immigration: the changing demographics of the nation. Fans and foes of the new order, including Social Darwinism and the Social Gospel.

16. **Urban Society in the Late 19th Century:** Like the old adage says, "The city makes free." City growth and machine politics. Urbanization and the lure of the city, intellectual and popular entertainment, and cultural movements.

17. **Populism and Progressivism:** So we're making money and having fun, but what do we stand for? Farmer revolts and issues in the late 19th century. Roosevelt, Taft, and Wilson as Progressive presidents. The beginnings of municipal, state, and national Progressive reform. Women's roles in the family, politics, the workplace, education, and reform. Black America: city migration and civil-rights initiatives.

18. **The Emergence of America as a World Power:** The United States becomes a big dog. U.S. imperialism grows with political and economic expansion. The beginning of WWI in Europe and American neutrality, WWI at home and abroad, and the Treaty of Versailles. Society and economy in the postwar years.

19. **The New Era (1920s):** Everything old is new again. The consumer economy and the business of America. Republican presidents Harding, Coolidge, and Hoover. Modernism: the culture of science, the arts, and entertainment. Responses to modernism: nativism, religious fundamentalism, and Prohibition. The ongoing struggle for equality: blacks and women.

20. **The Great Depression and the New Deal:** A bummer of a time, but we'll get through it together. What created the Great Depression? The Hoover administration tries to do something. FDR and the New Deal. The New Deal coalition and its critics. Labor and union recognition. Living through hard times: American society during the Great Depression.

21. **World War II:** The "greatest generation" fights the good war. The rapid growth of fascism and militarism in Italy, Japan, and Germany. America's policy of neutrality. The attack on Pearl Harbor and the U.S.' declaration of war. Diplomacy, war aims, and wartime conferences. Fighting a multifront war. The United States as a global power in the Atomic Age.

22. **The Home Front during the War:** While you were out kicking some Axis butt, things changed at home. The mobilization of the economy for World War II. Women, work, and family during the war. City migration and demographic changes. Reduced liberties and civil rights during wartime. War and regional development. The expansion of government power.

23. **The United States and the Early Cold War:** Is it just me, or did things get really cold in here? The beginning of the Cold War. Truman's policy of containment. Strategies and policies of the Eisenhower and Kennedy administrations. The Cold War in Asia: China, Korea, Vietnam, and Japan. The Red Scare and McCarthyism. The impact of the Cold War on American society.

24. **The 1950s:** Creating all those high schools, roads, and baby boomers. The beginning of the modern civil rights movement. The affluent society and "the other America." Agreement and conformity in the suburbs and middle-class America. Nonconformists, cultural rebels, and critics. The impact of changes in technology, science, and medicine.

25. **The Turbulent 1960s:** It's a political demonstration at the love-in! Moving from the New Frontier to the Great Society. Developing movements for civil rights. Cold War confrontations in Latin America, Asia, and Europe. The beginning of *détente*. Hippies, the antiwar movement, and the counterculture.

26. **Politics and Economics at the End of the 20th Century:** America moves right. Nixon wins in 1968 with the Silent Majority. Nixon's challenges: China, Vietnam, and Watergate. Changes in the American economy: deindustrialization, the energy crisis, and the service economy. The New Right and the Reagan revolution. The end of the Cold War.

27. **Society and Culture at the End of the 20th Century:** America sees the social realities of being a rich nation. The changing face of America: surge of immigration after 1965, Sunbelt migration, and the graying and tanning of America. New developments in biotechnology, mass communication, and computers. A multicultural society faces the future.

28. **The United States in the Post-Cold War World:** Get ready for the future; it's starting right now. The American economy faces globalization. Unilateralism versus multilateralism in foreign policy. Home-grown and foreign terrorism. Environmental issues that affect the whole world.

Getting Ready for the Big Day

As test day gets closer, make the most of the time you have. Although you'd ideally be reading this on a calm day months before the test, chances are you're getting close to crunch time. Here's how to spend the precious time you have profitably.

Say you have only a month to go before the exam that spans the centuries. Now more than ever, paying attention to your schedule and timing determines your success. Here are a few basic tips to get you started:

- ✔ Be true to your school; stick with the AP History review your teacher has planned for you.

- ✔ Work your way through this book like you do your school review — a little each day.

- ✔ Plan a time to study that you can stick to. A lot of brainiacs spend a little time studying at night before they crash and a little time first thing in the morning while the bagels are toasting. That way, you can sleep on the information and double-check it in the morning with a clear mind.

At some time during this month, the age-old dilemma of "Study or a show?" will arise. Before you jump in the car, remember that you're on a mission for college credit. You can be saving a whole college course by getting a good score on the AP, and the college course you can avoid would otherwise have cost you and your dear parents thousands of dollars. And just think about how much better it'll be to party later with advanced credit (and money) under your belt. Meanwhile, do something you like that goes well with studying. Perhaps you can take a lovely run in the park or treat yourself with some double-good premium ice cream!

The following sections show you how to creep up on the AP with preparation so complete that the actual exam will come as naturally as opening a candy bar in the dark.

Building a winning study strategy

Yes, it's a bummer that you have to study. Studying is work, but hey, you get paid with grades. Think of it like you're working in sales on commission; the harder you work (study), the more money you make (the more college credit you get). Given the harsh realities, you should make it as fun and easy as possible by turbocharging your study time with a few choice moves.

How much should you study? That depends; how smart are you? Despite what you've heard or read and all the head banging you've done in school, smart doesn't mean good, brave, or even successful in the world. Henry Ford could barely remember the capital of his own state, but he built an industrial empire. You, my friend, have some facts to remember to get through the big test, but they should be facts that you know how to use — not just rote memory pop-ups.

The following list presents some tips to help you set up your studying schedule and strategies in order to maximize your strengths (and your grade):

- Even within the field of intelligence, there are different kinds of smart. Some people can photocopy facts in their head; you can call them Copy Machines. Some folks may not be able to remember facts as well, but they can write essays like Shakespeare. You have the kind of intelligence that The Force gave you, but you also can build up smarts through exercise — just like muscles at the gym. On the AP exam, you'll need to be a Copy Machine and a Shakespeare, so you need to study based on your strengths and weaknesses. If you're good on multiple-choice, you have your Copy Machine running strong. If you're shaky on essays, you want to work on your inner Shakespeare.

- Study enough to know the themes and topics outlined in the earlier section "Syncing your mind with the big test." That college course you can avoid by getting AP credit would've taken at least seven hours a week out of your life. It seems reasonable, therefore, to study an hour a day for the AP U.S. History exam — more if you have a thick head for facts, and less if you can already ace through the tests in Part V of this book.

- Studying should never be just reading; it should be work with a pencil in your hand. Write on this book; your kid brother can buy another when his time comes (Wiley would like that!). If you can't write in your school textbooks, mark key passages with sticky notes.

   Only highlight the most important parts (say, for example, the icon information); if you use the highlighter to turn the whole book yellow, you're just coloring, not studying.

- Make lists of key events and themes and write out their definitions and years (perhaps on notecards). Always quiz yourself. What was the first state to permanently allow women to vote? (Wyoming in 1869.) Who was the guy who took over after Lincoln? (Andrew Johnson in 1865.) When was the Constitution ratified? (1789.) What was the big deal about the Second Great Awakening? (It renewed personal salvation with ties to church and social reform — 1800 to 1830s.)

Planning out your timing

The AP U.S. History exam isn't like a surprise pop quiz; you should have a good idea of what the big test looks like and how it's run. You'll be invited to devote a chilling three hours and five minutes of your life to searching frantically but calmly through the history hard drive of your mind. You'll be under the control of the test proctor, who will give you the usual warnings about food, time, copying, and reading answers off your history tattoos. And you'll have to shift gears at least once in order to complete the two sections of the test.

Slicing up Section 1

First, you'll have 55 minutes to answer 80 multiple-choice questions. You'll receive a Scantron form with tons of little ovals to fill in (with pencil, of course). With the form comes a booklet that contains the 80 multiple-choice questions — each of which has five possible answers, helpfully labeled from *A* to *E*. The questions are cleverly arranged from easy to hard, with chronological years and themes sprinkled in all levels of difficulty. The changes in difficulty come gradually; don't expect to find yourself lost in genius palace all of a sudden. Don't forget, what's hard for somebody else may be easy for you, especially if you've studied.

In the bad old days, the AP had a repeating time sequence of questions. You could sometimes use this mini-chronological order of the questions like a screwdriver to pry open answers. Recently, the Test Mavens got wise to this strategy and begin to sprinkle time periods randomly throughout the different degrees of difficulty within multiple-choice. Drat, foiled again.

Even though the multiple-choice questions in Section I take less than a third of your test time, they're worth half your test score.

Sailing through Section 2

Exhausted (or should I say, well-exercised) by your spiral through multiple-choice levels, now you must begin to write history in Section II. You'll get a question book containing one DBQ, or Document-Based Question (Section A), and four regular essay questions arranged in two groups of two questions each (Sections B and C). You answer one question from Section B and one from Section C. You'll get 15 minutes during which you can only review the questions. During this time, you can't start an essay, but you can read and take notes in the question booklet. Trust me, you won't get bored.

The DBQ would be entertaining if it weren't so stressful. You'll see anywhere from seven to ten documents; they could be diaries, letters, speeches, charts, graphs, political cartoons — almost anything you can read. Maybe someday the test will be electronic and have videos and ring tones! For now, use the first 15 minutes to read those documents and think about how you can bring them together with some relevant outside knowledge to write a stunning DBQ essay.

If you have time in your 15 minutes of calm before the writing storm, you're allowed to begin choosing the one question from the latter two sections that you least hate facing. Don't bother; just concentrate on the DBQ during the reading period. The other essay questions will take care of themselves when you get to them. Don't cloud your brain — you have plenty of documents and outside facts to marshal for the DBQ. Starting with the DBQ, you have a total of 1 hour and 55 minutes to write the three essays.

The suggested time for the DBQ essay is 45 minutes. The suggested time for the two regular essays is 35 minutes a piece. You can discover everything you ever wanted to know about the DBQ in Chapter 5. You get the inside scoop on the regular essay questions in Chapter 6.

"Wait, I have something else to say!" Don't get caught out of time on the big exam. Nothing is worse than having important, grade-winning points to make in an essay and no time left to write them. Before the exam, practice writing five paragraph essays in 30 minutes. Get used to timing yourself as you write. Better to write short and smart than long and pointless.

Getting buff on test exercise

It helps to take practice tests to get ready for the Big AP. Part V of this book contains two tough exams. But better than any printed test are the exam questions you make up yourself while you study. Creating Challenge Questions means turning the history that you read into questions that challenge you to find the answers as you study.

Asking yourself questions as you study is the key to the Challenge Question study secret. Make every major heading you see into a question; that's what the big exam is going to do to you. For example, if the heading in the history text says *Jacksonian Democracy transforms the United States*, you say to yourself, "Name the ways Jacksonian Democracy transformed the United States." Find the answers about Jacksonian Democracy as you're reading the section and write them down. Close your eyes and repeat the question and the answers. Study the practice tests in Part V until you have the form down cold.

To get good at making your own Challenge Questions while you study, though, you need to actually take a

sample AP U.S. History Test. Study the 2001 and 2006 AP U.S. History Released Exams to find out what actual past tests looked like. These exams may be available at your school; ask your AP teacher or order them from the College Board Web site.

Also, sit down and take one of the tests in Part V. Time yourself and stick to the schedule you'll have to follow on test day. How many multiple-choice questions did you get right? Was there a certain time period you were a little foggy on? How did the essays come out? Ask somebody you trust who's wise in the ways of history to score them using the criteria in Chapters 5 and 6. Need more experience writing these short but loaded factual stories? Practice until writing them becomes easier.

Don't get too stressed if you didn't do well the first time through a practice test. That's why you call them practice. Use the knowledge you just gained to put the Challenge Questions studying method to work where it will do the most good for you. Visit U.S. History a little each day!

Bracing for test-induced panic

As the big day approaches, no matter how hard you study, you'll feel a bit scared. So much history to cover, so little time. What was that XYZ Affair? (Diplomatic tension with France, 1797.) How many Great Awakenings were there? (Two — one before the Revolution and one after.) The more you know, the more you know you don't know.

Pre-show jitters are normal; just ask any singer. Chill out, Chillsky! The AP exam isn't like the tests you took in school, where you were supposed to know everything. It's impossible to know everything about U.S. History. If you don't believe that, just ask your teacher. The AP exam is more like an endurance race; even if you limp over the finish line, you deserve applause. Nobody is supposed to get all the questions right. The test has a theoretical perfect score of 180, but you can get the highest grade of *5* with a raw score as low as 117. It's as if the grade of *A* on AP U.S. History starts at 65 percent.

For more on relaxing yourself before the exam, I present the Chillax approach to psyching the test in Chapter 3.

The AP U.S. History test is curved to ensure a certain proportion of high grades every year. You just have to finish ahead of enough other people taking the exam to get ahead of the curve. It's like the story of two guys running away from a grizzly bear. The first guy stops, takes out a pair of running shoes, and starts to put them on. The second guy says "Don't be stupid, you can't outrun a bear." Replies the first guy: "I don't have to outrun a bear; I just have to outrun you." Feel better?

Chapter 3

Psyching Yourself Up for the Big Test

The first two chapters of this friendly guide show you how to use Challenge Question history review and political, economic, and social (PES) information to squirrel away some choice information that you can put down on the big day. The next three chapters show you how to leap gracefully across each of the three question types standing between you and that golden moment when you hand in your completed exam with a secret thumbs-up. (You've got to keep that thumbs-up secret, because you cannot forget the Ironclad Rule of Fake Test Agony: Just act out mild despair with the other students as you leave the exam. Complaining that all tests are hard and unfair is the only way to maintain social respectability as you quietly ace your way to the top.)

Before you look at the next three chapters to get down to cases of slaying the exam demons — multiple-choice questions, Document-Based Questions (DBQs), and regular essay questions — it's time for a little talk: How is your AP U.S. History confidence level at this point?

Success comes from more than just what you know; it also comes from how you use what you know. (It's not just the meat; it's also the motion.) You'll succeed on the day of the big test because you're going to have an unstoppable combination of knowledge and attitude. This chapter gives you pointers on how to prepare yourself for exam day so you stay calm, cool, and collected. Don't worry if you're a little anxious; that's good. You can use that nervous energy to slay the test dragon. This chapter gives you pointers on how to do it.

Taking Advantage of the Way You Learn Best

As I outline in Chapter 2, your goal is to arm yourself with information by studying U.S. history and the AP exam for an hour a day. Think about your study time as powering up with items to beat the big test boss. You know you need Copy Machine smarts to remember PES events with the approximate times they happened. Copy Machine power comes from active review with its best friend: Challenge Questions.

But how is any dude or dudette going to remember all that history? The secret is *mnemonics*, the art and science of memory. Naturally, just to mess with your head, the big brains over in the Word Design Department picked a word for memory that's both hard to remember and tricky to say. Just pronounce it without the first letter, and you'll be close enough. You may remember a demon kneeing you in the stomach to get you to remember: *demonic mnemonics*.

Be a poet, and you won't blow it

Most people have heard this mnemonic: "In 1492, Columbus sailed the ocean blue." Sadly, basing an entire essay response around this fact is hard, but it's a hint: You can make facts as stick-to-your-brain as a song in your head you just can't stop singing. How about this one? "Thirty days hath September, April, June, and November. When short February's done, all the rest have thirty-one. . ." When is the last time you used *hath* in daily conversation? But there it is, stuck in your brain.

In addition to bad poetry, you can make up first-letter lists. Did you ever wonder *Why Ants Jump More and More All June*? Bet not, but the first letters of those silly words help you remember the first seven presidents: Washington, J. Adams, Jefferson, Madison, Monroe, J.Q. Adams, and Jackson. In the same way, *HOMES* can help you remember the Great Lakes: Huron, Ontario, Michigan, Erie, and Superior. This technique is stupid, perhaps, but what's un-stupid is being able to remember an impressive list when AP time rolls around.

Mnemonics is the psychological system behind psyching yourself up for the big exam. There are three basic ways of learning. You're going to lean naturally on the way you learn the best.

- ✔ It turns out about 65 percent of humans prefer to learn things visually and, therefore, are visual learners. That's why they invented writing instead of just singing or tap-dancing history to one another.

- ✔ Another 30 percent are auditory learners — that is, they prefer to learn things through sound. That makes them good at learning from lectures and songs, but not as good at grabbing facts through reading. Auditory folks would be in favor of singing history.

- ✔ That leaves the final 5 percent, whose favorite way of learning is through kinesthetic movement.

Sorry — no tap-dancing for history review. I cover these learning preferences in more detail in the later sections. Consider each of these preferences carefully and see whether any of them apply to you. If so, you can take full advantage of your preference to make studying for the AP U.S. History exam easier and less stressful.

Just because you have a preference for one kind of learning doesn't mean you can't remember facts in the other ways as well. Also, you can use strategies for maximizing the kind of learning that comes most naturally. Even better, visiting another learning style helps break up your intellectual traffic jam. You become DJ Mixmaster Smarty.

Studying by sight

Visual people remember colorful emotional images best. Make a picture of a bright, loud religious revival in your mind when you read about the First Great Awakening. You may people the scene with Jonathan Edwards holding a sign that says "1730 — Revolution's Coming." That's visual learning.

Writing key events into your own notes helps fix them in your mind. This technique can be especially useful for timelines. History is, at its core, the study of change over time. Write out a timeline for major topics so that you can see the big picture of how the changes in one field developed. You could make a timeline of women's rights, U.S. expansion, the 50-year run-up to the Civil War, and other key themes.

Flash cards don't work for everybody, but they have saved more than one determined student on the AP. At the very least, you get to write down terms and their meaning one more time. The more you write stuff down, the better you'll remember it. Studying is a great example of instant karma. Research shows that students who put 50 percent more time into preparation do 50 percent better on big tests. You may want to color-code your flash cards by era. Just don't go overboard and spend more time decorating beautiful flash cards than using them.

Studying by sound

If you're having trouble remembering the facts you read, you may be much better as an auditory learner (you need to hear to remember). If you're a passive learner, hunched over your desk watching the textbook pages of history facts flip slowly by, you'll be lucky to remember 10 percent of what you see. Even people who don't prefer to learn things by sound remember 20 percent of what they hear. So close your eyes, visualize the facts with their dates, and say them to yourself.

As an auditory fan, while studying, make sure to say things like "First Great Awakening, Jonathan Edwards, 1730 — Revolution's Coming" out loud repeatedly to yourself with your eyes closed. (Don't do this in a crowded coffeehouse; people may think you're crazy instead of brilliant. There's such a fine line.)

Even if you do prefer sound to sight, also try forming the words into a vivid picture in your mind; most folks can remember 30 percent of what they see.

A high-tech solution is available for auditory learners: You can actually scan text into a text-to-speech program and have the facts read to you by a friendly computer voice. Check out the programs at www.download.com.

Studying through movement

Kinesthetic learners are hands-on people who concentrate better and learn more easily when movement is involved. Although you can't dance your way through the Big AP, you can learn to use movement sense to help your memory.

Kinesthetic people can make a scene into a movie in their heads. Just imagine Jonathan Edwards pounding the pulpit and waving a "1730 — Revolution's Coming" banner. It doesn't matter how silly the image is; in fact, the sillier it is, the better. Humor is an easy emotion to remember, and anything out of the ordinary is better than trying to remember gray words on paper.

If you have to see the facts spatially because you are a kinesthetic learner, try putting color-coded sticky notes containing key facts in date order along a route that you take through your house. Walk that route several times, stopping to associate each fact with where you are standing. That way, you can associate facts with known locations. Don't leave the sticky notes up too long, though; your mother may come along and vacuum a hole in the 1800s.

Taking Advantage of School Resources

If your school offers after-class review sessions for AP U.S. History, be there. Your teacher can't slip and tell you exactly what is going to be on the test, because he doesn't know. He *does* know what has been on the test in the past, however.

Also, review sessions are great places to practice that other smartness that is going to win a clap-for-you score. I call this skill Shakespeare Jr., also known as short essay writing. You weren't very good at riding a bike until you had the chance to try again and again. You won't be really good at short history essays until you have written at least ten. You wouldn't want your first time on a bike to be at the bike races, and you don't want your first experience with a DBQ to be on the big test. If your school offers feedback on practice essays, make sure you are first in line.

Streamlining Your Learning Outside Class

The topic of study skills sounds about as interesting as lint collecting, but there are some moves that can help you get more miles to the gallon out of your learning time:

- ✔ Have a regular study place and time, and stick to them every day.

- ✔ When you study outside class, break up your hour time into two 30-minute chunks, with a 5-minute break between chunks.

- ✔ Review during the day, when you are really awake. An hour during daylight can be worth 2 hours at night.

- ✔ As New Agey as this sounds, tell yourself that you strongly intend to remember what you are studying. At the beginning of your study session, for example, say, "I am going to remember the presidents from Abe Lincoln to Teddy Roosevelt tonight." Research shows that the act of seriously committing to remember improves retention as much as 50 percent. Trying and not quite making it is okay; you can always do better tomorrow. What is not okay is just waiting to see what happens to you. You have to set a clear goal and push hard to make it. Dreams come true because people make them come true.

- ✔ Always associate a new fact with an old one, as in "Oh, I see. John Charles Fremont becomes the Great Pathfinder for the Republican Party as its first presidential candidate (1856) after he was the Great Pathfinder of the West on the trails to California (1836–1853)."

- ✔ Study the difficult stuff first. Set some reward milestones. After you make it through the Civil War, it's time for a small party!

- ✔ Get emotional about the events you are studying: Women's rights were awesome and long overdue; slavery sucked. You remember facts that mean something to your heart, not just your fine mind.

- ✔ Although your friends and family may not seem to be begging for the latest in your history insights, teach them about some of the important events you are learning. Teaching a concept to someone else more than doubles your memory of that concept.

Cramming the Night Before May Not Help

Just because lots of people cram the night before the test doesn't make it right. You, in fact, are much too calm for that. Or at least you're *going* to be that calm. Or at a minimum, you will fake it till you make it.

Because the AP U.S. History test involves Shakespeare Jr. (heavy writing) as well as Copy Machine (remembering facts), you're way better off with a rested body and fresh mind the day of the test than you are trying to tip just one more woozy date into your tired cerebellum the night before. As hard as it is to admit, Grandma was right: Diet, exercise, and rest are keys to success.

You'll want to benefit from maximum sleep the two nights before the test. If you usually sleep for seven hours on vacation, give yourself room for eight both nights. You need two nights of good sleep, because sleep deprivation can skip a day. People can have a low-rest night, skate through the next 24 hours on fumes, and run out of gas on the second day. You don't want to get stuck in AP Land.

Triathletes and marathon racers knock off training two days before their event to build up an energy reserve. You can study your regular amount up to the last day, but you should knock off anything that distracts your mind or body two days before the big test. Replace coffee, junk food, and media with exercise and relaxation techniques. Kick up your exercise routine by 50 percent; more exercise keeps you calm and helps you think.

Cooling Out Pretest Anxiety

If you're a worrier, be honest with yourself. Are you worried because you really haven't prepared for the test? Here's the reality check: Have you gotten decent grades in your high school AP U.S. History course? Are you following your hour-a-day test-prep schedule? If the answer to those two questions is yes, you need to deal with your real problem: chronic anxiety. This condition is nothing to be ashamed of; the United States itself once suffered from overwhelming anxiety. In the inaugural words of longest-serving president Franklin Delano Roosevelt, "We have nothing to fear but fear itself — nameless, unreasoning, unjustified terror which paralyzes needed efforts." If you have done the study basics but are restless, check out the relaxation techniques later in the following sections. Relaxation doesn't just keep you comfortable; staying loose also helps you perform better on the test. You are going to be too cool to be a fool for a feeling that paralyzes needed efforts.

If your worry is justified because you really haven't done the preparation you need, consider the words of somebody who was just the opposite of a famous president. That would be Death Valley Scotty. In the early 1900s, Scotty was a prospector in the hottest place in the United States: Death Valley, California. Scotty never found gold, but he did find a beautiful oasis and many adventures, laughs, and friends. Scotty said, "There's just two things ain't worth worrying about: things you can change and things you can't." If it is already too late to study, consider that the lesson you're about to learn, no matter how painful, is cheap tuition for the rest of your life. If you still have time to get a study program together, start working right now. The effort you make will take your mind off your anxiety.

In the following three sections are professional techniques to buy yourself some worry-free time while you improve your sleep and concentration in the weeks before the test.

Think they're having a good time overseas? They're not

While Americans are sweating the APs and SATs, students in Japan are attending *juku*, or private cram schools. Japanese students sometimes go to juku every day after school and up to 16 hours a day on weekends to prepare for "examination hell" in January, which will decide their university fates. Row upon row of quiet students stare at the blackboard. Kids in the back even look through binoculars to grasp every word.

Meanwhile, in jolly old England, students are obsessing the *A levels*. A levels come in a variety of subjects, just like the APs, and you need to pass at least three to get into a good university. U.K. schools have grades like those in the United States, except that the land of Harry Potter has not forgotten about *E*. Average grade distribution is 10 percent *A*, 15 percent *B*, 10 percent *C*, 15 percent *D*, and 20 percent *E*. A further 20 percent are allowed an O-level pass, which is sort of like saying, "Thanks for showing up." The real flunkies get a *U* and have to play in rock-and-roll bands.

Using progressive relaxation

Lots of people, auditory learners or not, feel better hearing progressive-relaxation steps read out loud to them. You can get a spoken recording of relaxation instructions on the Web (cdbaby.com/cd/jmartin). Many slightly different versions of this technique are available; all of them work if you let them.

Relaxation is a natural state: it's what you do when you are asleep. You can learn to do progressive relaxation while you're awake and use it to clear your mind. First, get into comfortable clothing and choose a quiet space. Then:

1. **Lie flat on your back, with your eyes closed.**

2. **Feel your feet getting heavy. Consciously relax them, and let them sink down. Start with your toes and move up your foot to your ankles.**

3. **Feel your knees getting heavy. Consciously relax them, and let them sink down.**

4. **Feel your upper legs and thighs getting heavy. Consciously relax them, and feel them sink down.**

5. **Feel your abdomen and chest while you breathe. Consciously let them relax. Let your breathing be deep and regular. Let your abdomen and chest sink down.**

6. **Feel your back down to your upper legs. Consciously relax, and let your back sink down.**

7. **Feel your hands getting heavy. Consciously relax them, and feel them sink down.**

8. **Feel your arms getting heavy. Consciously relax them, and feel them sink down.**

9. **Feel your shoulders getting heavy. Consciously relax them, and feel them sink down.**

10. **Feel your head and neck getting heavy. Consciously relax your neck, and feel your head sink down.**

11. **Feel your mouth and jaw. Pay attention to your jaw muscles, and unclench them if they are tight. Feel your mouth and jaw relax.**

12. **Feel your eyes. Are you forcibly closing your eyelids? Consciously relax your eyelids, and feel the tension slide off your eyes.**

13. **Mentally scan down your body. If you find any place that's still tense, consciously relax that place, and let it sink down.**

14. **Lie still for 5 minutes.**

Practicing deep breathing

As simple as it seems, deep breathing is a great way to relax your body and concentrate energy, which is why it's an important part of spiritual, meditation, and martial-arts traditions around the world.

1. **Sit comfortably, straight up, with a loose waist and your stomach relaxed.**

   Don't worry about looking fat; no one is watching. A chair is fine; you don't have to sit cross-legged on the floor, wearing a turban. Just check that your back is comfortably straight and your middle is loose and relaxed.

2. **Let your whole self relax.**

   You can work your way from bottom to top, as in the progressive-relaxation technique in the preceding section.

3. **Begin to inhale slowly through your nose. Count to four as you fill your lungs in four parts from bottom to top. Breathe in slowly, taking about 5 seconds for a full breath.**

4. **Hold your breath for a couple of seconds.**

5. **Quietly relax, and let the air flow all the way out through your mouth.**

6. **Wait a few seconds, and do it again.**

   Breathe in through your nose in four sections; let the air out completely through your mouth in a long, peaceful "Ahh" or "Ohm." (That's the dial tone of the universe.)

7. **If you get dizzy, you're going too fast. Slow down.**

8. **Imagine that you're floating, and pretty soon you will be.**

Using Quiet Ears

This technique works like listening to a seashell at the beach. Since it stills the world around you, Quiet Ears helps you connect to your own inner strength. This technique works for everybody, but especially if you are easily distracted by outside sounds:

1. **Close your eyes.**

2. **Place your hands loosely on top of your head.**

3. **Cup your hands and cover both your ears.**

   You hear the slow, rushing sound of your own blood circulating. This is a good thing.

4. **Listen to this sound while you count to 10, ten times.**

5. **Relax your arms, and do it again.**

   You may find yourself breathing peacefully.

Keeping Calm and Cool on the Big Day

On the day of the test, eat a medium breakfast. You're on your way to a performance, and you don't need heavy food to slow you down. Give yourself more time than you think you need to get to the test site; no last-minute parking problems or traffic tickets should spoil your mood. If you get to the site early, walk around. You'll be sitting for a long time, and you want to get your blood circulating. Don't drink a lot of liquid. You'll get a break in the middle, but you don't want to be going to the bathroom while the test clock is running. If you run into friends, be nice, but don't listen very hard to what they say. Watch the pros before a race. They acknowledge one another with a nod, but they're already in their own space.

Bring three No. 2 pencils and a good separate eraser for the multiple-choice questions. If you change a scan-marked multiple-choice answer, you want to make sure that the mark in the scan oval you rejected is erased completely. Bring a couple of your favorite ink pens for the essay section. Wear a watch. You won't be allowed to look at your cell phone, and time control is important.

Pick a spot in the test room with good light and a minimum of possibly distracting people. You'll get an exam packet with the Section I multiple-choice questions and the Section II essay questions. Section I has a Scantron answer form with more than enough spaces. You mark your answers to the 80 multiple-choice questions by filling in the correct ovals carefully with a pencil. Section II essay questions are on a green insert; you write your answers in the supplied pink essay book.

For both Section I and Section II, you can make notes in the question books but not on the answer pages. You have 55 minutes to answer as many of the 80 multiple-choice questions as you can. After a 10-minute break, you have 2 hours and 10 minutes to study and write three essays. The Section II essay time begins with a mandatory 15-minute reading period. During the reading period, you study the questions but are not allowed to begin writing the essays.

Staying wide awake in AP land

With the proctor's word "Begin," you open the Section I multiple-choice book and dive in. You discover the strategy for handling multiple-choice questions in Chapter 4. For now, just realize that the 80 questions each have 5 alternatives for a total of 400 possible answers. You are going to be reading 400 possible answers, each of which is designed to at least minimally suck you into picking it as the right match for its question. You will be answering multiple-choice questions for 55 minutes, which means you have 41 seconds per question and only 8 seconds per possible answer. Don't panic; the time is longer than it seems. Try holding your breath for 41 seconds; you'll feel how long that is.

You don't have to be right about everything to score a perfect 5 on the big AP. The test grade is curved; test mavens realize that few people are going to burn through all 80 multiple-choice questions at 41 seconds each and come up with a perfect score. You can skate by on Section I by getting fewer than 50 questions right and still pull it out with an aces 5 score just by getting two-thirds of the possible Shakespeare Jr. credits for essay writing in Section II.

Avoiding a multiple-choice panic

Panicking is something to avoid at all times during the test, but especially during the multiple-choice section. What panic can do to you on multiple-choice questions is make you lose concentration and stop reading carefully. The situation only gets worse; the reality is that the questions get harder as you move through the 80 mini-challenges.

Don't stop to freak out. If you aren't sure about a question, cross off the answer choices that you do know are wrong in the question book. If you can cross out only one, do it, and move on. Keep going. Most people don't get through all the questions. You are refusing to panic — just moving along harvesting all the good questions that you know. After you've got the low-hanging fruit, go back and work on the tougher questions. Use every minute to complete multiple-choice questions that you skipped earlier and to double-check the answers you've already marked.

Getting all the way to the end has a time-sequence wrong-answer elimination advantage. You learn what this mouthful means in Chapter 4.

Don't outsmart yourself on multiple-choice. Save double-checking for last, because you do not want to trap yourself by overthinking. Usually, your first hunch is your best shot; you don't get any smarter by squinching up your eyebrows. Obsessing over every question as you go only slows you down. If you have time for a recheck, don't change any answers unless you're sure those answers are wrong.

Tuning up at break time

When 55 minutes are up, the proctor will say: "Stop working. Close your booklet, and put your answer sheet on your desk." You've got a 10-minute break before the Section II essay section calls upon you to create great history fast. Use those 10 minutes to get up and walk as far as you can from the crowd. Practice deep breathing lightly as you walk: four-count deep inhalation through your nose and a long, peaceful exhale through your mouth. Shake your arms; roll your shoulders and neck. This is not a time to impress people or gossip; you are in the middle of a race. Make sure to hit the bathroom on your way back, if there's any chance you'll need to go in the next 2 hours.

As you walk, think about what was good about how you did on Section I. Congratulate yourself for the answers that you knew, and leave the other ones behind. Besides the preparation you already have, your strongest weapon going into the Section II essay section is a positive mind.

Cruising with Shakespeare Jr. in Section II

Shakespeare Jr. is what I call short essay writing, covered in Section II of the exam. You're going to be having fun and earning points in Section II. Part A is the famous Document-Based Question (DBQ). Chapter 5 is devoted to nothing but this single topic. The DBQ is perhaps the greatest moment of high art in any history exam. For now, you don't have to appreciate its beauty. Just remember: Prepare before you write.

In Section II, Part B and Part C each contain two regular essay questions. Here, you get to choose the rope with which you want to hang yourself. You're going to pick the one question from each of the two parts that seems the least scary. But not yet.

Before you can uncoil your pen, Section II wants you to spend 15 minutes alone with it, just reading. Your proctor will recommend that you take the entire time to read the documents and to scan the pictures and charts in the DBQ. This time, amazing as it may seem, the grownup is right. The proctor can't do anything to stop you from sailing right past the documents in Part A and having a peek at what question beasts await you in Parts B and C. Don't do it. Whatever is in Parts B and C will wait for you to get there. You don't need it hanging over your head while you do the DBQ.

As you work through the three essays, keep this positive thought in mind: Each of your compositions will be scored by a completely different reader who doesn't know who you are, what you've done on the other parts of the test, or even who graded your other essays. It's a new day every time.

Here's another tip on how to approach the essays: Plan before you write, making notes on the green question insert and not in the pink answer booklet, which is *only* for your essays. Look at the essays in this happy way: It's like 2 hours and 10 minutes to grab everything you can carry from your favorite store. You have nothing to lose. You can only gain points by weaving the themes and topics you know into a well-argued essay.

It's payday. Copy Machine and Shakespeare Jr. are singing together!

Part II

Answering the Questions: Three Kinds, Three Strategies

The 5th Wave   By Rich Tennant

"Remember, there are 4 types of questions on the Advanced Placement tests: multiple-choice, document-based, essay, and 'How would you like to drive big rigs for a living?'"

In this part...

Now it's time to get down to cases. Are you ready to look at some actual questions? Don't be scared — this part tells you how to answer them. By staring those challenging questions right in the face now, you can begin to get into the mindset of the evil Test Mongers who are, even as you read this, probably cackling about what they have in store for you. This part arms you with a strategy for taking on whatever the Test Mongers throw your way. By looking at the three parts of the exam out front, you can be thinking about possible questions and answers as you review history. No surprises; you'll be locked, loaded, and ready for action.

Chapter 4

Going with Good Odds on Multiple-Choice Questions

*I*t's funny, isn't it? Fifty-five minutes seems really long when you have to get through a whole period of that class you hate in school. But in the AP U.S. History exam, when you're faced with 80 multiple-choice questions, each with 5 possible answers lettered from A to E, those same 55 minutes don't even seem to be enough time for you to say hello.

Well, hello! Whether 55 minutes seems like enough time to you for 80 multiple-choice questions, in this chapter, I give you plenty of pointers and strategies to help you stretch the time to fit your winning answers.

Scoping Out the Multiple-Choice Question Troll

If you look at the big AP test as payday for all the studying you've done, Section I is where you can score some easy bucks. In only a third of the test time, you can earn half of the credits just by confronting your old friend and enemy, multiple choice. Your trick is to avoid turning multiple choice into multiple guess.

You're going to be getting a great grade on multiple-choice Section I because you'll be keeping your eye on the basics. Don't waste your time on hard questions. When you're in class, the teacher may think you're super smart because you remember the year the Farmer-Labor Party was founded (1918). Face facts: The big exam doesn't issue brownie points. You get the same credit for answering hard questions as easy ones. Get all the easy answers before you bang your head on the hard ones.

Think of each multiple-choice question as a tricky little troll holding a shiny piece of treasure: one point worth of credit toward that great score you're going to rack up on the AP. But wait — not so fast! Mr. Troll doesn't want to give up the treasure — and he can bite. Before you reach in to grab the credit, scrutinize that tricky little troll carefully. Check the Question Troll out with all the scopes: Use a periscope, a microscope, and even a telescope on each question before you answer it. In this section, I show you how.

If you get stressed during your run through the multiple-choice warehouse, do a couple of the deep-breathing exercises outlined in Chapter 3. Breathe in deeply through your nose in four sections. Breathe out completely through your mouth. Don't overdo it, and keep your eye on the test. You're going for a good score, not spiritual enlightenment.

Looking out for hidden points

The Question Trolls like to hide their treasure points in the most important spots. The AP folks want you to know the key trends in U.S. history, not a bunch of board game trivia. You don't have to remember battles or the name of every explorer who ever leaned on a tree. The right answer is often the broadest, most important concept.

What was the most important impact of the Great Depression of the 1930s on the United States?

(A) It led to Prohibition.

(B) Lots of Americans were depressed.

(C) Businesses did better with less competition.

(D) The Great Depression led to an expansion of the role of government and social programs to protect people from poverty.

(E) The United States got off the gold standard to make more money.

Even though some of the other answers contain a little bit of truth, the only one that can be the key concept is expansion of the role of government and social programs, choice (D). The key concepts to study for the AP are right there in extra-black type: They're the section headings in this book and your textbook.

Beware of tricky Question Trolls! Some answer choices are attractive bait to lure you into a quick wrong decision. You're too smart to be fooled into saying, for the question about the Great Depression, that it meant lots of Americans were depressed, but that answer could sound like a fit to the uninformed. Watch out for answers that sound a little too simplistic; they're there to trap the simple.

Taking a closer look at the points penalty

How come the nice College Board lets the Question Troll bite you when you reach in for one of his treasure points the wrong way? Test makers are the kind of people who worked hard to make good grades all the way through school. They hate the kind of people who party down instead of studying and then, on the day of the test, somehow get lucky and blow right through the exam with a good grade they didn't earn.

Here's an example: Mr. Party slouches back in his chair, picks up the Scantron answer sheet, and just makes a nice pattern of filled-in ovals without even bothering to read the questions (which may as well be in Greek, for the amount of time he's studied). For each question, he has a one-in-five possibility of being right purely by chance. Therefore, with average luck, out of 80 questions,

just blind chance should get him one fifth of 80, or 16 points, on the multiple-choice section. That score isn't enough for Harvard to call with a scholarship, but it's 16 points more than Mr. Party deserves.

With the Question Troll taking a well-deserved nip out of his score, our bad actor gets one quarter of a point taken away for each wrong guess. Because his average luck on pattern marking left him guessing wrong 64 times, he loses one quarter of 64 points for a score of 16 lucky points minus 16 penalty, or 0 points total — exactly what he deserves for knowing nothing about history.

You deserve better, of course, because you've studied. You may not know everything about U.S. history, but at least you know some things.

Paying close attention to the scoring

Each right answer you snatch from a Question Troll is worth *one point*. If you get bitten by picking a wrong answer, the troll takes away *one-quarter point*. Section I of the AP test has 80 multiple-choice questions. Suppose you answer 60 of them correctly, pick the wrong answer 12 times, and leave 8 question spaces blank because the Question Troll for those last 8 questions looks too mean to mess with. You'd get 60 points for your correct answers and lose 3 points for the ones you missed (¼ of 12 points is 3 points), for a total of 57 points. Not bad. If you had taken a shot at the last 8 toughie troll questions and missed every time, you'd lose one quarter of 8 points; you'd end up losing another 2 points, for a final score of 55 points. You get a lot if you're right, but being wrong costs a little.

Suppose that you're confronted by this tricky troll question:

Which treaty did away with most of the trade restrictions among the United States, Canada, and Mexico?

(A) SALT

(B) NBA

(C) The Gulf of Tonkin resolution

(D) SDI

(E) NAFTA

Oh, my gosh! It's alphabet soup. Your mind goes blank. Then a small light begins to shine: Isn't the NBA that league with balls, hoops, tall guys, and 3-point plays? Okay, you don't play basketball with trade restrictions, so choice (B) is wrong.

If you can eliminate only that one wrong answer, you've evened the odds: You have one chance in four of guessing correctly on the remaining four choices by pure chance and three chances in four of losing a quarter of a point. Guess this way 80 times, and you'll theoretically be 8 points ahead: 80 questions with one out of four average luck equals 20 questions right. Take away one quarter of 60 questions wrong, and you lose 12. You pick up 8 points on average just by eliminating one bad response.

The odds get better if you can eliminate two bad multiple-choice answers. With random chance, you pick up an average of 14 points on 80 questions if you can narrow each question down to three choices. Suppose that in addition to tossing the NBA off the court, you have a strong suspicion that the Gulf of Tonkin is a long way from the United States, Canada, or Mexico. And you may just sneak up on the right answer directly. Don't these three nations make up North America? With that information to go on, you may conjure up the North American Free Trade Agreement — also known as NAFTA — from the misty outlands of your mind.

The take-out lesson is this: *If you can eliminate even one of the five multiple choices, guessing pays.* If you really haven't got a clue, don't touch the troll unless you feel lucky. Your odds of doing damage are as good as your odds of scoring points.

Fortunately for your chances with the Question Troll, you have more than one way to get a clue.

Periscope up: Watching out for tricky words

Because trolls are tricky, make sure that you read each question carefully, twice, before you grab one of the five answer choices. In sports, *juking* is when you fake out an opponent by dodging in the opposite direction from where he thinks you're going. Question Trolls love to juke you. If you don't study their moves carefully from a safe distance (as though you were looking through a periscope) *before* you move in to grab an answer choice, you may well find yourself headed in the wrong direction.

Questions meant to juke you typically contain the words *EXCEPT, NOT,* or *LEAST.* Notice that these words are in capital letters. They're printed this way to give you a fighting chance to see them even if you're in a hurry. This convention also allows the trolls to laugh righteously if you miss something that's right there in plain sight, capitalized. Juking words change the direction of the question.

Gracefully dodging the EXCEPT juke

Take a close look at the following sample question:

All these important foods came to Europe from discoveries in the New World EXCEPT

(A) chocolate

(B) corn

(C) tomatoes

(D) coffee

(E) potatoes

So you're blowing by at the rate of a question every 40 seconds; you see the terms *foods, Europe,* and *New World,* and you think, "Oh, boy. I know — it's got to be tomatoes, because how did the Italians make pizza without tomatoes before they discovered the New World?" Or you think, "It's chocolate for sure, because I remember wondering how Europeans even bothered to keep living in a pre-New World era without chocolate."

This question has too many good answers — and that's the tip-off that you're the target of an attempted juke. Perhaps you were going so fast that you didn't see the word *EXCEPT,* even though it's in brazen capital letters. Even if you miss *EXCEPT,* all is not lost. If you read all the choices and don't just swallow the first bait that the troll tosses your way, you'll begin to notice that a lot of the answers seem to fit a little too well. Suspiciously, all but one of the answers look like they could work. Look back at the question, and you find the juke in all caps.

Read the whole question and all the answers. Twice.

NOT is not to be ignored!

In addition to the EXCEPT trolls, you need to watch out for questions with NOT in them.

Which of the following was NOT included in the Northwest Ordinance of 1787?

(A) procedures for organizing territory and state governments

(B) a ban on slavery

(C) guaranteed religious freedom

(D) the right to a jury trial

(E) specific reservations for American Indians

Like the *EXCEPT* troll, the *NOT* bomb is hoping you're reading too fast to notice it lurking there as inconspicuously as any word can that's forced to wear capital letters. The *NOT* bomb is banking on your seeing just the phrase "Northwest Ordinance of 1787," glancing down at the answers, seeing one of the attractive first four answers (A) through (D), and patting yourself on the back as you rush your wrong answer to the Scantron sheet.

But you're too smart for the *NOT* bomb. You've read the question twice, so you've definitely seen the giant *NOT*. You've also read the possible answers twice, and they mostly look too good to be true. You've saved yourself from disaster by careful reading. But how do you know which of the five answers is the right one? Here are some things to consider:

✔ You know the Northwest Ordinance of 1787 was written by the same lovable guys who brought you the American Revolution. Therefore, it should contain Declaration of Independence issues such as jury trials.

✔ Setting up state governments is a noncontroversial housekeeping matter; it had to be there.

✔ Slavery certainly was controversial, but — clue — you know the Northwest ended up without slaves.

✔ Perhaps the least-noble reason for the Revolution was to let the new Americans have at American Indian lands the British government had declared off limits. It wouldn't make sense to set aside specific reservations when the American Indians were still fighting to have no settlers at all.

✔ The most extreme answer is (E). Take it to the bank.

When you scan a list of possible answers, especially in juke questions, look for the most extreme outlier to be the answer you want. The most extreme choices tend to be extremely right when it comes to answering negatively phrased juke questions. They go beyond the list presented and just don't quite fit in.

Last but not LEAST

The final juke word to look out for is *LEAST*. You're sailing along normally, looking for the best match between the key word in the question and those tricky multiple choices when you come upon a *LEAST*. Big pause. *LEAST* switches up the meaning, so now you're looking for the worst match. But *LEAST* is even trickier than that. The answer can't be wrong, and it can't be from outer space; it just has to be the worst fit. Check out this example.

Which of the following was the LEAST important reason Andrew Jackson was popular with American voters in the 1820s and 1830s?

(A) opposed the Bank of the United States

(B) stood up to nullification

(C) dressed like a frontiersman

(D) supported more democracy for the common man

(E) won the Battle of New Orleans

You don't have to worry about one of these answers being false. Because this is a *LEAST* question, they're all at least partly true. Dressing like a frontiersman seems to be pretty trivial, even in a symbolic field like politics. The 1820s and 1830s had no TV and few pictures anyway, so not many people could have seen Jackson. Choice (C), dressed like a frontiersman, is the *LEAST* reason and your best answer.

Conquering bossy words

In addition to *EXCEPT, NOT,* and *LEAST,* watch out for bossy words like *complete, always, never, only, all, every,* and *none.* Because history almost always has exceptions, bossy words that seem to cover the whole story are often the sign of a wrong answer. Take a look at the following example:

Abraham Lincoln freed the slaves with the Emancipation Proclamation of 1863 because

(A) the only reason he wanted to win the Civil War was to abolish slavery

(B) Lincoln always sided with the abolitionists

(C) the Emancipation Proclamation completely freed the slaves

(D) emancipation made political and moral sense in 1863

(E) Lincoln never made a political decision when he could make a moral one

The bossy words in (A), (B), (C), and (E) mark them for extinction from your answer choices. Lincoln said he wanted to preserve the Union, whether it meant freeing all the slaves or freeing none of the slaves. Although Lincoln certainly was personally opposed to slavery, he put being President of a united America before the cause of abolition. The Emancipation Proclamation freed only slaves in rebel states. Lincoln was a great and honest person, but he wouldn't have won the Presidential election if he weren't also an experienced politician.

Reverse engines! Bossy words are your friends when a troll tries to juke you with one of those tricky *EXCEPT, NOT,* or *LEAST* questions. Here's a different take on the Emancipation Proclamation question:

Which of the following causes is NOT a part of the reason Abraham Lincoln freed the slaves in the Emancipation Proclamation?

(A) The North had better news from the battlefield.

(B) Lincoln always sided with the abolitionists.

(C) Freeing the slaves had popular support in the North.

(D) Lincoln was personally opposed to slavery.

(E) Fleeing slaves may weaken Southern war efforts.

In this version, the very word *always* that made choice (B) wrong in the first question makes it right in the juke *NOT* question.

Going with what you know

You're smarter than you think. You can usually come up with more than one way to figure out a question. When you hit a blank wall, try thinking outside the wall. Eliminating even one bad answer choice puts the odds in your favor. Sometimes, you can rule out answers by looking at them closely, like through a microscope. Here's an example:

Upton Sinclair's book *The Jungle* led to the passage of which law?

(A) the Clayton Antitrust Law

(B) the Northwest Ordinance

(C) the Pure Food and Drug Act

(D) the Stark Amendment

(E) the Hepburn Act

Oh, my gosh, how would you know? All those boring acts look like foreign arithmetic to you. Ah, but wait. On a slow Friday in literature class, the teacher was talking about *The Jungle* not being all about vines and monkeys and stuff, but about filthy food factories. That would lead you to (C), the Pure Food and Drug Act. Or you may just have been wrestling with the question about the Northwest Ordinance covered earlier in this chapter, and you picked up something about the ordinance from answering that question.

When it comes to defending yourself from the biting Question Trolls, don't get caught with no facts to go on. Although it's good to be thinky, it's even better to be knowy. When you study history, take note of the key terms, their approximate dates, and why they're important. You may make this note: "Northwest Ordinance (1787 — at the beginning of U.S. government) = rules for setting up new states from the Ohio River to the Mississippi River; no slavery; freedom of religion; jury trials."

Making a little knowledge go a long way

You don't really need to know something by heart to choose the correct answer. Sometimes, you can make a little knowledge go a long way.

American artists painting around 1900 in what was called the Realist school tended to paint which subject?

(A) American frontier life

(B) urban scenes

(C) rural family life

(D) wild natural landscapes

(E) pastoral scenes

The answer is (B). A little time with art can go a long way. You have a vague feeling that the late Victorians painted some pretty sentimental scenes, certainly not what you'd call Realism. Then-common subjects like (A), (C), (D), and (E) probably wouldn't earn a special name like Realist school; they all blend together and make (B) stand out.

Using common sense

Sometimes, common sense alone can help you solve a problem.

When a U.S. reporter coined the phrase *Manifest Destiny,* he meant that

(A) the struggle for racial equality should be the purpose of America

(B) the United States should set all of South America free from colonialism

(C) America must become either all slaveholding or all free

(D) it's the fate of the United States to cover the whole continent from ocean to ocean

(E) all Americans should pursue happiness until they're happy all the time

Okay, your best bet is to know that Manifest Destiny means (D). But what if you just knew that Manifest Destiny sounded like something you'd heard a lot? That would probably eliminate events that didn't happen, such as (B) and (C). You can eliminate (E) because it sounds like a smart-aleck answer. You may know that Manifest Destiny started way before the Civil War and that even 100 years after the outbreak of the Civil War, racial equality still didn't have full support. That pretty much leaves (A) out. Knowing a little and taking the time to use your common sense can be a lifesaver.

Making historic eras your friend

By knowing the approximate year of a key term, you give yourself power to pry the point from a Question Troll.

All the following were results of the First Great Awakening EXCEPT

(A) more and stronger churches

(B) the founding of new colleges and universities

(C) nationwide religious enthusiasm

(D) a return to the persecution of witches

(E) ministers with followings of thousands

The answer is (D). The First Great Awakening wasn't about a return to the persecution of witches. You could have scored on this question from several directions. First, the minute you see the word *EXCEPT, LEAST,* or *NOT,* you say to yourself, "juke." You're looking for an extreme that just doesn't fit with the rest of the answers.

If you don't know all about the First Great Awakening yet, don't worry — I get to that in Part III. Even if this were test day, and you still didn't really know, you could work with whatever dates you do have in your brain. You may know that the witch hunt thing died out in the 1690s and that the First Great Awakening didn't occur until 40 years later. You may realize that history is written by the winners and that they'd be unlikely to give the name Awakening to something as ugly as burning women. You may just figure out that persecution of witches is a standout in a list with unifying words like *churches, colleges, enthusiasm,* and *ministers.*

You know you're better off guessing if you can eliminate one of the choices. Because (A), (C), and (E) all sound like they belong to the same club, you can eliminate them from being the extreme. You'd be statistically way ahead even if you had to guess between (B) and (D).

Questioning illustrations

As though they just can't wait for the Document-Based Question later on the test, the Question Trolls usually throw in few questions illustrated with pictures or charts. These illustrated questions can actually be easier than regular multiple-choice challenges. The illustration contains most of the answer; you just need to know what it's telling you.

What does the following chart, which conveys the median personal income by educational attainment, illustrate about income and education?

Measure

Some High School	High-School Graduate	Some College	Associate Degree	Bachelor's Degree	Bachelor's Degree or Higher	Master's Degree	Professional Degree	Doctorate Degree

Persons age 25+ w/earnings

$20,321	$26,505	$31,054	$35,009	$43,143	$49,303	$52,390	$82,473	$70,853

(A) It's always better to stay in school.

(B) Many people older than 25 are rich.

(C) Everybody with a bachelor's degree makes at least $43,143.

(D) Income tends to rise with education.

(E) These figures are the minimum salaries for each education level.

The answer is right on the page: (D), income tends to rise with education. The important point with illustrated questions is to look hard at the picture and stick to what the illustration shows. Don't think too hard and outsmart yourself by overinterpreting. The chart shows *median* personal income, not a guarantee. Median is different from the average that most people earn. That's why the income advantage in this chart for a college degree is even better than the bucks dangled before your greedy eyes in Chapter 1. Keep studying!

Sometimes, the test will ask you to identify a picture's background information; check out this example:

What are the era and social orientation of this cartoon?

(A) Southern Confederates

(B) Northern Democrats

(C) Slave owners, before the Civil War

(D) Northern abolitionists

(E) Reconstruction education, post–Civil War

The heart-rending subject indicates that the orientation is Northern, with strong abolitionist sentiments.

Beating the Clock for a Good Score

Time management is a key to winning on the multiple-choice section of the test. Even though you have only 55 minutes, you have all the time you need to pull out the easy questions and have a good shot at the harder issues. In the following sections, I give you tips to help you get through the multiple-choice section quickly without sacrificing accuracy.

Because the minutes make a difference, bring your own watch to the exam. You won't be allowed to check your cell phone or PDA, and the clock in the exam room may be wrong. Having a watch lets you be your own time manager.

Why timing is golden

The multiple-choice section is like a run through a warehouse in which you get to keep everything good you can find in 55 minutes. Trouble is, if you get too hung up trying to grab cartons of gelatin, you may not get to the jewelry section. Section I moves in general from easier to harder questions, but toward the difficult end, you may find questions that you know by heart. That's why you need to swing past all the questions quickly, like looking for your friends in a crowd by panning with a telescope.

Don't get hung up arguing with your brain. Try to scan all the questions, and then go back and work on the issues that need a little more thinking. If ten more seconds of thinking don't solve the problem, move on. Hitting the side of your head with your palm won't loosen up the secret knowledge cave. Give quick insights a chance to arrive, but spread your attention over as many questions as possible.

Relax. Forty seconds is longer than you think. Look at a clock with a second hand. Watch that second hand twitch around the dial for 40 seconds. Boring, huh? That's the interminable time you'll have for each question. Remember, you have a lightning-fast brain. Just think of how fast your mind can move from school to that hot kid you see when you're changing classes. Now stop thinking dirty and get back to the AP.

Pacing yourself to win

As you know only too well, the AP exam has 80 multiple-choice questions. When you get your Scantron form, make a light mark next to the answer ovals for question 20. Make another light mark next to the answer zone for question 40. The first mark will put you one quarter of the way through the multiple-choice race. You have 55 minutes total for the 80 questions. If you're running on time, you should be at question 20 about 14 minutes out of the gate. When the testing starts, add 14 minutes to the time on your watch. When you get to question 20, check to see whether you're on pace. Check once more when you get to question 40. If you've used more than half an hour of your 55 precious minutes, you need to pick up the pace. If you've used only about 20 minutes when you hit question 40, you can afford to take a little more time.

Using a marking trick for faster progress

When grades are on the line, smart people write and mark while they read. You, my friend, are a smart person, so you should mark *in the question book* as you roll rapidly (but in a controlled fashion) through the multiple-choice questions in Section I of the AP exam. Here are some pointers to follow to make the process faster and easier for you:

- ✔ If you're sure that you're locked into the right answer after reading both the question and all the answers twice, just circle that for-sure answer in the question book, and carefully blacken its oval on the Scantron answer form.

- ✔ If you can eliminate some but not all of the choices, cross out the answers you know are wrong.

- ✔ If you have one or more wrong answers crossed out, mark your best guess for the answer on the Scantron sheet, circle it on the question sheet, and put the number of wrong choices you've been able to cross out next to the question. If you've crossed out three wrong answers, put a *3* next to the question; if you've crossed out two wrong answers, put a *2* next to the question.

- ✔ If you don't have a clue to eliminate any of the choices, put a zero next to the question and don't fill in the Scantron sheet for that question. Also, put a light mark opposite the Scantron number of the question you're not answering so that you don't accidentally put the answer to a known question in the wrong place. Putting the right answer in the wrong row can screw up every answer that comes after it. Make sure you have completely erased all these light marks before you hand in the answers; extra marks can make the grading machine get funky and reject your good answers.

When you've made it through all the questions, you should still have time to go back to the beginning and take another look at the questions you've numbered. Go through all the *3*s first, because these are the questions you're closest to being sure about. When you're through with the *3*s, go back and do the *2*s. If you have time, give a last once-over to the *1*s and zeros. Do you feel lucky?

Don't linger on any question after you've marked it. Instead, pause just long enough to see whether you want to change the answer you marked. Also, go with your first hunch unless you actually have a reason to change. Research shows that if you can't come up with any additional information, your first hunch is usually the best bet.

Getting all the way to the end quickly, using the numbering tips I give you, has a time-sequence-wrong-answer-elimination advantage. You'll actually pick up some history just from the juxtaposition of topics on the exam. You may be able to eliminate some wrong answers from early questions based on what you've noticed on questions closer to the end of the test. Also, answering later questions helps jog your memory.

Chapter 5

Scoring Big on Document-Based Questions (DBQs)

In This Chapter
▶ Making Document-Based Questions work for you
▶ Reading and interpreting documents under pressure
▶ Using the proof, analysis, and thesis (PAT) method
▶ Bringing in outside information for a higher score
▶ Writing the DBQ essay to make it grader-friendly

Depending on your level of preparation, the Document-Based Question (DBQ, for short) that appears on every AP U.S. History exam is either a beautiful chance for self-expression or a wordy invitation to the Dark Side. The sad truth is that most people who take the big test don't do as well as they could on the DBQ because they get freaked out by the detail.

Using the proof, analysis, and thesis (PAT) method introduced in this chapter (see the section "Practicing the DBQ"), you can prepare for DBQs. *PAT* is the essay-writing system that has what teachers look for: You use history with analysis to support a clear idea. You don't freak out; you laugh happily because you know how to blend the detail that the College Board gives you on the DBQ with outside information. To score high on the DBQ, you must create a thesis, analyze the documents as they relate to your thesis, and bring in outside evidence that supports your thesis.

Using Documents Like a Historian

Ever wonder what being a historian would feel like? The Document-Based Question is your chance to write history from primary sources, just like the famous professors in their ivy-covered towers. After bravely hacking your way through the 80 multiple-choice questions in Section I, you return from your all-too-short 10-minute break to face Section II, the free-response questions.

Free response doesn't mean you're free to write anything you want. You're free to write essays about what the AP tells you; you're not just picking among multiple choices. The DBQ essay comes first. On the DBQ, you combine what you know about history with what you can pull from a supplied set of documents to answer an assigned question. After you finish the DBQ, you choose two additional regular essays from four available topics. You discover more about the regular essays in Chapter 6.

History is what a people chooses to remember to explain who they are. The historian's job is to make sure what people remember is facts interpreted in as honest a manner as their current understanding of the world allows. History doesn't come from wizards with long white beards; it comes from scholars working patiently with primary source material to provide accurate facts plus reasonable analysis and interpretation. That's what you're going to do on the DBQs, just like a big-time historian.

On the test, you'll confront one interesting analysis question from an important period in U.S. history. To help build your essay on that question, you'll receive a set of eight to ten primary source documents. These documents could be letters, news reports, political cartoons, financial reports, pictures, diary entries, charts, graphs, love notes — almost anything you can get on paper. Your essay for the DBQ needs to combine your interpretation of the supplied documents with outside history facts you remember about the period and topic in question. You're the History Judge.

You may not feel like you're ready to be Judge Judy for everything that ever happened in U.S. history, but the DBQ is a good place to be as smart as you can. This is the most important essay on the AP exam; your score on the DBQ makes up 22.5 percent of your final grade. And remember, the AP U.S. History exam is graded on the curve. To get a *4* or a *5* as your final grade, you don't have to have a perfect score — just one that's better than the scores of most other AP test takers.

You have a chance to get ahead of the pack on the DBQ because people tend to wimp out on this question due to lack of organization. All essays on the AP are scored on a scale from *0* for awful to *9* for the rare perfect composition. The average score on the DBQ in recent years has been a pathetic *3* on the *9* scale. You can do better than that, and when you do, you'll feel your final score giving you a high five.

Knowing the Criteria for Scoring Big on the DBQ

The AP wants you to think, not just memorize. For that reason, the highest scores on the DBQ go to students who have developed a clear thesis or way of understanding the era of their assigned documents. Here are the guidelines for scoring on Section II, Question 1 (the DBQ). Scores range from a high of *9* to a low of *0*.

The *8-to-9* essay:

- Contains a well-developed thesis that may explain most of the changes within the DBQ era

- Supports the thesis with an effective analysis of economic and social trends

- Effectively uses a substantial number of documents

- Supports or proves the thesis with substantial (ideally, 50 percent) and relevant outside information

- May contain minor errors

- Is clearly organized and well written

- Scores: Only a few hundred students — about a tenth of 1 percent — get a *9*. A few thousand — still less than 1 percent — get an *8*

The *5-to-7* essay:

- ✔ Contains a thesis that explains many of the changes within the era

- ✔ Has a limited analysis of the information supporting the thesis

- ✔ Effectively uses some documents

- ✔ Supports the thesis with some outside information for proof

- ✔ May have some errors that don't seriously get in the way of main essay points

- ✔ Shows acceptable organization and writing; language errors don't stop understanding

- ✔ Scores: Fewer than 2 percent of test takers get a score of *7;* around 4 percent get a score of *6;* and 10 percent score a *5*

The *2-to-4* essay:

- ✔ Contains a limited or undeveloped thesis

- ✔ Lacks analysis and deals with questions in a simplistic way

- ✔ Just parrots back a laundry list of documents

- ✔ Contains little outside information or information that's wrong

- ✔ May contain substantial factual errors

- ✔ Is either poorly organized or poorly written

- ✔ Scores: Unfortunately, these scores are the most common. About 18 percent of test takers get a *4;* around 30 percent get a *3* (3.16 is the average DBQ score); and 27 percent get a pathetic *2*

The *0-to-1* essay:

- ✔ Lacks a thesis or just restates the question

- ✔ Shows the student doesn't really understand the question

- ✔ Shows the test taker has little understanding of the documents or just ignores them

- ✔ Contains no outside information

- ✔ Contains wrong information

- ✔ Badly written

- ✔ Scores: 7 percent of test takers get a *1;* about half a percent get a *0;* and another half a percent get nothing because they apparently drifted off before they got to the DBQ

Practicing the DBQ

As you know, *BBQ* stands for *barbecue,* which is lots of fun unless you're on the grill. Think of the Document-Based Question, often shortened to DBQ, as being sort of a BBQ for your mind. The DBQ is lots of fun as long as you stay away from the heat and enjoy the party. In this section, I first give you pointers on how to set up your answer. Then I give you a sample question based on Reconstruction in the South (see Chapter 14 for more information). Finally, I present tips on answering the sample question and tell you how to apply the proof, analysis, and thesis (PAT) method when writing your answer.

To write a winning answer for *any* DBQ, you first have to understand the question. Understanding the question is where a sadly large number of DBQers go wrong, so that's where you need start to go right. PAT can help in that regard, and the following steps explain how. I suggest you consider and follow these steps to prepare yourself before writing your answer (or even reading the question).

1. **Start sweeping the cobwebs of your brain for *proof,* or *proofreading,* which is the beginning of the PAT system.**

   Don't even read the documents until you have taken a sober inventory of what you know about the question. Don't worry — you'll remember more as you go. Just note on the green question book every event and theme you can think of off the top of your head.

2. **Read the documents twice; on the second round, circle words within the documents that you may want to refer to in your essay.**

3. **Do a little *analysis* — Step 2 in the PAT method.**

   What are some points you want to make about the question, and how does the information you have support these points? Jot quick notes in the green book.

   When you're looking for space to write in the green book, don't skip ahead to read the other regular essays. Deal with the regular essays when you get to them; you have no reason to get distracted now. I tell you all about writing the regular essays in Chapter 6.

4. **At *thesis* time — the final step and solid foundation in the PAT approach — you argue your thesis with analysis, using one major point in each body paragraph.**

   State your thesis in the first paragraph and restate it (with proof) in the last paragraph.

   Take a stand! It doesn't matter whether you're wrong; historians love to argue. A clear thesis stops a bored reader dead in her tracks and makes her pay attention to your analysis and proof. Your thesis provides a philosophy or road map for everything in your essay. In the Reconstruction example shown in the next section, the thesis could be "the South's resistance was too strong for Reconstruction to work" or "the North succeeded in changing a primitive slave society in the South into the beginnings of a modern, if racist, culture."

The benefit of structuring your DBQ argument under the PAT system is that you don't have to be right to win; *you* are the judge of history. The fact that you can corral evidence and use proof and analysis to support a clear thesis makes you a contender for a high score. And you don't have to be very high to get above the average score of *3;* just keep citing proof. A good paper successfully uses three pieces of proof in each body paragraph, taken from a mix of outside information and document analysis. Most DBQs are presented in chronological order. Because you'll arrange your essay by analysis points, you probably won't cite the documents in letter order, and your essay won't look like a laundry list. Just remember to use every document that fits into your analysis; it's even okay if you don't use them all.

Defend your point, but don't get *too* creative. Remember, your brave reader may be getting a little blurry from reading hundreds of versions of the same essay that you're writing. Don't confuse him. State your thesis clearly and simply. Cite lots of documents (with document letters bracketed) and underline your outside evidence. Stick to one major thesis; don't try to snow the reader with a bunch of mini-concepts. Your test scorer is looking for analysis and proof, and he doesn't have much time to find it. Don't just rewrite the textbook; make sure the facts you use prove your analysis and thesis points.

See "Answering the Reconstruction DBQ" later in this chapter to see how to apply PAT to the following Reconstruction sample question.

Sample Document-Based Question: The Reconstruction

Here's a DBQ like the one that a third of a million students like you will be answering on the upcoming AP U.S. History exam. As you read it, remember that you have 15 minutes to read the material and 45 minutes to write your answer on the real test. The documents are original source material, so they contain some misspelling and bad grammar — hey, that's the way people talked back then.

Directions: The following question requires you to construct a coherent essay that integrates your interpretation of Documents A through F *and* your knowledge of the period referred to in the question. Only essays that both cite key pieces of evidence from the documents and draw on outside knowledge of the period will earn high scores.

1. Discuss the experience of Reconstruction in the South following the Civil War. What factors influenced the lives of the people affected by Reconstruction in both the South and the North? How did Reconstruction change over time, and what motivated these changes?

Document A

Source: Letter from black Union soldiers

June 1865]

Genl We the soldiers of the 36 U.S.Col Reg^t Humbly petition to you to alter the Affairs at Roanoke Island. We have served in the US Army faithfully and don our duty to our Country, for which we thank God (that we had the opportunity) but at the same time our family's are suffering at Roanoke Island N.C.

1 When we were enlisted in the service we were prommised that our wifes and family's should receive rations from goverment. The rations for our wifes and family's have been (and are now cut down) to one half the regular ration. Consequently three or four days out of every ten days, thee have nothing to eat. at the same time our ration's are stolen from the ration house by Mr Streeter the Ass^t Sup^t at the Island (and others) and sold while our family's are suffering for some thing to eat.

2nd Mr Steeter the Ass^t Sup^t of Negro aff's at Roanoke Island is a througher Cooper head a man who says that he is no part of a Abolitionist. takes no care of the colored people and has no Simpathy with the colored people. A man who kicks our wives and children out of the ration house or commissary, he takes no notice of their actual suffering and sells the rations and allows it to be sold, and our family's suffer for something to eat.

Document B

Source: Andrew Johnson vetoing the Reconstruction Act of 1867

It is plain that the authority here given to the military officer amounts to absolute despotism. But to make it still more unendurable, the bill provides that it may be delegated to as many subordinates as he chooses to appoint, for it declares that he shall "punish or cause to be punished."

Such a power has not been wielded by any monarch in England for more than five hundred years. In all that time no people who speak the English language have borne such servitude. It reduces the whole population of the ten States — all persons, of every color, sex, and condition, and every stranger within their limits — to the most abject and degrading slavery. No master ever had a control so absolute over the slaves as this bill gives to the military officers over both white and colored persons.

Document C

Source: Charles Sumner on the Impeachment Trial of Andrew Johnson, 1868

I would not in this judgment depart from that moderation which belongs to the occasion; but God forbid that, when called to deal with so great an offender, I should affect a coldness which I cannot feel. Slavery has been our worst enemy, assailing all, murdering our children, filling our homes with mourning, and darkening the land with tragedy; and now it rears its crest anew, with Andrew Johnson as its representative. Through him it assumes once more to rule the Republic and to impose its cruel law. The enormity of his conduct is aggravated by his bare faced treachery. He once declared himself the Moses of the colored race. Behold him now the Pharaoh. With such treachery in such a cause there can be no parley. Every sentiment, every conviction, every vow against slavery must now be directed against him. Pharaoh is at the bar of the Senate for judgment.

Document D

Source: Ulysses S. Grant's first inaugural address, 1869

The country having just emerged from a great rebellion, many questions will come before it for settlement in the next four years which preceding Administrations have never had to deal with. In meeting these it is desirable that they should be approached calmly, without prejudice, hate, or sectional pride, remembering that the greatest good to the greatest number is the object to be attained.

This requires security of person, property, and free religious and political opinion in every part of our common country, without regard to local prejudice. All laws to secure these ends will receive my best efforts for their enforcement.

Document E

Source: Blanche K. Bruce, Black Senator Temporarily Elected under Reconstruction, Speech in the Senate, 1876

The evidence in hand and accessible will show beyond peradventure that in many parts of the State corrupt and violent influences were brought to bear upon the registrars of voters, thus materially affecting the character of the voting or poll lists; upon the inspectors of election, prejudicially and unfairly thereby changing the number of votes cast; and, finally, threats and violence were practiced directly upon the masses of voters in such measures and strength as to produce grave apprehensions for their personal safety and as to deter them from the exercise of their political franchises.

It will not accord with the laws of nature or history to brand colored people a race of cowards. On more than one historic field, beginning in 1776 and coming down to this centennial year of the Republic, they have attested in blood their courage as well as a love of liberty — I ask Senators to believe that no consideration of fear or personal danger has kept us quiet and forbearing under the provocations and wrongs that have so sorely tried our souls. But feeling kindly toward our white fellow-citizens, appreciating the good purposes and politics of the better classes, and, above all, abhorring a war of races. we determined to wait until such time as an appeal to the good sense and justice of the American people could be made.

Document F

Source: Nat Crippens, black historian after Reconstruction, 1880-1965

Until the civil rights movement overturned systematic segregation, thousands of African Americans and other minorities were brutally maimed or killed by white vigilantes taking the law into their hands. Established law, which codified white supremacy, failed to protect the civil rights of black citizens. In the end, white segregation rested on open violence.

At the turn of the century, lynchings occurred every week, and most of the victims, denied the due process of courts, were innocent of the charges held against them. Some were not even accused of having committed a crime.

Answering the Reconstruction DBQ

The secret to successful DBQ essays is using both the documents presented *and* relevant outside information from the period covered by the documents. To do this successfully, you need to have a plan. That plan includes the PAT method for scoring high on essay questions (see the next section).

First, the proof. The green question book that contains your essay challenges and documents is also the place for you to make notes during the AP exam. Use the pink essay-writing booklet only for your essays; make notes in the green question book.

Read the DBQ question twice. The second time through, carefully circle the key words in the assignment:

1. Discuss the experience of Reconstruction in the South following the Civil War. What factors influenced the lives of the people affected by Reconstruction in both the South and the North? How did Reconstruction change over time, and what motivated these changes?

Before you even read the documents, make notes in the green question book about themes and events you remember from this period. You're going to use these happenings as proof to support the thesis that forms the backbone of your DBQ essay. You're wise to record your outside history knowledge before the documents distract you from what you already know.

Now read the documents. Circle the most important points in each primary source. You'll weave references to these documents throughout your essay. Your writing, however, is not a shopping-list description of the documents. For maximum impact, base your essay on a thesis, analyzed in at least three main points and defended with proof from your outside history knowledge and the documents.

Using PAT for a good DBQ

Sailing along under the PAT method (discussed earlier in this chapter), you first marshaled your proof in the form of PES (political events plus economic and social trends; see Chapter 1). So you just do the PAT with the PES. (You're probably sick of acronyms!)

How to be a brain-fight referee

Historians like to argue about events and trends that are old enough to have developed some proof. Can't decide who should win the next election? That's nothing to a historian; we're still arguing about the causes of World War I. You need to remember two things about the person who grades your DBQ:

1. She'll be overwhelmed by piles of tests.

2. She'll be a historian.

When historians don't agree about causes (which is usually), they love to argue about trends and documents. For extra credit with your historian–grader, join in the brain fight by defining your terms clearly.

Another good trick is admitting that the other side may have a point counter to your thesis and then destroying that point with analysis. This method is the *straw-man argument*. Don't think that you need to neglect documents that seem to run counter to your thesis. You can deal with seemingly contrary proof through analysis and gain extra historian street cred. If your grader slows down long enough to notice, a historian is always happy when you analyze the documents by date, author, and any indication of how the author's date and bias fit into an ongoing cultural trend.

Don't reach for facts you're unsure of. When a teacher is grading lots of papers fast, he'll naturally glory in finding a fact that's completely wrong. Unfortunately for the test taker, teachers celebrate finding a giant error by clamping on a major decrease in score. If you're not sure of a name or year, use a generality such as *the president* or *around this time*. Never quote directly from a document; summarize.

Historians have bad memories too. In gatherings of old historians, you'll typically hear someone say, "You know that guy — the father of our country . . ." The other historians don't even try to remember the name. They just say, "Oh, yeah. That guy."

After you have your outside history knowledge written down and your document proof circled in the green book, you're ready to proceed to an analysis of the question; this produces your thesis. Read the question one last time, paying careful attention to the words you circled.

For the Reconstruction question, your thesis may be

> The North's initially tough Reconstruction rules provided some protection for blacks in the South but caused a violent reaction from white Southerners threatened by change. Northerners with their own political agendas were unwilling to maintain strict Reconstruction. In 1877, 12 years after the end of the Civil War, the last Northern troops were withdrawn from the South, leaving Southern blacks free but segregated, with little political or economic opportunity.

This thesis becomes the first paragraph of your five- or six-paragraph DBQ essay. The second paragraph could talk about the angry retribution with which the North applied Reconstruction immediately after the Civil War. It could show that the North came within one vote of impeaching its own Union President after Andrew Johnson opposed tough measures by the Radical Republicans.

You should cite documents clearly in brackets, like this:

> After the war, even black Union soldiers who had fought bravely were treated badly in the South by their own officers [Document A].

Bracket all references to documents, but don't waste time copying the titles of the documents. The reader who grades your essay is an expert on this specific DBQ question; she has seen thousands of essays on this year's DBQ, and she knows the document letters by heart. (See the nearby sidebar "Grading the AP U.S. History exam.")

Grading the AP U.S. History exam

During one week in June of each year, more than 1,000 determined history teachers and professors gather at a college, usually in Texas, to grade 1 million AP U.S. History essays. About one-third of a million students take this test — the largest single-subject College Board (CB) test in the world. Each student who doesn't pass out from the strain writes three essays, and all of these 1 million essays must be graded by hand.

If the teachers grade 1,000 essays each and spend 2 minutes reading and scoring each essay, the job will take them 33 hours of solid work. With training, consultation, and occasional trips to the buffet, that's a very full week. Some of the most experienced graders arrive early to serve as coordinators. These super-specialists develop specific criteria for each of the five exam questions. Coordinators and regular graders specialize in only one question; they learn the grading criteria for their question and stick to it.

The upside to this specialization is that each of your essays will be read by a different, custom-trained person who is guaranteed not to be mad at you for something your big brother did two years ago. The downside is that if you're blowing smoke, your grader has seen it all a hundred times before. Leaders double-check a random sample of each grader's work to keep the grading consistent and fair.

Even as hard as they try, graders can make mistakes. If you're sure you've been given a much lower score than you deserve, you can pay the CB a few bucks to have an independent reader rescore your test. Strangely, no one has yet complained about getting too high a score.

Even machines can make mistakes. The CB recently paid millions of dollars in damages after a scanning machine gave *A* students *F* scores because the answer sheets had gotten wet. But in general, the CB deserves high fives for hanging in there with a heavy load. If you've ever tried to grade even a small pile of hand-written essays, try to imagine what grading 1,000 would be like. That's why you bracket your document citations and underline important information. Help the grader see your strong points!

Don't analyze the documents like a laundry list. Weave your document evidence throughout your essay on Reconstruction as proof of your thesis. Some documents require explanation to show that you understand them. You're trying to show that you can analyze an era by using primary source documents, not just proving that you can read by spouting back what the documents say. You need to do more than just quote the documents to get a good score on the DBQ.

Bringing in outside proof

For this Reconstruction DBQ, you want to mention as outside proof the Thirteenth, Fourteenth, and Fifteenth Amendments to the Constitution, which ended slavery and gave equal protection of the law and the vote to all males. In economics, Reconstruction saw the end of the Southern plantation economy and the beginning of sharecropping. The North's industrial base continued to grow, and its own economy drew Northern attention away from trouble in the South. The Civil Rights Bill of 1866 didn't actually overturn Black Code laws in the South; the Supreme Court limited the application of this early civil-rights legislation to only national laws. Southern states later adopted Jim Crow laws to further limit the rights of blacks.

Here's more outside information: Under early Reconstruction rules, former slaves — but not Confederate leaders — could vote in Southern state elections. Southern blacks helped pass important social legislation, including the establishment of public schools for all citizens. After the Southern states officially rejoined Union, local white officials made their own laws and quickly found ways to keep blacks from voting. President Hayes agreed to withdraw all troops from the South in 1877 as part of a deal to win a disputed election. The Ku Klux Klan and other groups orchestrated repressive violence against blacks in the South. In reaction to what it viewed as harsh Reconstruction pushed by Republicans, the Solid South voted Democratic for 80 years until after World War II.

The length of a DBQ response should be five or six paragraphs. The first paragraph states the thesis; the last paragraph reiterates thesis and proof. The middle paragraphs provide point-by-point analysis, supported by document citations and outside information. Underline the names of all outside information and dates, like this: <u>Solid South</u>, <u>Civil Rights Bill of 1866</u>, <u>Jim Crow</u>. This method helps make sure that test graders clearly see the outside information you're submitting. Test readers score so many essays so quickly that they have only a minute to see information you've spent months absorbing.

Chapter 6

Creating Essays Teachers Love

. . . .

In This Chapter

▶ Understanding the AP U.S. History regular essays

▶ Giving proof, analysis, and thesis (PAT) answers to essay questions

▶ Handling two questions per hour

▶ Managing PAT for a high score

. . . .

*I*magine that the end of the AP U.S. History exam is in sight, and you have a little more than 1 hour to write answers to two regular essay questions. An hour doesn't seem like much time, does it? Now you have some choices; you get to pick one of the two questions in Part B, and then one of the two questions in Part C. This chapter gives you some tips on how to select and write your essay answers for a winning score.

Nailing Down Your Timing

Now that you've finished your insightful discussion of the Document-Based Question (DBQ — see Chapter 5), you get to spend the last golden hour of your test time writing two regular essays. These regular essays are officially known as Section II, Part B and Part C of the test. They're "regular" only compared with the DBQ; in these last two essays, you don't have any documents to worry about (or lean on). You *do* have thought-provoking history puzzles that require a combination of analysis and appropriate facts.

The time at which you get started on these last two essays is suggested on the test, but it's not mandatory. After the 15-minute required reading time that begins your Section II quest, you have a grand total of 1 hour and 55 minutes to write the DBQ and the Part B and Part C essays. The test proctor will pop up like a human alarm clock to remind you when the recommended time to move on to the next section has arrived. After the 45 minutes recommended for writing the DBQ, your test boss will say, "You should now move on to Part B." You want to follow the advice of Mother AP and switch questions around the time she tells you to.

Although the DBQ section has the most credit (22.5 percent of the total test) and the most writing time assigned to it (45 minutes), Parts B and C are definitely worth the effort. Each of these regular essays represents almost 14 percent of the exam — a total of 27.5 percent for both.

You have a recommended 70 minutes to devote to both regular essays. The College Board suggests you spend 5 minutes planning and 30 minutes writing each one. As on the DBQ, you have a chance to pick up some ground against a slow field on these essay questions. The AP U.S. History exam is graded on a curve. To win a *4* or *5* as your final grade, your score doesn't have to be perfect — just better than that of most other AP test takers.

The average student performance on the regular essay questions is even slightly worse than the bad scores on the DBQ, because people are running out of gas by the time they get to them. When *you* get there, though, remember that you're almost to the finish line; you just need one last burst of speed to take advantage of the situation. Remember that essays on the AP are scored on a scale from *0* (for no intelligence detected) to *9* (for Shakespeare reborn). The average score on the regular essay questions in recent years has been less than *3* on the 9 scale. You can do better than that even if you're a little spotty on a few facts. As the saying goes, in the land of the blind, the one-eyed person rules.

No rule says you have to work exactly 35 minutes on each of the essays in Part B and Part C. Just don't move too much time from one part to the other; both parts are worth the same number of points, and a great score on one won't make up for a *0* on the other.

Meeting and Beating the Questions

When the College Board says "regular essay," it doesn't mean easy topics like "What I Did on My Summer Vacation." The AP is, after all, a college test you take before you've had any college classes. The test geniuses have had all year to come up with four challenging and meaningful essay questions. Teachers even have a special language: essay questions are *prompts*.

You'll find two of these prompts lurking in Part B; you get to pick the one that terrifies you less. Part C holds two more questions; go with the one that's slightly less awful. Getting the best score on these essays takes a combination of knowledge and reasoning. If you want to know how common that skill combination is in the AP U.S. History test-taking population, just look at the average score: 2.86 on a scale of 9. Don't worry; you have a plan.

 You don't have to answer the two regular essay questions in order. The specialist essay readers will find the essay they grade by its number in your pink answer book. You can read all four essays and pick the one that seems easiest for you so you can get a running start. Just remember to do one essay from Part B and one from Part C. To leave time for both, it's best to switch within a few minutes of the 35-minute advisory you get from the test proctor. Even better, bring a watch and keep your own time.

Writing like a professor

You know that your essay will be graded by a slightly bleary-eyed history teacher. One thing that professors insist on in their professional journals is that writers define their terms. If your essay question asks for the impact of changes on the common man, offer a brief definition of that term. If you're writing about the Progressive movement, use a sentence in the first paragraph to say what that term means. You should signal your high-level understanding of academic protocol by using this well-loved professional prelude: "It is important to define terms. By the Progressive movement, I mean newly organized initiatives in the early 1900s that had a goal of efficiency and fairness in U.S. society, economy, and government." Defining a term takes only a sentence and could make a professor very happy.

If you're asked to assess the validity of a statement, you've just been given a nonvoluntary invitation to jump into the middle of an argument. You may see something like this: "Assess the validity of this statement: The New Deal brought an end to the Great Depression." Gosh, what do you think? Take a position, and make it your thesis statement. Here are two example theses:

> ✔ "Although economic problems remained that were not settled until after the U.S. entry into World War II, New Deal programs were effective in blunting the worst problems of the Great Depression."

> ✔ "Although New Deal programs created a public perception of progress, they were largely ineffective in dealing with the economic roots of the Great Depression."

Notice, AP seekers, that both thesis statements begin with the magic word *although*. The use of this gentle, reasonable word signals that you're being bend-over-backward fair in your thesis position by acknowledging from the start the limits of your argument. Professors know that modest arguments provide a safety shield from academic attack. Later in each thesis statement, you can use more weasel words to make the thesis argument easier to defend. The first example says "effective in *blunting* the *worst* problems." That way, you have to defend only *blunting* (not actually solving) and *worst* (but not all problems). In the second version, the thesis reads "*largely* ineffective in dealing with the economic *roots*," so that the essay can admit that the New Deal was effective sometimes on the little issues but not the answer for solving problems at the economic *roots*. Then the two opposed writers can go on to gleefully define *worst* problems or economic *roots* in a way that makes their thesis arguments seem like the gospel truth.

PATting your PES dispenser

Writing regular essays that teachers love is as easy as applying the proof, analysis, and thesis (PAT) approach in writing (see Chapter 5) to the political, economic, and social trends (PES) that score points with test graders (see Chapter 1). With the PAT formula, you select everything you know about the topic as proof, and then analyze that proof to support your own theory about the question. The proof you use includes all the political, economic, and social trends you can find in the PES dispenser of your brain. In the DBQ (Chapter 5), the documents themselves supply some of the PES points; with regular essays, it's just you and your fine mind.

The regular essay questions are an AP dance party of political, economic, and social (PES) trends. Here are some examples of what to prepare for:

> ✔ You need to combine developments in different areas, such as the political outcomes of social issues. An example could be changes in the U.S. government brought on by urbanization.

> ✔ You also have to analyze common themes that run through an extended period —how women's rights changed society from 1830 to 1930, for example.

> ✔ You may need to write about the economic experiences of different ethnic, gender, racial, or socioeconomic groups during a certain period of American history. An example could be the impact of the Great Depression of the 1930s on women, men, and minority groups in the United States.

On the regular essay questions, the grader judges you on the thesis you develop, the quality of your analysis supported, and the historic proof you support it with. When you're figuring out your essay, you'll probably plan what you're going to write in PAT order:

1. **List all the political, economic and social facts you can remember about the essay topic (proof).**

2. **Figure out how these facts can go together to explain the essay topic (analysis).**

3. **Make up an opinion to tie the facts together with the essay topic (thesis).**

Make sure your answer has at least a vague relationship to the question. It doesn't have to be perfect; you want to show off any knowledge you have in the general area. Just don't try writing about 1800s shipping if the question is about the Mayflower. When you actually write the essay, PAT turns into TAP: First you state your thesis and then provide analysis supported by proof.

The official AP line is that your supported argument is more important than the amount of factual information you produce. In other words: essay-padders beware. You can't just write down a laundry list of names, trends, and events; you have to show how they fit together. This idea is a great humanistic and holistic one. In the rest of this chapter, you see how it works in practice.

Knowing the Criteria for Scoring Big on the Essay Questions

In this section, I provide you with a list of grading criteria for an essay question. The list may look a bit daunting, but don't worry, because you can ensure you meet the criteria for the highest score by following the tips in this chapter. By recognizing that the AP values political, economic, and social connections even more than reciting historic facts, you can make your essays on any topic show how trends interact. Your essays should stay positive; you catch more bees with honey than with vinegar. Slavery and the Trail of Tears, for example, are blots on the U.S. record of freedom (see Chapter 11), but they're also parts of trends that need to be viewed within the context of their times. Save political speeches for political meetings; when you're taking a test with your grade hanging in the balance, emphasize unity and progress.

By starting and concluding with a clear thesis, you help your overworked, weary grader find what he's looking for: a sense of style and meaning. Make sure the hurried test grader sees the proof you're using by underlining it in your essay; by highlighting facts about trends and topics and dealing with them in paragraphs separated into political, economic, and social themes that all connect to your thesis, you provide an essay that clearly deserves a good score. These essays follow the same grading scale as the DBQ, with a high score of *9* and a low score of *0*.

The *8-to-9* essay:

- ✔ Contains a clear, well-developed thesis that deals with the question at hand

- ✔ Supports the thesis with a large amount of relevant information

- ✔ Analyzes the main categories completely (somewhat uneven treatment of the categories is okay)

- ✔ May contain minor errors

The *5-to-7* essay:

- ✔ Contains a thesis that deals with the question only partially

- ✔ Supports the thesis with a medium amount of on-point information

- ✔ Analyzes all categories at least somewhat; treatment of categories may be very uneven

- ✔ May contain errors that don't detract completely from the essay

The 2-to-4 essay:

- ✔ Restates the question without providing a clear thesis
- ✔ Provides either minimal facts or minimal application of the facts
- ✔ Doesn't analyze all the categories, maybe gets one or two in a general way
- ✔ Contains lots of errors

The 0-to-1 essay:

- ✔ Omits a thesis
- ✔ Doesn't make sense
- ✔ Displays little or no understanding of the question
- ✔ Contains major false statements

Converting Questions to PAT Answers

AP U.S. History essay-grading week is a busy time for the College Board. More than 1,000 teachers grade around 1 million essays in the course of a few days, sitting around tables with only one 20-minute break in the morning and afternoon. Talk about hard work and dedication! The average reader could be covering as many as 1,000 essays, with only around 2 minutes to read each contribution.

The graders look quickly for proof and analysis supporting an overall thesis (PAT). Grading leaders develop clear criteria that the graders use for each essay, and each grader spends the whole time scoring only essays covering one question again and again.

The College Board makes grading 1 million essays as fair as it can, but in the rush, no one has time to ponder garbled proof, vague analysis, or a thesis that's not clearly stated. For that reason, you want to make your PAT answers simple and direct.

Some football teams use a five-yards-and-glory strategy. They're not looking to score a touchdown on every play; they just want to gain five yards on each down with short passes and runs because if they keep doing that, they'll move on down the field and eventually score. AP U.S. History essays are like that. You write approximately five paragraphs with a goal of showing that you know and can analyze historic information. You're not trying to list everything that went on during the era you're writing about. You'll score higher on the AP if you organize and analyze your information.

Here are some tips to make sure your essay dodges the test potholes and cruises smoothly down the AP highway to a good score.

- ✔ Make sure you address all the parts of the free-response essay questions. Missing a subtopic can affect your grade. Get all three PES parts: political, economic, and social.
- ✔ If you can't remember a name or date, don't guess. A wrong specific is worse than a possibly incorrect general. If you can't remember Seneca Falls in 1848, for example, say "an important women's-rights meeting before the Civil War." Don't let your grader see a clear error that she can use to slap you down.
- ✔ Don't freak out if the essay questions look hard. If the questions are tough for you, they're tough for everyone. The test is scored on a curve, so grading is survival of the

fittest. You could even get lucky. If you did well on the multiple-choice part of the exam and score very low on an essay, the grading coordinator may automatically ask that your essay be reread to make sure you're not being underscored. You could have two chances to make an impression.

✔ Don't get all anxious and start to write before you really understand the question. You may be missing the main point of the prompt while you're rattling off random facts. Carpenters have a saying: "Measure twice, cut once." You won't have a chance for a second cut at your essay, so read the question prompt twice.

✔ Circle the key words.

✔ Make notes in the green question book before you write.

✔ The College Board doesn't want to see a hip-hop version of history, fun as writing that may be. Stick to what your English teacher taught you: The first paragraph is the introduction and includes your thesis statement. Each of the body paragraphs has a different theme that supports the thesis. A good goal is to have three proof facts in each of the body paragraphs.

✔ Sometimes, the prompt decides the themes for you. If a question asks how post–Civil War government policies affected American Indians, Western settlement, and economic development, for example, the middle paragraphs of your essay need to deal one-by-one with American Indians, settlement, and development.

If no clear division is obvious from the prompt, you're always safe if you have a paragraph on each of your PES friends: *political* events, *economic* conditions, and *social* trends.

✔ The final paragraph of your essay restates the thesis in slightly different words and provides a summary that mentions the themes of the middle paragraphs.

✔ Don't let your essay wander around the subject like some drunk in a bar. Check back during the writing of each paragraph to make sure what you're saying supports the thesis in the introduction.

✔ Don't introduce historic facts just to prove you know something. Tie each trend or event to the theme of your essay. You shouldn't have to exclude too many random facts; you can usually find a way to use creative logic to tie almost any trend or event to the theme you're supporting.

✔ Keep PATting your essay. Make sure you tie your proof together with analysis to support your thesis. You get no penalty for having a wrong thesis, but you sink fast if you don't use proof and analysis to support your theme.

Analyzing an essay question

Test day marches on. You've been multiply chosen and DBQed half to death, and now it's time for a final burst of essay brilliance. Here's what you may face in Part B:

Directions: Choose ONE question from this part. You are advised to spend 5 minutes planning and 30 minutes writing your answer. Cite relevant historical evidence in support of your generalizations, and present your arguments clearly and logically.

1. How did the New Deal (1932–1944) change U.S. society? Consider TWO of the following factors in your response:

   Social movements, economic development, political change

2. The period from 1824 to 1848 is often called the era of Jacksonian democracy. What social and political changes characterized this era?

For the sake of this example, assume that you choose Question 2, because you think you can recall more about this era and have a thesis point you want to make. Check out Chapter 11 to familiarize yourself with the important things to know from this era.

First, read the prompt twice. Circle the terms that are key parts of the prompt.

> 2. The period from 1824 to 1848 is often called the era of Jacksonian democracy. What social and political changes characterized this era?

Make a list of what you know about this era. You could list many other PES topics, but the following points would more than get you started:

- ✔ Election of 1824 (the Corrupt Bargain)
- ✔ Andrew Jackson elected in 1828 and 1832
- ✔ Trail of Tears
- ✔ Nullification
- ✔ Spoils system
- ✔ Increased voter turnout
- ✔ 1848 women's rights meeting at Seneca Falls
- ✔ Universal male suffrage
- ✔ Defeat of the Bank of the U.S.
- ✔ The spoils system

Now that you have your PES, you're ready to apply the PAT formula. The PES list you have made forms most of the proof. Your analysis supports your thesis.

Settling on your thesis

Now you need a thesis. You're the historian now. You know what you've been taught, but what do you *believe* about Jacksonian democracy? Pretend you're some kind of authority.

Relax. Forming a thesis isn't something you can get wrong. Historians love to argue, and one of the topics they argue about is the era of Andrew Jackson. History changes: Andy Jackson has gone from American hero to dangerous redneck to rough but effective champion of the common man. The only thing you can do wrong on an AP essay question is fail to have a clear thesis.

A thesis — your point of view — unifies your essay and makes it worthy of a higher score. Just think about your grading audience as one tired teacher who has endured hundreds of unfocused fluff-a-thons loosely connected to the Jackson era. Give him something clear and decisive, and he'll thank you with a better grade.

For most history questions, you can go in either of two broad directions with a thesis: mainstream history or counterculture. In the case of the Jackson era, you can argue for a mainstream view

> The 1820s to 1840s was a time when the United States began to move toward being true to its democratic ideals.

Or you could go with a counterculture approach and say

> From the 1820s through the 1840s, the United States made some surface changes toward greater representation for the common man, but these changes were largely symbolic. The real economic and social conditions of slavery and sectionalism changed little during this period.

As much as you may hate to agree with the Man, you should go with the mainstream view on this one. The Jackson era really did involve a move toward democratic ideals.

Planning the essay

Now you're ready to plan the essay. You want to have a five-paragraph essay, structured as follows:

- ✔ The thesis anchors the first paragraph.
- ✔ The three body paragraphs support your central point (ideally with three pieces of analysis each).
- ✔ The final paragraph reiterates and amplifies the thesis.

Look for the subjects of the three body paragraphs. Sifting through the PES topics in your notes, you see that they can be arranged in political, economic, and social categories. Political events include elections, increased voter turnout, universal white-male suffrage, and the spoils system. Economic trends include nullification and the defeat of the Bank of the U.S. Social happenings include the Trail of Tears, the Second Great Awakening, and women's rights.

Writing the essay

Okay, your five minutes of planning are up, and you're ready to write the essay. Keep the PES terms that form the proof for your thesis in capital letters to make them easier for the grader to see when she's reading quickly. Let the English teachers complain; this exam is about history, and you're in a high-traffic situation. Capitalizing provides a road marker to help direct your reader to the destination.

In another high-traffic detour from the refined world of English composition, you're going to start your essay with the thesis sentence, not keep it waiting demurely for the end of the first paragraph. Also, you're going to label it *Thesis*. That way, it's difficult to miss. The thesis doesn't repeat the question; believe me, after reading hundreds of essays, the grading teacher knows what the question is. Your thesis restates the prompt in your own words to show that you understand it.

Consider beginning your thesis with the magic word *although*. In Chapter 5, you see how to admit that the other side may have a point counter to your thesis. This argument makes you look fair and allows you to counter possible objections to your argument on your own terms. In full debate, developing your opponent's argument and then destroying it is called the *straw-man argument*. The use of the word *although* is a quickie version of the straw-man move.

Give your essay a title. A title doesn't cost anything and makes the essay look official.

Checking out a sample essay

Here's a sample essay that contains a clear thesis, reasonable analysis, and enough historical proof to ring the test grader's bell.

Democracy Comes to the United States in the Jackson Era

Thesis: Although important issues like slavery and states' rights remained unresolved, the period from the 1820s to the 1840s, known as the Jackson era, was a time when the United States began to move toward being true to its democratic ideals. This era saw the increase in the power of ordinary people in political, economic and social areas. These power changes were brought home to people through Religious and Moral Reform movements and through Political Campaigns that were conducted on a large public scale for the first time. Citizens began to see themselves as having real freedom to change their own lives and the course of the nation in which they lived.

The most important political event was the introduction of white Universal Male Suffrage in most states in the early 1820s. Although it was a far cry from the voting rights we enjoy now, it was an unimagined freedom in earlier days, when voting was limited by property and class. The newly enfranchised citizens responded by increasing Voter Turnout by large numbers. People began to see themselves as more powerful, not just as the pawns of destiny. Greater democracy spelled the end of leaders selected by small elites and the beginning of the election of popular national leaders like Andrew Jackson in 1848 and 1832. Even the Spoils System can be seen as a democratization of public employment.

The Second Great Awakening increased social as well as spiritual growth by getting people together away from the farm in newly organized religious congregations. These congregations in turn provided a religious base for small but growing Temperance, Abolitionist, and Women's Suffrage movements. The era ended with a symbolically important women's meeting at Seneca Falls, New York, in 1848. Even an event that we now view as negative, such as the Trail of Tears removal of American Indians from the South, had its beginning in increased public social pressure for land.

Economics are never far from any social or political change. The birth of the Industrial Revolution with factory jobs offered urban alternatives to rural isolation. Rapidly improving transportation by Canal, Railroad, and Steamship made the sale of crops and manufactured goods into the beginning of a National Economy. Transportation allowed ordinary people to move where they wanted to go to seek a new fortune. Even the Nullification Crisis, with its argument about tariffs, was a sign of the economic strain on sectionalism brought by an increasingly powerful National Interest.

When Thomas Jefferson wrote "Life, Liberty, and the Pursuit of Happiness," most of his upper-class congressional colleagues could recognize the theory of freedom only as it applied to them and people of their class. Most common people could not vote and had no time for economic and social betterment. That's why the Founding Fathers created the Electoral College and chose senators and presidents in private meetings. But with the new nation, the theory of freedom had become an ideal. As reform improved the power of ordinary people, those people were more likely to use their power to improve social, political, and economic life. The era of Jacksonian Democracy, with its emphasis on personal beliefs and more universal suffrage, brought the idea of freedom that had begun in the American Revolution to reality: the beginnings of real democracy in the United States.

Steer clear of funny history answers

Apparently, some people studied even less for their history exams than your slacker friends. Here are some essay responses gone terribly wrong:

It was an age of great inventions and discoveries. Gutenberg invented removable type and the Bible. Another important invention was the circulation of blood. Sir Walter Raleigh is a historical figure because he invented cigarettes and started smoking. And Sir Francis Drake circumcised the world with a 100 foot clipper.

Later, the Pilgrims crossed the ocean, and this was called Pilgrim's Progress. The winter of 1620 was a hard one for the settlers. Many people died and many babies were born. Captain John Smith was responsible for all this.

One of the causes of the Revolutionary War was the English put tacks in their tea. Also, the colonists would send their parcels through the post without stamps. Finally the colonists won the War and no longer had to pay for taxis. Delegates from the original 13 states formed the Contented Congress. Thomas Jefferson, a Virgin, and Benjamin Franklin were two singers of the Declaration of Independence. Franklin discovered electricity by rubbing two cats backwards and declared,

"A horse divided against itself cannot stand." Franklin died in 1790 and is still dead.

Soon the Constitution of the United States was adopted to secure domestic hostility. Under the constitution the people enjoyed the right to keep bare arms.

Abraham Lincoln became America's greatest Precedent. His mother died in infancy, and he was born in a log cabin which he built with his own hands. Abraham Lincoln freed the slaves by signing the Emasculation Proclamation.

The nineteenth century was a time of a great many thoughts and inventions. People stopped reproducing by hand and started reproducing by machine. The invention of the steamboat caused a network of rivers to spring up.

World War I broke out around 1912–1914. Germany was on one side of France and Russia was on the other. At war people get killed, and then they aren't people any more, but friends. Peace was proclaimed at Versigh, which was attended by George Loid, Primal Minister of England. President Wilson arrived with 14 pointers.

Wrapping up the essay plan

Use simple, short sentences. Your audience of one grader has seen a lot of convoluted essays and is probably already verging on cranky. Make it easy for her to follow your theme.

Throw in a big history term, if you know one. Here are some themes beloved to teachers: expansionism; utopia; ratification; peculiar institution (slavery); oligarchy; nativism; mercantilism; jingoism; imperialism; egalitarian; capitalism; and the all-time American favorite, Manifest Destiny. Don't try to force in terms you don't understand; you'll get caught.

Take the time to write clearly and neatly. Graders hate chicken-scratch writing and love clear printing. Your grader will probably be right on the edge of surly by the time she gets to your essay. Make it easy for her. Write the whole sentence in your mind *before* you put it down on paper. If you absolutely have to cross something out, do it neatly. Try not to cross out at all. For sure, don't cross out bad spelling. This test isn't English class; if the grader can recognize the word, she won't count off for bad spelling. By making too many corrections, you only call attention to your mistakes and make yourself look like a ditz. If, heaven forbid, you have to insert a line or even a paragraph, do it neatly. Write the words to be inserted clearly away from the main body of the essay; circle them; and draw a neat arrow to where they go in the essay. Don't use carets to crowd text on top of what you have already written. Keep your essay readable by taking a deep breath and thinking before you write.

Smooth out the flow of your writing by using transition phrases such as "in addition," "furthermore," "also," and "in another example." When you're changing directions, use "however," "yet," and the magic word "although."

Number your points, as in this example: "First, the New Deal never claimed to solve all the problems. Second, the Great Depression was caused by world as well as national problems. Third, even the best programs often took time to work." Numbering lists of arguments makes it look like you have a plan.

Use examples to back up your idea. Nothing gets wooly faster than academic papers that are all about concepts without real-life examples. You start with this: "Third, even the best programs often took time to work." Then you add this: "Two examples of programs that had delayed effects were the WPA and CCC. In these programs, government-supported jobs eventually helped lift the economic fortunes of certain communities, but these examples took time to work."

Make sure your last paragraph directly addresses the question. This paragraph is the applause section, when you set yourself up for your well-earned reward of a high essay score. Bring the essay back home by answering the original question clearly as you restate your thesis.

Yay! Hurrah! You're ready with a good battle plan for the AP U.S. History exam.

Part III
Early U.S. History: From Dinosaurs to the Civil War

The 5th Wave   By Rich Tennant

"Help me out here. Are these guys Pilgrims or Puritans? I can never tell them apart."

In this part . . .

If the exam questions were in the form of a car you were going to drive on Test Day, history would be the gasoline you put in the tank. Fortunately for your memory, U.S. History is a very cool story starring Thomas Jefferson, George Washington, Abe Lincoln, and a cast of thousands, probably including some of your ancestors.

About 20 percent of the questions of the test will cover the period up to 1789. The story starts with American Indians having the whole place to themselves for about 30 times as long as any Europeans have lived here.

Another 30 percent of the questions on the test will be from Independence through the Civil War. That means the history in this section is about half of your tank full of knowledge. It's an exciting story, but read Chapters 7 through 13 slowly and carefully. Test day is a-comin' . . .

Chapter 7

Living on the Land: American Indians from 35,000 BCE to 1491 CE

In This Chapter

▶ Understanding the first people

▶ Building empires down south

▶ Losing the battle with disease

*T*he AP U.S. History exam doesn't thump heads too much on American Indian history before Christopher Columbus, partly because high-school AP courses vary too much on pre-Columbian American history for the test makers to be sure what students have learned. Also, we historians are a little shaky on just what did go on back then. Nobody took notes.

Although the AP may not have many questions on pre-Columbian America, you'll want to scan this chapter anyway as insurance, should an early-times question arise. You want to know as much as you can about the long years of our American Indian forebears. After all, if the room you're sitting in were the history of human beings in North America, the amount of time settlers have lived here would be the space behind the curtains.

Encountering the First Americans

Christopher Columbus wasn't looking for a new world in 1492; he was just trying to get to China without having to walk, as his Italian predecessor Marco Polo had done more than 200 years before. Polo had reported in his book *The Million* that China was full of untold riches. Columbus had a well-thumbed copy of Polo's story by his side as he contemplated a cruise to the jewels of the East. He also saw a map based on one that Polo had brought back with him years before. On this map, you can still make out Europe, Asia, and Africa in blobby form, right where they're supposed to be. What's missing is the entire New World.

Not surprisingly, when Columbus landed, he called the people he met *Indians*. They didn't look Chinese, so they must be Indians from the East Indies, related somehow to the India that Polo had visited and Alexander the Great had fought way back in Greek times. Columbus took six years of return voyages before he had to confront the fact in a message to his royal sponsors: "I have come to believe that this is a mighty continent which was hitherto unknown . . . .Your Highnesses have an Other World here."

35,000 years before Columbus

The people Columbus called Indians didn't think they were in a strange new world; they were home in the land that legends told them had been theirs since the beginning of time. They knew every rock and tree and had a name for every valley and river. These first people had well-practiced ways of surviving with the thousands of plants and animals around them. Actually, even the first American Indians were relative newcomers to their lands compared to the history of the Old World; human beings have lived in the New World for less than a tenth of the time they have been settled in Asia, Europe, and Africa.

Human beings have lived in China and Northern Asia for at least 300,000 years and for as long as 1 million years. About 35,000 years ago, an ice age froze over the water between what are now Siberia and Alaska. Native hunters, probably following migrating herds of game, walked across this convenient ice bridge to Alaska. Because it was cold, they kept heading south.

When the ice age melted about 10,000 years ago, the Bering Straits went back to being water, and the New World was cut off from the Old. This was okay for the American Indians; the same big thaw opened passes through the mountains to the south. Roaming gradually through the beautiful wilderness that still covers much of North America, the first people reached the tip of South America by 9,000 BCE, some 15,000 miles from the land bridge they had crossed from Siberia. That means they averaged about 1 mile of migration every 2 years.

In the year before Columbus landed, 100 million first people probably inhabited the New World. More people lived in North and South America than in Europe. Not all these first people whom Columbus called Indians were hunter–gatherers. The New World had cities before the Egyptians built the pyramids.

At the time of Columbus, the Aztec capital city (in what became Mexico City) was larger than any city in Europe. Unlike the dirty European cities of the 1400s, the Aztec capital had running water, clean streets, and botanical gardens. This beauty didn't lead to mellow living; as many as 5,000 human beings were sacrificed every year to please the Aztec king and his gods.

2,000 cultures

Whereas kingdoms like the Aztec were able to control large areas of land for a time, many American Indians were split into small tribes that spoke at least 2,000 different languages — ten times the number of languages spoken in Europe. American Indians spoke a lot of languages because they had little reason to conquer and consolidate with neighboring groups. Hunter–gatherers aren't very interested in dominating their neighbors. What are they going to get — more room to hunt and gather? Only with the beginning of agriculture did property become worth seizing, and people were vulnerable to domination because they couldn't move away from their crops to avoid being conquered.

Agriculture also fed the large population centers. The Aztecs in Mexico, Mayans in Central America, and Incas in Peru built networks of roads and amazing cities with incredible buildings and artwork. They were experts at raising more than 100 varieties of corn — one kind for every taste and climate. One modern scientific journal calls the American Indians' development of many corn types from a barely edible wild plant the greatest feat of genetic engineering in history.

If the AP test has a question on pre-Columbian American Indians, it may well contain that favorite buzzword of people who write early-history tests: *Mesoamerica*. Relax. *Meso* just means *middle* of the New World, as in south Mexico and Central America. This term throws a lot of people because it's not part of the current United States that you thought you were studying.

Blame those advanced southern American Indians; they're just more interesting than the hunter–gatherers and early agriculturalists who peopled what's now the United States. The Mesoamerican culture area included some of the most complex and organized people of the Americas, including the Olmecs, the Mayans, and the Aztecs. These cultures developed advanced political systems; discovered technological, scientific, and mathematical concepts; and participated in long-distance road networks that covered hundreds of miles and resulted in the transmission of ideas and products. Way to go, Mesoamerica!

The Original Empires Were American Indian

So why do you have to know about the three great American Indian empires that happened 1,000 miles south of the Rio Grande U.S. border? Because these southern American Indian superstates influenced the development of the United States, both directly and indirectly.

The riches that the American Indian empires amassed with the gold they discovered attracted the Spanish conquistadores like flies to a picnic. Easy conquests of large civilizations emboldened Europeans armed with only primitive guns and swords. The Spanish won partly because the American Indians were surprised by their weapons but mostly because the American Indians couldn't believe how ruthless the Europeans were. Spanish riches sped the development of the New World and provided rich plunder for the buccaneers of other European nations.

The American Indian empires funded the Spanish empire. After the defeat of the Spanish Armada by England in 1588, other nations started colonies in the New World in hopes of finding similar riches. Many of these colonies were investor-owned joint stock companies — undertakings that wouldn't have found support were it not for the Spanish experience with rich American Indian empires. More on that in Chapter 8.

Tales of cities of gold eventually led explorers overland into what's now the American Southwest. Accounts of distant civilizations and new worlds to discover always stirred European adventurers into action.

Digging the Big Three cultures: Mayan, Incas, and Aztecs

The Mayan, Incan, and Aztec Empires were the three large American Indian empires encountered by Spanish explorers. A predecessor civilization called the Olmec died out two thousand years before the Spanish arrived but started some of the traditions common to later American Indian empires.

The Mayan

North of present-day Panama and extending into what's now southern Mexico, the *Mayan* (800 CE) built temple cities with tall pyramids surrounding wide plazas in the deserts, mountains, and rain forests. About 700 miles south of what's now Mexico City, the Mayan were a Mesoamerican civilization noted for having the only fully developed written language of the pre-Columbian Americas. They were also known for their intricate art, building techniques, and mathematical and astronomical developments. Mayan civilization ran until the arrival of the Spanish more than 2,000 years later.

Mayan writing used a system similar to that of the early Egyptians and Chinese. Mayan scribes had picture words, called *glyphs,* that could stand for a noun or a syllable sound. The Mayan were talented farmers who grew early corn variants, called *maize,* in raised fields. The Mayan people never disappeared, neither with the rise of other powerful American Indian kingdoms nor with the arrival of the Spanish conquistadores and the subsequent Spanish takeover. Today, the Mayan and their descendants form sizable populations throughout the Mayan area and maintain a distinctive set of traditions and beliefs that are the result of the merger of pre-Columbian and post-conquest ideas. The Mayan may seem to worship in Christian churches, but many of their beliefs are thousands of years old.

The Incas

The *Incas* (1400) are the second-oldest civilization of the big three, beginning their empire in about 1000 CE. At its height, the Incan empire stretched for 2,500 miles, almost as long as the distance across the continental United States. From 1438 to 1533, the Incas used both conquest and peaceful assimilation to influence a large portion of western South America. The center of their empire was in the Andean mountain ranges, including modern Ecuador, Peru, western and south-central Bolivia, northwest Argentina, north and north-central Chile, and southern Colombia.

Incan palaces were surrounded by high walls made of huge, closely fitted stones. Like their empire neighbors to the north, the Inca connected their vast holdings with paved roads. Their mountain towns include the stunning Machu Picchu. The Incas developed a system of terraced agriculture fed by canals and aqueducts to allow farming in the mountains; they gave the world the tomato and the potato. Incan government and agriculture were well developed by the time the conquistador *Francisco Pizarro* (1532) stopped by and led his force to victory over the Inca.

The Aztecs

The *Aztecs* (1300) were the youngest of the Big Three American Indian empires. They hit the big time in modern-day Mexico City in about 1300 CE, just in time for a couple of hundred years of fun before Hernan Cortez and his Spanish buddies arrived to spoil the party. Mexico City was a city in the middle of a lake, with beautiful temples built along canals and a system of floating island gardens that fed much of the population. As the northernmost empire in Mesoamerica, Mexico City was connected with its provinces and tributary states by a good system of roads usually maintained through tribute from local rulers. Because the people had no horses or any kind of wheeled vehicles, the roads favored fast travel on foot. By order of the Aztecs, travelers had places to rest, eat, and even use a latrine at regular intervals — roughly every five to seven miles. Couriers with messages constantly traveled along those ways, keeping the Aztecs informed of events and reporting whether the roads needed work. Due to this steady surveillance, even women could travel alone — a fact that amazed the Spaniards because lone women hadn't been safe in Europe since the time of the Romans.

The Aztecs were a warlike people with a king, priests, tax collectors, and a merchant middle class. They captured prisoners in constant conflicts and used them for human sacrifices. Their American Indian enemies helped Cortez, with his small band of brave and bloodthirsty soldiers, conquer the Aztecs and kill their king. This event led to an uprising in Mexico City, from which Cortez barely escaped with his life. Other American Indians were glad to see the Aztecs removed from the complete power they'd enjoyed for only a few years.

Don't get caught confusing the Big Three American Indian empires. Just remember this: I'm not confused, AM I? From north to south, the three empires spell AM, I. The Aztecs are in Mexico, the Mayans are in Central America, and the Inca are in South America. In terms of age of the empires, they run MIA, as in missing in action. Mayans are the oldest, followed by the Incas and then the Aztecs. Both the Incas and the Aztecs got to rule for only a short time before the Spanish arrived. The Mayans had thousands of years to enjoy the limelight and were in serious decline when the Spanish arrived to end the party.

End of an empire

With just 180 men, 27 horses, and 1 cannon, Pizzaro often had to talk his way out of potential fights that could have easily wiped out his little band. The main type of battle in the Andes consisted of siege warfare, in which large numbers of drafted men were sent to overwhelm opponents.

Along with material superiority in the form of armor, weapons, and horses, the Spaniards acquired tens of thousands of native allies only too glad to end the Inca control of their territories. Combined, all of their resources and tactics allowed the Spanish to capture the emperor and subsequently throw the Incan ruling classes into a political struggle. The Spanish also kept increasing their native allies until they had enough people and resources to launch a successful attack on the Incan capital city.

The American Indian empires ended, but their cultural heritage lives on. Most Mexicans and Central and South Americans have American Indian ancestors. Anyone who has ever eaten a burrito, a taco, or even a french-fried potato has eaten American Indian food. Chewing gum, chocolate, and brightly patterned clothing left their American Indian-empire beginnings to become part of the world.

Question: What were the major American Indian empires encountered by Spanish explorers in Mesoamerica?

Answer: The Mayan, Incan, and Aztec empires.

Nothing Corny about Civilization Advancements

Corny as it sounds, corn made all the difference to American Indian civilization. The first planted-corn agriculture occurred in the Mexican highlands in about 5,000 BCE — a full 30,000 years after the first people got to the New World and around the time large-scale crop-raising got going in Egypt and the Middle East. Corn-growing took 4,000 years to reach the American Southwest, where corn supported an advancing culture 1,000 years before the birth of Christ.

The Anazazis in what's now New Mexico managed to build an apartment house with more than 600 interconnecting rooms. When the Spanish explorers reached the Southwest, they found villages of terraced multistory buildings. (*Pueblo,* the Spanish word now used for these American Indian settlements, means *village.*)

Another 2,000 years later, the American Indians in what's now the Eastern United States got the good news about corn-planting. In 1,000 CE, corn helped support a settlement of 25,000 people near modern-day St. Louis. By the time agriculture got to the eastern section of what's now the United States, the American Indians had only a few hundred years to enjoy cultivation in peace before the arrival of the Europeans.

Charting American Indians in North America

The American Indians living in North America before Columbus' arrival were divided into Northeast, Southeast, Great Plains, Southeast, Great Basin, Plateau, California, and Northwest Coast civilizations. They consisted of thousands of small groups loosely connected into tribes. Western American Indians were mostly hunter-gatherers. The Eastern American Indians devised a clever system of what they called *three sisters* agriculture: corn, beans, and squash. Beans grew on the stalks of corn, and squash covered the planting mound to hold moisture in the soil. This method supported some of the largest tribes, including the Cherokee, Creek, and Choctaw in the Southeast.

In the northern woodlands of what are now New York and New England was a remarkable alliance called the *Iroquois Confederacy* (also known as the *League of Peace and Power,* the *Five Nations,* the *Six Nations,* and the *People of the Longhouse*). This group of First Nations/ American Indians originally consisted of five tribes: the Mohawk, the Oneida, the Onondaga, the Cayuga, and the Seneca.

A sixth tribe, the Tuscarora, joined after the settlers came. Their constitution, called the Great Law of Peace, was handed down from the Middle Ages, when Europe was just a collection of feuding local rulers. The Iroquois Confederation actually served as one model for the development of the U.S. Constitution.

Although what's now the United States had some centers of development, the American Indian population of this area before Columbus probably never exceeded 4 million. Agriculture simply arrived too late to support large urban areas. In some areas, planting never arrived at all. The California American Indians spoke more than 200 languages and lived in small, stable communities near rich seashore and mountain food sources. These early Californians had the chance to develop agriculture but never bothered. Surf's up, man.

Carrying Death in a Handshake

Explorers are biological weapons. They don't mean to, but they carry diseases for which native populations have no immunities. These diseases killed many — perhaps most — of the American Indians in the New World before they had ever seen a European.

Good roads in the American Indian empires and nomadic migration by the plains American Indians allowed diseases to spread like wildfire. American Indians had no tradition of quarantine, which Europe had learned to use for epidemics; American Indians stayed close to their sick friends. Although staying close to those who are ill is good for human support, it's bad for the transmission of infectious diseases. Europeans brought smallpox, measles, bubonic plague, influenza, typhus, diphtheria, and scarlet fever to the New World, and close American Indian communities spread these diseases.

When explorers spread out to settle new lands, their diseases went with them. Friendly Taino natives met Columbus when he landed on Hispaniola, the island the Spanish named for themselves. Within 50 years, the estimated 1 million local people on Hispaniola were reduced to a pathetic and lonely 200. The conquistadores managed to defeat big American Indian empires largely because these empires were already collapsing from within. With friends and allies dying all around them, the American Indians fought desperate wars among themselves for the few resources left. Fighting and illness left them relatively easy conquests for the Europeans.

Europeans had fished in southern New England for more than 100 years before the Pilgrims landed in 1620. They met the American Indians and, without meaning to, passed on some diseases. The native inhabitants had no resistance to the illnesses brought by the Europeans, and within a few years, a plague wiped out 90 percent of the inhabitants of coastal New England. This death rate was unknown in all previous human experience. Even the Black Plague in the 1300s left 70 percent of Europe's population alive. The American Indians who met the Pilgrims were a confused and disorganized remnant, fighting among themselves.

When most of your friends are dead, part of your spirit dies with them. American Indians felt that their Supreme Being must have abandoned them. Some survivors of the Cherokee lost all confidence in their religion and destroyed the sacred objects of their tribe. American Indians were so reduced in numbers that they offered little real opposition to European invaders; some even looked upon the settlers for possible salvation.

Before the arrival of European explorers, the native population of North and South America may have been 100 million in 1491. The entire population of Europe at the time was 70 million. If colonists hadn't been able to take over lands that the American Indians had already cleared and cultivated, and if the American Indian population hadn't suffered devastating epidemics, the landing of the explorers may have been a very different story.

Question: What was the largest cause of death for American Indians during the European conquest?

Answer: The largest cause of death was disease unintentionally spread by explorers.

By 1900, the American Indian population of the New World was less than 1 million — a drop of 99 percent from Columbus's day. The United States had only 250,000 American Indians. Today, people are proud of their American Indian blood. In the 2000 U.S. census, more than 4 million Americans listed themselves as all or part American Indian.

Uneven Gift Exchange

What settlers brought to the New World versus what they took home leaves the American Indians way ahead on the gift exchange. The Old World brought death and domination to the people who lived in North and South America; the New World gave the Old World a new life. Eventually, European ideas of individual freedom would bring more options to American Indian survivors, but in the short run, the settlers profited far more than the American Indians.

Spain was poor and barely united when Columbus sailed. Through New World gold and silver, Spain was the richest country in Europe within a few decades. After the importation of corn, potatoes, pineapples, tomatoes, beans, vanilla, and chocolate from the New World, Europe had a chance to get fat and happy. The population of Europe more than doubled while Europeans spent the money and passed around the great food. Tobacco and syphilis also came from the Americas, but getting involved with either was generally a personal choice. Europe got tomato sauce for spaghetti and pizza, potatoes to go with meat, plus vanilla and chocolate for ice cream. What a deal!

Chapter 8

Sailing to a New Home: 1492–1690

• •

In This Chapter

▶ Planting the United States, one state at a time

▶ Seeing how early Americans made a living

▶ Getting into the political, economic, and social minds of the early Americans

• •

*W*hen Christopher Columbus sailed the ocean blue in 1492, he almost ended up in a great big stew. He landed half a world away from where he was heading (he originally intended to land in Asia, in the East Indies), and he got to the Bahamas but forgot his swimming suit. These missteps were forgiven after the Spanish found gold and realized that they'd discovered a whole new world, which was named for explorer–mapmaker Amerigo Vespucci. Maybe the song should say "God Bless Vespucciland," but *America* sounds better. (See more about Columbus later in this chapter.)

When European nations established colonies in America, the Spanish chose first and went south, where they found gold and silver. The British had a little navigation problem getting through the Spanish Armada, but eventually they went north and found mostly rocks and swamps. Clearing their way through American Indians, the Dutch, and some mighty lean years, British settlers built homes and livings in unique ways in different colonies. These colonies forged a particular trend toward freedom, even while slavery grew. This trend helped make the New World a major influence on the whole world.

Don't miss the forest for the trees. The AP exam concentrates on overall political, economic, and social (PES) trends, not so much on individual personal or state history. You need the whole story to have PES ammunition for writing essays. Don't try so hard to memorize everything that you lose the big picture.

In this chapter, you discover history from Columbus through the establishment of all the early colonies, all the way to the Salem witch trials on the eve of the 1700s. Pay special attention to early U.S. colonial trends; questions about this period are bound to show up on the big AP test.

Europeans Settle into the New World

Explorer *Christopher Columbus* (1492) was a little late and a lot short. He originally intended to land in the East Indies, but after six weeks at sea, the East Indies were still a cool 10,000 miles away, and his sailors were beginning to get a little testy. Just when Columbus looked as though he may end up on the sharp end of a pike, over the horizon loomed history's greatest consolation prize, the New World of North and South America.

The AP U.S. History exam isn't going to dwell much on Columbus. He gets too much competition from Leif Eriksson and his voyaging Vikings of 1000 CE for first-discoverer naming rights. The AP likes to concentrate instead on What It All Meant. Columbus in 1492 was important because he represented the beginning of permanent settlement in the New World.

Finding the New World changes the whole world

The settlement that began with Columbus eventually changed nearly all the world's continents in the following ways:

- ✔ North and South America through conquest and new communities
- ✔ Europe through gold and food from the Americas
- ✔ Africa through slavery and trade
- ✔ Asia, Australia, and the South Seas through commerce encouraged by New World discoveries

The New World was actually more of a team effort: Europe provided the money and the markets; Africa furnished a lot of the labor; and the New World produced gold and land for growing high-profit, bad-for-you crops like sugar cane and tobacco. Additionally, more than half of all the food grown in the world today originated in the New World. Fed by potatoes, tomatoes, corn, and beans first grown in the Americas, the population of Europe doubled. Although Africa suffered from slavery, it also benefited from new foods like cassava and sweet potatoes. For better or worse, the whole world became new.

In addition to colonization, the biggest impact that the European colonists had on the New World was the introduction of diseases against which American Indians had no defense. Within a few hundred years of the October morning when Columbus' ship sighted land, as much as 90 percent of the American Indian population was dead. This situation made the conquest of America much easier for the Europeans, leaving room for settlement, not just military victory. Many of the American Indians whom the Europeans did meet were dazed and confused survivors of ancient cultures that had been lost forever. Tribes moved and intermingled, but they had limited resources for taking united action against the European invaders.

Settling in with the Spanish and Portuguese

Before colonizing America, Europeans had been fighting one another for hundreds of years. Due to some smooth-sailing explorers, Spain and Portugal were in the lead for international conquest moving into the late 1400s.

So that these two leading-explorer countries wouldn't step on each other's toes, the pope helpfully issued a decree in the year after Columbus' first voyage, dividing the New World between Spain and Portugal. Because the pope's line managed to miss pretty much all the land, leaving Portugal holding nothing but waves, the two countries got together and amicably signed the *Treaty of Tordesillas* (1494). This agreement moved the dividing line a few hundred miles west, so that Portugal at least got Brazil, plus a little bonus land in Africa and Asia. Spain got the rest of the "heathen" world and immediately got down to some heavy-duty conquistadoring.

Spanish explorers spent a lot of time in hot armor looking for gold. Some looked in all the wrong places in North America, but all managed to make some interesting discoveries:

- ✔ *Vasco Balboa* (1513) made it across Panama to become the first European to wade into the Pacific Ocean. He found pineapples and pearls.

- ✔ *Ferdinand Magellan* (1519) sailed west from Spain with five small boats and an international crew of Portuguese, Spanish, Italian, French, English, and German sailors. After making it around South America (the Strait of Magellan is named for him), he died in the Philippines, but a few members of his crew made it all the way around the world and home again in 1522 with a cargo of cinnamon and cloves.

- ✔ *Ponce de Leon* (1513) checked out Florida.

- ✔ *Francisco Coronado* (1540) spent years marching around the Southwest. Coronado found the Grand Canyon and millions of buffalo but nothing he could put in the bank.

- ✔ *Hernando de Soto* (1539), with 600 men in bright armor, checked out the middle South. De Soto ended up sunk in the Mississippi River, but after three years, a few of his men made it back wearing animal skins.

- ✔ *Francisco Pizarro* (1532) persuaded the Incan king to turn over his gold and then turned over his whole kingdom looking for more.

- ✔ *Hernán Cortés* (1519) took over the Aztec Empire, centered in Mexico City, happily trading the lives of his men and thousands of natives for gold. For variety, the mines in what's now Bolivia produced tons of silver.

Soon, Spain and the rest of Europe were glittering with precious metal. New World treasure made Europe rich. Having money to explore, trade, and conquer made Europe even richer.

Bringing Christianity to the New World

The *encomienda* system assigned groups of American Indians to colonists who were supposed to Christianize them but who actually used them as slaves. Conquistadores signed agreements with the Spanish king, raised money from investors, and then marched off looking for plunder. Only about 10,000 of these mercenaries existed, but they had guns, horses, and no hesitation about killing anybody who got in their way. To turn a profit for themselves and their investors, the conquistadores were experts at getting American Indians to fight one another. Many sincerely believed they were bringing the gift of true Christianity to a savage world; any gold they picked up along the way must be their just reward.

A Black Legend historical theme popular in the 1900s said that the Spanish killed, raped, and looted for treasure, leaving nothing but suffering behind. Although some Spaniards certainly were cruel and greedy, Spain hardly had a monopoly on those bad habits. Spanish settlers who thought they were spreading the word of God founded missions and settlements in places that had no gold, including New Mexico and California. (Ironically, gold was discovered in California just nine days before Spain's successor, Mexico, turned the territory over to the United States.)

Blending cultures and blending people

The conquerors also married American Indian women. The women converted to Catholicism, couples got married, and the Spanish–American Indian children were called *mestizos*. This wonderful mixture of cultures forms much of the population of Mexico, Central America, and South America to this day.

La Malinche was a native Aztec woman who accompanied Hernán Cortés and played an active role in the Spanish conquest of Mexico. La Malinche smoothed the way for Cortés as an interpreter and intermediary. She also was the mother of Cortés' son, who's considered one of the first mestizos. In Mexico today, people both love and hate La Malinche. She's remembered alternately as a traitor, a sellout, a heroine who helped save at least some of the

Aztecs, and the symbolic mother of the new Mexican people. The Mexicans also celebrate Columbus Day as *Día de la Raza* — the birthday of what they see as their whole new race of people.

Spaniards' ideas of civilization often backfired on them. The Pueblo Revolt, also known as *Popé's Rebellion* (1680), was an American Indian uprising in New Mexico that killed hundreds of Spanish settlers and priests. The American Indians rebuilt their sacred *kiva* (ceremonial chamber) on the ruins of the Spanish plaza in Santa Fe; Spain needed almost 30 years to regain control. In the New World as a whole, the influence of a Spanish culture willing to intermarry with native society is still evident from San Francisco 8,000 miles south to the tip of South America.

Dealing with pirates of the Caribbean

No more than 50 years after Columbus discovered the Bahamas, hundreds of small Spanish and mestizo towns had sprung up, especially near the gold and silver in Mexico and Peru. The Spanish founded the first universities in the New World, 85 years before the English got around to starting Harvard. In fact, the Spanish get the credit for the first permanent town in what would become the United States. They built a fort at *St. Augustine, Florida* (1565), way before Disney World came around. The Spanish fortified St. Augustine to hold off real-life pirates of the Caribbean.

All that Spanish treasure attracted fortune hunters with ships who didn't mind stealing from the Spanish (who had stolen it from the natives anyway). Privateers (a name they preferred to *pirates*) operated from around 1560 to the mid-1760s. The period during which pirates were most successful was the 1640s through the 1680s. Caribbean piracy arose out of conflicts over trade and colonization among the rival European powers, including England, Spain, Holland, Portugal, and France. Most of the privateers who had permission from their governments to attack foreign ships were from Holland and England.

Because Spain controlled most of the Caribbean, most of the attacked cities and ships belonged to the Spanish Empire. Some of the best-known pirate bases were in the Bahamas (1715 to 1725), Tortuga (established in the 1640s), and Port Royal (after 1655). Among the most famous Caribbean pirates were Edward Teach (also known as Blackbeard) and Henry Morgan.

Having trouble with the neighbors

Closer to home, the Spanish were having trouble holding their European domination over the Protestant country of Holland. They sent their great fleet — the *Spanish Armada* (1588) — to invade and subdue England, Holland's Protestant supporter.

In a battle just north of the English Channel, the English and Dutch attacked the armada. Even though they were outnumbered, the attacking ships managed to scatter the armada and sink some of the ships. More armada ships were lost in storms that showed up just in time to help the defenders. When England and Spain finally signed a peace treaty in 1604, the English were free to move to unclaimed North America. Spanish power began a slow decline that lasted for more than 300 years.

Getting colonial with the English

Poor and distracted by local conflicts, the best the English could do to get into the exploration game was to send out a ringer. A captain the English called *John Cabot* (1497) (even though he was really an Italian named Giovanni Caboto) sailed along the coast of what's now Canada. The exploration received funding from British businessmen eager to make a profit trading with the Spice Islands. When Cabot didn't come back from a second voyage, England decided to put the whole exploration thing on the back burner for a while.

Spain and Portugal had a 100-year head start in colonizing Mexico and South America, but nothing much was happening north of there. The Spanish had sniffed around but hadn't found anything glittering and immediately saleable. Then, at almost the same time, Europe came to stay in three corners of North America:

- ✔ The French built a fur-trading post at *Quebec, Canada* (1608).
- ✔ The Spanish built a mission at *Santa Fe, New Mexico* (1610).
- ✔ The English established their first permanent colony at *Jamestown, Virginia* (1607).

Jamestown wasn't England's first shot at New World colonization:

- ✔ *Sir Francis Drake* (1580) had done so well as a pirate of the Caribbean that Queen Elizabeth I knighted him as a way of saying thanks for all the Spanish gold he brought back.
- ✔ *Sir Walter Raleigh* (1585) founded a short-lived colony of 100 men and women on Roanoke Island. The colony survived long enough for the birth of Virginia Dare, the first English child born in the New World. When a ship carrying supplies arrived after a 3-year absence, the crew found everybody gone, with houses and fortifications neatly removed. The only clue was the word *Croatoan* carved into a post of the fort and *Cro* carved into a nearby tree. The survivors of the colony may have gone to live with a nearby friendly tribe of Croatoan American Indians and intermarried.

The latter point, if it's true, represents last major intermarrying the English did with the American Indians because, unlike the Spanish, the English brought their wives with them to America. The English did enough reproducing by themselves; in the 50 years up to 1600, the population of England increased by one third. At the same time, a change from growing crops to growing sheep displaced a lot of English farmers. People were looking for a place to go, and settling in America seemed like an ideal solution.

Staying on in Jamestown

The English went to Jamestown for all the wrong reasons. Their privately financed joint-stock Virginia Company wanted to find gold or at least a passage to the rich Spice Islands of Asia. The colonists were under some pressure to produce riches; if they didn't, they could be abandoned in the wilderness.

Question: Who owned Jamestown?

Answer: A joint-stock company eager for profits owned the colony.

In the great tradition of brown-nosing, the name *Jamestown* paid tribute to then-ruling English King James I. The territory's name, *Virginia,* honored the alleged lovemaking status of the previous ruler, Queen Elizabeth I, the Virgin Queen. (Imagine if people still named places for love status — say HotToTrot Land or Dreamyville.)

The Charter of the Virginia Company guaranteed the colonists basic rights as Englishmen. The colony had about 100 settlers to start, all of them men. They were too busy looking for gold to gather much food, so a lot of them died from hunger and the diseases that go with it.

In 1608, Captain John Smith took over and whipped the surviving colonists into shape with a simple rule: "He who shall not work shall not eat." Earlier, Smith had been saved by the American Indian princess Pocahontas, who went on to marry another settler, help protect the colony, and visit England to meet the king.

Still, times were tough: Of the 400 settlers who had gone to Jamestown by 1609, only 60 survived the "starving time" winter. Twelve hundred English people lived in Virginia by 1625, but an additional six thousand died trying to live on this edge of the New World.

Forming and breaking alliances with the American Indians

Pocahontas tried to keep the peace, but after she died during her trip to England, the colonists and American Indians fought a series of wars. By 1650, the Chesapeakes had been banished from all the land around Jamestown; by 1685, few American Indians remained. This pattern repeated as English colonies came in contact with American Indians across North America: first cooperation, then conflict, and finally removal and severe population decline for the American Indians. As outlined in Chapter 7, disease often destroyed native people and culture before they ever saw a European settler.

American Indian tribes moved, made and broke alliances, and fought wars with one another for thousands of years before the Europeans came. The arrival of the settlers was like introducing an elephant into the living room; everyone had to shift around. Looking for land to live on, tribes moved hundreds of miles and fought other tribes. For some American Indians, this migration was good; they got guns from settlers and made good profits delivering furs and acting as scouts for the Europeans. Competition for shrinking hunting grounds led to increased American-Indian-on-American-Indian violence.

Lots of American Indians moved west toward the Great Plains as English settlements spread out from the East. Tribes like the Sioux, who previously led quiet lives on the edge of the forest, learned to ride escaped Spanish horses and became Great Plains buffalo hunters and raiders. The Iroquois Confederation in the northern colonies benefited from alliances and trades with settlers, and actually grew in power for 100 years. But for most American Indians, the arrival of Europeans was an unmitigated disaster. In a world governed by survival of the strongest, the concept of human rights was still a long way off.

Setting up as offshore sugar daddies

As the first wave of settlers left Britain, twice as many English pioneers went to the West Indies as came to the rocky, swampy shores of North America. They didn't go because they had timeshares; they went to grow sugar, the other bad-for-you big money-maker of the New World. Although they could grow tobacco in their Virginia backyards, sugar cane required large plantations and thousands of workers. New World slavery really got its start in the West Indies. While small farmers were working their own land in the mainland colonies during the late 1600s, West Indies plantation owners were busy importing more than 250,000 enslaved people from Africa. Before long, blacks outnumbered whites four to one.

The inhuman *Barbados slave code* (1661) required that slave owners dress their slaves. That was about it. The code denied slaves even the most basic right guaranteed under English common law: the right to life. It allowed slaveholders to do whatever they wanted to their slaves, including mutilating and burning them alive for punishment, without fear of the law.

Plantation owners were so busy growing sugar that they squeezed out most of the small farmers who grew food for the islands. These farmers moved to the North American colonies, bringing a few slaves and the slave code with them.

Germany and Italy didn't start colonies in the New World because these nations didn't even get themselves organized until the late 1800s. The English settlements along the American coast grew because they had more settlers who came to stay. The French were either happy at home (the food was better) or would have left if the king hadn't forbidden them to go to America (like the French Protestants). The Spanish and Portuguese saw the New World as more of a money mine than a place to start a new life. The English began to settle down and build some permanent family homes in the New World, whereas Spanish colonial administrators just sent money back to the central government in Europe. When English colonies were mostly self-governing in politics and religion, Spanish colonies were ruled centrally from the mother country.

Question: What were some differences between the Spanish and English colonies?

Answer: The English operated politics and religion locally (instead of reporting back to the central mother country like Spain) and used their New World settlements to build personal wealth rather than sending everything back to Europe.

Establishing the Future States: The American Colonies

If you were choosing where to settle in the new colonies during the 1600s, you probably wouldn't pick the Northern colonies for their climate or chances of supporting your shot at tobacco riches. What the North had was a place to raise a family and own your own land. As the country grew up, the Northern colonies made up for what they lacked in agricultural riches with smart money from commerce and industry. Meanwhile, they also offered the purifying search for spiritual truth.

Maryland, Virginia, the Carolinas, and Georgia all developed as large plantation colonies focused on growing and exporting agricultural products. Whereas independent North Carolina and reform-born Georgia protected the rights of small farmers, the economic system of the South favored large landowners. With lots of slaves and not many citizens, developing a system of schools or even alternative types of religion was hard. The standard Church of England dominated the South and collected taxes to ensure its support. By growing tobacco, rice, and eventually cotton, the South made a lot of money for a limited number of rich planters. These planters controlled politics because nonlandowners couldn't vote. Because big planters weren't interested, the South had virtually no industry and no public school system until after the Civil War.

Pennsylvania, New York. and New Jersey came to be known as the *bread colonies* because they grew grain for the rest of the Eastern Seaboard. But their industry wasn't all agriculture. They had forests of big beautiful trees to cut down, and the lumber from these trees built houses, businesses, and ships. All these crops and construction opportunities gave business to the growing ports of New York City, Philadelphia, and Albany. The middle colonies were midway between small-farm New England and the big-plantation South. Government fell midway between the superdemocratic town meetings of New England and the autocratic rich-man's government of the South. The middle colonies weren't middle in freedom. Especially in Pennsylvania, people enjoyed religious freedom and a cosmopolitan tolerance for minorities.

Pilgrims, Puritans, and Massachusetts: Leading the way

America was built in the smoke from the great fire of the Protestant Reformation. A German priest named *Martin Luther* (1517) broke with the Roman Catholic Church, which had ruled Christianity since the late Roman Empire. Luther said that individuals had to have a personal relationship with God and the Bible; priests and popes couldn't tell them what to think or sell them a ticket to heaven. In his *Institutes of the Christian Religion* (1536), John Calvin went further. Calvin said God had already chosen who would go to heaven and who would burn in hell; this theory was the *predestination of the elect*. God knew everything, and no amount of good works would change his mind.

Conveniently for English believers, *King Henry VIII* (1533) had just kicked the Catholic church out of England over his multiple-marriage issue. As England scrambled to piece together its own church, religious beliefs were up for grabs. This confusion drove both radical Protestants (who didn't think the English church was changing fast enough) and out-of-favor Catholics (who felt it was changing too fast) to the New World for a little spiritual breathing room.

First out the door were the most radical Protestants, a small group of Separatists who wanted nothing to do with the new Church of England. They headed in the opposite direction from America and spent 12 years in Holland. The Dutch were tolerant of their religious rights, but the Pilgrims didn't like that their kids were assimilating to the Dutch lifestyle. After a short stop back home to load some supplies on a little boat about 35 steps long called the *Mayflower,* 50 Pilgrims and 52 other settlers sailed for Virginia.

After two months of bobbing across the Atlantic, the *Mayflower* crew landed 700 miles north of where they were aiming, on a peninsula now called Plymouth in a land now called Massachusetts. Before they even got off the ship, the settlers signed the *Mayflower Compact* (1620), agreeing to make decisions by the will of the majority. From this simple agreement and the open town meetings that followed came a feeling for participatory democracy that now has a history of almost 400 years in the United States. The Pilgrims had great leaders: a short non-Separatist soldier named Myles Standish (also called Captain Shrimp) and William Bradford, an eloquent self-taught scholar who could read five languages. More than half of the Pilgrims died the first winter, so when they brought in a good harvest the next year, they really did have a happy Thanksgiving. Their little Plymouth colony never had more than a few thousand people; late in the 1600s, it merged with the Massachusetts Bay Colony a few miles to the north.

The *Massachusetts Bay Colony* (1630), which would become Boston, was settled by Puritans who didn't think they actually had to leave the Church of England to follow the word of God. They came to America to escape political repression, a bad economy, and restrictions on their religion. They got off to a strong start with almost 1,000 well-equipped settlers arriving on 11 boats. They also had an excellent leader in John Winthrop, who served for 19 years. Around 20,000 more settlers arrived during the first 12 years of the colony, although twice as many headed south for the warm breezes and easy sugar living of Barbados.

Question: Were the Puritans Separatists?

Answer: No. They wanted to purify the Church of England from within.

The Bay Colony offered freedom but no easy living. All freemen who belonged to the Puritan church could vote. That meant about two out of five people — a much higher percentage of voter participation than anyplace else at the time. The catch was that to be in the church, you were supposed to have had a conversion experience that identified you as one of the *visible saints*. In other words, God had to pick you to go to heaven before you could go to church. And yes, you took a test. Prospective church members had to explain to an interview panel how they knew God had chosen them (without sounding stuck-up, of course).

Question: Why did the Puritans leave England?

Answer: They left to escape political repression, recession, and religious restrictions.

Back in the early days of Puritan orthodoxy, the freethinking *Anne Hutchinson* (1638) took on the leaders of the Bay Colony. She actually may have been more spiritual than the leaders were, because she felt she had a direct revelation from God that if predestination were true, everybody had a duty to follow his or her own conscience. Leaders banished her from the colony for challenging their religious authority; she happily left with her whole family. *Roger Williams* (1635) was another purifying spirit. He said the Congregationalists (a more modern name for the church that started with the Puritans) should make a complete break from the corrupt Church of England, treat the American Indians fairly, and not try to legislate religious behavior. Hounded out of Massachusetts, he helped found the new colony of Rhode Island (discussed later in this chapter) to protect freedom of thought and expression.

Question: Why did Anne Hutchinson get in trouble with the leaders of the Bay Colony?

Answer: She challenged their religious authority.

Freethinking Rhode Island

Helped by sympathetic American Indians, Roger Williams fled to what would become the colony of *Rhode Island* (1636) in the midst of a bitterly cold winter. He built the first Baptist church in America and established complete religious freedom of thought, even for Catholics and the Jewish. Nobody had to believe a fixed creed; no one had to go to church or pay taxes to support a state religion. These freedoms sound normal now, but they were rare at the time.

Rhode Island also started with universal male suffrage; any man could vote. This right was limited later, but from the start, Rhode Island was a progressive beacon in an already-freedom-loving country. The colony grew with people who didn't fit in other locations, including Anne Hutchinson and her family. Critics from other colonies called it Rogues' Island. Originally highly unofficial, Rhode Island somehow managed to win a charter from Parliament in 1644; a statue of the Independent Man tops its statehouse.

Connecticut comes to order

The Connecticut River valley is one of the few really fertile spots in New England. A mass migration of Puritans from Boston settled near the river, and some Dutch and English immigrants followed. In an open meeting, the new colony drafted the *Fundamental Orders* (1639), the beginning of a modern constitution. So-called substantial citizens were to democratically control the new government. The Connecticut colony was soon joined by another attempt at godly government in New Haven. Together, these colonies mark the small beginning of the migration of American settlers to the west.

Puritans versus Pilgrims: Telling them apart

To remember the difference between Puritans and Pilgrims, just remember that Puritans wanted to purify the Church of England from within. Pilgrims thought they had to be grim Separatists and leave the established church on a long pilgrimage to find a godly place to live.

Puritans believed (rather like modern fundamentalists) that the whole purpose of government was to enforce God's laws. Still, they cut some slack. Congregations hired and fired their own ministers; thus, they could have local control over what the church was saying. Contrary to what people think now, the Puritans were actually heavily into food, drink, songs, and married love. A "Protestant ethic" supported willpower and hard work, but after the responsibilities were taken care of, nothing was wrong with having fun. Because they never had to answer to any central dogma, the Congregationalists eventually evolved into the most liberal Protestant denomination.

Dutch treat in New York and New Jersey

The practical Dutch actually got where everybody else thought they were heading: to the East Indies. For 300 years, the Dutch had a profitable colony far from home. Casting their eyes across the Atlantic, they sent Henry Hudson (1609) exploring up the great Hudson River and eventually into Hudson Bay. While he was starting up what would later be called the Hudson River, his navigator wrote down the American Indian name for an extended island they passed. The American Indians called it "island of many hills," or *Manhattan*. Later, the Dutch thought they'd made a great deal when they bought the island from the American Indians for a chest full of flashy trinkets. However, the American Indians had the last laugh. They didn't really own Manhattan; they'd just stopped by to fish.

New Amsterdam (1623), the Dutch city that would become New York City, wasn't a beacon of liberty. The Dutch ran business for a profit and had no real interest in religious tolerance, free speech, or voting in the colony they called New Netherland. The Dutch had trouble with American Indian attacks in New Amsterdam, so they built a high wall. The street that ran along that wall is called Wall Street. The uptown country on Manhattan reminded them of a place in Holland, so they named it Harlem. They had to boot out a small Swedish settlement (1655) on the Delaware River, but then the Dutch themselves were booted when the English came, first as settlers and then in warships.

In 1664, the surrounded and already-profitable Dutch peacefully surrendered New Netherland to the English, who renamed it New York after an island off the British coast. Ownership of New Jersey came along with New York when the English took over from the Dutch. The large landholding tradition of New York state discouraged heavy settlement of the inland area during the early colonial period. Upstate New York was still a frontier when the Revolution came.

Question: Why did the Dutch found New Netherland?

Answer: The Dutch had commercial and mercantile goals: They wanted to make money.

Quaking in Pennsylvania and Delaware

After the Catholics lost control of England, the religious cat was out of the bag. Among the many sincere groups that tried to discern the word of God were the Quakers. They called themselves the Religious Society of Friends, but everybody else called them Quakers because they allegedly became so full of the Holy Spirit that they quaked. They had no mandatory beliefs and no preachers; Quakers took turns speaking in their Sunday meetings when the spirit moved them. They refused to fight or join the military and tried to live peaceful lives.

This Christian behavior made everybody hate them. William Penn was a serious-minded English boy from a family with money. He decided to become a Quaker and worked to get a colony where Quakers could live in peace. Amazingly enough, King Charles II owed Penn's father some money, so he gave William a choice piece of land that the king called *Pennsylvania* (1681). Penn tried to change the name because it sounded too egotistical but eventually settled down to attract good settlers. He carefully laid out Philadelphia, "the city of brotherly love," which quickly became the largest and most beautiful city in the colonies.

The Quakers treated the American Indians so fairly that some tribes from the South tried to move to the colony. Unfortunately, Pennsylvania had only a minority of Quakers, so trouble soon began. The government was fair, with freedom of religion, no church tax, and a representative legislature elected by all male landowners. The death penalty was levied only for treason or murder; by comparison, more than 200 offenses could result in beheading in

England at the time. Within 19 years of its founding, Pennsylvania was the third-richest colony in British America. After the English ousted the Dutch from New York, the future Delaware became the Lower Counties of Pennsylvania and got to be an independent area in time to be the first state to ratify the Constitution after the Revolution.

Merry Maryland

The rich English Catholic Lord Baltimore founded *Maryland* (1634), conveniently located up the Chesapeake Bay from Virginia. He hoped to make a profit and provide a haven for his fellow Catholics, who were still heavily discriminated against in England. He was thinking of vast feudal estates, but colonists didn't want to come unless they personally got to own some land. Tobacco was growing before long. To work the fields, the Maryland settlers imported indentured servants, generally poor white Englishmen who agreed to work for 4 to 7 years for free in exchange to a ticket to the New World. In the early days, three of every four English immigrants to the Chesapeake Bay came as indentured servants.

Sadly, only 40 percent of the indentured servants lived to win their freedom; the early death rate from disease was that high. As indentured servants died out in the late 1600s, Maryland began to import larger numbers of slaves. Even with servants working and slaves on the way, Maryland managed to make a stand for freedom with the adoption of the *Act of Toleration* (1649). The act guaranteed freedom of religion to everyone, Catholic or Protestant, as long as they believed in Jesus. Tough luck if you were Buddhist or Jewish, though; the act threatened nonbelievers in Jesus with death.

Smokin' Virginia

When he wasn't bankrolling failed colonies, Sir Walter Raleigh liked to smoke a pipe. Back then, people called it *drinking tobacco,* but by any name, the habit has always been hard to quit. Smoking really took off in England after John Rolfe, the husband of Pocahontas, figured out a way to grow smoother-tasting tobacco in the Jamestown colony. He made so much money that pretty soon people were planting tobacco in their front yards and even in the street. As the market for the "bewitching weed" grew, colonists pushed for more land to grow it on. With more land, they needed more labor: Virginia finally had an economic hit.

Just in time, a ship appeared off Jamestown and sold a cargo of 20 Africans to work for hungry Virginia planters. It was still a year before the Pilgrims came to New England seeking freedom. In the same year the slave ship arrived, London authorized the *House of Burgesses* (1619) in Virginia to be the first representative government in the New World. America was already on a two-track system.

Carolina, North and South

The colony of Carolina officially adopted a version of the Barbados slave code in 1696. *Carolina* (1670) was the third middle colony in a row named in honor of the then-current English ruler: Charles II had replaced Charles I, who lost his head. The colony served as a supply station for the hugely profitable sugar plantations of the West Indies. Carolina even tried its hand at supplying slaves. Over the objections of its London proprietors, the colony shipped as many as 10,000 American Indians to the cane fields of the sugar islands. Carolina learned to grow rice with the help of West African slaves; by 1710, the colony had more Africans than whites.

Carolina divided into North and South in 1691. North Carolina people were small farmers who often just claimed land, built a cabin, and planted a few crops. They were rugged individualists, hiding out between the landed aristocracies of Virginia and South Carolina. The North Carolina folks were even accused of harboring pirates along stormy Cape Hatteras, the "graveyard of the Atlantic." When the local Tuscaroras attacked a North Carolina town, the settlers fought a bloody war and ended up selling hundreds of the American Indians into slavery. The survivors traveled north looking for protection and became the sixth tribe in the Iroquois Confederacy.

Reforming Georgia

Georgia (1733) was the last of the original 13 colonies and the only one founded in the 1700s. Named for the foppish King George II (new king, new colony name), Georgia was a buffer against the Spanish in Florida and the French in Louisiana. The colony had as a founder James Oglethorpe, a fair-minded reformer who used his own money to develop a land that would let debtors get a new start. Oglethorpe helped design the beautiful city of Savannah, banned slavery, and fought off Spanish attacks. He invited reformers to visit, including the young John Wesley, who would go on to found the Methodist Church. Over his objections after he left the colony, Georgia allowed slavery in 1750. Oglethorpe lived long enough to be a friend of the American Revolution in England.

Early Challenges to the New Colonies

The early days of the colonies were far from smooth sailing. Settlers had problems with American Indians, autocratic English government, diseases, slavery, the economy, and even witchcraft. The following sections summarize topics that may come up on the AP exam.

American Indian troubles

American Indians resented being driven off their land, and they fought back from time to time with vicious attacks. Shortly before the Pilgrims arrived, an epidemic swept through the New England coastal tribes and wiped out three-quarters of the native people. With no strength to repel even the weak Pilgrim settlement, the local American Indians were friendly. *Squanto* (1620), who had been kidnapped by an English ship's captain years before, greeted the Pilgrims in perfect English and helped them through to the first Thanksgiving.

As the settlers pushed the American Indians off their land over the next 50 years, the son of the chief who had welcomed the Pilgrims lost his patience. The settlers called him King Philip because they couldn't be bothered to learn his American Indian name, Metacom. Backed by an alliance of fed-up American Indians, he launched *King Philip's War* (1675). By the time the war ended a year later, his forces had attacked 52 towns and destroyed 12. One out of ten settlers of military age was a casualty; women and children were carried off by American Indians. Even Plymouth itself, site of the Pilgrims' landing, fell victim.

Bacon's Rebellion of 1675 had tied down the Virginia government, the only other significant English presence in North America. Canada was still mostly French and rooting for the American Indians. The New England colonies had to defend themselves on their own.

In the end, the settlers fought together through the *New England Confederation* (1643) and held on. In the south, the first capital of Virginia, Jamestown, was burned in 1676, but the government eventually regained control. Although nightmare fears of Indian attacks lasted for years, actual Indian power in New England ended with the death of Metacom. For the first time, settlers in separate colonies began to think of themselves as Americans.

Locals get together; England cracks the whip

The first colonial union was the *New England Confederation* (1643), a partnership of the Massachusetts Bay Colony, Plymouth, and two Connecticut colonies for mutual defense and problem solving. The colonists were proud of that.

Years later, the royal government in London imposed a very different *Dominion of New England* (1686). The head of the new dominion was Sir Edmund Andros. His job was to enforce the law, especially the *Navigation Act* (1660), which made it illegal to send anything to the colonies that hadn't first passed through and been taxed by England. This Navigation Act and the later *Molasses Act* of 1733 supported a policy of *mercantilism* that forced colonies to buy and sell with their mother country so that the mother country could make a profit off the colonies.

Question: What did the Navigation Acts (1660) and the Molasses Act (1733) support?

Answer: These acts furthered the policy of *mercantilism.*

The colonists hated Sir Edmund, and he responded by closing down meetings, schools, the courts, and the press, and revoking land titles. He issued taxes without consulting the local assemblies. The colonists were on the verge of revolt. Fortunately, the English did the revolting for them. In the *Glorious Revolution* (1689), they dethroned the unpopular James II and brought on the mellower William and Mary. Sir Edmund was caught trying to sneak out of town dressed as a woman; the boots sticking out from under his dress gave him away. He was booted back to England.

Disease and money

The Chesapeake area was a money-maker but not a very healthy place to be. The colony history earlier in this chapter discusses the short life of indentured servants; that short life went for everybody in early Virginia and Maryland. Half the people born in the early years didn't live to see their 20th birthdays. Few of those who lived past 20 made it to 50, and women were lucky to see 40. Most marriages ended in the death of a partner within 7 years. Without many parents or any grandparents for moral guidance, more than one third of girls were pregnant when they got married.

Meanwhile, the money kept rolling in to those who survived to spend it. The Chesapeake Bay already shipped 1.5 million pounds of tobacco a year in the 1630s; by 1700, the colony shipped 40 million pounds a year. Both Virginia and Maryland employed the *headright system* (1670) to encourage the importation of servant workers. Whoever paid to bring in a servant received the right to 50 acres of land. Hungry for land and labor, big planters brought some 100,000 indentured servants into the region by 1700; most of those servants didn't live long enough to serve out their contracts. In all, these indentured servants represented three quarters of all newcomers to the region in the 1600s.

Early rebellions

Leisler's Rebellion (1689) was an uprising in colonial New York City in which militia captain Jacob Leisler seized control of lower New York from 1689 to 1691. The uprising, which occurred in the midst of Britain's Glorious Revolution, reflected colonial resentment of the policies of King James II. British troops sent by James' mellower successor William III restored royal authority in 1691.

Virginia's governor, William Berkeley, had a good thing going. To keep his profitable fur-trade monopoly with the American Indians flowing smoothly, he looked the other way when American Indians killed settlers on the frontier. In *Bacon's Rebellion* (1676), a group of about 1,000 planters took on the American Indians; they then drove Berkeley from his capital at Jamestown and burned the place. After Bacon died of all-too-prevalent natural causes, Berkeley defeated the rebellion and hanged the surviving leaders. This small rebellion sent a wake-up call to the big planters; they needed to find workers who lived longer and couldn't fight back. The answer was slaves.

Slaves in the land of the free, Part 1

Only about 5 percent of the 8 million human beings stolen from Africa to be enslaved in the New World during the 1600s and 1700s went to the colonies or their successor, the United States. One-third of the slaves went to Brazil; most of the rest worked the sugar plantations of the Caribbean.

As late as 1670, slaves made up less than 10 percent of the population of Southern plantations. That started to change in a big way as indentured servants died off. By 1750, half the population of Virginia was African. Many slaves in the Deep South died from hard work in the rice and indigo fields (cotton came a century later) and had to be replaced with new imports. In the Chesapeake Bay, the very place that killed so many white indentured servants, slaves lived much longer. By the mid-1700s, the slave population of this area was capable of sustaining itself without the new importation of human beings.

Slaves brought more than just labor to the New World. Without call-and-response singing, the rhythmic ringshout dance, hand drums, and the banjo, all of which came from Africa, America may still be doing the minuet. Long live rock-and-roll!

Slaves fought back when they could. A revolt in New York City in 1712 cost the lives of a dozen whites and 21 Africans. The *Stono Revolt* (1739) saw 50 self-liberated slaves marching toward Florida to be free, only to be stopped by the militia.

New England living

In contrast to the middle Southern states, New England added 10 years to the average life span of new settlers. The first generation of Puritan colonists lived an average of 70 years — pretty close to a modern life span. Because of this unprecedented longevity, some say New England invented grandparents, who were still around to play with the kids. Family morality is reflected in the low premarital pregnancy rate, again in stark contrast to the experience in the South. Massachusetts started the first college, Harvard, in 1636, just 8 years after the colony's founding. It took Virginia 83 years after staking out Jamestown to get around to starting the College of William and Mary in 1693.

Witches and religion

With all this goodness came a little New England fanaticism. The Puritan light burned bright, but it also could be blinding. After about 40 years of accepting only the select, Puritan churches had to offer a *Half-Way Covenant* (1662), which opened church attendance to people who couldn't prove they were among God's elect. As time went on, the doors of the churches opened wider, perhaps sometimes even admitting sinners.

At about this time, a new type of sermon began to appear — something that speakers called a *jeremiad* after the always-scolding Old Testament prophet Jeremiah. Preachers thundered about the wrath of God and the hellfire that awaits the sinner, just as though sinners walked among the elect. This kind of angry shouting soon showed its ugly face in the town of Salem, north of Boston.

A group of teenage girls, under the influence of voodoo talk by a West Indian slave, claimed to have been bewitched by certain older women in the town. This claim triggered a hysterical witch hunt that led to the legal murders of 20 people. Most of the victims were hanged, but one was pressed to death under a huge rock. The girls claimed they could see devils in the courtroom ceiling, and Puritan judges believed them.

The *Salem Witch Trials* (1692) helped save other people by introducing the pejorative term *witch hunt* into the language. When ordinary people say that the government is going on a witch hunt, they unconsciously refer to a hard time in colonial America.

Chapter 9

Growing Up and Getting Revolutionary: 1691–1775

*F*rom shaky settlements clinging to the edge of a wild continent, the 13 colonies grew to become prosperous and increasingly feisty. Surviving colonial wars with the French and their American Indian allies gave colonists confidence. Making a good living by farming, building ships and trading showed the early residents of British North America that they could take care of themselves. Life was good, and as the new country grew, so did the population's strength in numbers: More than five times as many people lived in the colonies in the 1770s as had made their homes there in the 1690s. People began to feel like acting independent.

Stirring the Melting Pot: Population Expansion

The early colonies of New England included Massachusetts, Rhode Island, Connecticut, and New Hampshire and were mostly into fishing and small family farming. The early Southern colonies of Virginia, Delaware, Maryland, North Carolina, South Carolina, and Georgia made their money on large plantations growing rice and tobacco. The Middle colonies of New York, Pennsylvania, and New Jersey were actually in the middle, with medium-sized farms growing medium-sized crops of grain and raising cattle.

During the years between 1691 and 1775, the American colonies grew like rabbits, thanks mostly to immigration. In 1700, the 13 original colonies had only 250,000 people. Just 50 years later, the population had quintupled to 1.25 million. The colonists had plenty of children, but America also attracted immigrants by the thousands. Irish, Scots, and Germans came to join the party, along with 200,000 slaves from Africa. Canada was the biggest British colony, and Jamaica was the richest, but the 13 colonies were the most popular places to settle because their good land grew rich crops. The colonies were 90 percent farms; the population of New York City in 1700 was all of 5,000 people.

Another 5 percent of the settlers were Europeans, such as Swedes, Dutch, Irish, Welsh, and Scots. None of these non-English people felt any great love for their English rulers. The colonies were the most multicultural country in the world, especially the ethnically rich Middle colonies of Pennsylvania and New York. Beyond the fittingly named New England, half the people of the colonies weren't from England — about a third of the signers of the Declaration of Independence originated from the world beyond England. In the following sections, I cover the most prominent groups to move to the American colonies during this time.

England, Britain, the United Kingdom . . . how many names can a little-but-mighty island have? Don't get all confused; here's what you need to know. England is the biggest part of the island called Britain, which is about the size of California and a few miles off the west coast of Europe. Great Britain evolved politically from the gradual union of England and Scotland, which started in 1603 with the Union of Crowns and slid into the Acts of Union in 1707, when the parliaments of the two nations merged into the Kingdom of Great Britain. Over time, the kingdom added Wales and Northern Ireland, and decided that the name *United Kingdom* sounded classy. After 1700, the mother country of the colonists can be referred to by either the more inclusive *Britain* or by its original name, *England.*

The Scotch-Irish

Perhaps the most aggressive immigrants to search the frontier for farms to settle were the Scotch-Irish. The United States has had 12 presidents with a Scotch-Irish background. These English-speaking people were originally from the Scottish lowlands. (Ay, Scotland isn't all highlands.) The only thing high about the lowlands was the land rents charged by greedy Scottish lords. Many of the Scotch-Irish moved to Northern Ireland, where their Protestant ancestors still make up the majority of the population. Some kept going to America.

With little money, the Scotch-Irish kept traveling until they found cheap land on the frontiers of Pennsylvania, Virginia, and Maryland. Having been pushed around plenty themselves, they tended to solve potential American Indian problems by shooting first and asking questions later. By 1750, the Scotch-Irish had spread out along the *Great Wagon Road,* a path for immigration they helped build through mountain passes from Philadelphia to Georgia. By the Revolution, they represented 7 percent of the population of the colonies.

Having moved more than once, the Scotch-Irish didn't originally build to stay. They threw up rough log cabins, chopped down trees, and planted crops between the stumps. As they gained title to their lands and confidence that no lords would boot them off, the Scotch-Irish built Presbyterian churches.

The rough-and-tumble Scotch-Irish caused heartache for the original Quaker settlers of Pennsylvania (see Chapter 8) when they killed peaceful American Indians and led the *Paxton Boys'* (1764) march on Philadelphia to protest lenient treatment of the natives. The Paxton Boys wanted to punish American Indians in general, regardless of whether they'd actually done wrong; luckily, Ben Franklin and the Philadelphia militia stood up to the Paxton Boys and protected the friendly American Indians. The Scotch-Irish also shook things up with the *Regulators' Uprising* (1764) against aristocratic domination of their rural settlements in North Carolina. Many of the Regulator hotheads, including a young Andrew Jackson, later joined the move toward revolution.

Germans

Germans were the largest non-English-speaking immigrant group in the colonies. Faced with war and oppression in their homeland, they delighted to find out about the rich soil of Pennsylvania. They built sturdy homes and barns, some of which still function today. German Americans eventually became one third of the population of the Quaker State (Pennsylvania); some neighborhoods in Philadelphia had German street signs. German Americans brought the Lutheran religion, adding to the Protestant mix of religious toleration. By the time of the Revolution, German Americans were about 6 percent of the population of the colonies.

The Pennsylvania Dutch are so called because English-speaking Americans got confused by *Deutsch,* the German name for *German.*

French Canada had about 1 person for every 20 in the 13 colonies, but it helped form what would become the United States. *La Salle* (1682) was a French explorer who navigated down the Mississippi, establishing French claims to the Louisiana territory that the French government would eventually sell to the young U.S. French *courers de bois* (runners of the woods), who ranged over North America trading animal pelts with the American Indians. French Acadians resettled by the British from Canada would become the Cajuns of New Orleans. The French founded Detroit, New Orleans, Pittsburgh, and other towns; if more of them had come, maybe U.S. drive-throughs would serve French cuisine. French settler Crèvecoeur observed in his *Letters from an American Farmer* (1782) that the "strange mixture of blood, which you find in no other country" was an "American, this new man."

Africans and the ongoing issue of slavery

Africans made up 20 percent of the population by the Revolution, mostly in the South but also with at least a few representatives in all the other early colonies. Slaves worked all their lives with no pay, and their children automatically became slaves too. Slavery grew because slaves made money for their masters, who then had more political and social power.

When they could get together at the end of long workdays, slaves created their own American African culture different from anything in Africa. Africans were brought to America as slaves, but when they could, they fought for their freedom. Slaves revolted in New York in 1712 and 1741; during the *Stono Rebellion* (1739) in South Carolina, slaves under a flag of freedom fought a pitched battle with white slaveholders. This led slave owners to tighten the rules so that slaves found it hard to get together or even learn to read. Slaves who revolted were tortured and/or killed.

Question: Where was slavery legal in the colonies?

Answer: Slavery was legal in all British North American colonies in the 1700s.

Question: What did slaves do besides hard work?

Answer: Slaves in early America maintained African social customs and even created a hybrid African American culture.

Question: Why did slavery grow in the colonies?

Answer: Slaves made money for their owners, which increased the owners' social and political power.

Question: How did owners' power over slaves change in the colonies?

Answer: In the 1700s, slave laws became more repressive and owners expanded their legal power over slaves.

Question: Name some slave rebellions that occurred in the colonies.

Answer: The Stono Rebellion (1739) in South Carolina and the New York slave conflicts (1712 and 1741) are examples of slave rebellions.

Daily Life in the Colonies

Colonial Americans lived in drafty houses heated in the winter by fireplaces in one or two rooms. Bedrooms, churches, and schools had no heat, air conditioning, or even fans. The bathroom was an outhouse 20 feet out the back door, and baths, when they happened, meant boiling a lot of water and pouring it into a tin tub. Garbage disposal meant tossing garbage out the window, where it was taken care of by hogs or buzzards. Light at night may be a flickering whale-oil lamp, and everybody had to ask whether what they were doing instead of going to bed was worth the candle. Going to bed early was easy, because most people were tired from a workday that ran from first light until sundown, when they couldn't see anymore.

Entertainment meant getting together with a good excuse like a militia muster, when citizen soldiers drilled and partied, or a barn-raising, quilting bee, funeral, or wedding. All these events could be accompanied by a good deal of drinking and flirting. Northerners liked sleigh rides and skating; Southerners went for fox hunts and playing cards. Southerners thought that plays and dancing were just fine; Northerners took a few years to warm up to those ideas.

The Middle states were, as usual, in the middle when it came to entertainment. Not much fox hunting happened, but plays and dancing were okay with most people. Everybody played the lottery. Lotteries were used to fund churches, hospitals, and colleges like Harvard.

Having a Chance at Success and Education

Unless you were one of the growing number of slaves, America in the 1700s was the place to be. Most people were farmers, but more jobs were always available in towns for skilled craftsmen. Even if you were an indentured servant, you could potentially earn your freedom and rise to prominence, which is what two originally indentured signers of the Declaration of Independence did. George Walton was only 26 when he risked hanging by the British to sign the Declaration; he was an orphan who had been indentured to a builder. George Taylor had to indenture himself to earn his ticket from Ireland, but as an old guy of 60, was important enough to sign the Declaration.

Although everyone had a chance for success, the number of rich people (who earned far more than the average farmer) grew with time and opportunity. Between the late 1600s and the Revolution in 1776, the colonies seemed to be dragged into one European war after another.

Wars burn up lots of military supplies, so the merchants in the big cities made big money by supplying the troops. By 1750, the richest 10 percent of the people in Boston and Philadelphia owned more than half of the property. They got reserved seats in the churches and schools.

Poverty: Not as bad as in Britain, but bad enough

A few poor people in the cities were supported by charity and sometimes had to wear a large red *P* on their clothes. Still, poverty in the colonies was nothing like it was in Britain in the 1700s, where as many as one out of three people lived with next to nothing. The colonies were rife with land that could be farmed and opportunities in trade and skilled jobs. The idea that anybody had a chance to make a good life in America started in the early 1700s. It was true; by the time of the Revolution, the early states had, overall, the most prosperous people in the world.

The government in London tried to drop its problems on the colonies by sending over 50,000 convicts. These convicts included real hard cases as well as plenty of people who received harsh sentences for little more than stealing a loaf of bread. Some of them became upright citizens in the New World, but they had no love for their British persecutors.

The worst poverty was within the growing slave population. White people were afraid of slave violence like the Stono Rebellion in 1739 and made periodic attempts to limit the importation of more slaves, but British leaders vetoed these attempts. Thomas Jefferson tried to put language opposed to slavery in the Declaration of Independence, but he was overridden by Southern slaveholders (see Chapter 10).

Education and vocations

Most people were farmers, but colonists learned technical skills on the job. This didn't always mean you had to be an indentured servant to gain a skill; Ben Franklin (the youngest boy of 16 children) learned to be a printer by working for his brother.

In England, education was viewed as being a privilege of the elite, not as a basic right for everyone. Things were different in New England, where public elementary schools supported by towns and counties started in the 1600s. In the Middle colonies, schools were sometimes free and sometimes private for-pay institutions. In the South, where distances between plantations could be large, families tended to rely on private tutors.

Early Puritan religion taught that everyone should be able to read the Bible. Students went to school when they could spare time away from their chores on the family farm. In all schools, whipping was the rule. Students memorized Latin and Greek, and didn't talk back to their teachers for fear of being whipped.

Christian ministers were the most respected professionals in the colonies. Harvard, Yale, Princeton, Brown, and almost all the other original colleges were established to train ministers. Lawyers weren't universally loved in the pioneer societies; some colonies even passed laws against them. Some early settlers even thought that lawyers made disputes get worse just so they could make money from them. Physicians learned their trade from hanging around other doctors in the early days; the first medical school in the colonies wasn't founded until 1765. Making patients bleed deliberately was a favorite form of treatment, and epidemics were common.

Smallpox affected one in five people; George Washington was a heavily pockmarked survivor of the disease. The first crude inoculation for smallpox was given in 1721.

An epidemic of diphtheria in the 1730s took thousands of lives and helped scare people into the First Great Awakening, which I cover in "Changing Attitudes toward Religion" later in this chapter.

Establishing American Arts

The 1700s brought more than just independence to the colonies; during this period, American art, architecture, and writing took off. The following sections describe the cultural flourish of this era.

American painters

Fine-arts painters got their start in America during the 1700s. At first, colonial artists focused on portraits — settlers wanted to be remembered, and cameras weren't an option. Benjamin West was the first American artist to train in Europe; when he saw a statue of Apollo, he realized it was no more handsome than an American Indian warrior. You can check out early American art at www.artcyclopedia.com/artists/American-artists-17th-18th.html and www.nga.gov/collection/gallery/amer.shtm; the following are a few prominent painters of early America:

- *John Trumbull* (1785) painted pictures of the American Revolution, in which he served briefly.

- *Charles Willson Peale* (1780) served in the Revolution too, painting all the while. Peale could accurately be described as a Renaissance man, having developed a level of expertise in such diverse fields as carpentry, dentistry, optometry, shoemaking, and taxidermy.

- *Benjamin West* (1770) painted large-scale historic pictures. He said that when he was young, American Indians showed him how to make paint by mixing clay from the riverbank with bear grease in a pot.

Architecture

Early American architecture styles were imported from Europe; even the log cabin appears to be based on a Swedish model. Nobody lived in log cabins in most of Europe; the idea came from the northern Swedes during their short-lived colony in America.

The popular *Georgian architecture* (1750) was named after the Georges who were kings of England around that time. Georgian style usually is defined by reddish brick walls that contrast with the white used for window trimming and cornices. A small porch often emphasizes the entrance. *Regularity* was a term of praise for Georgian architects, who used mathematical formulas to figure the proportion of windows to wall size. Georgian is the architecture of Williamsburg, Harvard, and many colonial buildings.

Literature, libraries, and the birth of American journalism

Colonial literature was very much in the shadow of the mother country; for years, many Americans assumed that only the English had the sophistication to write. This assumption began to change with the prejudice-shattering poetry of *Phillis Wheatley* (1772), a slave who had learned to write. Her memorial poem for George Whitefield (see "Changing Attitudes toward Religion" later in this chapter) caused such a stir that John Hancock and others examined her to make sure a black person could actually write such a work.

Benjamin Franklin (1776) would be remembered even if he weren't a famous Revolutionary War leader. His *Poor Richard's Almanack,* which he edited beginning 45 years before the Revolution, contained gems of thought quoted throughout the colonies. Among them is his reaction to the Great Awakening: "Serving God is doing good to man, but praying is thought an easier service, and therefore more generally chosen." Franklin proved that lightning was electricity and invented bifocal glasses, the efficient Franklin stove, and the lightning rod. He also started the first privately supported library in the country.

By the Revolution, around 40 simple newspapers were published in the colonies. Most of these papers were one-page weeklies, but they begin to reflect and mold public opinion. *Peter Zenger* (1734) was a New York newspaper printer who attacked the corrupt royal governor. He was hauled into court and charged with libel. The government didn't deny the truth of what he said but planned to throw him in prison anyway. In a landmark day for freedom of the press, the jury set Zenger free. Ever since, newspapers have had the right to publish the truth even if it upsets the government.

Changing Attitudes toward Religion

The problem with all the education that ministers received in the American colonies (see "Education and vocations" earlier in this chapter) is that they got so smart that they started to question what their own churches believed. The gloomy predestination doctrine got harder to support; fewer and fewer people went along with the idea that nothing they could do in life would alter God's prebirth judgment about whether they were going to heaven or hell. The Puritans' (see Chapter 8) original belief that predestination meant only a small group of people preselected by God for salvation should get to be in their church didn't leave a lot of room for free will or more church members. They tried the *Half-Way Covenant* (1662) to let in a few new members who couldn't swear they'd undergone a conversion experience, but the churches were losing their power over a people busy making a living in the early 1700s.

The *Great Awakening* was a spiritual revival complete with preaching and conversions all over the colonies. Awakening was so important that it actually happened at least twice. The *First Great Awakening* (1734) began when the colonies were becoming well established in the 1730s; the *Second Great Awakening* occurred in the 1820s. First Great Awakening ministers were set up for their success by the toil, loneliness, and heartbreak of life on the frontier. The movement had more power in the country than in the cities, but America was practically all country in the early 1700s. Great Awakening preachers left in their wake a spiritually charged citizenship eager for change. By traveling throughout the colonies, they gave the separate sections a sense of belonging to a whole nation. The Great Awakening set the emotional stage for the American Revolution. Two men in particular were very influential in this movement:

- ✔ The First Great Awakening began with *Jonathan Edwards* (1734), a well-educated theologian and Congregationalist minister from Massachusetts. Edwards came from Puritan roots but spoke with the power of immediate, personal religious experience. His fiery sermons, including "Sinners in the Hands of an Angry God," attracted a large following.

- ✔ Methodist preacher *George Whitefield* (1738) was even more electric than Edwards. Whitefield traveled across the colonies and spoke in the dramatic, emotional style of a modern revival preacher, often in outdoor camp meetings. He was the first nationwide American star, accepting everyone into his audiences and preaching a simple message of the power of God. He gave more than 18,000 sermons. Whitefield was the most widely recognized public figure in America before George Washington.

Edwards, Whitefield, and others who used a similar style started a new trend in American religion. Previously, so-called *Old Light* ministers droned on in their sermons, using only rationality and arguments from theology. Modern *New Light* preachers spoke with emotion and showmanship. Princeton, Brown, Rutgers, and Dartmouth were all *New Light* schools.

On the more open end of spirituality, the Quakers (see Chapter 8) believed God was so close to love that everyone should be free to worship him in the way that was best for them. Quakers supported women's rights and freedom of worship. They opposed slavery and war, but they did pay taxes and worked to influence local governments. Although some Quakers were actually put to death in New England for their tolerant beliefs, more worked to build a peaceful society in Pennsylvania, the colony established by Quaker William Penn.

As freedom in the colonies grew, so did tolerance for neighbors who may have a different way of worshiping God. The colonies in the 1750s represented many religious denominations, generally liked the king, opposed aristocrats from England, and were open to settlement by non-English people.

Question: Who were the biggest followers of the First Great Awakening?

Answer: The First Great Awakening of the 1730s and 1740s appealed more to poor and rural people and less to rich urbanites.

Question: What did the Quakers believe?

Answer: Quakers were against war and slavery; they paid taxes, tried to influence local governments, and supported women's rights and freedom of worship.

Question: Was Quakerism the official religion of Quaker Pennsylvania?

Answer: Because it was founded by Quakers, who believed in freedom of worship, colonial Pennsylvania had no established official church.

Question: What was the political and social atmosphere of the colonies by the 1750s?

Answer: In general, the colonies in the 1750s represented many religious denominations, disliked aristocrats from England but were okay with the king, and were receptive to settlement by non-English people.

Early Politics

Three colonies had governors appointed by their official proprietors, and two colonies elected their own governors. In the other eight colonies, the king appointed usually competent governors (not counting the dunderhead governor Peter Zenger exposed in New York — see "Literature, libraries, and the birth of American journalism" earlier in this chapter). The colonies had two legislative bodies like the modern U.S. Senate and House of Representatives (see Chapter 10). The Senate-type legislators usually were appointed, and the House-type representatives were elected by all the people who had the right to vote.

Property wasn't too expensive in a land with miles of open space, so getting the right to vote wasn't hard. The House, elected by the people, had some major power over the governor; it controlled his salary. The colonies had the most democratic government known in the world up to that time.

Making Money in Colonial America

Due in large part to the plentiful goods they produced and traded, the colonies also provided the highest average standard of living people had ever seen. Here's a list of the most profitable goods of the period:

- The Middle colonies produced enough wheat to make all the bread the colonists could eat and still export thousands of barrels of flour.

- Tobacco was a big money-maker for Virginia and Maryland. Taxes on tobacco made up one third of U.S. government revenue until long after the Civil War.

- It seemed as though the supply of codfish off the coast of New England would never run out, and boatloads were exported to Europe. Although cod is no longer as plentiful, the fish was so important to the growth of New England that a "Sacred Cod" still hangs in the Massachusetts House of Representatives.

✔ New England fishing led to shipbuilding and provided training for thousands of Yankee sailors to man American ships. With a plentiful lumber supply, by the time of the Revolution, the colonies were building a third of all the ships in the British trading fleet.

✔ North America had a lock on beaver pelts, and anyone who was cool in Europe just had to have some beaver fur.

✔ Making cloth at home, American women outfitted their families for free and often had extra linen to sell.

✔ Before the Revolution, America had more small iron forges than England did. One famous place — Valley Forge, Pennsylvania — was even named for its iron works.

✔ The United States was (and is still) the world's leading wheat exporter.

The triangular trade

From the earliest days, rum and other forms of alcohol had an enthusiastic following in the New World. Early Americans could drink most modern people under the table. The infamous *triangular trade* was the shipping of New England rum to Africa in exchange for slaves, who were sold in the West Indies for money and molasses, which was taken back to New England to make more rum. This three-legged voyage was hugely profitable but made up only a minority of New England trade. Most Yankee traders exchanged food and lumber for manufactured goods, which they sold in the colonies

Mercantilism

Early Americans couldn't have been all that drunk from the rum trade, because the colonies managed to make more money per person on average than anyplace else in the world. Long before they knew it, the colonies were on a collision course with the interests of their mother country due to England's policy of *mercantilism*. Under this policy, the colonies were supposed to supply England raw materials and buy expensive manufactured stuff only from the mother country. If the colonists wanted to sell anything to another country, the trade was supposed to go through England. England controlled trade, got the markups, and treated the colonists like cows. After the colonists got it together, they weren't about to let this practice keep happening.

Dealing (or not dealing) with trade tension

America was growing fast; Britain was growing slowly. Pretty soon, the British had all the American food and other stuff they needed, and Americans wanted European finery that Britain didn't produce. Yankee businessmen wanted to trade with other countries, especially the rich French West Indies. This situation produced the beginning of trade tension between the colonies and their mother country — tension that eventually was one of the precipitating causes of revolt.

Beginning in 1650, the English passed a series of Navigation Acts to support mercantilism. The *Navigation Acts* (1650) tried to regulate trade with the colonies to make more money for England. As part of the program, Parliament passed the *Molasses Act* (1733), which imposed a tax of sixpence per gallon on molasses (about $1 in modern money) to make English products cheaper than those from the French West Indies. Colonists largely opposed the tax and rarely paid it; smuggling to avoid it was a huge business. The growing corruption of local officials and disrespect for British law caused by this act and others helped lead to the American Revolution in 1776.

American tobacco filled the pipes of Europe, but the smoking trade was less troublesome; most of the leaf shipped through England, giving British merchants a nice little rake-off.

Fighting All Over North America

Special as the colonies felt they were, they were actually pawns in a world-domination power struggle among the great nations of Europe — mostly England, France, and Spain. Spain got the early lead by finding gold and silver all over South America (except for Brazil, owned by its Portuguese buddies), plus Mexico and other hot parts of what would eventually become the United States. On the East Coast of North America, England started late but was catching up fast, with no gold but plenty of valuable crops in the West Indies and 13 mainland colonies. In Canada and other parts of North America, France went north of everybody else for the furs and the fish.

Everybody was frontier fighting

The English colonists got left alone by Britain for 30 years, during which time they learned to kind of like being on their own. Being left alone also meant that at first, the kings didn't bother to send any troops over to help the colonists, which would be like getting involved in a war between the squirrels in your backyard.

In both *King William's War* (1690) and *Queen Anne's War* (1710), French woodsmen and their American Indian buddies raided English settlements. Fighting back, English colonists and their American Indian allies attacked Canada without doing much damage. The French and American Indians managed to kill a lot of settlers in Schenectady, New York, and Deerfield, Massachusetts, but averaging out the rest of the conflicts, the British won. They got frozen northern Canada around Hudson Bay and the island of Nova Scotia, north of Maine, for their troubles.

The prize for the best war name goes to the *War of Jenkins's Ear* (1739), fought over British outrage that the Spanish cut off the ear of a British sea captain named Jenkins. During this conflict, great Georgia reformer James Oglethorpe skillfully repelled Spanish raids into the southern Atlantic colonies. (See Chapter 8 for more on Oglethorpe and Georgia.) When the war spread, New Englanders hitched up their pants and, with the help of the Royal Navy, invaded Canada again. This time, they captured a large French fort, but the British gave it back at the end of the war in 1748. The colonists felt betrayed by Britain (and not for the last time).

The French and Indian War

In 1754, the governor of Virginia gave a 21-year-old surveyor named George Washington a mission to scout out French forces who were building forts on land on the Pennsylvania–Ohio border — land that Virginians (including Washington's family) liked to think they owned. Washington, with 150 Virginian volunteers, spied some Frenchmen resting in the woods and took a shot at them. The Frenchmen called for reinforcements and eventually surrounded Washington. They could have killed him; his men had killed their leader in the sneak attack. Instead, they let Washington and his men go — ironically enough, on July 4.

The French Empire

In Canada, the French were held up by religious and internal political hassles, but *Samuel de Champlain* (1608) got a town going in the natural fortress of Quebec. Almost right away, Champlain did something that seemed so good but turned out so bad: He helped the local Huron American Indians by kicking some booty on their traditional enemies. Unfortunately, the Hurons' traditional enemies were the megapowerful Iroquois nation. Sure, only a few Iroquois were around when Champlain got involved, but tens of thousands more lived farther south, and after Champlain's little faux pas, they tended to side with the British.

The mostly Catholic French were pretty comfortable back in France, and the French Protestants who would have loved to get out of town to the New World weren't allowed to go. The French who did make it to the New World were more interested in paddling around and partying with the American Indians than settling down and raising a family. This fact made for slow population growth in the French colonies: By 1750, French Canada boasted only 60,000 settlers, as opposed to the 1.25 million in the English North American colonies. Like the British, other French were getting rich on rum and sugar down in the Caribbean, and most of them weren't all that big on going on freezing beaver hunts.

Although farming wasn't their main thing, the French managed to float a surprising amount of grain down the Mississippi to feed their sugar colonies in the West Indies. French fur trappers traveled farther and farther for fur. French trading posts were established all across Canada, up to the British settlements in America and down to the Rio Grande in the south of what's now Texas. They moved around a lot, because when you trap too many beaver, they tend to disappear.

Antoine Cadillac (1701) founded Detroit and fittingly enough got a car named for him. *Robert de La Salle* (1682) floated down the Mississippi and named Louisiana for his king. The French also established a well-placed fort at *New Orleans* (1718).

That incident was the beginning of the largest international war the world had yet seen; the U.S. called it the *French and Indian War,* but it was the *Seven Years' War* in the rest of the world. The war raged so hot and heavy in Europe that the French couldn't do much more in the New World than unleash their American Indian allies. The British, fearing a stab in the back from French people living under British rule in Canada, forced some 4,000 of them to move to New Orleans, where they became the Cajuns.

To unite the colonists and impress the (hopefully) loyal Iroquois, the British called the intercolonial *Albany Congress* (1754). The American Indians stayed mostly loyal, and Ben Franklin got to present his *Albany Plan of Union,* an early attempt to form a union of the colonies. It was a nonstarter, but everybody agreed that the idea was interesting.

The British blew it repeatedly in the early French and Indian War. A major British attack against Fort Duquesne (Pittsburgh) was cut to ribbons by a much smaller force of French and American Indians who knew about hiding behind bushes and rocks. In that battle, Washington had two horses shot out from under him, and four bullets tore through his coat. Miraculously unwounded, he rallied his men for an orderly retreat. A later major British attack on outposts all over Canada also failed.

Finally, new Prime Minister William Pitt the Elder directed British forces to make a coordinated assault on the key French fortress at Quebec. In one of the most important battles in British and American history, the British–American force won. The French were thrown completely out of northern America, and William Pitt got Pittsburgh named after him.

During this long war, some 20,000 local troops from all the colonies learned to work and fight together. They saw that the British could lose, and they experienced British arrogance firsthand. British General James Wolfe, for example, called members of the American militia "contemptible, cowardly dogs." And despite Washington's heroic war record, the British demoted him to captain. These actions weren't very good ways to make friends.

With the French and most of the hostile American Indians out of the way, the colonies didn't need much protection from mother Britain. When the *Treaty of Paris* (1763) ended the war, the colonies were psychologically on their way to 1776. With the French defeated, the English tried to make peace with the American Indians by prohibiting the colonists from settling west of the Alleghenies in the *Proclamation of 1763*.

Question: What was the Proclamation of 1763?

Answer: The Proclamation of 1763 was a British royal decree that forbade the American colonists from settling west of the Alleghenies. Its goal was to promote peace with the American Indians and a clear line of defense for the British.

The British halt Western expansion

The Treaty of Paris (see the preceding section) was a tough blow for the American Indians. The warriors who had sided with the French lost an ally, but even American Indians who had been neutral or pro-British had lost the French counterweight to colonial expansion.

In the same year that the French admitted defeat, the great Ottawa American Indian leader Pontiac launched a last-ditch attack against the British advance into the Ohio country. It almost worked. Pontiac's warriors overran all but three British outposts west of the Appalachians, killing 2,000 soldiers and settlers, and coming close to taking heavily fortified Detroit. Pontiac's name became another car.

Almost as though they were going into extreme defensive mode right after a victory, the British issued the Proclamation of 1763, flatly forbidding any settlement west of the Appalachians. The British were just trying to be fair to their American Indian allies and to prevent more bloody uprisings like the one Pontiac had led. For the land-hungry Americans, the law was a slap in the face of their long-fought-for dreams. They disobeyed the law and moved West by the thousands. The British were in no mood to put up with insolence. Neither were the Americans. It was head-butting time.

The Colonies Become Fighting Mad

By 1770, the 13 colonies were no longer just a fringe experiment out in the wilderness; together, they were a country of 2.5 million well-fed, educated, and experienced people. The American population was one third as big as that of the mother country, and America had a lot more land. The problem was that the English couldn't recognize a grown-up nation when they saw one; they insisted on treating America like a spoiled child. Now it was time for the child to make himself useful and do his chores.

These chores had to do with raising 140 million pounds (billions of dollars in modern money) to pay for the debt Britain had run up fighting its wars. Up until this time, the colonies had skated by without paying any dues to the mother country — sort of like buying something tax-free on the Internet. No more. Mother Britain was coming up a little short, and those pesky colonies were certainly big and strong enough to help.

Also, because the American Indians were still kicking up a fuss — and who knew whether the French and the Spanish would stay defeated — it was time for the colonies to pay for the standing army of 10,000 troops that Britain was helpfully sending over.

New thoughts about freedom

Schools in the colonies spent a lot of time teaching students about classical life in Greece and Rome. Athens and Rome were often viewed as democracies where the people helped decide on their own government, and teachers drilled this idea into the heads of the colonists.

Settlers also had a selective idea of their rights as Englishmen — rights that had been slowly expanding since the Magna Carta in 1215. The colonists' idea of English liberty was selective because they concentrated on their lack of representation in Parliament without proposing an alternative solution to funding the army that Parliament had sent to defend them.

Finally, the colonists were influenced by the left-wing of British politics — the radical Whigs, who distrusted everything the king did as a potential attack on their freedom. The Whigs saw corruption everywhere in the royal government, and they weren't always wrong. Although the British government hadn't seen a lot of tax revenue from the colonies, it had enjoyed a fair amount of profit. This profit made the colonies worthwhile based on the theory of mercantilism (discussed earlier in this chapter), which held that the power of a country can be measured by how much money it has.

London was a long way away, and the colonists had no trouble slipping a little trade to other places where they could make a profit. No matter how many Navigation Laws the British passed, they couldn't control the colonies. As the colonies got richer, their side business of trade around the Navigation Laws got larger. Britain felt as though it had paid to take a date to a dance, but that date was dancing with everybody else.

Stampin' on the Stamp Act

With victory in their pockets and billions of dollars of debt making a hole in their purses, the British decided to tax the colonists directly for the first time. Here are the legal actions that Britain took:

- ✔ First, the prime minister ordered the British navy to start strictly enforcing the Navigation Laws to end the colonies' profitable side trade.

- ✔ Second, London enacted the *Sugar Act* (1764), the first law for raising revenue for Britain in the New World. The Sugar Act taxed the sweet stuff Americans were just as addicted to as everybody else. When the colonists screamed, the government lowered the duties, and the outcry died down.

- ✔ Third, the *Quartering Act* (1765) attempted to give the 10,000 British soldiers in the New World places to stay: with the colonists. Nobody wanted soldiers crowding into the house and eating all the food. Colonial legislatures dragged their feet and refused to cooperate.

- ✔ Fourth, Parliament passed the *Stamp Act* (1765). People in Britain had already been paying stamp taxes for almost 100 years, but to the colonists, shelling out a few cents to the king for every newspaper, playing card, lease, will, and even marriage license seemed to be a major insult.

Colonial legislatures had passed plenty of taxes without trouble, but in those cases, the colonists were taxing themselves. Now a bunch of snooty big shots an ocean away were reaching into their pockets without permission. Chanting "No taxation without representation," the colonists were fighting mad.

To remember all the legislation in order, consider this scene: You navigate to the store (Navigation Laws) to buy some candy (Sugar Act), but a soldier stops you (Quartering Act) and stamps your hand (Stamp Act). This analogy is silly, but it works.

With years of experience in self-government and the precedent of the Albany Congress setting them up for cooperation, nine colonies quickly assembled the *Stamp Act Congress* (1765) in New York City. The congress mostly just talked and passed some resolutions, but it did get 9 of the 13 colonies working together.

More to the point of protest were the unofficial *nonimportation agreements* (1765). Americans agreed among themselves not to buy products from the mother country that was making them so mad. These local agreements were enforced by a gang called the Sons of Liberty, which wasn't above applying tar and feathers to the bodies of people who tried to break the strike by buying imported goods. The British were hit hard by the boycott; one quarter of their exports had gone to the colonies, and now almost nothing was selling.

The Stamp Act, though, was a nonstarter. Under mob persuasion, all the stamp sellers had been forced to resign before the act took effect. Because the law wasn't working anyway, Parliament revoked the Stamp Act in 1766. Although this repeal could have been an occasion to make nice, the government instead petulantly enacted a resolution called the *Declaratory Act* (1766), which declared that although it may be cutting some slack now, Parliament had the power "to bind" the colonies "in all cases whatsoever." It wasn't long before Parliament tried a little more binding.

Question: What was the purpose of the Stamp Act?

Answer: The purpose of the Stamp Act of 1765 was to raise money to support British troops in America.

The Boston Massacre

In 1768, the British landed about 1,200 troops in Boston — one soldier for every four residents. *The Boston Massacre* (1770) occurred when citizens started throwing rocks at ten British troops and the troops fired back, killing or wounding 11 citizens. The Townshend Act that had everybody so upset (see the following section) produced almost no revenue, and the cost to the British of occupying the colonies continued to rise.

The Boston Tea Party

If the colonists wouldn't pay direct taxes, why not skim a little more off the top before the products got to the New World? The *Townshend Act* (1767) put a light import tax on glass, lead, paper, paint — and, most importantly, on tea. This tax eventually led to the *Boston Tea Party* (1773). When the injury of the tax was combined with the insult of granting a monopoly on tea to the British East India Company, citizens responded by dumping a shipload of tea into Boston Harbor.

Gearing up for a revolution

Samuel Adams was a Boston hothead with shaky hands but a firm resolve. While talking revolution in the bars at night, he organized the first *Committee of Correspondence* (1772). Soon, committees of correspondence were exchanging revolutionary ideas in and among all the colonies. They had lots to talk about.

A couple of years later, the British passed what the colonists called the *Intolerable Acts* (1774), designed to be a spanking for Massachusetts in general and Boston in particular. The acts closed Boston Harbor until Boston paid Britain back for all the tea lost in the Tea Party. The acts also took away the rights of the legislature and of town meetings, and allowed any English officials who killed an American to be tried back in friendly Britain.

Showing less than zero political sensitivity to the feelings of America, the British also passed the Quebec Act. This act expanded Canada down into Ohio on land the colonies thought they owned. Something had to give.

The Committee of Correspondence set the groundwork for the first *Continental Congress* (1774). After seven weeks of drinking and deliberation, the first congress passed a Declaration of Rights and sent appeals to the British king and people. The congress also established something called *The Association* to oversee a boycott of everything British. Americans weren't going to buy, sell, or even use British goods.

Determined to slap down growing resentment with a surge of strength, in April 1775, British troops marched out of Boston to seize some arms and to arrest protest leaders Samuel Adams and John Hancock. They met colonial militia in the towns of Lexington and Concord. After taking some casualties, the militia fired back, and with American help running in from the hills in all directions, the militia pushed the outnumbered British back to Boston. With 300 total casualties for both sides, the British had a war on their hands.

War wasn't going to be easy for the Americans. They had one-third of the population of the British army and not one-tenth of the money, and they were facing the most successful fighters in the world. The British had an experienced standing army of 50,000 men, which they made even stronger by hiring 30,000 German mercenaries. The colonies were far from united: The British had as many as 50,000 American loyalists ready to fight their fellow colonists to stay linked to Great Britain.

Contrary to some modern National Rifle Association beliefs, America in 1775 wasn't a nation of dead-eye marksmen. Only a small minority of households owned firearms. The colonies had no gun factory, and an imported rifle cost the modern equivalent of $5,000. Only 1 out of 12 colonists reported for duty with their own rifles.

The colonists had the advantage of fighting on their own grounds. Eventually, they would get help from the French and other nations. But mostly, the American advantage was that a dedicated minority of the citizens of the New World colonies believed in freedom so much they were willing to die for it.

Working Early Colonial History into Essay Subjects

Social-history themes make great essay fodder for the big AP U.S. History showdown. This section covers a couple of ideas that historians love to chew on, based on the information in this chapter. You may be able to work them into an assigned essay subject.

The Great Awakening seems to be about religion and, thus, about following cosmic rules, but it also really shook things up socially. Public emotion wasn't something that had been big in Britain, but it was the common experience of religious deliverance in the Awakening. This swept-away feeling helped set the stage for the emotion connected to the Revolution, which would be fought by the grandchildren of the people who attended the Awakening. Awakening preachers often came from congregations outside the religious mainstream. Their very presence outside the church implied that people could be true to God without following all the cues of the established churches. In fact, maybe people had to follow their own hearts to be connected with God's will. The Awakening led to new schools and the beginning of new light ministers. Could a new country be far behind?

One of the greatest questions in U.S. history is the slavery/freedom paradox. How can one country be the light of freedom in the world *and* a major exploiter of African slaves? One answer is to see New England as the tower of freedom and abolition and to view the South as the basement of slavery and reaction. But what about Patrick Henry, Washington, Jefferson, Madison, the other architects of freedom, and all those Southern slaveholders? Another answer is that slavery blurred the boundaries between rich and poor in the South and made the idea of equality possible (for everybody but the slaves, of course). This idea gets some support when you consider two other slaveholding beacons of democracy in the ancient world: Greece and Rome.

Historian Edmund Morgan said, "Americans bought their independence with slave labor." A more balanced statement may be that America got economic power from a large-scale application of the system of slavery that was legal in most of the world and far larger in the West Indies and South America. The North and the Middle states didn't need large-scale slavery to make money; they were quite capable of winning their freedom without it. Only four generations after the Revolution, while slavery was making more money than it ever had before, the United States fought the bloodiest war in its history — the Civil War — to free the slaves. That war is one of the only times in history when one people (white Northerners with freed black help) fought for the rights of another people (enslaved black Southerners) — not for conquest or glory, but to put an end to slavery in the land of the free.

Chapter 10

You Say You Want a Revolution? Freedom and Change, 1776–1815

In This Chapter:

▶ Following the Revolutionary trail

▶ Fighting for survival

▶ Understanding the Articles of Confederation and the Constitution

▶ Becoming the United States

▶ Discovering the power of democracy

*W*hen George Washington heard the news about the fighting at Lexington and Concord (see Chapter 9) he wrote from Mount Vernon to a friend, ". . . the once-happy and peaceful plains of America are either to be drenched in blood or inhabited by slaves. Sad alternative! But can a virtuous man hesitate in his choice?"

Washington didn't hesitate. The *Second Continental Congress* (1775) met in Philadelphia a month after the battle and appointed Washington to command the 30,000 militia troops currently bottling up 8,000 British soldiers in Boston.

The patient 43-year-old Washington was a good choice. He may not have been history's most brilliant general, but he was competent and sometimes even daring. Most important, he had the strength of character to hold the army together through hard times and the aristocratic bearing to assure people with money that the rebels were more than just an angry mob. Those tough times, and their aftermath, are covered in this chapter.

Exciting as they are, battles and military campaigns seldom appear in the big AP exam. The test mavens are more interested in the meaning of conflicts and what social conditions contributed to and came out of the fights. Still, some knowledge of how the Revolution went down can provide handy ammunition for answering political, economic, and social questions. This chapter gives you the short version of the American war for independence.

Power of the Pen: Common Sense and the Declaration of Independence

The Continental Congress could have just mailed King George III a polite letter telling him to get the heck out of America, but educated people know giving reasons is always better when they want to make some major changes. The explaining-why-you've-got-to-go job went to 32-year-old Virginian Thomas Jefferson, who wrote the Declaration of Independence. Before the Declaration, though, people were talking about the writings of Thomas Paine.

Showing the power of an idea whose time had come, patriot Paine published a pamphlet called *Common Sense* (1776), arguing that it just made common sense for the colonies to be separated from Britain. Britain was a small island compared with the vast expanse of the colonies. Where in the universe does a small star control a large planet? Paine had a dream of a new kind of government — a republic in which power came from the people, not from some corrupt king.

America was ready to hear Paine's words. People in Britain had slowly been increasing their freedom for years; many colonists knew the words of progressive British thinkers who supported the theory of a republic. Freedom was no theory in America; New England town meetings and elections throughout the colonies prepared patriots to launch the world's first true republic.

In the Declaration of Independence, Jefferson wrote that all men are created equal, with the right to life, liberty, and the pursuit of happiness. He called these *natural rights,* not theoretical or British or pie-in-the-sky-when-we-die rights. Jefferson's *Declaration of Independence* (1776) has served as a model for progressive people around the world ever since. In the Declaration, Jefferson calmly listed the ways the British king and government had trampled on America's natural rights. The Declaration was officially approved on July 4, 1776.

Notice that both Paine and Jefferson referred to natural rights and common sense. They viewed the world as being rational, made for humans, and capable of being improved by people. They were children of the *Enlightenment* (1760), a giant wake-up call that started in the early 1700s and spread around the world. Despite the continued presence of fear and intolerance, people still live with the ideas of the Enlightenment.

Britain versus the Patriots: The Fighting Escalates

The fighting between the patriots and the British loyalist forces began to look like more than just a family feud when the patriots surprised some British forts in northern New York and hauled off their cannons. With the extra firepower, the patriots marched up Bunker Hill (actually, Breed's Hill), overlooking Boston.

The British eventually dislodged the patriots, but not without losing a lot of men. The British burned a couple of seaports; the patriots invaded Canada and kicked some Loyalist butt in the South. Then the British hired German professional soldiers, called Hessians, to help them whip the colonists.

Problems the British faced

Like any occupying power, the problem for the British army was that it really controlled only the ground it was standing on. Although as many as 50,000 Loyalist colonists fought alongside the British at one time or another, their numbers weren't enough to keep any large part of America loyal to the king after the king's army left town.

Things got pretty hot for Loyalists when the British army wasn't around to protect them. Patriots weren't above going from tar-and-feather parties to destruction of Loyalist property and violence that bordered on terrorism. Some 80,000 Loyalists moved out of the country to Canada or Britain.

Cutting it close to find freedom

Congress didn't officially declare the United States independent until 14 months after the first shots were fired. With both sides firing away, Congress's hesitation for more than a year shows how close the colonies still felt to Britain.

Another sign of how difficult it was to break the bond with Mother England was the fact that around one in six colonial people were loyal to the British crown. Not only did Loyalists not want to leave Britain, but they were also ready to fight the patriots who did.

Problems the patriots faced

The problem for the patriots was that the British had a larger and better-trained army — at least 35,000 British and Hessian troops supported by 500 ships. Washington had at most 18,000 men, mostly poorly trained and equipped. Although by the end of the war, Washington had around 8,000 properly trained regular-army Continental soldiers, many of the minuteman volunteers who made up most of the army were good for little more than a minute in a stand-up battle. Sniping from behind rocks went only so far in a real war; sooner or later, the armies faced each other across an open field. Minutemen volunteers tended to fire a round or two and then head home to their farms. Developing soldiers who would stand up to British cannon and massed musket fire took years of drilling and combat experience.

Slaves: Fighting for both sides

Thousands of African slaves fought with the British because they were promised freedom if they did. Many, but not most, were helped out of the country when the war ended. The black Loyalist Colonel Titus Tye became legendary for capturing supplies and patriots. Blacks fought for the Revolution as well: A black soldier is shown right next to Washington in the famous picture of Washington crossing the Delaware.

Winning the American Revolution, in a Nutshell

Surrounded by angry colonists, the British cleared out of Boston and sailed to New York City, where they had a lot more fans. George Washington tried to defend New York but was quickly pushed out, almost losing his army and his life in the fallback. As winter closed off the ability of the armies to maneuver, Washington struck back bravely against detachments of the British army in New Jersey; famously rowing across the ice-clogged Delaware River at night on December 26, 1776.

Meanwhile, the British planned to cut troublesome New England off from the rest of the colonies by marching an army down from Canada through New York. Didn't work. In the important *Battle of Saratoga* (1777), a patriot army forced the British to surrender in northern New York. That victory gave the French the courage to enter the war on the side of the patriots. French help was huge, because the French had the weapons, navy, and well-trained regular army that the patriots desperately needed. After their loss at Saratoga, the British offered the Americans home rule within the British empire, but it was way too late for that.

Question: What was the most important outcome of the Battle of Saratoga?

Answer: The win by the patriots in the Battle of Saratoga gave the French confidence to enter the war to help the rebels.

Valley Forge and help from France

Another British army managed to take Philadelphia, forcing the members of the Continental Congress to run for their lives. Washington's army stayed gamely nearby, freezing through a terrible winter at its Valley Forge camp. With the French threatening them, the British high-tailed it back to the safety of New York City, fighting a hot battle with Washington along the way. For the next three years, Washington stayed close to New York, tying down the British troops there. The French landed a powerful army of 6,000 soldiers to help the patriots.

Obviously, the British couldn't win the war by sitting around New York. Because New England hadn't worked for the British, and the Middle states were a little tough, they decided to try the South, where a large Loyalist population promised a happy welcome.

Cornwallis and losing morale

British General Charles Cornwallis took the South's most important city, Charleston, forcing the surrender of the entire Southern patriot army. Then he marched through the Carolinas and Virginia constantly harassed by patriot forces who attacked any time they could isolate a bite-sized British force. Patriots stung Cornwallis but couldn't stop him.

After four years of war, the patriots were running out of steam in 1780. Despite French help, the powerless Congress was so broke that it announced it could pay off patriot debts only at the rate of 2.5 cents on the dollar. Without food and supplies, Washington's army was close to mutiny. Rich American merchants sold the patriots bad-quality supplies at huge profits. The South seemed to be going to the British. Many of the once-gung-ho revolutionaries despaired of ever winning their freedom. Soldiers worried about how their families were doing without them, the chronic lack of guns and food, and the fact that they got paid in almost-worthless paper money.

Question: What were the complaints of the Continental soldiers in Washington's army?

Answer: Continental soldiers' discontent came from home worries, not enough weapons, paper-money pay, and little food.

Victory and the Treaty of Paris

Then Cornwallis decided to do something really safe: He marched his army to what he thought was shelter and resupply in Yorktown on the Virginia coast. Instead of being met by the protective, well-stocked British fleet, he found the French navy controlling the escape routes by sea. Washington and his French allies marched 300 miles from New York in a few weeks to attack the trapped British.

Cornwallis surrendered with about one quarter of all the British troops in North America. After another year of small-scale fighting, the British government gave up. The Americans went from despair to joyous celebration.

In the *Treaty of Paris* (1783), the British formally recognized the independence of the United States. They took a satisfyingly broad view of what the new United States owned, signing over everything from the Atlantic to the Mississippi and from the Great Lakes to Spanish Florida. America began its independence with the largest area of rich land in the world and with a priceless heritage of freedom.

Question: What were the major parts of the 1783 Treaty of Paris?

Answer: Under the Treaty of Paris, the United States was free and owned all the lands to the Mississippi.

Designing a New Country

The American Revolution introduced the reality, not just the theory, of democratic government to the world. The Revolution challenged the old order in Europe and South America by opposing inherited political power with the democratic idea that government rests on the consent of the governed. The example of the first successful revolution against a European empire provided a model for many other colonial peoples, who realized that they too could become self-governing nations. In the 20th century, revolutionaries sometimes even quoted Thomas Jefferson as they fought against American economic interests.

America won its independence with the help of the endless fights between European countries; it provided the model for what would become, 200 years later, the peaceful European Union. The United States remains the leading example of the extent to which a country with people from all around the world can remain a free society.

Before America could do all that, though, it had to figure out exactly what changes to make after it became independent. In their enthusiasm for new-found freedom, some lawmakers got ahead of the times.

After the Revolution, with 1 out of 30 of the American people (the most conservative Loyalist residents) taking a permanent vacation to Canada or Britain, the new United States had a distinctly progressive bent. Once, for example, the titles *Mr.* and *Mrs.* were reserved only for the upper classes; now everybody got called that. Even more social changes were to come.

Separation of church and state

Church and state were separated. Although the Congregationalist denomination hung on for a few years as the official religion of Massachusetts, one by one, the states dropped any affiliation with a particular denomination. One of Jefferson's proudest accomplishments was the passage of the *Virginia Statute for Religious Freedom* (1786), which separated religion from government in what was then the largest state. It served as a model for other states.

Early attempts to abolish slavery

The Continental Congress of 1774 called for the abolition of the slave trade. Some Northern states ended slavery as early as 1776. In writing the new Constitution, Southern slaveholders got a *Three Fifths Compromise* that allowed them to count part of each slave toward the representation they'd get in Congress.

Question: What was the Three-Fifths Compromise?

Answer: The Three-Fifths Compromise meant that slaves counted toward Congressional representation.

Even a few forward-thinking Southerners freed their slaves in a burst of Revolutionary zeal. Washington arranged for his slaves to be set free after he and his wife died. Although the U.S. set a deadline of 1808 to abolish the importation of new slaves, a slave rebellion in *Haiti* (1791) scared a lot of slave owners into harsher treatment of slaves. The slave revolt also made Napoleon rethink his involvement in the New World.

> Question: What was the influence of the slave rebellion in Haiti on the U.S.?
>
> Answer: The rebellion scared Southern slave owners into increasingly brutal treatment of slaves and gave Napoleon a reason to want to sell out of his interests in the New World, paving the way for the Louisiana Purchase.

Jefferson was embarrassed that he couldn't free his slaves. Enslaved workers were worth as much as $50,000 each in modern money. A poor businessman, Jefferson had been forced to mortgage his slaves to the bank, which wouldn't let Jefferson set them free. The Polish American Revolutionary war hero Thaddeus Kosciusko spent his army pay to help buy the freedom of slaves.

Women's gains and republican motherhood

Women made some early gains. New Jersey's Revolutionary constitution of 1776 even briefly granted women the right to vote, 100 years before the rest of the world. Although that early right was overturned, women played a role in the freedom fight. John Adams's wife, Abigail, warned him in her so-called Remember-the-Ladies letter before the Declaration of Independence that women were ready to start their own revolution. During the war, some women dressed like men fought in both the artillery and the infantry for the patriots. Two sisters dragged a British messenger off his horse and smuggled his secret dispatches through enemy lines to the Americans. He never knew what hit him.

> Question: What did Abigail Adams, wife of future president John Adams, write about in a famous letter to him?
>
> Answer: In an early call for women's rights, Abigail advised John to "remember the ladies."

The idea of *republican motherhood* (1780) elevated women to the role of keeper of the nation's conscience and first educator of future patriots. The concept of republican motherhood resulted in increased educational opportunities for American women. By 1837, women had their own source of higher education: Mount Holyoke Female Seminary, the predecessor to Mount Holyoke College.

> Question: What was the meaning of republican motherhood?
>
> Answer: Republican motherhood meant that it was the important responsibility of women to raise the next generation of freedom-loving patriots.

Although republican motherhood kept women at home rearing children, it also produced an initiative that legitimized political activity. The Abolitionist movement, which began to gain strength in the 1830s and 1840s, found many of its strongest voices among educated Northern women. The *Seneca Falls Convention* (1848), which began the women's-rights movement in the United States, owes some of its origin to the emphasis on republican motherhood at the time of the Revolution.

Trade, industry, and economic democracy

The rich Loyalists who split the country left behind some oversized chunks of land that were divided among deserving patriots. Although land that the king and his unrepentant subjects had owned was sold to help pay off the war debt, few attacks were made on former Loyalists who chose to stay in the new country. Economic democracy meant sharing fairly in the wealth of the land; because America didn't have royalty or an aristocracy, it had some measure of economic democracy even before the political democracy of the Revolution got going. That may be one reason why the United States didn't experience as much violence after its change of government as France did.

Trade and industry got off to a good recovery after the Revolution. Although the United States was outside the British family, it still had the whole non-British world with which to trade. American ships were landing in China as soon as they could get out of port after the peace treaty was signed. River-powered industry was encouraged in New England as soon as the restrictions of old England were gone. Building industry wasn't always easy. The new country had to compete with British manufacturers that were dumping products that had been bottled up by the war for cheap prices.

Looking to make the country larger

The ink had barely dried on the peace treaty that ended the Revolution when Congress sat down to plan for the expansion of the United States into its western lands. The Land Ordinance of 1785 provided that the land in the old Northwest Territory — covering what are now Ohio, Indiana, Michigan, Illinois, and Wisconsin — should be sold to help pay off the national debt. The proceeds from the sale of 1 out of 36 sections went to support local schools, a gift to education that was unheard-of in the rest of the world.

The even more important *Northwest Ordinance* (1787) let government of the new lands pass quickly from dependent territories to full partnership states as soon as any state had 60,000 residents. It also banned slavery in the Northwest Territory.

Question: What was the major purpose of the Northwest Ordinance?

Answer: The Northwest Ordinance of 1787 provided rules for admission of new states and prohibited slavery in the Northwest Territory.

Setting Down the Legal Foundation of a Nation

To get a fresh start, the Continental Congress in 1776 asked the states to rewrite their state constitutions as republican documents. Written constitutions serve as the fundamental rules — laws that don't change with the day-to-day ideas of ordinary legislation. Most of the state constitutions were similar, being contracts that defined the powers of government and the rights of citizens.

Massachusetts came up with the new idea of having the people of the state ratify any amendments to the state constitution. The amendment process for the U.S. Constitution still works that way: The legislatures of three-quarters of all the states must approve any changes. After the states began to think in a new way, almost half of the 13 original colonies decided to move their capitals to be closer to the people in the center of each state.

The Articles of Confederation

To set some permanent rules for the new nation, Congress had taken the time, between running the war and running from the British, to draft the *Articles of Confederation* (1777). The big deal at first wasn't so much how to govern the new country as how to handle the land it was sitting on. Most colonial governments liked to think of themselves as extending all the way over the Appalachian Mountains to the Mississippi, if not to the Pacific. They each had claims on Western land. The central government got the states to give up these claims so that new states could be formed and land sold to settlers to support the central government. The individual states pooled their Western land resources for the common good.

This was an important start, because the Articles of Confederation gave no power to Congress to collect taxes. Congress established a tax quota for each state and then used the time-honored negotiating strategy of begging and pleading to get the states to pay up. How well this system worked is reflected in the number of brave Continental soldiers who were never even supplied shoes by the government. And tax collecting wasn't the end of the Confederation government's weakness. Congress wasn't allowed to regulate commerce and set tariffs; each state did that individually. Oranges could be taxed at 10 cents in New York and $10 in Pennsylvania — possibly both ways if a cargo moved across state lines.

Question: What was the major government revenue weakness of the Articles of Confederation?

Answer: Under the Articles of Confederation, the United States couldn't levy taxes or control commerce.

If the British have it, we don't want it!

The Confederation was an anti–King George machine; whatever the colonies didn't like about the British government, they left out of the Articles of Confederation. Dictatorial administration? No problem. The articles allowed for no president, king, or executive at all. Crooked judges? Got it covered. The articles established no national judicial system; each state did its own thing. The central government got to negotiate treaties and run a postal system, though it was a little unclear where it would get the money to print the stamps.

The Articles of Confederation contained good things as well. First, the articles existed, giving the states a unified platform to work with. Second, pitiful as they were, the articles clearly spelled out the powers of the government. Unlike the unwritten, hard-to-define British Constitution, the articles were right there in black and white. They held the union together through a tough war and gave the states a stepping stone to something stronger and more permanent.

The states rebel

When the war was over, the states' attentions drifted back to their own interests. Quarrels over boundaries generated minor battles between discharged state militias. A large but mostly peaceful uprising in western Massachusetts, led by a captain in the war, scared the government and the local courts.

Shays' Rebellion (1786) was a series of armed demonstrations led by small farmers angered by debt and taxes. Failure to repay debts often resulted in imprisonment in debtor's prisons or loss of the family farm. The rebels freed their friends from prison and stopped courts from ordering evictions. The rebellion lasted about six months before it was violently put down by a private army paid for by rich landowners. Without a standing army, the national government could do nothing. This scare helped lead to support for the *Constitutional Convention* (1787), which began a few months after the rebellion.

Question: What was Shays' Rebellion?

Answer: In Shays' Rebellion, debt-ridden Massachusetts farmers attacked courts. The Rebellion helped show the need for a more powerful federal government.

The Constitutional Convention

Delegates from all the states came to the Constitutional Convention, including Revolutionary superstars Ben Franklin (then 81 years old), Alexander Hamilton, and James Madison. George Washington chaired the meeting.

The delegates knew they needed a strong central government, but they wanted to preserve the maximum rights to states and their individual citizens. Proposals broke down into a large-state plan and a small-state plan. Under the Confederation, the rule had been one state, one vote. The big states wanted representation by population size. In the end, the great compromise split the difference. Big states got the House of Representatives, based on population; the small states got the U.S. Senate, with two senators for every state no matter how small. As a tip to the big states, all tax and revenue bills had to start in the House. The many compromises took years to be finally approved.

Question: Did all the delegates agree with the new Constitution at the first meeting?

Answer: No, the Constitution was controversial and required compromise and years of discussion to be ratified by all 13 states.

Getting over King George-o-phobia, the delegates established a strong president who could appoint judges and other officials, serve as commander in chief of the military, and veto legislation. This strong president was to be chosen by the people indirectly through an electoral college as a supposed safeguard against mob rule.

Slavery: Reduced but not gone yet

The Southern states wanted to count slaves as part of their population to get more representatives in the House. The North said it was nice that the South finally wanted to count slaves as people, but the way Southerners treated slaves, Northerners may as well request representation for their horses.

The two sides split the difference: Slaves were partly counted in the *Three-Fifths Compromise* (1787). All but two of the states wanted to shut down the African slave trade; the compromise was to stop stealing people from Africa in 20 years (1807).

Reining in the states

The Constitution needed the approval of nine states to get going. Eventually, it was approved by all 13 states, but it took 3 years and some mighty close votes. In general, wealthy, well-educated people liked the strong central government called for by the new Constitution; people who supported the federal Constitution were *Federalists* (1788). They wrote the *Federalist Papers,* arguing that a large republic can best protect minority rights.

In the end, the laws that didn't change in the Constitution served all the people. You can count on one hand the countries in the world that have had stable governments for the past 200 years. Although it's far from an economic democracy, the United States has provided a shield for freedom and a chance for success to millions of people.

Question: What was the main point of the Federalist Papers?

Answer: The Federalist Papers argued that a large republic best protects minority rights.

As weary old Ben Franklin was leaving the convention hall, a woman asked him, "Well, doctor, what have we got — a republic or a monarchy?" The elder statesman replied, "A republic, madam, if you can keep it."

First president: George Washington

George Washington became the first U.S. president in 1789. His ride from quiet Mount Vernon to the nation's temporary capital of New York City was one big party: Bells rang, bands played, and the roads were strewn with flowers. Washington took the oath of office on a balcony overlooking Wall Street — something that some people have seen as a bad omen for economic democracy. Washington appointed the first Cabinet: Thomas Jefferson, Alexander Hamilton, and Henry Knox.

Bill of Rights

The *Bill of Rights* (1791), the first ten amendments to the Constitution, was approved by all the states to guarantee that the new Constitution would mandate basic rights for all citizens. Spelling out these rights put critics of the new Constitution at ease by mandating freedom of speech and religion and other liberties.

Although the AP exam probably won't trick you with individual amendment numbers, the Bill of Rights makes excellent essay fodder and can come in handy on multiple-choice questions. Here's the short version:

- **First Amendment:** freedom of religion, speech, and press

- **Second Amendment:** right to keep and bear arms

- **Third Amendment:** protection from mandatory quartering of troops in private citizens' homes

- **Fourth Amendment:** protection from unreasonable search and seizure

- **Fifth Amendment:** due process under the law

- **Sixth Amendment:** right to criminal trial by jury and other rights for the accused

- **Seventh Amendment:** right to civil trial by jury

- **Eighth Amendment:** no excessive bail or cruel and unusual punishment

- **Ninth Amendment:** establishes that amendments don't limit rights, just suggest some

- **Tenth Amendment:** establishes that powers not listed belong to the states and people

Moving Along with the Young Republic

One thing that America was good at was growing people. By the time of the first official census in 1790, almost 4 million people inhabited the U.S., up from just over 2 million in 1770. Although business was picking up, the government was still deep in debt from the Revolutionary War.

Treasury Secretary Hamilton had a unique idea: He actually wanted to pay off the national debt. Even though the United States had won the war, investors still didn't think government bonds were worth much more than 10 cents on the dollar. Hamilton proposed to pay them all back and got Congress to approve a duty on foreign imports and U.S.-made luxury items such as whiskey and carriages to raise money. The credit of the United States improved. Hamilton supported the development of a national bank, partially funded by the government, that could keep money in circulation and help boost the economy. He also wanted to give subsidies to business, but Congress wouldn't buy that. Jefferson argued against the Bank of the United States, but it passed. Although he got the nation on a firm financial footing, Hamilton's policies were seen by poorer farmers as serving the rich Eastern merchants.

Question: What was Alexander Hamilton's economic policy?

Answer: Alexander Hamilton's economic program included a Bank of the U.S., plus excise and tariff taxes. Congress rejected his idea of direct subsidies to manufacturers.

Question: How was Hamilton's financial program viewed by poorer voters?

Answer: Alexander Hamilton's fiscal policy was seen as favoring Eastern merchants.

As a states'-rights *strict-constructionist,* Jefferson believed that anything not specifically mentioned in the Constitution was prohibited. Hamilton took a broad interpretation or *loose-construction* view of the Constitution. He thought the Constitution had *implied powers,* which allowed the government to do whatever was necessary to carry out the general tasks assigned in the Constitution. A modern example of implied power is the federal road-building program; the only power enumerated for this in the Constitution is the maintenance of postal roads. Therefore, every freeway is officially a postal road.

The Whiskey Rebellion

The *Whiskey Rebellion* (1794) was a protest on the western Pennsylvania frontier against the tax Hamilton had gotten passed on booze. At almost $4 a gallon in modern money, the tax was more than most self-respecting moonshiners could come up with in a barter economy. Whiskey was distilled money for the frontier farmers, who had little cash and almost no transportation; whiskey was the easiest and most profitable thing to do with a crop of grain. Even preachers got paid with jugs of booze, which they could then exchange for food or supplies.

Hamilton's tax may have raised money, but it really hurt small-time farmer/distillers. With local protests spreading throughout the states, Hamilton and Washington personally led an army of 13,000 armed men on a fruitless search for whiskey criminals near Pittsburgh. They didn't catch many people, but they made their point. The whiskey business paid up for a while in Pennsylvania. On a larger scale, the new federal government showed it could use force to back up laws. But in other places without soldiers, the tax was difficult to collect, and it was repealed in 1803.

Forming political parties

Hamilton's ambitious big-government programs created opposition from people like Jefferson, who believed in more individualism and less government. Political parties began to form around these opinions. People who liked Hamilton's ideas were called *Federalists* (1795), and Jefferson's followers called themselves *Democratic-Republicans* (1800). The Federalists died out around 1816. After trying silly party names like *Whigs* (1834) and *Know-Nothings* (1855), American's factions divided the names of Jefferson's party. Political parties weren't an idea of the framers of the Constitution, but they've been a handy addition to democracy, always scraping just to the right or left of whoever is in power.

Trying to stay out of other people's wars

The French had a bloody revolution of their own, occasioning yet another war with Britain. The *Franco-American Alliance* (1788) that was key in helping the United States win its independence was still on the books, but Washington decided not to take sides and issued his *Neutrality Proclamation* (1793). That was okay with the French, who figured that the baby United States wouldn't be much help anyway.

Meanwhile, on the Ohio frontier, the American Indians had gotten together in the *Miami Confederacy* (1790) and had twice beaten up small U.S. armies sent against them. The British were still lurking in forts on American soil, arming the American Indians. Finally, a serious U.S. force beat the American Indians at the *Battle of Fallen Timbers* (1794), and the American Indians sold most of their lands in the *Treaty of Greenville* (1795).

Rolling along the treaty trail, trying to stay out of trouble, the United States signed *Jay's Treaty* (1794) with Britain to stop the British from lurking in forts. The agreement didn't stop Britain's nagging bad habit of seizing American ships at sea and forcing U.S. sailors to join its navy, but it did let the United States into the valuable trade with the British West Indies. Spain cut the United States a break with *Pinckney's Treaty* (1795), giving the new country all the land down to Florida and free use of the Mississippi. America was getting a little respect. That little respect was more than Washington was getting from many people in the country he helped create.

Question: What was Pinckney's Treaty?

Answer: Pinckney's Treaty of 1795 with Spain fixed Southern boundaries and gave U.S. ships the right to use the Mississippi River.

Washington leaves office

Facing criticism and tired of politics, Washington left office at the end of his second term. His *Farewell Address* (1796) warned the nation to stay out of permanent alliances and asked people to be governed by moral religious principles.

Washington himself was a freethinking Freemason who welcomed all religions and avoided communion with sectarian statements of faith in his later years. He was an example of good behavior; after 200 years, his pure character still shines. He liked a good time, however; his major retirement project was the construction on his property of one of the largest whiskey stills in the country. His last words were "It is well."

John Adams takes over

John Adams (1797), the second American president, sent envoys to France to try to solve a hissy fit. Angry that the Americans would be dating the British with Jay's Treaty when they should be going steady with them under the Franco-American Alliance, the French were taking a leaf from the British playbook and seizing American ships at sea. After an aborted negotiation called the *XYZ Affair* (1797), for the coded names of three French envoys who tried to extort a bribe from the United States, both sides got over their emotions and signed the *Convention of 1800,* which ended their formal alliance.

Don't miss the forest for the trees. The AP exam cares about trends, not a whirlwind of treaty names. The individual names are like a bonus round: you get extra points for remembering. The main trend to understand from all this early U.S. diplomacy is that the new nation was wisely avoiding war and slowly gaining respect. If the United States had fought a war with France in 1800, the French surely wouldn't have sold America the Louisiana Purchase in 1803.

What with all the international and domestic political tensions, the ruling Federalists in Congress freaked out and passed the *Alien and Sedition Acts* (1798). These acts made criticizing the president a crime, raised the waiting time for citizenship from 5 to 17 years, and allowed the government to deport any noncitizens it didn't like.

The U.S. appeared to be on the path to becoming a police-state, but Jefferson fought the repressive laws every step of the way, and they expired at the end of Adams's one term as president. Jefferson and James Madison secretly wrote the *Kentucky and Virginia Resolutions* (1798), which were passed by these states to protest the repressive Alien and Sedition Acts. In fighting the laws, Jefferson took an extreme turn in the antigovernment direction and introduced the concept of nullification, saying that any state could refuse to follow a federal law it didn't like. This concept would come back to roost in a bad way before the Civil War.

Question: What were the Kentucky and Virginia Resolutions?

Answer: Kentucky and Virginia Resolutions championed states' rights against the Alien and Sedition Acts.

Thomas Jefferson: Moving into the 1800s

Thomas Jefferson (1801) narrowly squeaked past Federalist attacks to become the third president. This election marked the first change in political parties for the United States and was an important landmark for peaceful political transition. Jefferson believed in small government, and he reduced government programs; he pardoned the martyrs to the expired Alien and Sedition Acts, and the government returned many of their fines. A new naturalization act again let immigrants become citizens after only five years. In 1804, Alexander Hamilton was killed in a duel with Vice President Aaron Burr; Burr fled the country.

Question: What was Thomas Jefferson's political approach?

Answer: Jefferson reduced the activities of the federal government.

During his last days in office, Adams had appointed a new chief justice of the Supreme Court, John Marshall. Marshall had only six weeks of formal legal training; he was President Adams's last choice after three other men couldn't take the job. Jefferson didn't like Marshall's strong-government views but couldn't get rid of him.

Empowering the Supreme Court

Marshall had suffered from hunger and cold as a soldier at Valley Forge; he knew governments had to be strong enough to deliver for their people. Marshall's first landmark case was *Marbury v. Madison* (1803). In rejecting an appeal from a fellow Federalist, Marshall overturned a previous law as unconstitutional because it didn't agree with the 15-year-old U.S. Constitution. This set the precedent that the Supreme Court can review all laws for their constitutionality.

Question: What was the importance of the case of Marbury v. Madison?

Answer: This decision gave the Supreme Court the power to review all laws for their constitutionality.

Jefferson's small-government followers tried to strike back by filing impeachment charges against a judge they didn't like. Congress dropped the charges, and the principles of independent judicial review and separation of powers got under way.

Making a deal with Napoleon

In France, famous Napoleon Bonaparte had two troubles on his mind: He was fighting almost every other country in Europe, and he had just lost a war to an island of slaves. Haiti was a rich sugar island where thousands of slaves had risen up in revolt against their French masters. Napoleon's troops could shoot their way in, but diseases and guerilla warfare meant they really couldn't stay. Napoleon needed money and wanted out of the New World.

Jefferson had sent negotiators to France to try to buy New Orleans. They had authorization to pay as much as $10 million (half a billion dollars in modern money) for the city. Napoleon surprised them by offering all of France's holdings in North America, from the Mississippi to the Pacific Ocean, for $15 million. What the heck? They bought a wilderness to get a city.

Question: What was the background of the Louisiana Purchase?

Answer: The Louisiana Purchase resulted from Napoleon's loss in Haiti, opened the whole trans-Mississippi area, and showed Jefferson's flexibility with his own strict-constructionist views.

Lewis and Clark

Meriwether Lewis and *William Clark* (1804) explored the new territory with the help of the American Indian woman Sacajawea. They wouldn't have survived without her. The fact that Lewis and Clark's expedition was traveling with a woman and her child showed the American Indians that the expedition wasn't a hostile war party. Their 2½-year epic adventure pointed the way west for future settlers. Other early explorers, including *Zebulon Pike* (1805), brought back reports of the immense and unknown new territory of the United States. Pike showed the value of publicity; although Pikes Peak was only one of over 50 tall mountains in Colorado, it became the one everybody knows.

Caught between Britain and France

After winning a landslide reelection victory in 1804, Jefferson and the nation were caught between France and Britain in their seemingly endless war to control Europe. Jefferson was unpopular for keeping the United States out of an early war with the great powers; America couldn't trade with either power without facing the other's guns. Both sides grabbed American merchant ships and sailors. The British forced some 6,000 American sailors to join their navy between 1808 and 1811 alone.

> Question: How was Jefferson's policy of avoiding war received by the public?

> Answer: Jefferson was unpopular for neutrality toward Britain and France.

Too weak to fight, the United States passed the *Embargo Acts* (1807), which were meant to stop all trade with foreign nations. While the United States held its breath and turned blue, the British and French managed to do without American goods. American exporters either smuggled goods or went out of business; many saw the acts as attacking Americans to fight foreigners.

To the extent that they kept foreign goods out, the Embargo Acts helped infant U.S. industries grow without competition. Some traders actually liked the cops-and-robbers aspects of the smuggling business; it was exciting, and the profits were great if you didn't get busted. Just before Jefferson left office, Congress passed the *Non-Intercourse Act* (1809), which limited the embargo to Britain and France.

James Madison steps in

James Madison (1809), friend and follower of Jefferson, took over as president of a nation still caught in the French/British nutcracker. The 15-year U.S. headache of foreign entanglement without any foreign alliances showed the impossibility of separating the United States from the world, as both Washington and Jefferson had wished. As a trading nation, America couldn't avoid the crossfire of belligerents.

Congress tried a finesse that was too tricky by half. *Macon's Bill No. 2* (1810) said that if either Britain or France would end its commercial blockade, the United States would restore its embargo against the nation that didn't stop blocking trade. In other words, America would take sides, but it was first come, first served. France promised to be good; Britain didn't. America was drawn closer to another conflict with Britain.

Britain's deal with Tecumseh

Meanwhile, in the green forests of the frontier, a strong Shawnee leader named *Tecumseh* (1811) united tribes from Canada to Mexico and prepared to push the settlers back. The British were more than happy to supply guns to the American Indians. William Henry Harrison, U.S. governor of Indiana, led a band of militia toward Tecumseh's headquarters on the Tippecanoe River while the chief was away gathering together his allies.

Tecumseh's brother unwisely attacked the militia before the American Indians could get together, telling the braves that his medicine-man powers would keep them from being wounded. When magic didn't stop the militia's bullets, the American Indians fled, and Tecumseh's rebellion was over before it started. Tecumseh fought on, eventually charging alone into the middle of an American army. An old American frontiersman helped the American Indians give Tecumseh's body an honored burial.

The U.S. versus Britain — version 1812

After being pushed around for years, the United States declared war on Great Britain in 1812. The United States could hardly have been more divided; war resolutions barely passed in Congress. The war was most popular in the South and in the Middle and Western states. New England greeted the news of war with mourning.

The young United States faced a war with its old enemy Britain, still the most powerful empire in the world. New England refused to let its militias fight and probably loaned more money to Britain than to the U.S. government. New England food helped supply British invaders from Canada.

How could New England, the hotbed of freedom and revolution, as well as a major shipping area, turn against an American government that was determined to preserve the freedom of international shipping? A lot of the answer was politics. New England was Federalist territory; the people there would rather lose a war than see Jefferson's Republicans win. Faced with the experienced British military, the young United States was in trouble trying to go to war without the support of the whole country.

Like slipping on a banana peel and sliding into a gold mine, the *War of 1812* was an embarrassment that turned out fine. New England didn't want to fight; inexperienced American troops often ran from a British army hardened by years of combat with Napoleon, and old generals from the Revolutionary War proved that they needed to retire. U.S. invasions of Canada failed miserably; the British army burned Washington, D.C., and the British navy raided and blockaded.

The good news was that the United States got some victories to remember:

- The *USS Constitution* (Old Ironsides), with a crew that was one sixth free blacks, blew away proud British ships.

- The star-spangled banner continued to wave over Baltimore Harbor and inspired the national anthem.

- A thrown-together force of sailors, frontiersmen, free blacks, Frenchmen, and pirates smashed a larger force of experienced British regulars to save New Orleans.

When the smoke cleared, the United States and Britain signed the *Treaty of Ghent* (1814), without any formal gains for either side. The United States gained respect for standing up to the great British Empire, and Americans felt a new sense of national pride.

It had been a close thing. Toward the end of the war, the *Hartford Convention* (1814) was an angry meeting of the New England states demanding more power. Those states shut up when news of the victory at New Orleans reached the capital at about the same time as their complaints. Ironically, New England started all the talk about nullification and secession that would become popular in the South with respect to the issue of slavery.

Hopeful in the Era of Good Feelings

With so many years of embargo and blockade, the United States had time to develop its own industries. Following the war, Congress passed the protective Tariff of 1816, which taxed foreign imports to make American goods more competitive. Congressman Henry Clay launched the *American System* (1824), which included easy credit, increased tariffs, and roads and canals to move American products. An added bonus: Roads and canals were the most important way to encourage settlement of the West.

Question: What were the most important new forms of transportation in the early United States?

Answer: Roads and canals were the most important new avenues of transportation.

James Monroe (1817), the last of the Revolutionary War soldiers to be president, served two terms mellow enough to be called the *Era of Good Feelings.* Nothing with humans in it is really mellow all the time; Monroe faced plenty of debate about tariffs, the Bank of the United States, where and how to build canals and roads, and how much to charge for the sale of the millions of acres of public lands that were up for grabs.

Whatever its political challenges, the nation was on a transportation roll. The Cumberland Road began in 1811 and eventually stretched from Maryland to the frontier at Illinois. The first steamboat to make it down the Ohio River and on to New Orleans also sailed in 1811.

Chapter 11

Rough and Tumble: The United States Grows Up, 1816–1845

- -

In This Chapter

▶ Getting the drop on Manifest Destiny

▶ Checking out Andy Jackson's tough guy act

▶ Discovering how the Supreme Court shaped the law

▶ Connecting inventions to events in young America

- -

*T*he years between 1816 and 1845 were a time of tremendous growth and expansion for the United States. In this chapter, you find out about events that changed the landscape of the country, pointing the U.S. in the direction it still follows today. AP tests always have questions on *Jacksonian democracy;* this chapter contains what you need to know to be ready for them.

As you review this period of U.S. History, remember the power of *PES:* political events, economic realities, and social trends (see Chapter 1). Don't just memorize names, dates, and places. *When you see themes, connect them:* Manifest Destiny was the social trend connected to American Indian removal. The Gibbons v. Ogden decision on interstate commerce was the economic reality brought about by the invention of the steamship and better transportation. Jacksonian democracy was the consequence that stemmed from the shift toward more universal voting rights. Connect themes as you review so you'll be ready to connect to a high score on the big day.

Manifestin' Destiny

You're almost sure to see a question on the AP test about Manifest Destiny, a theme that runs through much of U.S. History. *Manifest Destiny* means that lots of Americans felt God obviously meant for their country to control all the land between the Atlantic and Pacific Oceans. With the giant Louisiana Purchase speeding America toward the West Coast while the country was still only on its third president, the U.S. seemed to be on a transcontinental roll. (See Chapter 10 for more on the Louisiana Purchase.)

Manifest means a fact any kid can tell just by looking at it (like it's manifest that this book is meant to get you past the AP exam), and *Destiny* is a fate nobody can avoid. Because Manifest Destiny meant that citizens of the U.S. would have to fight not just the British but thousands of American Indians and Mexicans as well, a substantial minority of citizens was against the idea at any given time and would have been just as happy to pass up the honor. Many more thought America was doing the non-Americans a favor by forcibly inviting them to the party.

Manifesting on the AP exam

For the AP exam, remember that Manifest Destiny showed up early in the 1800s, super-charged by Jefferson's huge Louisiana Purchase, and hung around until the U.S. finished grabbing land during the Spanish-American War at the end of the 1800s. You can use the concept as part of the official AP theme of American exceptionalism: Americans thought they were so special that they deserved to rule the continent.

Hooking up Manifest Destiny to the big picture

When you think you're driving Destiny's limo, you're on a mission, and nothing can get in your way. To show this strong trend on an essay question, you could mention Manifest Destiny in the context of the Trail of Tears (covered later in this chapter), the long trail West (Chapter 12), and the willingness of both sides to fight to the death in the Civil War (Chapter 13), and as a cultural influence on America becoming a world power (Chapter 17). Hooking up a trend to later events warms the heart of test-grading teachers.

On multiple-choice questions, watch out for wrong choices that tie Manifest Destiny to slavery, independence, or an overseas empire. Manifest Destiny is just about territorial expansion from the Atlantic to the Pacific, sometimes called *overspreading the continent*. Manifest Destiny is part of the larger topic of *American exceptionalism*. Consider this when writing the inevitable social history essay involving Manifest Destiny: All nations think they're special; powerful nations have in the past expressed their *exceptionalism* by taking over more land. Manifest Destiny was an American expression of exceptionalism. Exceptionalism can be good; feeling moral has inspired America to help other nations, and feeling free has led the U.S. to support freedom for other people. You can still hear the ghost of Manifest Destiny/exceptionalism in talk of using force to bring American values to other countries.

Even the name of the subject you're studying changed from American History to U.S. History to avoid sounding like exceptionalism. Professors realized, duh, 20 other countries in North and South America have claim to being Americans, too. For easy understanding, I still refer to U.S. citizens as Americans in this text, but be ready to write sensitively to score points on essay questions.

Kick-Starting Political Action

History shows how social developments influence political outcomes. Factories allowed for the growth of towns. The growth of towns provided a place for social movements like abolition, labor unions, and temperance organizations. Women who came together for the Second Awakening got interested in women's rights and abolition, often at the same time. (See "Transcendentalism and the Second Great Awakening" later in this chapter.) The U.S. grew and changed rapidly, which may explain why the country went through so many different presidents, and why the Supreme Court gained so much power during this era.

Question: Some artists say, "I don't care who makes the laws as long as I can write the songs." How did social developments in the 1820s and 1830s influence the development of the United States?

Answer: In addition to the connections outlined just before this sample question, you can also point to the growth in Jacksonian democracy that brought down the Bank of the U.S. (see "War on the Bank of the U.S."), the cotton farming that pushed American Indians off southern land (see "Slavery Grows with Cotton" and "Ethnic Cleansing, American-Style: The Trail of Tears"), and the improvements in transportation that allowed the spread of culture (see "Early Emo: Feeling in Art, Education, and Belief").

The Presidential parade

Besides Andy Jackson, only one president in this period stuck around for a full two terms. That would be *James Monroe,* Mr. Era-of-Good-Feelings (1817 to 1825). Other than presiding over the Missouri Compromise and issuing the Monroe Doctrine, Monroe had a cruise (literally. He was the first president to ride on a steamboat.)

Other Presidents of this era:

- *John Quincy Adams* (1825–1829) had the honor of losing to Andy Jackson twice. The first time, it didn't take; Adams squeezed into the White House. (Check out the section "Looking at the Back Story on Jackson" later in this chapter.) During his one term, the U.S. got a ride on the Erie Canal and the Baltimore & Ohio railroad, revolutionizing transportation.

- *Andrew Jackson* (1829–1837) was the superstar of this era and the godfather of Jacksonian democracy. Andy threw such a big populist party on inauguration day that he had to crawl out a back window of the White House to find a place to sleep. Check out "Andy Jackson: Bringing Tough-Guy Democracy to Washington" later in this chapter for more info.

- *Martin Van Buren* (1837–1841) had the bad luck to be president during the depression economy following the Panic of 1837 and during the infamous Trail of Tears. With bad vibes like that, one term was enough.

- *William Henry Harrison* (1841) didn't even have time to get to the buffet. He delivered an almost two-hour inauguration speech, caught pneumonia, and died. Vice President *John Tyler* (1841–1845) took over, annexed Texas, fought against a national bank, and found time to have 15 children. The population of the nation grew almost as fast as Tyler's family.

The Marshall Court shows it's supreme

The Supreme Court became a powerful third branch of government largely through the 34 years of service of John Marshall. Marshall was Chief Justice from when the United States was a baby in 1801 until the country and its government were pretty grown up in 1835. In Chapter 10, I discuss the establishment of judicial review with the Marbury v. Madison decision in 1803. Here are a few more key decisions from the Marshall era:

McCulloch v. Maryland: 1819

Maryland didn't much like the Bank of the United States doing business in its state. Maryland couldn't shoot the bank, so it decided to tax the bank out of existence. James McCulloch, the bank's cashier, refused to pay tax to Maryland because his bank was chartered by the United States government. Maryland said that it didn't see anything in the U.S. Constitution about a national bank and that the bank was therefore illegal and certainly couldn't hide behind the robes of the U.S. Supreme Court.

McCulloch v. Maryland held for *implied powers* in 1819. In its 1819 decision, John Marshall's court held that the Constitution doesn't have to flat-out specify everything the government can do; Congress has implied powers for Congress. After all, the Constitution says the U.S. government can do anything "necessary and proper" to carry out its specifically listed duties. In this case, the specific duties were to tax, borrow, and coin money. If the Marshall court hadn't established implied powers, the Feds wouldn't be building roads or flying rockets because none of that's in the Constitution.

Cohens v. Virginia: 1821

Lotteries didn't start behind the counter at the gas station; they were big business even in the early days of the U.S. The Cohens got busted selling illegal lottery tickets, and they appealed their Virginia criminal conviction to the Supreme Court. The Marshall court heard the appeal and thus established the principle that state criminal decisions could be appealed to the federal Supreme Court. This allows mobsters to yell: "Mess with me, and I'll take you all the way to the Supreme Court!"

Gibbons v. Ogden: 1824

Gibbons v. Ogden held for interstate commerce in 1824. Imagine if everybody in New York had to pay one person to get to New Jersey. Aaron Ogden had that kind of a deal with New York State; before the area had bridges, crossing meant taking Ogden's boat or swimming. Trouble was, Thomas Gibbons had a license from the Feds for the same route. Ogden sued Gibbons, and the New York state court said Ogden had the power to stop the Fed's guy Gibbons. The federal Supreme Court said no way: Federal law is supreme, especially in interstate commerce (also known as trade that crosses state lines.)

You will see questions on Supreme Court decisions on the AP exam. Memorize the key decisions, which you can find in Chapter 27.

Question: What Supreme Court decision established the principle of federal regulation of interstate commerce?

Answer: Gibbons v. Ogden determined that the federal government had jurisdiction over trade that crossed state lines.

Nobody's Happy: Missouri Compromise of 1820

As early as the beginning of the 1800s, the increasingly industrial Northern states and the slaveholding agricultural Southern states were anxiously watching the balance of power between them. They each had exactly 11 states, so the balance of power in the U.S. Senate was even. Problem: Missouri wanted to be admitted as a slave state, throwing the balance of power to the South. Henry Clay, the Great Compromiser, was sort of neutral because he came from what was then the Wild West of Kentucky. He came up with this deal:

Missouri would come in as a slave state, but Maine would enter as a free state to keep the balance. From then on, an imaginary line would cross the middle of the U.S. Any territory north of that line would be free; anything south would be open to slavery. This was called the *Mason-Dixon line.*

Question: What new free state was added as the result of the Missouri Compromise?

Answer: Under the Missouri Compromise, Maine entered the Union as a free state.

Neither side liked the *Missouri Compromise* (1820), but both sides lived with it for the next 30 years. That makes it important and a cinch to get on the AP test. The Compromise led to fights within the previously united Democratic-Republican party. Things had been so mellow before the Missouri Compromise that the country had only one political party; the period was even called the Era of Good Feelings. Afterwards, the good feelings wore off in a political fight between Andrew Jackson and John Quincy Adams. The states'-rights issue had been hidden in the closet with the failure of the Articles of Confederation (see Chapter 10). Now it came out of the closet and became part of the law.

Remember, the Missouri Compromise is early — 1820 — and it deals directly only with Missouri and Maine. It helps divide, not unite, the political process, but it remained the general law of the land for 30 years. After that, the new Compromise of 1850 took over and dealt with the Western states and the Fugitive Slave Law.

Keep Your Hands Off Our Hemisphere: The Monroe Doctrine

Although it had once been the playground of the European powers (see Chapters 8 and 9), the New World of North and South America was relatively free of colonial ownership by 1820. Following the American Revolution, most countries gained their independence from foreign masters.

As a small but aspiring big dog, the United States wanted to keep it that way. To this end, President James Monroe posted a stay-out warning on the Western Hemisphere to the rest of the world. The *Monroe Doctrine* (1823) said the United States wouldn't tolerate further attempts by European powers (the only powers there then were) to colonize the New World. That it worked in the 1800s was more bark than bite, but it established a precedent still cited to this day.

Question: What was the Monroe Doctrine?

Answer: The Monroe Doctrine was a declaration issued by President James Monroe warning European powers not to establish any more colonies in the New World.

Ethnic Cleansing, American-Style: The Trail of Tears

American renewal usually meant American Indian removal. In fact, President Andrew Jackson made his reputation as a frontier American Indian fighter and signed a bill called the Indian Removal Act in 1830. The act set aside a big share of the federal budget to have the Army force all the American Indian tribes to move out of the fertile river valleys the settlers wanted and into dusty prairies west of the Mississippi River. By 1850, most of the American Indians east of the Mississippi were gone, forced to either move west or die along the way. For more than 100,000 American Indians, including civilized tribes who had their own schools, newspapers, and farms, this journey west was called the *Trail of Tears* (1838).

In 1832, the Supreme Court held for the American Indians in the case of *Worcester v. Georgia*. A lot of anti-Manifest Destiny people applauded this decision, but that didn't stop President Jackson. He declared that Chief Justice John Marshall could say anything he wanted to, but "let's see him enforce it."

After gunpoint negotiations, the Cherokee families were forced to leave their homes in 1838 to 1839 and walk the 1,200 mile Trail of Tears to barren land in Oklahoma. With no supplies, half of the families died on the forced march to what was then called Indian Territory. Later on, even that would be taken away from them (see Chapter 15).

Andy Jackson: Bringing Tough-Guy Democracy to Washington

Andrew Jackson never went to college, and he's in good company — neither did Washington or Lincoln. Although he wasn't as nice a guy as Washington or Lincoln, he did usher in the *age of the common man.* The emphasis here is on the word *man,* because Jacksonian democracy certainly didn't include blacks or women. But under Jackson, a majority of white men voted for president for the first time; previously, you had to own property to vote in many states.

Jackson was a self-made Western fighter with few ideas but strong convictions. He ignored his appointed Cabinet officers and relied on the advice of a shifting group of buddies known as the *Kitchen Cabinet.* He had no problem appointing friends to government jobs in what was called the *spoils system,* as in "to the victor belong the spoils." Jackson didn't even think this system was wrong because to him any man should be equal to doing any job. The Founding Fathers said they believed in equality, but those were just words — most of them, including Washington, were rich guys. Jackson made the little guys feel like they owned the government.

After the U.S. allowed greater voting participation under Jacksonian democracy, it started to have issues that until then had been swept under the parlor rug. These problems included the right of individual states to nullify or ignore federal laws, fights within the administration, and the future of an unpopular national bank.

Looking at the back story on Jackson

Andrew Jackson was a popular guy who had actually won the most votes for president in 1824, the first time the whole country voted directly for the presidential electors. Unfortunately for him, he didn't have a majority — the three other candidates pooled their support in the House of Representatives to elect John Quincy Adams. Adams had ties to the beginning of the country: His father was the second U.S. president.

Just say no, no, nullification

John Quincy Adams did what he could to protect the American Indians, but the pressure from Jackson and his followers never let up. Plus, Adams had his hands full with a Civil War prequel led by his own vice president (John Calhoun) protesting *tariffs* (federal taxes on imports). Southerners called the 1828 tax the *Tariff of Abominations* because it made stuff that Southern planters bought from overseas more expensive (and an *abomination* is something you consider hateful, which is how the South felt about the tariff). By beginning to challenge the right of the national government to make laws the South didn't like, Southerners came up with a political time bomb that would tick for 30 years until it blew up in the real Civil War of 1861.

Here's how the South saw the situation: The federal government was a collection of independent states that had united under the catchy name United States to get a few things done. If states felt like de-uniting over a certain issue, they could just sit that game out (or even leave the team if necessary). *Nullification* (1830) meant any state could just refuse to follow (as in nullify or declare null and void) any federal law with which it didn't agree.

The nullification time bomb ticked on in a debate over selling cheap land to settlers in the west. Jackson supported cheap land. He was the first president from outside the original 13 colonies, the first tough-guy frontiersman with no ties to the polite, educated founders of the country. On the possibility of nullification, he had support from the best people. When states talked about nullification if they didn't get their way, famous Congressman Daniel Webster spoke against it, crying, "Liberty and Union, now and forever, one and inseparable!"

Threatening to hang the vice president over tariffs

Jackson was stuck with the same uncooperative Vice President Calhoun his rival John Quincy Adams had endured (you can see why presidents now pick their own vice presidents). Calhoun quit over a new tariff bill and went home to South Carolina, where he got an *Ordinance of Nullification* passed ordering federal customs officials in that state to stop following federal law.

Old General Jackson never blinked; he had Congress authorize a Force Bill to use the army to enforce the collection of taxes. Jackson talked loudly about hanging his former vice president. Having learned a few things in politics, he also offered some cuts in the tariff. South Carolina backed down, and both sides claimed victory.

War on the Bank of the U.S.

Currently, the U.S. has a Treasury Department that works with independent banks, but when Jackson was president, it had an official Bank of the United States. Jackson hated the national bank because it was tight about loaning money that expansion-minded Americans needed. He abolished the bank and sold Western land to settlers on a low payment plan. When money and good land started to run out, Jackson changed the rules to cash-only. That move burst the real-estate bubble, and the country went into a recession that lasted for years beyond Jackson's presidency (and made voters think twice about tough-guy presidents).

Question: Which event best illustrates Andrew Jackson's idea of expanded democracy?

Answer: Jackson saw the Bank of the U.S. as a rip-off by rich guys (and he wasn't too far off). His abolition of the bank is a great example of his view of expanded democracy.

Watch out for smart-aleck professor questions on Jackson. He marks a turning point in U.S. politics because he's the first president to come from a Western state (Tennessee looked Western back then), and he fought the American Indians, nullification, and the Bank of the United States. Because we teachers like to have our cynical little laughs in the teacher's lounge, we often try to fool you with a multiple-choice question that has Jackson as a founder of the country or in favor of one of the issues he fought. Don't fall for it.

Embracing Modern Conveniences

In the days before today's modern transportation, telephones, and TV, messages and products had to arrive on foot. The Battle of New Orleans took place after the War of 1812 was over — the news of peace was a little slow getting around. You could own the best crops or raw materials in the world, but having stuff wouldn't do you any good if you couldn't get it to where somebody was ready to buy it. In the early days of the U.S., transportation moved as slowly as it had thousands of years ago in the Roman Empire.

Several inventions helped the U.S. grow. In 1838, an Illinois blacksmith named John Deere invented the steel plow, good for helping grow crops. For harvesting crops, Pennsylvania farmer Cyrus McCormick invented a mechanical thresher that did the work of 15 men. A New York painter named Samuel Morse invented the telegraph in 1844, and the world became instantaneously connected. In new factories, the same kind of steam engines that chugged along in boats and trains helped make new jobs.

These inventions changed the world more than battles, bills, or presidents. They're concrete examples of the non-political *themes* that will be the key to your success on the AP U.S. History exam.

Got me a job in the factory

Commuting wasn't really an issue before the Civil War. Most people worked where they lived: down on the farm. Sounds nice now, but back then for a lot of people it was boring and made them a little short on cash. With improved transportation for products and steam power to run machines, factories in New England began making cloth, tools, and guns. For example, the whole town of Lowell, Massachusetts, popped up around a cloth factory that supplied jobs for hundreds of *Lowell girls* who came from farms and immigrant ships beginning in 1813.

Getting ahead 1.0

People chose to work in factories and stores because, hard as the work was, it gave them some freedom to change their lives. Before the Industrial Revolution, most of the money and power belonged to the people who owned land. People were stuck where they were born: lucky landholder or landless farm laborer. The Industrial Revolution gave people the chance to move around, change jobs, and maybe even save up enough money to start a small business. Most poor people stayed poor, but some of them managed to get ahead — in the U.S., no fixed social classes held them back. The Industrial Revolution, with all its pollution and overwork, was the beginning of the American Dream.

Cruising along canals

The Dutch, French, and British all had big canal systems before the American Revolution. The United States was late to the party but made up for it with enthusiasm, beginning in 1825 with the completion of the *Erie Canal* (1825), which connected over 300 miles between the Hudson River in New York and Lake Erie. Between 1825 and 1840 the United States dug more than 3,000 miles of canals. Making an artificial river may not seem that high tech, but canals were a hundred times faster and stronger than trying to get little wagons down muddy and often-frozen dirt roads. Before canals, crops and resources never got far from home; after canals, the idea of a national marketplace emerged.

Churning the sea with steamships

In 1807, American inventor *Robert Fulton* (1810) built the double-paddle-wheeled steamboat *Clermont* which went smoking up the Hudson River from New York way faster than a canal or horse wagon. By the mid-1850s, steamboats driven by large paddle wheels were carrying passengers on all major U.S. rivers. Oceangoing steamships, constructed with strong iron hulls, reduced the time needed to travel to Europe from weeks to days. The *Savannah* in 1819 was the first ship equipped with a steam engine to cross the Atlantic Ocean. By 1838, several steam-powered paddle wheelers were crossing the Atlantic, and in 1840, the first regularly scheduled steamship service began.

Riding the rails

Canals got to be cool for only about 25 years, because railroads were faster and could go anywhere. In 1830, the first little American steam engine pathetically lost a race with a horse. Getting it right didn't take long: By 1840, the U.S. boasted 400 railroads and more miles of track than canal. By the time of the Civil War, America was the railroad leader with close to 30,000 miles of track.

No guns necessary — it's an industrial revolution

Industrial work was a new way of life — not exactly fun, but at least a ticket to town. Men, women, and children worked 12-hour days, six days a week. The first labor unions originated to fight for better working conditions, but that battle took decades to win. Factories made products people wanted, and people made money they needed to buy the products. *Skilled workers* like steam engine builders, printers, and carpenters did much better than the more common *unskilled workers,* who had to take any job they could get and were easy to replace.

The first *Industrial Revolution* in the United States started off, humbly enough, making thread in small water-powered mills at the time of the American Revolution. Fast forward 30 years, and steam-powered factories provided jobs off the farm for around 5 percent of the people. This was the small beginning of the get-ahead capitalist spirit that still drives Americans.

Slavery Grows with Cotton

There was no American Dream during this period, only an endless nightmare for human beings stolen from Africa and forced to work all their lives without pay as slaves. They were beaten, raped, and killed with no protection and no hope for the future; they'd work until they died, and their children were doomed to be slaves like them.

The irony of proclaiming freedom in a land where one out of four people were slaves wasn't lost on the leaders of the American Revolution. The U.S. banned the importation of new slaves from Africa after 1808 and waited for what they called the peculiar institution to go away, much like people now wait for someone else to fix global warming. Slavery was too much a part of the country to deal with right away; eight of the first ten presidents owned slaves. Enslaving people while fighting a revolution for freedom was bad, but then it got worse.

While George Washington was president, a teacher named Eli Whitney invented a cotton engine (*cotton gin* for short) that got the seeds out of cotton balls and allowed Southern plantations to grow 50 times more cotton than they ever had before. Trouble was, without ready labor or machinery, every 10 acres of cotton needed another slave to grow it.

A technical invention like the cotton gin led to millions of people being enslaved, and that growth in slavery plus the social movement of abolition eventually brought about the Civil War, which I discuss more thoroughly in Chapter 13.

Slavery becomes synonymous with power

Slavery became big money; by the Civil War, the U.S. had five times more enslaved people than it did during the Revolution. A slave was worth as much in modern money as an SUV costs today. The slave states had extra political power grandfathered into the Constitution — slaves counted as ⅗ of a person in determining representation for slave states. This kind of power forced careful balancing legislation like the Missouri Compromise outlined earlier; slave state representatives wouldn't even let the subject of abolition come up in Congress. The few slave rebellions like that of Nat Turner in 1831 were put down with devastating force. Most Southern states made it illegal for a slave to learn to read and write.

Waking up to the evil

Northern blacks lived with racism even though they weren't technically slaves. Free blacks had trouble finding jobs, schools, or places to live in the North. Eventually, as ex-slaves learned to write and speak about conditions in the South, they began to gain Northern white supporters. Some highlights:

- *Frederick Douglass* (1850) escaped from slavery in 1838 and wrote his moving life story.
- *Harriet Tubman* (1860) escaped ten years later and went back to help more than 300 other slaves (including her parents) make it safely to freedom.
- Both races worked together on the *Underground Railroad* (1855), sheltering former slaves on the way to freedom.
- *William Lloyd Garrison* (1855), a white newspaper editor, and *Sojourner Truth* (1851), a freed slave woman, both spoke eloquently in support of abolition.

Although most white Southerners were too poor to own slaves, they were willing to fight for slavery anyway. In the North and West, opposition to slavery grew steadily stronger.

Early Emo: Feeling in Art, Education, and Belief

For the first time, ordinary people could learn about culture in free public schools. Before the 1830s, schools were mostly for rich kids — if you wanted to get an education, daddy had to pay. Horace Mann started the common school movement of tax-supported mandatory free education for all children. By the 1850s, every state outside the South had free education and teacher training.

Advances in art and literature

In the 1820s, America got its own art after years of kissing up to Europe as the only seat of real culture. The Hudson River School produced artists like Thomas Cole, who painted man and nature in harmony along the Hudson River in rural upstate New York. George Caitlin painted American Indians in natural settings, and John James Audubon did the same for birds.

The U.S. cut a fine trail in literature as well; James Fenimore Cooper, Washington Irving, Nathaniel Hawthorne, Edgar Allan Poe, Herman Melville, and Henry David Thoreau (among others) wrote influential works during this period that are still popular today.

Transcendentalism and the Second Great Awakening

Henry David Thoreau, author of *Walden,* shared a philosophy with his New England neighbor *Ralph Waldo Emerson:* Transcendentalism. The *Transcendentalists* believed God was an inner voice, leading people to do the right thing and live in harmony with nature, if they'd just listen.

Strong feelings about spirituality were part of the *Second Great Awakening,* which encouraged that religion should be felt as well as thought. (America must have been taking a nap, because even though the country was only a few years old, it was already on its Second Awakening. For the story of the First Awakening in colonial America, see Chapter 9). Evangelists traveled the country speaking at deeply spiritual meetings. This period also saw the birth of Mormonism and the spread of the Methodist church, as well as the beginning of groups devoted to abolition, education, and temperance.

Chapter 12

From Sea to Shining Sea: 1846–1854

In This Chapter

▶ Inventing the future

▶ Riding along on the trail of continental expansion

▶ Seeing how social and cultural changes affect history

▶ Watching the disaster of the Civil War approach

America was bursting at the seams in the 1840s. In one 10-year period, the country suddenly had 35 percent more people, including almost a million immigrants from Ireland and half a million from Germany. The Irish mostly settled in Eastern cities and brought a motivated labor force willing to do a lot of work for low pay. The Irish also expanded Catholic churches and schools, making the mostly Protestant United States stretch to include the Church of Rome into its accepted religious mix. The Germans went straight for the good farmland of the Midwest and brought along the Christmas tree, German beer, opposition to slavery, and support for public education, including kindergarten (a German word).

The population surge was driven by *revolutions in Europe* (1848) and the *potato famine* (1845) in Ireland; people were drawn to the United States by the promise of opportunity. Much of this opportunity was created just by people who were looking for it, especially because the United States needed both workers and consumers, and new inventions were ready to be used.

Social history, like much of the information covered in this chapter, scores points on the big AP exam. Knowing the leaders of the women's-rights and abolition movements, for example, is huge. You're sure to find multiple-choice questions in these areas, and you should be able to work these topics into essay answers. The authors and poets mentioned in this chapter and elsewhere in the book are extra-credit items. The test probably won't have many multiple-choice questions about art, but showing that you know how literature fits into the American story in essays rings college bells. Hint: American literature gets more up-front on issues of race and gender as Americans challenge the conventions they inherited from the Old World.

Changing Lives with New Inventions

Eli Whitney was only getting started when he invented the cotton gin in 1793 (see Chapter 11). He went on to pioneer the concept of *interchangeable-parts manufacturing* (1800) by making identical musket guns with identical parts for the Army. Up till then, guns were handmade, with each part machined to fit only its own rifle. After Whitney had his second bright idea, you could trade triggers or barrels without risking an embarrassing misfire just as the bear was getting ready to eat you. This bright idea led to a surge in inventions and manufacturing that would become prevalent between the mid-1840s and 1850s.

Interchangeable parts supported mass production, which Northern factories had down by the 1850s. Whitney's cotton gin allowed the South to become a rich slave empire and spurred him on to greater inventions. His interchangeable parts allowed the North to become an even richer manufacturing empire, complete with the rifle power the North needed to defeat the Southern slavers in the Civil War. You could say Whitney solved the problem his cotton gin created in the first place.

Producing in mass in factories

The North wasn't just making guns. The *Singer sewing machine* (1846) revolutionized clothes-making; it was the first practical way to sew clothes without making everything by hand. You pumped the first sewing machine with your foot; electricity wasn't available. Even made with interchangeable parts, however, the sewing machine was still expensive. Singer revolutionized the way products were sold by allowing families to buy the new sewing machine on time payments. This system magically linked the first must-have home technology with the first must-pay credit debt. Before the mid-1800s, most purchases had to be made with cash up front.

Mass production also sped the introduction of *the reaper* (1834), which Cyrus McCormick manufactured to allow one man riding on a horse-drawn machine to cut as much wheat as five men swinging the hand scythes that had been the only way to harvest grain since the days of the Romans. This invention allowed the extensive large-scale agriculture that made the Midwest rich. Even an invention as humble as John Deere's *steel plow* (1837) greatly improved food-growing by reliably turning the soil for better crops.

Making electricity useful: Telegraphs

Samuel Morse was the first person to put electricity to work with the invention of the *telegraph* (1844). For the first time, news could travel across the nation in seconds, not weeks. The talking wire drew opinions closer together in the decade before the Civil War. Getting instant feedback may actually have heightened the disagreements between North and South. Morse's telegraph got an international boost with the laying of the Atlantic cable to Britain. The cable broke before the Civil War but was restored permanently right afterward. The telegraph reached the West Coast in 1861.

Making Strides in Transportation

In the early years after the Revolution, you could get out and walk if you didn't like the roads. Or maybe you could swim; early roads turned to giant mud puddles when it rained. Horses and wagons got stuck up to the middle, and drivers would have to crawl through mud to get food to feed the stuck animals while they waited for help. Once in a while, a carriage would just sink out of sight. But highways, canals, and railroads soon came along, allowing farm products to get to big-city markets and urban inventions to get to people everywhere. By the 1850s stagecoaches and the Pony Express crossed the country. Clipper ships sailed the oceans faster than steamships could. The world was getting more and more connected.

Traveling the long and winding road

The first transportation break came with the privately owned *Lancaster Turnpike* (1795), 60 miles of hard-surface road heading west from Philadelphia. In 1811, the federal government began to build the Cumberland (or National) Road from Maryland. By 1852, the road stretched across the old Northwest territory to Illinois and was the beginning of many a wagon train. Most roads were dirt or logs placed side by side (a very bumpy ride). Even city streets were mostly unpaved. During a particularly wet and muddy time in San Francisco, a citizen erected a sign that warned his city street was "not passable, not even jackass-able."

Creating canals

Robert Fulton's pioneering idea of a *steamboat* (1807) on New York's Hudson River (see Chapter 11) proved even more valuable on the great Mississippi. As early as 1820, 60 steamboats regularly traveled on the Mississippi; by the time of the Civil War, the big river had the regular service of 1,000 boats. This type of transportation led to settlement; people could get their crops to market, and the local stores could get manufactured stuff to make life a little easier.

With the beginning of the *Erie Canal* (1817), Americans started to make the rivers come to them. Hooking up to the Hudson River at Albany, the Erie Canal went all the way to the Great Lakes. What used to cost a dollar to ship now cost a nickel. Rocky New England farms couldn't compete with the lush produce of New York and Pennsylvania floating into town on canal boats. New England farmers either moved west to the land along the canal path or worked in growing industries — the first sign of how better transportation could hurt as well as help local producers.

Having made their own rivers with the canals, the states began to get over the need for a water path. The *first railroad* (1828) chugged along three years after the Erie Canal was finished. By 1850, the northern United States was more interconnected by rails than it was by canals. The cotton-growing South started to build late; by the Civil War, the South had just a skeleton of railroads, whereas the North had a spider web. For more about railroads, see Chapter 14.

Dealing with Social Change

With all the freedom and change, sometimes a new idea for utopia seemed to be around every American corner. But these perfect worlds were a little hard to live in — not surprisingly, because *utopia,* from Thomas More's fantasy novel *Utopia* (1516), meant *no place.*

Improved communication brought about by the telegraph and more efficient travel (discussed earlier in this chapter) didn't always lead to improved understanding. The South saw strengthened trading ties along the Mississippi and across the Atlantic as economic insurance that outsiders would have to allow slavery to continue to support Northern and British profits. Difficult as perfection was to achieve, however, people in the United States kept moving in what they saw as the right direction.

Doing the right thing

Here are some of the major social movements that started in the mid 1800s:

- The first women's rights conference was held in Seneca Falls, New York, in 1848.
- The first large labor unions started in the 1840s.
- *Dorothea Dix* (1845) published reports that led to so many reforms in mental institutions that she was made superintendent of nurses for the Union Army during the Civil War. Women and men worked to reform treatment of prisoners and the mentally ill.
- *Neal Dow* (1851) got a prohibition law passed in Maine and ten other states; these laws were rescinded when the stress of fighting the Civil War made lots of people need a drink.
- Utopian communities were established in several places in the U.S. Named for Thomas More's novel, utopian communities tried to build happy places to live and work by creating a new social structure. Among the hopeful utopias were

  - *New Harmony* (1825). On the Wabash River in southern Indiana, New Harmony produced limited perfect community but lots of education. The progress of entomology, geology, and the Smithsonian Institution in Washington are all associated with this attempt by Welsh industrialist Robert Owen to build a better world.

  - *Brook Farm* (1841) near Boston had a literary influence from authors like Henry Thoreau and Nathaniel Hawthorne. They were better at writing than at farming.

  - *The Oneida Community* (1848) in New York practiced community marriage and shared jobs and child raising. Although the commune broke up, the members went on to found Oneida Silver, one of the largest silverware companies in the world.

  - *Mother Ann Lee of the Shakers* (1840) at one time inspired 19 different communities making furniture and other housewares that are still in demand. Since Shakers didn't have children, they've largely died out. The Shaker song "Simple Gifts" is still sung to remind people of quiet peace.

Moving from farm to factory

Life wasn't all domestic bliss, of course. Thousands of hungry workers shifted from job to job and city to city. Workers were needed almost everywhere during the fast-growing 1840s and 1850s; they were rewarded with wages that grew slowly but steadily.

Factory owners tried to meet increased demand and improve their incomes by working factory employees for 13 or 14 hours a day. Unions weren't legally allowed to organize until the 1840s, and the "easy" 10-hour day, long fought by employers, slowly started to be accepted.

The willingness of single men to do whatever it took to earn a living and support the nation without turning into a mob was a key reason the United States grew so much during this time. Peaceful, willing workers without families — an often-overlooked strength of any society — made up half the labor force.

Going to school: Public education and one-room schoolhouses

Public schools were growing against a very real backlash among people who thought education was wrong, at least if they had to pay for it.

As late as 1860, the United States had only about 100 real high schools. Education got a boost from *Noah Webster* (1828), whose reading lessons and dictionary taught Americanism as well as letters. *McGuffey's Readers* (1850) taught patriotism along with language and were used all over the country for 100 years. *Horace Mann* (1850) established the model for free public education that eventually spread across the country.

Don't confuse Noah Webster (1758–1843), the teacher and dictionary-maker, with Daniel Webster (1782–1852), legendary congressman and leader of national compromise. Noah brought people together with a common approach to language; Daniel tried to keep the Union together with common laws. Noah got his name on almost every American dictionary; Daniel wasn't around to see his compromise laws fall apart in the years before the Civil War.

As the country expanded, public education was a proud part of most new settlements. The little red one-room schoolhouse got its start teaching farm kids the three *R*s: reading, 'riting, and 'rithmetic. All the grades were in one room, and some kids could spare only a few months to learn in between helping out with the crops.

Oberlin College (1837) in Ohio was the first college to admit women and blacks; Ohio's *Antioch College* (1852) had the first female faculty member. The fact that Oberlin College's second president was the famous Great Awakening preacher *Charles Finney* (1840) (a committed abolitionist, early champion of women's rights, and the most powerful revivalist in an age of renewed faith) and Antioch's first president was Unitarian educator Horace Mann demonstrates the connection between religious revival and social action at that time.

Expanding religious diversity

In 1850, three out of four Americans attended church every Sunday. The idea that one sect contained all the special people and that everyone else was going to hell had loosened up as the United States learned to live with many different denominations. The Enlightenment-inspired founding fathers hadn't been all that big on religion, but they — and members of new American movements like the Unitarians, Transcendentalists, and Mormons — certainly did believe that spiritual and material life could be improved right here on Earth.

The *Second Great Awakening* (1830), a powerful nationwide spiritual movement put the emphasis on salvation through personal change (see Chapter 9 for information on the First Great Awakening). Both the spirit of the movement and the connections that people made at tent meetings helped found several middle-class movements, often led by women, including those for temperance, prison, asylum reform, abolition, and women's rights. Methodists, Baptists, Mormons, and members of other new religions gained strength, and members of America's first religions, such as the Congregationalists and Anglicans (see Chapter 11), loosened up. The Second Great Awakening stressed *perfectionism*, the belief that free will can create a better life on Earth. Free will Perfectionism encouraged reform movements and was directly opposed to the original Puritan belief in predestination.

Question: Why was the belief in perfectionism important in the Second Great Awakening?

Answer: Perfectionism supported social movements, presented the idea that free will could improve life, and marked a departure from the Puritan belief in predestination.

Question: What were the social movements that came out of the Second Great Awakening?

Answer: The women's-rights, antislavery, temperance, and education movements were all supported by middle-class women coming out of the Second Great Awakening.

The notion of predestination (see Chapter 8) faded away in favor of emotional activism. Middle-class women were enthusiastic revivalists, charged up by spiritual services and the community of believers. Their awakened talents helped spur both religious and social causes. No social cause received more attention than slavery. By 1845, the issue of slavery split national denominations like the Methodist and Baptist churches into Northern and Southern branches. First the churches split, then the political parties, and finally the nation.

Earning Expanded Roles for Women

Women didn't get much education in the early days beyond what you would need to make a shopping trip. Male physicians said that too much learning could injure the female brain. By 1850, around 20 percent of all women had worked outside the home by the time they were married. After they were married, women didn't work; they were locked inside the household. Women seemed to be trapped on a pedestal: They were supposed to be more morally refined than men but were limited to being the keepers of families. They got some input on social responsibility with the *cult of domesticity (*1850), which held that, by being virtuous, women could change the world through their families.

Gaining control of their own lives

Of little breakthroughs is freedom made. Under the belief in *republican motherhood* (1780) at the time of the Revolution (see Chapter 9), women were valued as teachers of children, especially the sons who were needed for the new democracy. With the cult of domesticity, however, women began to use their power as queens of the household to make decisions about things that mattered outside the family as well. They gained more power to plan children and choose their own mates; families arranged fewer marriages.

Question: What were the positive benefits of the cult of domesticity for women?

Answer: American women gained power from the 1700s to 1860 as they moved from republican motherhood to the cult of domesticity. Changes in women's rights over this time included their own choice of husbands, activism outside the home, and more control over childbearing.

Women were often factory workers, and they participated in early union activities. As public education spread in the 1840s, the hitherto male profession of teaching began to admit some females. Women could also work as cooks or maids. About one Northern family in ten was rich enough to pay a domestic servant to help with the housework.

Women had only half as many children during the 1800s as during the 1700s; family planning was beginning to take hold. Couples used timing and early barrier methods to keep from getting pregnant. These methods had been passed down for hundreds of years; in the mid-1800s, women just got more assertive about using them. With fewer children, mothers could spend more time rearing their kids. The idea of helping children develop began to take hold; parents no longer just survived the rugrats until they could be sent out into the fields.

Founding women's rights

As women got some power, they wanted more. *Lucretia Mott* and *Susan B. Anthony* were Quakers who stood up for women's rights. Mott fought for women and abolition from the 1820s until after the Civil War, and Anthony carried the movement into the 1900s. *Elizabeth Cady Stanton* was a mother of seven who insisted, with the full support of her husband, on leaving the word *obey* out of her marriage ceremony. Stanton and Mott were leaders of the groundbreaking *Seneca Falls Convention* (1848), which proclaimed the rights of women. Seneca Falls was the first meeting of women to adopt a program designed to lead to votes for women. The Convention's Declaration of Sentiments echoed the U.S. Declaration of Independence.

Watching the Arts Bloom

Art defines a culture, and culture is a pretty good predictor of the actions people will take. In the 1800s, the United States developed a national culture of music and writing that helped the young country identify its own character.

Stephen Foster and the American songbook

Stephen Foster (1850) was one of the most popular composers in American history and the only songwriter to try to make a living from the art until modern times. He wrote "Oh! Susanna," "Camptown Races," "My Old Kentucky Home," "Beautiful Dreamer," and "Old Folks at Home (Swanee River)" — songs so popular 150 years after their composition that an album of them won a Grammy award in 2005.

Showing how thoroughly mixed American culture was on the eve of the nation's tearing itself apart in the Civil War, Foster wrote about the South but was from the North. The man who wrote the music used in the North's "Battle Hymn of the Republic" was from South Carolina. "Dixie," the theme song of the South, was written in New York City by a Northerner.

The rise of American literature

American literature came onto its own with the increased popularity of Henry Wadsworth Longfellow, Walt Whitman, Ralph Waldo Emerson, and many others:

- Emerson was a giant of American letters for almost 50 years. His *Transcendentalist* (1840) philosophy stressed self-reliance and personal spiritual unity.

- Emerson's friend and colleague Henry David Thoreau wrote *Walden* (1854), about man's connection to nature, and *On the Duty of Civil Disobedience* (1849), a book that influenced Mahatma Gandhi and Martin Luther King Jr.

- Walt Whitman wrote *Leaves of Grass* (1855), which broke down the conventions of poetry with bold language:

   "Fresh and strong the world we seize, world of labor and the march,
   Pioneers! O Pioneers!"

- *Henry Wadsworth Longfellow* (1850) was an American poet who was also widely popular in Europe. He wrote "Paul Revere's Ride," "A Psalm of Life," "The Song of Hiawatha," "Evangeline," and "Christmas Bells."

- *John Greenleaf Whittier* (1838) was a poet of human freedom who stood up to angry mobs for the abolition of slavery.

- Louisa May Alcott showed the man-centered Victorian world that women can write beautifully with *Little Women* (1868).

- *Emily Dickinson* (1870) showed the universality of even a quiet human heart with more than 1,000 poems published after her death.

Not all writers saw much good in human beings. All these darker writers served a good purpose in helping the world see that good and evil are never pure and that living well means making moral choices every day:

- *Edgar Allan Poe* (1845) lived on the dark side of madness and evil with stories like "The Fall of the House of Usher" and poems like "The Raven."

- ✔ Nathaniel Hawthorne wrote *The Scarlet Letter* (1850), about a woman who had a secret affair with a minister, bore his child out of wedlock, and had to wear a scarlet *A* for adultery.

- ✔ Herman Melville's *Moby-Dick* (1851), one of the greatest American novels, tells the story of a sea captain's obsessive hunt for a great white whale.

Painting began to show the beauty of the American landscape. The Hudson River School, active from 1850 to 1875, painted dramatic American landscapes, especially featuring the Hudson River area in northern New York. This movement made more people stop to appreciate the wonders of nature.

Question: What was the Hudson River School of painting?

Answer: The Hudson River School painted dramatic American landscapes, especially featuring the Hudson River area in northern New York.

Understanding Early Ethnic Group Issues

As a nation started on the ringing words of freedom, the United States was never proud of slavery, even though many of its founding fathers owned slaves. Like a bad habit you mean to give up next year, slavery just kept getting bigger and harder to shake. Opposition to the peculiar institution (as slavery was politely called) grew in the North, which didn't have any slaves. In the South, it was considered too profitable to be publicly debated.

A similar moral double standard affected grabbing land from American Indians and foreign governments. What started out as 13 states grateful for their own freedom turned into a continent-wide rush for more territory. See Chapters 10 and 11 for more information.

The *Indian Removal Act* (1830) provided federal assistance to move more than 100,000 American Indians from their ancestral homes east of the Mississippi to the specially created Indian Territory in what's now Oklahoma. The government was supposed to supply food and transportation help with the forced migration, but many died on the long trek.

In the *Trail of Tears* (1838), 17,000 Cherokee were forced to travel 1,200 miles to Oklahoma from their homes in Georgia. More than 4,000 of the American Indians died in concentration camps or on the trail itself. In the southern U.S., the Choctaw, Creek, Chickasaw, and Seminole tribes were relocated in addition to the Cherokee. In the north, evicted tribes included the Shawnees, Ottawas, Potawatomis, Sauks, and Foxes. Chief Black Hawk led American Indians back to their homes in Illinois to fight for their land, but they were defeated by the army.

Expansion by war occurred with the *Mexican-American War* (1846). Texas gained independence from Mexico in 1835 and joined the United States in 1845. With the excuse of a border dispute and the real desire for more land, the U.S. declared war on Mexico in 1846. After some tough fighting, the U.S. defeated Mexico and in 1849 got California and all of the Southwest.

Irish, Polish, and Italian immigrants weren't always welcomed by all the people in the land of the free. The Know-Nothing Party campaigned against Catholic immigration in the 1850s. Signs for jobs often said, "No Irish Need Apply". When Irish workers hungry for jobs replaced striking women textile employees in New England, prejudice against the new immigrants soared. Italian and Polish immigrants often spent generations living in ethnically segregated communities. In the years before the Civil War, multi-ethnic neighborhoods and towns were rare.

Question: How did textile mill owners inflame prejudice against the Irish?

Answer: New England textile mills replaced striking local workers with Irish immigrants.

The economics of slavery

Northern ships carried Southern cotton to market in Britain and New England. To a large degree, the extra profits of merchants in all parts of the United States before the Civil War depended on the crushing work of slaves.

Cotton represented half the value of all U.S. exports in the years before the Civil War. The profits of slave labor didn't stop at the border: About one of five jobs in Britain was tied to manufacturing cotton cloth, most of it from raw cotton grown in the American South. Southerners assumed that Britain would have to support them in any break with the North to keep Britain's vital supply of cotton raw materials coming.

Thomas Jefferson, slaveholder, said this about slavery: "The whole commerce between master and slave is a perpetual exercise of . . . despotism on the one part and degrading submissions on the other. . . . I tremble for my country when I reflect that God is just; that his justice cannot sleep forever." People often see more than a little moral disconnect between Jefferson's proclamations against slavery and the fact that he kept slaves. Sadly Jefferson — a good president but a poor businessman — couldn't free his slaves in his will. He had mortgaged them to get enough money to live on.

Fewer than 2,000 families in the South owned more than 100 slaves. Three of four families owned no slaves at all. Because the South was basically a one-crop economy, even large landowners could suffer reversals when that crop did poorly.

The South was at the mercy of the North for basic manufactured supplies; even cotton clothing came from New England. Most immigrants avoided the South so they wouldn't have to compete with slave labor on the one hand and rich landowners on the other. That situation left the South short of new blood and any kind of cheap labor except slavery.

Even slavery could be a money-loser. A slave cost as much as $80,000 in modern money. If slave traders missed the market or some of their charges died, they were in trouble fast. Economically as well as morally, the slavery/cotton empire was a bet with the devil. It continued to be very profitable right up to the time of the Civil War, but it was a house of cards.

In a seeming paradox, some of the strongest supporters of slavery were the small Southern farmers who owned no slaves. On closer examination, this situation is no paradox at all. The small farmers had someone to look down on in the slaves who lived around them and a shallow brotherhood of white people with their richer neighbors. The poor whites could look forward to the day when they could get ahead enough to turbocharge their earnings by buying a slave or two. It was a sick application of the American dream of upward mobility.

Problems faced by free blacks of the era

About 250,000 free blacks lived in the South and another 250,000 in the North. Blacks gained freedom through Northern emancipation laws and the occasional goodwill of Southern owners; their children were then free as well. They were in a precarious position. Free blacks couldn't testify in court. If they were assaulted by whites, unless other whites showed up to defend them (which was rare), the blacks never got justice. In the South, they were in constant danger of being kidnapped into slavery. In the North, mobs of poor Irish and other immigrants who resented the competition from free blacks for low-wage jobs often beat them up. Blacks couldn't go to most white schools, stores, or churches. Frederick Douglass, the distinguished black abolitionist, was beaten by Northern rowdies more than once.

Question: How did some blacks become free before the Civil War?

Answer: The number of free blacks in the United States grew because Northern states ended slavery, some Southern slaveholders freed their slaves after the Revolution or in their wills, and freed blacks had children who were then themselves free.

Blacks fought for their own freedom whenever they could. They didn't have much opportunity to fight back; slaves were guarded and whipped for the slightest infraction. Informant slaves who brought news of any trouble were rewarded and potential troublemakers punished without mercy. Even walking on the road at night could spell death to a black man who didn't have a ready excuse. Despite these barriers, at least 11 slave revolts were attempted from colonial times to the Civil War:

✔ In 1800, an armed insurrection in Richmond led by a tall, strong blacksmith slave named Gabriel was foiled by informants. Gabriel had carefully planned to take Virginia's governor (later president) James Monroe hostage and ask for freedom for slaves in the name of the American Revolution. He was questioned under torture but refused to submit. He, two of his brothers, and 24 others were hanged. After Gabriel's bid for freedom, Virginia kept slaves under tight surveillance.

In 2007, Virginia governor Tim Kaine informally pardoned Gabriel and his co-conspirators. The modern governor said that Gabriel's motivation had been "his devotion to the ideals of the American Revolution; it was worth risking death to secure liberty." The governor noted that "Gabriel's cause — the end of slavery and the furtherance of equality of all people — has prevailed in the light of history." He added, "It is important to acknowledge that history favorably regards Gabriel's cause while consigning legions who sought to keep him and others in chains to be forgotten."

✔ In 1822, Denmark Vesey, who had managed to buy his freedom after winning a city lottery, was within days of launching a revolt that could have included more than 1,000 slaves in Charleston. Vesey had been able to plan the revolt because he was a free black who worked as a carpenter. He had tried to live with whites, but he was angry because they had repeatedly closed the black church he had helped start. Betrayed by frightened slaves, Vesey and more than 30 of his followers were hanged. Vesey's son survived to reopen the black church after the Civil War.

✔ Nat Turner was a black slave who could read and who served as a preacher. He had visions that told him to fight for freedom, and in 1831, he led a rebellion of at least 100 slaves in Virginia. The slaves fought for 2 days, killing around 60 white civilians, before they were defeated by an overwhelming force of soldiers, sailors, and militiamen who rushed in from all directions.

After the battle, Virginia actually debated proposals to end slavery but decided to go the other way instead. The state forbade teaching a slave to read and instituted regular slave patrols that stopped any blacks found on the roads.

Abolition in the North

The movement for the abolition of slavery began with calls for freedom from Quakers and Mennonites before the Revolution. An American Colonization Society was formed in 1817 to send blacks back to their now-forgotten home; a few years later, the society founded the Republic of Liberia on the west coast of Africa.

In 1832, a rare group of people got together at Lane Theological Seminary in Cincinnati and held an 18-day debate on slavery. They included Theodore Weld, who had been evangelized by Charles Finney, the same Great Awakening preacher who would go on to be president of Oberlin College. Based on what he learned from slaves just across the river from Cincinnati in Kentucky, Weld wrote *American Slavery As It Is* (1839). He greatly influenced a young lady whose father was the head of the seminary.

That young lady was Harriet Beecher Stowe, and she would go on to write the best-selling novel of the 1800s: *Uncle Tom's Cabin* (1852). That book burst upon society like a star shell, lighting up thinking all over the North. It sold more than 300,000 copies in its first year. Watching thousands of stage productions in every little town in the North, people in the audience gasped as Eliza carried her son across the shifting river ice to freedom and cried at the death of kindly Uncle Tom. Showing the power of an idea whose time has come, *Uncle Tom's Cabin* crystallized opposition to slavery in the North. For more information about *Uncle Tom's Cabin,* see Chapter 13.

On New Year's Day 1831, uncompromising publisher William Lloyd Garrison, another spiritual child of the Great Awakening, launched the antislavery newspaper *The Liberator.* He said, "I will be as harsh as truth and as uncompromising as justice." The cause soon had black heroes:

✔ Sojourner Truth, a freed black woman in New York, fought for both emancipation and women's rights.

✔ Frederick Douglass, an eloquent escaped slave, wrote his early life story in *Narrative of the Life of Frederick Douglass* (1845). He went on to be a respected spokesman for blacks through the Civil War and for years after.

Question: Who was William Lloyd Garrison?

Answer: Garrison was the uncompromising abolitionist who founded the antislavery newspaper *The Liberator.*

Abolitionists were beaten, burned out of their houses, and sometimes killed, but they didn't back down. At first, wise politicians like Abraham Lincoln avoided them, but by the 1850s their cause was beginning to be accepted in the North. With the birth of the Republican Party in 1854, that cause found a national voice. See Chapter 13 for more information on the rise of abolition.

Acquiring More Land for America

Destiny hadn't finished manifesting itself at the beginning of the 1840s, but after that, the United States picked up a lot of land in a short time. First came the lumberjack battles in northern Maine called the *Aroostook* War (1842). These battles were settled with the British masters of Canada in a way that left Maine with plenty of north woods, Canada with room to build a winter road to Quebec, and the U.S. with the nice surprise of major iron deposits in Minnesota.

As outlined earlier, Texas won its independence from Mexico in 1836, but between then and 1845, Texans had to cool their heels down on the border while Congress debated whether to admit Texas as a slave state. In 1845, Texas switched from being the Lone Star Republic to being the 28th star in the American flag. Mexico couldn't stand the transition of their former territory to the United States and war broke out soon after.

One of Andrew Jackson's last political acts was recommending his friend and neighbor James Polk as the Democratic presidential nominee in 1844. Polk was victorious over a terminally frustrated Henry Clay and efficiently carried out his four-point presidential agenda: lower tariffs, establish an independent treasury, grab California, and settle the Oregon border.

Polk got legislation to lower the tariffs and restore an independent treasury. Then he went to work on grabbing California and the Oregon Territory. In 1846, the British settled the Oregon Territory question by splitting the difference with the United States on the northern border of what became the state of Washington.

California looked beautiful even before gold was discovered in 1848. Its inhabitants included around 13,000 Mexicans, 1,000 Americans more or less poaching on Mexican territory, and 100,000 American Indians. Polk managed to stir up a border incident with an angry Mexico down on the Rio Grande in Texas, and the Mexican-American War was under way in 1846. The war was unpopular in New England; Henry David Thoreau spent a night in jail to protest it.

Most of the rest of the country was spoiling to finish off Manifest Destiny with a good fight. The renegade Americans in California seized the province, aided by Captain John Fremont, who just happened to be in the neighborhood with an armed patrol.

An American army fought its way into Mexico City by September 1847. Mexico reluctantly signed the *Treaty of Guadalupe Hidalgo* (1848), turning over an area that amounted to about a third of the United States in exchange for $18 million (offered rather guiltily by the United States). When the treaty was signed, neither side knew that gold, ultimately worth billions of dollars, had been discovered 9 days earlier on the American River in California.

Sliding Closer to Civil War

An enormous new piece of the United States meant an enormous fight over whether it would be slave or free. Almost all the free states passed resolutions called the *Wilmot Proviso* (1846), an anti-slavery move calling for all the new land to be admitted as free states. This contentious amendment easily passed the U.S. House of Representatives but couldn't get through the carefully balanced Senate.

Question: What was the first resolution to split the North and South on the slavery issue?

Answer: The Wilmot Proviso of 1846 was the first purely sectional vote (which never passed) to block extending slavery to territory acquired from Mexico.

Politically, the South was fighting with its back to the wall. The free-state population now far outnumbered that of slave states, even with the three-fifths provision for nonvoting slaves (see Chapter 10). Therefore, the North had more votes in the House, and if more free states were admitted, it soon would have more votes in the Senate as well. The South couldn't back down.

Meanwhile, hatred for slavery had reached the point in the North at which many people couldn't stand the thought of creating another state under the grip of slaveholders. The Mexican land was becoming a gigantic poison pill for compromise in the Union.

In the election of 1848, the Whigs ran a hero of the Mexican-American War, Gen. Zachary Taylor. Taylor had no political liabilities, having never held public office or, for that matter, even voted in a presidential election. The Democrats ran an old veteran of the War of 1812 who believed in *popular sovereignty* (1850), the principle of letting the people of any territory decide whether they wanted the territory to be slave or free.

Question: What is popular sovereignty?

Answer: Popular sovereignty allowed local voters to choose whether their state would be slave or free.

A new Free Soil Party came out squarely against the extension of slavery to even one more square inch of the United States. The Free Soilers diverted enough votes from the Democrats to elect Zachary Taylor of the Whig party. Taylor hadn't made any speeches about slavery during the election, but he was a slaveholding plantation owner from Louisiana. That was enough to attract most Southern votes.

With the discovery of gold, California rushed toward statehood as a free state. The territory had plenty of people, had written its own constitution, and was ready to more than pay for itself. But if California were admitted, the balance in the Senate would swing to a majority for the nonslave states.

The Southerners were also stressing about the issue of runaway slaves. They had plenty to be steamed about:

- *Harriet Tubman* (1849), a fearless runaway slave, had helped rescue more than 300 other slaves from the South, including her aging parents.
- The *Underground Railroad* (1850), a series of safe houses and hiding places for escaping slaves, was helping a small number of slaves escape. The total number of slaves who made it North in a year was around 1,000 — a small loss to freedom from a slave population of 4 million.

The South was also steamed about the North's nonstop campaign to outlaw slavery in the nation's capital, Washington, D.C. The South was whirling around, looking for a fight almost as though it had a guilty conscience.

The Compromise of 1850

The situation didn't come to fighting yet. Most Northerners in 1850 were willing to let slavery remain in the South, as long as it didn't spread to other states. The old peacemakers of the Congress, Henry Clay (73), Daniel Webster, and Southerner John Calhoun (both 68), cobbled together the *Compromise of 1850*. They'd been working tirelessly to hold the nation together for 40 years, but now they were running out of time, both in their own lives and in the lifespan of compromise. Some highlights of the compromise:

- The North got California as a free state, finally tipping the balance toward free-state votes in the Senate.
- The slave trade, but not slavery itself, was outlawed in Washington, D.C.
- New Mexico and Arizona could join the Union under popular sovereignty by deciding to be slave states if they wanted to.

The big Southern win in the Compromise of 1850 was the *Fugitive Slave Law,* which allowed slaves who had escaped to the North to be grabbed by federal marshals and dragged back

South in chains. When a Boston runaway slave was dragged off in 1854, the shocking scene made previously peaceful compromisers into instant abolitionists.

> Question: What was the most common Northern position on slavery in 1850?
>
> Answer: For most Northerners in 1850, slavery could remain in the South as long as it didn't spread.
>
> Question: What was the most pro-slavery part of the Compromise of 1850?
>
> Answer: The Fugitive Slave Law allowed escaped slaves in the North to be returned to the South.

The Fugitive Slave Law was a public-relations disaster for the South, delivered in spite over a few slaves. The South became even more spiteful when Northern states refused to enforce the law.

Democrat Franklin Pierce won the presidency in 1852 and pledged to enforce the Fugitive Slave Law. This election was the end of the road for the Whigs; they had too many abolitionists to do well in the South and not enough antislavery zeal to win the North.

The South looked desperately for new slave-state territory, even sending military expeditions to Central America and Cuba; these expeditions were easily beaten back, to the embarrassment of the United States. The United States tossed another $10 million Mexico's way for a chunk of desert containing Tucson, which made a good route for a railroad west if you wanted to build it from the South.

Stephen Douglas and the Kansas-Nebraska Act

Stephen Douglas, senator from Illinois, wanted the western railroad to go from the North (specifically, from his state's big city, Chicago). To do this, the United States would have to organize the Nebraska Territory that the railroad would run across. The South wasn't going to settle for any more free states, but the Missouri Compromise said that slavery was banned from Nebraska.

Douglas, a Northerner from Abe Lincoln's home state, proposed that the compromise be disregarded and the Nebraska territory opened to popular sovereignty. That could mean that Kansas, due west of slaveholding Missouri, would become a new slave state. Over angry opposition from the North, Douglas rammed the *Kansas-Nebraska Act* (1854) through Congress, doing away with the Missouri Compromise.

The Kansas-Nebraska Act was a self-defeating victory for the South. The North felt betrayed: The Missouri Compromise clearly said that there would be no slavery in the Nebraska territory, but now Southerners were flooding into Kansas to claim it for the South. The North hadn't liked the Compromise of 1850 in the first place; from now on, they would openly ignore it.

A new political party sprang up spontaneously in 1854 in the Midwest to fight against slavery. Within two years, the Republican Party would have enough strength to elect the speaker of the House of Representatives. The compromises were over.

Chapter 13

Fighting to the Death over Slavery: 1855–1865

• •

In This Chapter

▶ Understanding the causes of the Civil War

▶ Marching with the troops through horrendous battles

▶ Seeing the political, economic, and social background of the Civil War

• •

*T*he Civil War was four years of brutal fighting with clear a cause and bravery on each side. The first cuts of the Civil War were delivered with medieval broadswords near a peaceful river in Kansas, a thousand miles from the debates in Washington. The political decision that made the war inevitable came not from the divided Congress or the compromising president, but from the one place where the South had complete control: the Supreme Court.

When John Brown and his sons hacked five Southern slavery advocates to death in 1856, Northerners showed that at least some of them would shed blood to defeat slavery after the court blew the cracked lid off the Missouri Compromise of 1820, which had bought time by dividing the country into slave and non-slave sections (see Chapter 11). With the 1857 Dred Scott decision (discussed later in this chapter), middle-of-the-road peacemakers no longer had a place to meet. When the new Republican Party elected a worried-but-determined anti-slavery president in 1860, Southern guns were already being moved into position.

Although the political, economic, and social focus of the AP exam limits your need to know the Civil War's specific battles, you may be asked about the *causes* of the Civil War. Well, duh — slavery, of course. Also be sure to mention the political impact of the polarizing 1860 election, the economic influence of cotton profits, and the social dynamic of Northern immigrants wanting more free land in the West. Most of all, the growing Northern population threatened to swamp the South with more voters and more free states. In this chapter, I cover this information in more detail to give you the basic information you need to know.

How Reading Led to Fighting

In 1852, author Harriet Beecher Stowe had a hit on her hands. *Uncle Tom's Cabin,* about the plight of a Southern slave, was the most popular book in the United States. *Uncle Tom's Cabin* (1852) was a best seller not only in the United States but also in England and France and the best-selling novel of the entire 1800s. One copy of the book was in print for almost every voter in the North; *Uncle Tom* was banned in the South.

The impact of *Uncle Tom's Cabin*

What made Stowe's book so powerful? *Uncle Tom's Cabin* (1852) put a human face on slaves for the first time in literary history. Most people don't like to see other people suffer. The way Americans coped with the cruelty of slavery was to pretend, without thinking too hard, that slaves were work animals without feelings. In *Uncle Tom's Cabin,* the slaves have names, families, hopes, and spiritual souls. Uncle Tom is never the kiss-up that his name has come to signify in modern times; he stands up for his beliefs and his friends even though he doesn't have the power to fight back physically against the slave masters.

Tom is an older Christian slave separated from his wife and children when his master falls on hard times and is forced to sell Tom down the river to a life of hard labor and punishment on a cotton plantation in the Deep South. A slave mother belonging to Tom's master who is about to have her son torn away from her manages to run north to freedom, carrying her son across the dangerously shifting ice of the Ohio River. On his way south, Tom saves a 6-year-old white girl named Eva from drowning. Eva's family buys Tom. By the time young Eva dies of natural causes several years later, she and Tom have developed a faith in goodwill that inspires everyone around them. Eventually, Tom is sold to an evil slave owner named Simon Legree. When Tom refuses to tell about two slaves who have escaped from the plantation, Legree has Tom beaten to death. Like Christ on the cross, as Tom is being killed, he forgives the slave drivers who are whipping him. The slaves who escaped from Legree meet the slaves who escaped from Tom's first master in Canada and realize they're all from the same family. Moved by Tom's story, the son of Tom's first master frees all his slaves.

Part of the power of *Uncle Tom's Cabin* for contemporary audiences came from readers' feeling that they were learning the truth about the taboo subject of slave life. The subtitle of the book is *Life among the Lowly,* making the cause sound plaintive and nonthreatening. The main title is a poem in three words. *Cabin* is the humble home familiar to all Americans; several U.S. presidents benefited in elections because they'd been born in log cabins. *Tom* is as simple as any male name; it was the name of both Thomas Jefferson and Thomas Didymus, a disciple of Christ. *Tom* incorporates the *ohm* sound used in meditation and as part of *Amen;* the name means *twin* in Latin and Greek. *Uncle* is a favorite relative, kindly without having to carry the emotional baggage of a mother or father.

Uncle Tom's Cabin followed the format of then-popular writing called *domestic* or *women's fiction;* it could have been a hit even if it didn't have so much meaning. It was as though a James Bond movie featured a suffering yet kindly alien who unites society and, with his death, saves the world from global warming.

The book had even more impact because *Uncle Tom's Cabin* was the first novel many people had ever read: Literacy was just becoming common for average people due to the growth in public schools. It would also be the last book many young Northerners read before they went off to enlist in the Union Army. The book not only helped start the war but also helped win it by causing Europeans to side with the North.

Because of the popularity of the book in Britain and France, those governments were morally afraid to intervene on the side of the South. The book was translated into languages around the world, including Chinese. Stowe had a simple answer when asked how her book came about. "God wrote it," she said.

People didn't even have to read the book to get the message; Tom appeared in thousands of plays performed in every Northern town before the Civil War. The message was so popular that *Uncle Tom's Cabin* was still in theaters during the 1900s, 50 years after the Civil War.

Another book, *The Impending Crisis of the South* (1857), written by middle-class Southerner Hinton Helper, argued that slavery was bad for the Southerners who didn't own slaves. The book was banned in the South but used by the Republicans in the North as campaign publicity. Southerners were fighting mad about exposés they considered to be falsely libelous.

Question: Why was *Uncle Tom's Cabin* important?

Answer: The book turned Northern opinion firmly against slavery.

Turning Words to Bullets in Bleeding Kansas

After the *Kansas-Nebraska Act* (1854) opened new territory for settlement, with popular sovereignty deciding whether the states to be formed would be slave or free, settlers poured into Kansas (see Chapter 12). Most of the Northern settlers just wanted land, but they included some well-armed partisans who were ready to fight to make Kansas a free state.

The South sent tough gangs of men to raid Northern settlements and fix elections with the goal of making Kansas a slave state. Northerners fought back, and the resulting sporadic violence won the area the name *Bleeding Kansas* from 1854 to the beginning of the Civil War in 1861.

For several years, Kansas lived under the proslavery *Lecompton Constitution* (1857), a railroaded partisan document forced through by crooked votes and supported by the U.S. president but not accepted by Congress.

Responding to raids by proslavery Southern bands, militant abolitionist John Brown and his sons brutally killed five Southern sympathizers in 1856 (see the discussion on John Brown later in this chapter). Brown wasn't arrested and continued to lead antislavery defenders in pitched battles with Southern forces. Although plenty of property destruction and beatings occurred, fewer than 60 people were killed during the years of Bleeding Kansas.

Having let the genie out of the bottle by pushing through the Kansas-Nebraska Act, Senator Stephen Douglas threw away Southern support for the Democratic Party in general and for his presidential campaign in particular by insisting on real popular sovereignty for Kansas. Douglas was from Illinois, like Abraham Lincoln, but he was willing to compromise on slavery. That made him a popular opponent, but Lincoln beat him in the presidential election of 1860.

Violence even reached the Senate floor when a Southern congressman named Preston Brooks beat abolitionist Senator Charles Sumner almost to death in 1856 over a virulent speech Sumner made against Southern-sponsored Kansan "hirelings picked from the drunken spew and vomit of an uneasy civilization." For some reason, that speech made Southerners mad. Outrage over the beating of Sumner contributed to the growth of his antislavery Republican Party in the North.

In the end, Kansas settlers were allowed to vote in a fair election in which they supported a free-state constitution by a margin of two to one. The territory never had more than a few slaves; no slave owner would risk his valuable property on such dangerous ground. Kansas was admitted to the Union after the beginning of the Civil War and was the scene of raids and reprisals by both sides during the war. Kansas contributed more than its share of volunteers to the Union Army.

The Dred Scott Decision

In the presidential election of 1856, the Democrats cast around for someone nobody knew enough about to hate and came up with James "Old Buck" Buchanan, who had been out of the country serving as ambassador to Britain. Buchanan beat John Fremont, the first presidential candidate of the new Republican Party.

Had Fremont won, the Civil War would have been off to an early start. Fremont believed in action and was so antislavery that he had to be recalled as a Union general during the Civil War for freeing slaves prematurely. He could have created so much animosity that the North may have let the South leave peacefully. Buchanan generally supported slavery and its extension to the territories under popular sovereignty, so the South stayed put during most of his presidency. He couldn't have done much else to save the Union, though; sectional conflict was barreling down the tracks like a runaway freight train.

As he took the oath of office, Buchanan was looking forward to the Supreme Court's decision on the Dred Scott case, issued only two days after he became president. *Dred Scott* (1857) was a slave who had been taken by his master to live in free Illinois and Wisconsin. Scott sued for his freedom, because he had spent years living with his master in places where slavery was illegal. The Supreme Court could have just ruled that Scott couldn't sue because, in the twisted world of pre–Civil War law, Scott wasn't a person. Legally, he could no more sue for freedom than your cat can sue for cat food. The law, bad as it was, was clear on a slave's lack of standing to sue in court.

The Supreme Court chooses sides

The high court may be supreme, but that doesn't mean the judges are blind to politics. Having lost its majority in the Senate, and with abolitionists nipping at Southerners' heels in the House, the South still ruled in one place: the Supreme Court. Most of whose justices were Southern sympathizers. They took this opportunity to strike a legal blow against anybody who questioned slavery.

The Supreme Court ruled that because slaves were private property, and because the Fifth Amendment prohibited Congress from depriving people of their property without due process of law, every restriction on slavery, every hard-fought compromise, and every choice of the people in any state or territory was null and void. *Due process of the law* means that lawmakers must respect all of a person's legal rights, not just some or most of them, when passing laws. If a slave owner had an unrestricted legal right to own a slave (and of course the slave, being property, had no rights at all) then the slave owner could take his slaves anywhere he wanted and work them as slaves as long as he wanted.

 The ruling in the Dred Scott case probably is the worst decision the Supreme Court ever made. First, it was a bananas interpretation of the Fifth Amendment to the Constitution, the amendment that protects life, liberty, and property. Due process of the law is exactly what the Congress and the territorial and state legislatures had gone through in debating and passing laws banning slavery from jurisdictions under their control. The legislature clearly had the right to legally deprive people of their property for the public good; that's what taxation and eminent domain are. Second, the ruling on the Dred Scott case virtually guaranteed that civil law would lead to civil war; the Supreme Court was stripping the power of the law by making it politically absurd.

The fallout from the Dred Scott decision didn't take long to hit. Stephen Douglas, the Democratic cheerleader for popular sovereignty, felt stabbed in the back and fought back furiously in the Senate. The Republicans had a field day, calling the previously respected Supreme Court nothing but a Southern debating society. The South was first delighted and then aghast that the North wouldn't follow the ruling of the august Supreme Court when the South was winning. Talk on both sides moved farther in the direction of "We can't live with these people."

Question: What was the overall legal importance of the Dred Scott decision?

Answer: The Dred Scott decision meant Congress could put no limits on slavery in the territories, or technically, anywhere else in the United States

Question: What laws did the Dred Scott decision overturn?

Answer: The Dred Scott case effectively repealed the Missouri Compromise of 1820, the Compromise of 1850, and the Kansas-Nebraska Act of 1854.

The Panic of 1857

Just in time to increase the misery index in the North, the short but sharp Panic of 1857 brought financial collapse and unemployment. The South rode out the down market on the back of King Cotton, figuring that its relative prosperity was further proof that God was on its side. Hungry people in the North renewed their cries for the federal government to make cheap land available for settlement. Congress passed a Homestead Bill in 1860 to do just that, but President Buchanan vetoed it. Buchanan's friends in the South didn't want more settlers to vote against slavery in the territories.

An Election and a Division

With fights brewing in all branches of government, everyone looked anxiously toward the presidential election of 1860. Would the Democrats find a bring-us-together candidate? Could the Republicans possibly win when they weren't even allowed south of the Mason-Dixon line? Who was going to save democracy?

Abraham Lincoln runs for president

Abraham Lincoln described himself as ugly. He towered above the short but determined fire-plug figure of Stephen Douglas (see "Turning Words to Bullets in Bleeding Kansas," earlier in this chapter) during their debates for the Senate in 1858, which turned out to be a prequel of the 1860 presidential race between the two.

Lincoln wasn't exactly spending all his time splitting logs before the debates, but he wasn't any superimportant guy, either. He had risen from his humble beginnings on the Illinois frontier to become one of the better-known local lawyers. In the House of Representatives, where incumbents usually kept getting reelected, he had managed to serve only one term. Up until the passage of the Kansas-Nebraska Act in 1854, he didn't stand out from a thousand other lawyer–politicians.

Lincoln was against slavery, but he shied away from the troublemaking abolitionists. When the passage of the Kansas-Nebraska Act threatened to extend slavery, the Republican Party rose in opposition, and Lincoln became a tiger. He debated the famous Senator Douglas all over Illinois and came close to knocking him out of the Senate.

John Brown

Meanwhile, the abolitionist anger of John Brown could wait no more. Brown had been the bad-boy hero of peaceful-but-well-funded abolitionists since he chopped up a few slavery supporters during the war for Bleeding Kansas (see "Turning Words to Bullets in Bleeding Kansas," earlier in this chapter). He went to Kansas to help protect the free-state settlers, including some of his adult children, from violent Southern raids.

Brown had a legitimate concern for the welfare of his sons and the free-state settlers in their vicinity, especially because the sacking of the free town of Lawrence seemed to signal an all-out campaign of violence by proslavery forces. After he murdered five proslavery men, he skillfully led the free-state settlers in defending themselves. When he captured a detachment of armed slavery raiders, he treated them well and negotiated for the return of two of his own sons who were being held by the slavery forces.

Brown put together a loony plan to start a slave uprising by marching through Virginia, handing out guns that he would steal from the federal armory at Harpers Ferry, north of Washington, D.C. Brown and a few men took the armory but were quickly arrested after a shootout with an army detachment under the command of (dramatic foreshadowing!) then-Union Col. Robert E. Lee. Brown's Harpers Ferry idea could never have worked; during the Civil War, slaves didn't revolt even when the Union Army was near.

Brown was quickly tried and hanged, but his spirit electrified the antislavery North and totally teed off and frightened the slaveholding South. His last words as the noose was being tied around his neck were "This is a beautiful country." His death raised an anger in the North that helped elect antislavery Abraham Lincoln.

When a guy like Brown does something violent, labeling him crazy is natural. Maybe he was crazy, but how crazy and violent was the slave system he hated? People seem to have more tolerance for institutionalized violence than they do for attacks against violent institutions. Brown just thought *somebody* had to do *something;* he was driven crazy by the crazy system of slavery.

Lincoln gets elected, and the South says goodbye

It took two conventions for the Democrats to nominate Stephen Douglas for president in 1860. The Southerners walked out of the first convention and nominated John Breckinridge, a moderate who was willing to run on a Southern Democrat platform calling for the extension of slavery. The Northern Democrats who were left behind nominated Douglas. Desperate compromisers threw together a Constitutional Union Party, to put a fourth candidate in the race. The Republicans thought they were playing it as safe as possible by picking Abraham Lincoln; their other choices were better known but were radicals.

During a bitter campaign, the Southerners announced that if "that baboon" Lincoln became president, they were going to start their own country. Although Lincoln scored less than 40 percent of the popular vote, he got electoral votes from every free state. Even with Lincoln elected, the South was under no real danger of having its slavery institution taken way. That would take a constitutional amendment, and the slaveholders had almost twice as many states as they needed to defeat an amendment. The Republicans were a minority in both the House and Senate, and the Southerners still controlled the Supreme Court. But the South was fed up.

Within days of Lincoln's election, Southern states had started to secede. Eventually, 11 states left the Union, taking with them most of the U.S. Army guns and supplies on Southern soil. To tell the truth, the army didn't have much to grab. The entire U.S. Army consisted of only 15,000 men, and lots of them were scattered across the frontier, looking out for American Indians. The Union held on to one major fort guarding the approach to the hotbed of the rebellion: Fort Sumter in Charleston harbor.

Even as soldiers drilled, the sides made one final attempt at compromise: the *Crittenden Amendments* (1860), which would have allowed slavery in the Southwest and in territories to be acquired (watch out, Cuba). That law was a nonstarter.

Fighting the Civil War

Most Southerners actually thought they could just say, "Well, it's been a nice country, but gotta go," and the North would wave a peaceful goodbye. Although three quarters of the soldiers from the South owned no slaves, they were still ready to fight for those who did. Southerners figured that Northern businessmen would want to hold on to Northern middle-man profits from the cotton trade and the millions of dollars owed to them by the South. They found out that money talks, but not as loud as a cause does. For the North, saving the Union and opposing slavery were causes worth fighting for.

Five border slave states chose to stay with the Union — luckily for the North, because border-state people, manufacturing, and horses would have added more than a third to Southern Confederate strength. As it was, the North had more than twice as many people as the South, three times as much money, and ten times as many factories.

Those figures didn't mean that the North was sure to win, though; Britain had those kinds of advantages over the colonies, and the Revolution still triumphed. As in the Revolutionary War, the South didn't really have to win; it just had to not lose. The North was forced to attack the South on the South's own soil; the South mostly fought from behind prepared defenses with short internal lines of supply and communications. The Union Navy blockaded Southern ports, but the South had enough food and weapons to last a few years.

The hotheads of South Carolina fired on *Fort Sumter*, the key to Charleston harbor held by the Union, thereby rousing Northerners into feeling that their nation's flag was under attack. Lincoln asked for 75,000 volunteers. After the Union troops had a few months of training, they marched off to take the Confederate capital of Richmond, Virginia, and end the war quickly. At *First Bull Run* (1861) in Northern Virginia, the first battle of the war, one unit of Confederates held firm like stone, earning their talented general the nickname "Stonewall" Jackson and buying the South enough time to win the fight.

The Union regrouped under Gen. George McClellan, who was good at organizing parades but not much at actually fighting. About a year after Bull Run, he lost the *Peninsula Campaign* (July 1862) to the Confederate Army under Robert E. Lee. Lee beat the Union again at *Second Bull Run* (August 1862) and headed into Union territory, only a few miles from Washington, D.C. In one of the two most important fights of the Civil War, Lee was turned back, barely, at *Antietam* (September 1862). Second Bull Run and Antietam showed that both sides could defend their own territory.

Britain and France were talking about getting involved on the Southern side, but Antietam made them shut up. It also gave Lincoln the backing he needed to announce his plan to free the slaves in the states then fighting the Union. On New Year's Day, he officially issued the

Emancipation Proclamation (1863). With the Union on record as fighting for the cause of freedom, average people in Britain and France made sure their governments wouldn't help the South. They had read *Uncle Tom's Cabin* (see "How Reading Led to Fighting" earlier in this chapter).

Question: What was the significance of the Battle of Antietam?

Answer: It helped convince England and France not to support the Confederacy, and it gave Lincoln the political strength to issue the Emancipation Proclamation.

Meanwhile, the North tightened its blockade to cut off Southern supplies. Southerners had figured that Britain would have to help them because something like one out of five jobs in Britain was tied to Southern cotton. Even though some British working people went unemployed and hungry, the British refused to help. The Northern states shipped Britain extra food; they had plenty to share.

The South tried to break the blockade with a homemade iron-sided ship called the *Merrimack*. Just in time, a Union ironclad arrived to fight. The *Monitor* and the *Merrimack* (1862) fought to a tie. After this first fight between metal ships, it was clear that warships of the future would be made out of iron, not wood.

As slaves were freed, many of them enlisted in the Union Army. Paid less than whites until the last year of the war, they fought bravely in difficult battles. About 10 percent of Union forces were black, and they suffered more than their share of casualties. Southern slaves never rose up against their masters, but they did run away to freedom when they could.

The Union lost badly at *Fredericksburg* (December 1862) by attacking an unbeatable Southern entrenchment and at *Chancellorsville* (May 1863) by being suckered in a brilliant flank attack by Lee. Up to that time, Union generals deserved a grade of about *F*+.

Lee was feeling his oats and decided to have another go at invading the North. At *Gettysburg* (July 1863) in Pennsylvania, he attacked Union troops who would not be moved. For three days of ferocious fighting, the Union held. The battle was very close; the South had peace commissioners ready to take the Union's surrender. Instead, Lee's army was forced to retreat to Virginia. Gettysburg, the South's last real chance to win the Civil War, joined Antietam as the other key battle of the conflict.

Question: What were the two key battles of the Civil War?

Answer: Antietam, where the North held the line against the South, and Gettysburg, where the South was defeated in Northern territory.

The day after Gettysburg, General Ulysses S. Grant took the Confederate fortress at *Vicksburg* (1863), splitting the South at the Mississippi River. With the twin victories at Gettysburg and Vicksburg, Britain and France even stopped taking Southern money to build them warships. The Confederacy was on its own. Union General William Tecumseh Sherman marched across the Confederacy from *Atlanta to the sea* (1864), leaving a 60-mile-wide path of destruction and freeing 25,000 slaves. His tactics were brutal, but they helped shorten the war and save lives. He said, "War is all hell."

Lincoln won reelection in 1864 on the Republican ticket, cleverly including a loyal border-state Democrat as vice president. When Lincoln won, desertions from the Confederate Army increased. General Grant, now in command of the main Union Army, hammered relentlessly at Lee throughout 1864. Finally, in April 1865, the Confederacy surrendered. Lincoln visited the defeated Southern capital of Richmond. When grateful slaves tried to kneel in front of him, he pulled them up and said, "You must kneel to God only, and thank Him for the liberty."

People will tell you the AP never asks about battles, but that isn't necessarily true. Don't get lulled into studying nothing about the way the Civil War unfolded. At a minimum, remember Antietam, which kept out foreign intervention and let in the Emancipation Proclamation, which I talk about in the next section. The battle of Gettysburg stopped the South's invasion of the North and marked the last real chance for the South to win the war.

Question: How many Southerners owned slaves?

Answer: Only about one quarter of Southern whites owned slaves.

Question: What was the role of black troops in the Civil War?

Answer: Black soldiers made up 10 percent of the Union Army. They suffered more than their share of casualties and by the end of the war were paid the same as white troops.

Emancipation and the Loss of Lincoln

Although the Emancipation Proclamation of 1863 (see "Fighting the Civil War" earlier in this chapter) technically only freed slaves in the Confederacy (which was out of the reach of the law), more and more slaves were freed as the Union Army rolled up Southern territory. More than 200,000 freed slaves joined the Union Army and fought to free those still held in bondage. More important, the proclamation showed that the North was fighting to end slavery, not just keep the Union intact.

Question: What was the most important immediate impact of the Emancipation Proclamation?

Answer: Issuing the Emancipation Proclamation showed that the North was fighting to end slavery, not just to preserve the Union. This increased support from ex-slaves and from foreign nations opposed to slavery.

A few days after he knew the war would end, Lincoln was assassinated by John Wilkes Booth, an actor with Southern sympathies who thought he could somehow revive the Confederacy by killing Lincoln. Actually, killing Lincoln hurt the South. Lincoln had planned to let Southern states rejoin the Union on relatively easy terms. With Lincoln gone, Democratic Vice President Andrew Johnson would have to try to manage *Reconstruction,* the rebuilding of the South with free blacks (see Chapter 14), through a Republican-controlled Congress eager to make sure that the South learned a lesson.

Question: What was the impact of the assassination of President Lincoln?

Answer: Without the forgiving Lincoln to guide the process, Reconstruction of the South after the war became a partisan political controversy.

More than 600,000 men died in the Civil War — close to the total for all the other wars the United States has ever fought. Family members fought one another. Mary Lincoln, the president's wife, had three brothers killed fighting for the Confederacy. Four million slaves were freed, although real social freedom took another 100 years to accomplish, which I talk about in the following chapters. Extreme states' rights were abolished, and the twin national challenges of nullification and secession, which first threatened while George Washington was still alive (see Chapter 10), were finally laid to rest.

The Union's victory in the Civil War expanded federal power. The first 12 amendments to the Constitution, in place before the war, all limited the power of the government. The next three amendments, passed after the war, all expanded national power.

The Civil War led to a national banking system with national currency; the first income tax (3 percent, starting in 1861); the first draft (1863); and, through attempts to help freed slaves, the beginning of a national welfare system.

Before the Civil War, the term *United States* was plural. People said, "The United States — *they* have decided to expand." After the war, *United States* was singular, as in "The United States — *it* has decided to grow." Small words can make a big difference.

Part IV
U.S. History from After the Civil War to the Days of the Internet

In this part . . .

The United States put back the pieces after the Civil War, but it was never the same: it was better. Despite economic destruction, the South planted new crops and even built some industry. Former slaves suffered from discrimination and occasional terror, but they were technically free, which was progress toward civil rights. The North and South got together again to take on the Spanish. After holding back from Europe's endless fights, the U.S. eventually entered World War I and tipped the balance for the Allies.

You'll want to remember that about 20 percent of the questions on the AP exam come from the post-Civil War through World War I period.

There were up times like the 1920s and down times like the Great Depression. World War II shook the planet, and the U.S. was right in the middle of it. After the victory came the social challenges and the Cold War. The Cold War ended, but terror expanded. Prosperous, diverse, and challenged, the U.S. now stands fully part of a difficult world.

About 30 percent of the AP exam questions deal with the post-World War I world. There aren't a lot of questions about what happened after 1985; history takes a while to digest.

Chapter 14

Reconstructing and Moving Westward, 1866–1880

As you can probably determine if you read Chapter 13, the results of the Civil War were pretty uncivil! Because everyone who died on both sides was an American, the Civil War cost as many U.S. lives as all the other wars the country has ever fought combined. Both sides lived for years with chips on their shoulders. And what about those 4 million newly freed slaves? The Civil War resulted in Reconstruction, and also set the stage for U.S. expansion west, and I tell you all about that in this chapter.

After the Civil War, besides Reconstruction and Western expansion, industry grew, and even farmers started using machines. More people moved to the cities, trading all-day farm chores for nighttime bright lights. Railroads crossed the country, American Indians were pushed onto reservations, and immigrants streamed onshore. Hard-to-remember presidents who looked like walruses debated about hard-to-remember things like tariffs and silver coinage. Meanwhile, the rights of women and labor advanced in fits and starts. This chapter covers the beginnings of all of these things. Pay special attention to social trends that can be useful in both multiple-choice and essay success on the big test.

Reconstruction: Rebuilding the USA in a Brand-New Way

What with the actions of Union Generals Sherman and Grant, plus the South's own destructive fighting (see Chapter 13), the Cotton Belt was pretty torn up after the war. Southern plantations needed five years to get back into full cotton production. The *Reconstruction* (1865–1877) of the South included new national and local governments, as well as social help. And the *Thirteenth Amendment* (1865) made Lincoln's Emancipation Proclamation into a national ban on slavery.

Slaves who were worth billions of dollars to plantation owners before the war were now officially free, so how was the South going to plant and harvest all that valuable cotton? Well, after the Civil War, blacks with no clothes, shoes, education, food, or places to live weren't really all that free. Former slaves often didn't have any choice but to sign up to work for very low wages, often for their former masters.

Reconstructing a new South

A month before the Civil War was even over, Congress created the *Freedmen's Bureau* (1865) to help educate and take care of freed slaves. By the time the bureau packed it in, it had taught 200,000 former slaves to read with the help of volunteer teachers from the North. In one classroom, four generations of a family, from child to great-grandmother, all learned to read together. Union Gen. Oliver Howard ran the Freedmen's Bureau and later started Howard University in Washington, D.C.

The issues of Reconstruction included the changes that Southern states would have to implement to be readmitted to the Union, how much help the former slaves would have from the federal government, and how Northern troops could contain Southern terrorist attacks by groups like the Ku Klux Klan.

Expect a question about Reconstruction on test day, especially about the amendments that I discuss in this section. Remember that the amendments were passed in the order you would expect if you freed someone: The Thirteenth abolished slavery, the Fourteenth granted citizenship, and the Fifteenth provided the right to vote. The Thirteenth Amendment, representing the unlucky number, got rid of a very unlucky thing that can happen to a person: slavery.

Off to a bumpy start: The Radical Republicans

With Abraham Lincoln gone (see Chapter 13), his Democratic vice president, Andrew Johnson, took over as president. Lincoln had generously planned to let the Southern states rejoin the Union on easy terms. Johnson went along with the Mr. Nice Guy policy; he issued pardons to hundreds of ex-Confederates.

That wasn't what the *Radical Republicans* (1866) in Congress wanted, however; they wanted to change the South radically, punish the former slave masters, and protect the blacks with federal power. To the disgust of these Republican lawmakers, new delegates from the South came knocking on the Capitol door in December 1865 — the very same year in which the South was finally defeated and Lincoln was shot.

And who should be there asking for admission as congressmen but several Confederate generals, members of the Confederate Cabinet, and even the Confederate vice president? ("Well, it was quite a war, but we were only kidding. Can we come back now?") The Radical Republicans threw them out. The radicals had two reasons for hanging tough:

- ✔ The unreconstructed Southerners had passed ugly *Black Codes* (1866) that made blacks almost into slaves again. Blacks had to sign one-year labor contracts, and if they didn't come through, they could be fined and put so deeply in debt that they would never earn anything. They could be punished for "idleness" by being sent to work on chain gangs.

- ✔ Now that the slaves were officially free, the South actually got more representatives in Congress than it had before the war, when a slave counted as only three-fifths of a person. Working with Northern Democrats, the South could even take control of Congress and undo all the progress that the North had fought to gain.

The Fourteenth and Fifteenth Amendments

To nail down blacks' rights, Congress passed the *Fourteenth Amendment* (1866) to the Constitution. It guaranteed the citizenship of freed slaves, reduced the representation of

Southern states if they kept blacks from voting, disqualified anyone who had left public service in the North to join the Confederacy from ever holding office in the Union again, and guaranteed the debt of the Union while repudiating the debt of the Confederacy. The Fourteenth Amendment encouraged universal male voting; the Fifteenth Amendment made it the law.

Congress was determined to not let any Confederate state back in unless it endorsed the Fourteenth Amendment. President Andrew Johnson told the former rebel states not to sign it. Johnson had been the only senator from a Southern state to remain loyal to the Union; now that the fighting was over, he wanted to go easy on his Southern buddies. Even though Johnson was from a different political party, Lincoln had made him vice president as a show of national unity. Now Lincoln was dead and Johnson was unexpectedly president. The Republican Congress headed for a showdown with the president they never wanted.

Johnson had hoped to pick up some support in the fall congressional elections, but the Republicans won big. After whites attacked blacks in vicious riots in the South, Congress divided the South into five military districts and sent in the Army to keep order. It also passed the *Fifteenth Amendment* (1869) to guarantee blacks the right to vote. To get back into the Union, representatives of former Confederate states had to sign both amendments.

Question: What was the purpose of the Fourteenth Amendment?

Answer: The Fourteenth Amendment guaranteed citizenship and civil rights for former slaves.

Question: What was the most serious constitutional issue following the Civil War?

Answer: How the former Confederate states would be readmitted to the Union.

Women, former slaves, and the limits of freedom

Women's-rights leaders like Susan B. Anthony and Elizabeth Cady Stanton put their own cause on hold to work tirelessly for emancipation of the slaves. Although women's rights were a growing concern before the Civil War, most politically involved women were even more concerned with ending slavery and preserving the Union. Women from outside the women's-rights movement also served during the war. For example, Dorothea Dix was the leader of Union nurses; the Woman's Loyal League gathered nearly 400,000 signatures on a petition for a constitutional amendment banning slavery. Many of them were just a little peeved that the new Fourteenth and Fifteenth Amendments gave black males the right to vote, but not white or black women. Women would have to wait almost 60 years before their election rights became part of the Constitution.

Meanwhile, more and more Western states let women step up to the ballot box, starting with Wyoming ("The Equality State") in 1869. Black women, voting or not, helped rally black political participation in the South until they were silenced by the heavy hand of segregationist governments.

Question: Name a female leader who was not greatly involved in the women's-rights movement.

Answer: Despite being the leader of the Union's nurses, Dorothea Dix wasn't a women's rights pioneer.

Northern troops in the South supported "radical" state governments that allowed blacks freedom and passed public education bills to help everyone. But by the time federal troops finally withdrew from the South in 1877, Southern state governments were quickly seized by Redeemer or home-rule segregationist groups, which took as many rights as they could away from blacks. Before these groups struck, however, blacks enjoyed a brief period of being elected to Congress and local offices, which outraged former slave masters.

White Southerners called anyone from the North who helped Reconstruction a *carpetbagger* (1870), taking dig at the image of outsiders arriving with cheap luggage made out of carpets. Southerners who cooperated with Reconstruction were called *scalawags* (1870). The most important and lasting contribution of the carpetbagger governments was the establishment of a system of public education in the South.

Although Reconstruction Southern state governments did have their share of mismanagement, they were no more outrageous than the scams going on in some Northern capitals at this time. Reconstruction governments got some important work going in public education and road repair.

Blacks as well as poor whites in the South were forced into sharecropping. In a system reminiscent of feudalism, they worked their small parts of a large plantation owned by a landlord and turned over a third or more of their crops to the landlord. Worse, sharecroppers were required to buy supplies from the landowner and sell their own crops to the landlord at prices that the landlord set. Because the landlord kept all the accounts, any halfway intelligent landlord could make sure his sharecroppers stayed perpetually in debt.

Question: What lasting accomplishments of carpetbagger governments remained even after the Redeemers took over?

Answer: The greatest accomplishment of the carpetbagger Southern governments that survived the Redeemer segregationist takeover was a lasting public education system.

Question: How did blacks earn money after the Civil War?

Answer: Most of them were sharecroppers close to where they'd been slaves.

Fighting against Reconstruction

Southerners struck back at Reconstruction with violence through secret terrorist organizations such as the *Ku Klux Klan* (1867). The original Ku Klux Klan lasted only for about six years before federal troops put it down, but its terrorist hatred did a lot of damage. Hundreds of blacks and their white helpers were beaten and murdered. Congress passed the *Force Acts* (1870), which used federal troops to largely stamp out the Klan, but white intimidation of blacks lasted well into the 20th century (see Chapter 15).

By the 1890s, blacks were blocked from voting in the South by technically legal methods like rigged literacy tests and poll taxes. A hate-filled white minority didn't limit itself to legal methods; lynchings and beatings continued for 100 years after the Civil War.

Frederick Douglass on the end of Reconstruction

"As the war for the Union recedes into the misty shadows of the past, and the Negro is no longer needed to assault forts and stop rebel bullets, he is in some sense, of less importance. Peace with the old master class has been war to the Negro. As the one has risen, the other has fallen. The reaction has been sudden, marked, and violent. It has swept the Negro from all the legislative halls of the Southern States, and from those of the Congress of the United States. It has, in many cases, driven him from the ballot box and the jury box. The situation has much in it for serious thought, but nothing to cause despair. Above all the frowning clouds that lower about our horizon, there is the steady light of stars, and the thick clouds that now obscure them, will in due season pass away."

President Johnson made himself so unpopular with the Republican Congress that it moved to impeach him. Fearing that Johnson would fire the Republican members of the Cabinet he had inherited from Lincoln, Congress passed the *Tenure of Office Act* (1867), which made that move illegal. Johnson fired Republican Secretary of War Edwin M. Stanton anyway because Stanton wanted strong Reconstruction measures. The House of Representatives voted to impeach Johnson. Amid much drama, the Senate came just one vote short of voting Johnson out of office. Tempers ran high, but the country stuck to democracy. No violence broke out among the Union and former Confederate leaders.

The national government's attempts at Reconstruction lasted until the disputed election of Rutherford Hayes as president in 1877 caused the Republicans to make a deal to pull the last Union troops out of the South.

The political gains that blacks made during the 12 years of Reconstruction didn't last much longer than the last federal rifle to defend them. No way were powerful Southern whites going to swallow the blacks' change from slaves to citizens in one generation. In fact, it took 100 years for blacks to be really free to vote, go to school, and live with the rest of society.

The legacy of poverty had a lot of staying power. In the words of the distinguished ex-slave Frederick Douglass, a freedman was "free from the individual master, but still a slave to society . . . free from the old quarter that once gave him shelter, but a slave to the rains of summer and the frosts of winter. He was, in a word, literally turned loose, naked, hungry and destitute, to the open sky." Delayed but not forever denied, the gains of the 1960s civil-rights movement had their basis in the faltering reforms of Reconstruction in the 1860s.

Reconstruction comes to an end

The political fight that ended Reconstruction was the *Hayes-Tilden Compromise* (1877). Hayes was a Republican political hack running under the burden of Grant-administration corruption. Samuel Tilden was the Democratic reformer who had cleaned up the Boss Tweed scandal. Tilden racked up more popular votes, but the numbers in the Electoral College were about even.

The Democrats made a deal to let Hayes win in return for the Republicans' agreeing to withdraw the last federal troops from the South. In reality, the determination of the North to protect blacks in the South had faded with time.

The last-gasp *Civil Rights Act* (1875) was mostly overturned by the South-leaning Supreme Court in the *Civil Rights Cases* (1883). Even the Fourteenth Amendment was found by the court to apply only to government violations of civil rights, not to the denial of rights by individuals. Blacks were pretty much on their own in a hostile society for the next 100 years.

Civil War General Turns President: Ulysses S. Grant

In 1868 (before the end of Reconstruction), former Union Gen. Ulysses S. Grant ran for president as a Republican under the slogan "Vote as you shot" and was elected by a grateful nation and an army of Union veterans. Although Grant had most of the electoral votes, his popular-vote majority came from former slaves. The Republicans, on only their second elected president, realized that they would have to play politics carefully to stay in office.

Unfortunately, politics (then as now) meant hanging around with rich people who were out for their own good.

Grant proved to be better at fighting battles than watching over money. He had been in office for only a few months when speculators tried to corner the gold market on *Black Friday* (1869), causing a business panic. Other problems followed Grant through his presidency:

- ✔ The *Crédit Mobilier scandal* (1872), which involved Union Pacific railroad payoffs to politicians.
- ✔ The *Whiskey Ring scandal* (1875), in which politicians robbed the U.S. Treasury of excise taxes on booze.
- ✔ The forced resignation of Grant's secretary of war William Belknap in 1876 after he was caught pocketing bribes from suppliers to American Indian reservations.

Although Grant himself was not dishonest, he did enjoy drinking Old Crow whiskey and had complete trust for all his relatives and friends. The crooks who always hang around politics took advantage of Grant's easygoing character. After *Boss Tweed* (1872), leader of the Tammany Hall ring in New York City, was finally sent to prison, one of his cronies explained how it worked: "I seen my opportunities, and I took 'em."

Living in the Gilded Age

Author Mark Twain (see "Increasing literacy" later in this chapter) called the period of the 1800s after the Civil War *the Gilded Age* (1875), for all the gold-painted furniture and fancy living. The country was evenly split between Republicans and Democrats; although the Republicans won most of the presidential races, control of Congress changed hands in more than half of the elections.

Most people voted, and the issues, though deeply felt at the time, seem pretty small in retrospect. Republican voters tended to be rural Protestants, believers in personal morality, and veterans of the Civil War. Democrats tended to live in big cities and in the South or to be recent-immigrant Protestants and Catholics, and were more easygoing in their judgments.

The self-betterment dreams of early modern Americans were modest; people didn't dream of a mansion, just a home. Even so, the country grew and changed in ways that many people found surprising, as covered in the following sections.

America gets used to paper money

An economic panic that started in 1873 introduced an issue that would continue for the rest of the 1800s. During the Civil War, the Union had issued millions of dollars in paper money. People who owed loans wanted more paper money, because that would increase inflation. Inflated cheap money would make the debt they owed easier to repay. Businessmen who loaned money wanted all paper money paid off in gold, so that the money they loaned would be worth more when it was paid back. The cheap-money people also supported the coinage of silver to bring about more inflation. The U.S. Treasury, backed by businessmen, redeemed paper money for gold so regularly that after a while, people got tired of carrying jangling coins and just used paper money.

Immigration

When a country loses 600,000 men in a war, you'd expect the population to go down for a while. The South lost 1 out of 10 adult males, the North 1 out of 30; the equivalent loss in today's U.S. population would be 6 million people. But the United States was the most popular immigration destination in the world. The population of the country actually went up by more than 25 percent during the Civil War decade; by 1870, the United States had almost 40 million citizens. Lots of these people were moving to Eastern cities or opened Western land. With no real danger of foreign attacks or internal dissolution, the United States turned to wrangling about money and voting rights.

The history of the post–Civil War United States centered on moves to the cities and to the West. The Civil War was a fight among farm boys; 80 percent of Americans lived in the country. But by 1900, the United States was only 60 percent rural and boasted several cities over 1 million in population. New York had become the second-largest city in the world.

Europe was growing too. Thanks in part to food imported directly from America and to European cultivation of that New World feeding wonder, the potato, the population of Europe doubled in the 1800s.

Many Europeans were moving around that continent, looking for new opportunities. For some people — like the Irish living in famine — the choice was immigrate or die. Aided by the ease and cheapness of steamship travel, 20 million Europeans made the jump across the Atlantic to the United States between 1820 and 1900.

As in the Know-Nothing days before the Civil War, the increase in immigrants and the growth of cities worried some traditionalists. As the 1870s drew to a close, calls to restrict immigration grew louder.

Industrialization and the birth of labor unions

The world's petrochemical future began with the first rickety oil well in Pennsylvania in 1859. Cars didn't exist yet, but kerosene made from petroleum oil burned brighter than the expensive whale oil that had been the only thing used in lamps since before the days of *Moby-Dick*. The oil business was off to a good start; within a few years, kerosene was the fourth-leading export of the United States.

Slowly, American products begin to show up all over the world. Among the first to arrive were five-gallon kerosene cans from Standard Oil Co. The growth in industry was trailed by a growth in labor unions. The National Labor Union was formed just after the Civil War and helped to win the first eight-hour working day, initially just for federal government employees. Workers in the period after the Civil War were often made to work ten or more hours a day, six days a week, without overtime.

By 1872, labor unions had hundreds of thousands of members, and more than 30 national unions represented typesetters, hat-makers, cobblers, and other skilled craftspeople. Business depressions in the 1870s and the inability of unions to raise wages while profits were shrinking caused the union movement to lose momentum for a while. In the 1870s, a new national union coalition called the Knights of Labor gained strength. The Knights tried to unite all laboring men behind a program of worker-owned stores; health and safety regulations; and, most important, the eight-hour working day. The eight-hour workday didn't become standard until the 1900s.

Older U.S. history texts (and some older U.S. history teachers) may not pay enough attention to the labor-, women's-, and minority-rights movements that the politically up-to-date AP U.S. History exam expects you to know. Don't get caught short. Because this exam gets you the college credit you want, take this opportunity to memorize some key names and dates from the evolving history of people's movements. Progress is like a dance between the leaders and the people: Sometimes the rulers lead; sometimes the people do.

Increasing literacy

Public schools spread throughout the nation in the 1870s. The change was especially important in the South, where public education was a lasting benefit of Reconstruction. Adults too old for school were so eager to learn that they flocked to public lectures called *chautauquas* held in hundreds of locations all over the country. The number of Americans who couldn't read dropped from 20 percent in 1870 to about 10 percent in 1900, despite the influx of millions of initially poorly educated immigrants. However, in 1900, almost half of nonwhite Americans still couldn't read.

College education got a big boost from the *Morrill Act* (1862), which reserved some of the proceeds from the sale of public lands to found land-grant colleges in new states. *Land-grant colleges* are state schools with public backing in all of the United States that allow people to get higher education even if they come from poor families. *Johns Hopkins University* (1876) provided the first serious graduate-degree programs in the United States.

More people could read than ever before. They chose books with stories that seemed to speak to their own lives and dreams. The books they read then proceeded to reshape the way readers saw the world.

- Horatio Alger wrote more than 100 novels with titles like *Luck and Pluck* (1869) and *Tattered Tom* (1871). The young heroes of Horatio Alger stories advance through hard work and honesty from poverty to middle-class economic safety, not from rags to riches, as people who have never read the stories have come to believe.

- Walt Whitman continued his poetic tributes to natural humans and his native land through the 1870s.

- America and the world found a new literary friend when a failed silver miner named Samuel Clemens took the pen name Mark Twain. His writing, from *The Innocents Abroad* (1869) to *The Adventures of Tom Sawyer* (1876) to *The Adventures of Huckleberry Finn* (1884), helped make reading widely popular and broadened the meaning of great literature.

The impact of Charles Darwin

Charles Darwin's theory of evolution upset religious traditions as it spread through America after the Civil War. Darwin said that all living things have evolved to their present form through a dazzling process of natural selection. The Christian Bible says literally that God created the world in six days, but evolution covers millions of years. Religious fundamentalists felt that their faith would be shaken if they didn't take those six days in the Bible literally. Religious modernists, on the other hand (including Catholics, the Jewish, and most of the major Protestant denominations), saw evolution as just an advance in understanding the grand workings of God.

The fight over human evolution that started during this period is part of an evolutionary battle between literal and spiritual interpretations of religious teaching that has been going on since the writing of the first holy books. In the United States, evolutionary theory led to political, educational, and religious polarization. *Social Darwinists* (1875) carried natural selection to a literal extreme and taught that survival-of-the-fittest competition was the law of society. Speakers toured the U.S. to promote science and Darwin's theory. Toward the end of the 1800s, fundamentalist churches increasingly opposed evolution.

Question: How was Darwin's theory of evolution used to explain society?

Answer: Social Darwinists said society functions on Darwin's survival-of-the-fittest theory.

Censorship and women's rights

The forces of new morality took on the forces of censorship in the 1870s. Winning the right for women to vote was a crusade for eloquent *Victoria Woodhull* (1872), who became the first woman to run for president (with the amused support of Cornelius Vanderbilt). She and her sister published a magazine that crusaded for equal rights and outed respected minister Henry Ward Beecher for having an affair with a female parishioner.

Armed with the *Comstock Laws* (1873), Anthony Comstock tried to arrest Woodhull for indecency. The *Comstock Laws* include federal and state laws against indecent material. For 50 years, these laws were also used to suppress information about birth control. Woodhull escaped Comstock's clutches and represented progressive causes for the rest of her life. Comstock's censorship laws survived into the 1960s, when they no longer seemed necessary in a free society. Family planning information and most kinds of literature are no longer prohibited in the U.S. Woodhull's feisty feminism is still alive today in books, movies, songs, and politics.

The temperance movement gains strength

People on the frontier often drank too much, and the United States had been a frontier for all its existence. The National Prohibition Party organized in 1869 and the more-moderate Women's Christian Temperance Union (WCTU) in 1874. Temperance allows a little social drinking for those who can control it; Prohibition means no booze for anybody. Throughout the late 1800s and early 1900s, people against drinking gained political strength. In the early 1900s, the Prohibitionists won big. With the passage of the *Eighteenth Amendment* (1920), alcohol became illegal in the U.S. America's "dry" period lasted only 13 years. In 1933, the Eighteenth Amendment was repealed, because making alcoholic beverages illegal seemed to lead to more problems than it solved.

Workin' on the Railroad

At the end of the Civil War, most of the railroads were north and east of the Mississippi; none of them crossed the West. California could be reached only by weeks of sailing or riding in a bumpy stagecoach. By 1900, the United States had more railroads than Europe, and people could ride the rails to the West Coast in a matter of a few days.

Beginning right after the end of the Civil War in 1865, a crew of 5,000 (mostly Irish) workers pushed the rail lines west from Omaha, while 10,000 Chinese workers labored over the Sierras from Sacramento. By 1869, the railroad across America was complete.

The Crédit Mobilier scandal tainted the westbound-from-Omaha owners of the Union Pacific Railroad. The Central Pacific Railroad from Sacramento made a lot of money but avoided the large-scale political bribery of the Crédit Mobilier scandal.

Cornelius Vanderbilt had made a fortune in steamboats. In his late 60s, when he should have been happily enjoying the money, he decided to build some railroads. He pioneered the use of steel instead of iron rails for the important New York Central, making train tracks safer and less expensive to build. In the years after the Civil War, the railroads finally got it together and agreed on a standard width or *gauge* for rails so that people didn't have to keep getting out and changing trains. Westinghouse air brakes helped trains stop, and Pullman cars made them comfortable.

Railroads made the United States the largest integrated market in the world. Food, resources, and products could move anywhere in the country, which stimulated growth. Building the railroads also helped develop the U.S. steel industry. When Vanderbilt first used steel rails, he had to buy the steel from England. Settlements sprung up like strings of pearls along the railroads, just as they'd done in the past along rivers. Corn, wheat, and cattle replaced tall-grass prairies and buffalo. Forests were cut down and rolled over rails to build cities.

Question: How did the railroads contribute to economic growth?

Answer: Transportation sparked growth from 1860 to 1900 by creating the world's largest connected market system, by allowing settlers and businessmen to reach any part of the country quickly, and by fueling the business involved in the very act of building the world's largest railroad system.

The profits of progress attracted rip-off artists. Jay Gould made a fortune buying railroads, inflating their stocks, and then selling them. The scam was called *stock watering,* after the farmer's trick of getting cattle really thirsty and then letting them fill up with heavy water just before they hit the scales to be sold by weight.

Railroad stock wars led to bare-knuckle fights between capitalists. Tough old Vanderbilt said: "I won't sue you; the law takes too long. I'll ruin you." Railroads had almost unlimited political power; they bought influence by giving out free passes to politicians and reporters. Without competition on most routes, they could charge whatever they wanted. They angered small shippers and farmers by demanding more money from them than from their large business cronies.

Moving Out West

The *Homestead Act* (1862) allowed half a million settlers to buy 160 acres of land from the federal government for the bargain price of $30 (about $900 in modern money). Around two out of three of these families couldn't make a go of farming marginal Western land. Another 2.5 million settlers bought land from the railroads, land speculators, or state governments.

Farming increased everywhere. As with any real estate, location was everything. Land west of the 100th meridian, the imaginary dividing line that runs north from the Texas Panhandle, was just too dry for regular farming without irrigation. Ranchers held on by planting tough strains of wheat and fencing their land with the new barbed wire invented in 1874.

Cattle drives moved beef to the nearest railroad terminals all over the West. The spectacular Long Drive covered 500 miles from Texas to Kansas, with crews of black, white, and Mexican cowboys moving herds as big as 10,000 head to market. The Long Drive was just one of thousands of trails that connected cattle range in the farthest corners of the West to railroad lines and finally dinner plates. These cattle drives built the real-life legend of the cowboys. The cattle drives died out in the 1880s as the open range was broken up by homesteaders, but by that time, more than 4 million steers had made the big roundup.

Historian Frederick Turner, who specialized in the American West, thought that the constant push against the Western frontier defined America. Although Turner's specific conclusions are no longer current, his approach to looking at how social and economic issues influence history is very important. The frontier spirit of tough self-sufficiency and belief in the power of new directions wasn't limited to the West. As the 1800s drew to a close, the formerly rural United States moved closer to world leadership in social and industrial development (see Chapter 15). By the end of the 19th century, the once-little republic on the edge of the New World began to move toward center stage in world affairs.

Question: What was the biggest change in the agricultural landscape in the post–Civil War era?

Answer: Settlers cultivated more and more land to grow crops.

Question: What was the role of the federal government after the Civil War with regard to race relations, economic development, and Western expansion?

Answer: The Homestead Act and quick admission of new states supported Western expansion; a strong dollar, railroad support, and high tariffs boosted economic development; Reconstruction and the Freedmen's Bureau were federal efforts in race relations.

The American Indians Get Crowded Out

At the end of the Civil War, close to half a million American Indians were scattered across the West — 1 American Indian for every 60 Americans. Twenty-five years later, the Western homes of the American Indians were on reservations, and their homelands were carved into states and territories.

American Indians didn't really live in tightly organized tribes, and they mostly didn't stay put for long. Tribes were made up of family-based bands that numbered as few as 25 people. They came together with other bands that spoke the same language for periodic hunts, wars, or parties.

The various tribes also often had no permanent leaders, which made the settlers' need to have someone to negotiate with difficult to satisfy. American Indians not only didn't have permanent leaders, they also lacked obedient followers who could be made to stick to treaty agreements. Most of all, the American Indians lacked any political power to make the United States abide by its own agreements. Many treaties were signed by compromised and self-appointed leaders on behalf of tribes that barely knew what was going on except that their life of freedom was being ruined by relentless settler aggression.

Settler inroads pushed American Indians into being aggressive with one another as well as with the whites, resulting in a sort-of domino effect:

 ✔ Before the settlers arrived, the Comanches had driven the Apaches off their land on the central Plains in the 1700s.

 ✔ Pushed by other tribes, the Cheyenne abandoned their villages along the upper Mississippi and Missouri rivers in the early 1800s.

 ✔ The Sioux, displaced from the Great Lakes, learned to ride horses and, like the Cheyenne, became swift buffalo hunters.

Far more American Indians died from diseases than from the bullets of settlers; explorers are biological weapons even if they don't want to be. Europeans often encountered American Indian tribes reduced by two-thirds or more by recent epidemics. Most American Indians died before they ever saw a settler.

In the 1860s, the U.S. Army pushed to move American Indians either to the Sioux Reservation in Dakota Territory or to Indian Territory in Oklahoma — the end of the trail for Eastern American Indians from the 1830s on. Mounted Plains Indians resisted skillfully when they could and tried to live in peace when they were surrounded.

In one of the most brutal and cowardly acts in the West, Colonel John Chivington's Colorado Militia murdered almost 200 women, children, and elderly men in an attack on an American Indian encampment living under the American flag on Sand Creek in Colorado. Because the camp was at peace, the warriors were off hunting. Reaction to Chivington's massacre turned public opinion away from a general war against the American Indians and toward a somewhat more even-handed treatment of peaceful natives.

The Sioux struck back a couple of years later, wiping out a detachment of 81 soldiers who were building a trail through their land in Montana. Stung, the federal government actually signed the *Treaty of Fort Laramie* (1868), with the Sioux. The U.S. government agreed to stop the trail and guaranteed a Great Sioux reservation on the land around it.

Within years, Colonel George Custer's Seventh Cavalry was back on Lakota Sioux land for a "scientific exploration." Custer announced that he had discovered gold, and treaty be damned, greedy miners rushed onto land given to the Indians forever in the treaty signed only a few years before. Custer attacked the Sioux and got killed, along with 264 officers and men. The Sioux were eventually hunted down and returned to the reservation.

Also hunted down by settlers were the Plains buffalo that fed the American Indians. Buffalo were 15 million strong at the end of the Civil War. By 1885, fewer than 1,000 buffalo were left.

Chapter 15

The U.S. Goes Big Time: 1881–1899

The time between the end of the Civil War in 1865 and the beginning of the Spanish-American War in 1898 was the longest period of peace in U.S. history, and America used the time to grow. New inventions transformed the country. Industry, pushed originally by flamboyant capitalists, began to take on the look of modern big business. Women and working people also fought to make progress. Blacks endured endless persecution, but they weren't slaves anymore. Lost causes like the Populist Party and protests by laborers and farmers sowed the seeds for later reform.

As the United States grew more powerful, it got a bigger role to play in the world. The country that started as colonies becoming independent ended up fighting Spain to take over *its* colonies and, a little embarrassed, eventually set those colonies free. The United States became strong and stable enough to help lead the world into the 1900s. This chapter gives you the rundown on what happened during those years.

Social Change in the Gilded Age Scramble

Some see the time after the Civil War as a time of complacency, when the U.S. caught its breath and concentrated on making money and inventing things. Mark Twain called it the *Gilded Age* for a reason. Even though the pace of change slowed down, people who saw injustice often worked to improve society.

> ✔ The American Society for the Prevention of Cruelty to Animals was founded in 1866.
>
> ✔ Human beings got some protection, too, when the American Red Cross began in 1881 under Clara Barton, a beloved nurse from the Civil War.
>
> ✔ The *Anti-Saloon League* (1893) won some temporary victories, but Prohibition, when it came in 1919, lasted little more than a decade (see Chapter 17).

Separate but not equal

Politics didn't help blacks in the closing years of the 1800s. They weren't slaves anymore, but society was still holding them down. According to the chilling phrase used until the 1960s, keeping blacks "in their place" meant, for many Southern whites, that blacks would be kept poor, segregated, and unable to vote. Blacks were forbidden to mix with whites in Southern schools, buses, trains, and parks by *Jim Crow laws* (1890). These laws also erected phony literacy tests and poll taxes to keep blacks from voting.

Despite many challenges, Jim Crow laws were finally cleared away only by the Civil Rights Act of 1964. An early attempt to appeal to the Supreme Court, *Plessy v. Ferguson* (1896), failed when the court ruled that "separate but equal" facilities were legal under the Fourteenth Amendment. This ruling was a good day for the segregationist South but a bad day for justice. (See Chapter 26 for the best Supreme Court rulings). The lives of blacks were separate but almost never equal. Just to make sure blacks and their Northern supporters were too frightened to fight back, whites lynched more than 1,000 blacks during the 1880s and 1890s.

Question: What was the significance of the Supreme Court decision in *Plessy v. Ferguson* (1896)?

Answer: The decision said that "separate but equal" public facilities were okay under the civil-rights laws.

Blacks were left to pull themselves up by their own bootstraps, and they did so:

- *Booker T. Washington* (1885) taught hundreds of blacks to make a living at his Tuskegee Institute in Alabama. His *Atlanta Compromise Speech* (1895) called for blacks to better themselves through education even while they remained separate but linked to whites, like the individual fingers of a hand. Blacks mostly attended special black colleges until they began to be admitted to traditionally white institutions in the 1960s.

- *George Washington Carver* (1900) became a respected agricultural chemist who publicized many uses for peanuts and sweet potatoes at a time when the South needed a crop to replace cotton.

- *W. E. B. Du Bois* (1910) got a PhD from Harvard and helped found the National Association for the Advancement of Colored People (NAACP).

- Writer Paul Dunbar made the literary world appreciate the experience of blacks through poetry and dialect in *Lyrics of Lowly Life* (1896).

Question: What did Booker T. Washington support in his Atlanta Compromise Speech?

Answer: He favored black self-help and separate but cooperative development with whites.

Dealing with change on the railroads

Railroads were so important that they actually changed the time. Before the 1880s, every major city had its own local time, based on calling it noon when the sun was right over city hall. Noon in Philadelphia was a few minutes later than noon in New York; when the clocks in St. Louis said 11:50, the clocks in Chicago said noon. This customized time didn't matter much in the days of stagecoaches, but railroads needed to run on schedules that everybody understood. In 1883, the major railroads laid out four time zones for the United States; these time zones are still basically what Americans set their watches by today.

The year 1877, when the last federal troops protecting blacks were withdrawn from the South, was a bad time for many white railroad workers. The four largest railroads in the United States cut their pay by 10 percent. When union members went on strike, federal troops were called in to break up the picket lines. In the fighting that followed, more than 100 people died.

Chinese workers also had problems. After they finished building the Central Pacific railroad west from Sacramento, the jobs for low-paid Chinese far outnumbered those for other workers. When the Chinese population of California reached nearly 10 percent of the state total, jobless white residents launched violent attacks against the competitive Asians.

Under pressure, Congress passed the *Chinese Exclusion Act* (1882), barring all further settlement from China; this first law to limit national immigration stayed in effect for 60 years. Some exclusionists even tried to take away the citizenship of Chinese born in the United States, but the Supreme Court slapped them down in *U.S. v. Wong Kim Ark* (1898), saying that all people born in the United States are citizens.

Progressing with the immigrants

Immigrants brought progress as well as strong backs. They were willing to challenge entrenched interests, if necessary, to better working conditions. Most immigrants came from European towns and farms, and some newcomers took the money they earned and went back to their home countries. Almost half the Italian immigrants returned to Italy; perhaps 20 percent of other immigrants went back home in the 1800s.

The new Americans who stayed had help from urban settlement houses like *Jane Addams' Hull House* (1889) in Chicago and Lillian Wald's *Henry Street Settlement* (1893) in New York. Florence Kelley worked at both places and for 40 years led the fight for the welfare of ordinary people. Reformers slowly got laws passed to improve the treatment of the poor.

Question: From what social and economic background did most late-1800s immigrants come?

Answer: They came mostly from rural and small-town Europe.

Giving the women's-rights movement a boost

In 1820, the United States didn't have a single female college graduate. By 1900, however, one out of every four college graduates was a woman.

The women's-rights movement got a platform in *Women and Economics* (1898), written by feminist thinker Charlotte Gilman. Gilman said that women have no biological differences that necessarily keep them from full participation in the world. She called for child care and takeout food 100 years before fast food and drop-off preschool became available to working parents.

In 1890, pioneer feminists Elizabeth Cady Stanton and Susan B. Anthony passed on the torch of the Seneca Falls Convention of 1848 (see Chapter 12) by founding the National American Women's Suffrage Association. Women cleverly linked their role in the family with getting the vote. The concept had its roots in *republican motherhood* (see Chapter 10), but the arguments were now both clear and not about to go away.

Hull House hero Jane Addams said men were as sloppy at running government as they were in the home and that voting needed a woman's touch. Carrie Catt said the growth of city life meant that women couldn't confine caring about the future of their families to their houses: Family life now extended into the community, and women needed to be represented there. The movement gained strength; most Western states allowed women to vote even before the passage of the women's suffrage amendment in 1920.

The AP exam will include questions on women's rights and other social issues. Knowing the names of the primary leaders of these movements in the 1880s will help your score. At minimum, remember from the women's movement Abigail Adams, Harriet Tubman, Elizabeth Cady Stanton, and Susan B. Anthony. From the black freedom movement, keep in mind W. E. B. Du Bois, Booker T. Washington, William Lloyd Garrison, and Frederick Douglass. For labor (discussed later in this chapter), remember Samuel Gompers, Eugene V. Debs, and Terence Powderly.

Educating the population

The Morrill Act of 1862 (see Chapter 14) provided money from the sale of public land to state universities; the Hatch Act of 1887 added agricultural experimentation and education to the government-funded mix. College and high school graduation both tripled between 1870 and 1900, although those increases still meant that only 6 percent of the U.S. population stayed in school long enough to get a high-school diploma.

Bicycles: Providing transportation for everyone

Before the automobile, bicycles set people free. Riders could tear along on dangerous-looking high-wheel bikes at speeds that are hard to reach today. "Safety bicycles," with two equal wheels like the ones we ride today, made riding the rage for both men and women. By 1893, the United States had as many bicycles as horses.

Arts and Entertainment, Late-19th-Century-Style

Greater education meant greater interest in reading and in entertainment in general. Newspapers grew as most people learned to read. The invention of the *linotype* (1885), which automatically set type for newpapers, caused papers to get cheaper and more colorful.

The Associated Press, founded in the 1840s, allowed newspapers all over the world to share stories from reporters on the scene. Unfortunately, newspapers sometimes resorted to sensational and often misleading *yellow journalism* (1895) to grab readers. The term *yellow journalism* comes from an early color newspaper comic strip featuring a character called the Yellow Kid.

The rise in newspapers also led to a boost in literature and in access to public interest in art and music, because news on these items was suddenly more public. I cover these topics in more detail later in this chapter. Following are some other notable achievements in art and entertainment:

- ✔ Henry Richardson designed massive civic buildings decorated with Gothic arches.
- ✔ The Chicago World's Fair of 1893 presented the dream of a beautiful future city and sold enough tickets to admit almost half of the population of the United States.
- ✔ *Buffalo Bill's Wild West Show* (1885) brought cowboys and Indians to the world, including the crack shot Annie Oakley.
- ✔ The Barnum and Bailey Circus hit the road in 1881.
- ✔ Professional baseball got its start in the 1870s; college football was big by the 1880s; and basketball was invented by YMCA instructor James Naismith in 1891.

Literature leading to action

Civil War General Lew Wallace thought that Christianity needed defending from attacks by Darwinists (see Chapter 14), so he wrote a moving book called *Ben-Hur* (1880) that became, like *Uncle Tom's Cabin*, a best-selling international hit. The book's main character, Judah Ben-Hur, accidentally injures a high-ranking Roman commander, for which he suffers a life of punishment, only to be redeemed in the end by an encounter with Jesus. *Ben-Hur* was the first work of fiction to be blessed by the pope.

Following are other notable authors and works of the period:

- ✔ Low-profile but still beloved was *Emily Dickinson* (1886), whose poetry still moved people despite the fact that she hardly left her home.

- ✔ *Henry James* (1889) used authentic characters to explore the world of Americans, Europeans, and even women's rights in *Daisy Miller* and *The Bostonians.*

- ✔ California writers brought fresh Western ideas:

  - Jack London wrote about nature in *The Call of the Wild* (1903).

  - Frank Norris took on the railroad monopoly in *The Octopus* (1901).

  - Theodore Dreiser pioneered social realism with *Sister Carrie* (1900).

- ✔ Upton Sinclair created public uproar with his novel *The Jungle,* a muckraking exposè of the meatpacking industry.

- ✔ Jacob Riis took pictures that changed society's view of the poor in *How the Other Half Lives* (1890). His book led a young police commissioner named Teddy Roosevelt to close dangerous flophouses.

Question: What was Jacob Riis's *How the Other Half Lives*?

Answer: The book was a photographic study of poverty in New York in the 1890s.

Artists and music

Music and art grew in popularity. Now competing with photographers, artists mixed feeling with realism:

- ✔ *Thomas Eakins* (1895) ignored Victorian fashion to paint a world he considered beautiful beyond the need for idealization.

- ✔ *Winslow Homer* (1890) painted life near the sea in beautiful watercolors.

- ✔ *Augustus Saint-Gaudens* (1890) made moving sculpture, including memorializing the heroics of blacks in the Civil War.

Symphony orchestras and opera houses were founded in major American cities in the late 1800s. As black musical traditions merged with white folk music, "ragged music" became ragtime, spirituals became blues, and rhythm became jazz (and, eventually, rock-and-roll).

A Presidential Do-Si-Do

Although the plump, stuffy, walrus-mustached presidents who ran the country from the Civil War to the end of the 1800s may not seem very heroic, their very lack of conflict gave the nation time to heal and grow.

James Garfield, Chester Arthur, and William McKinley

James Garfield didn't get to be president long; he was shot in the back by a crazy guy from one of the factions in Garfield's own Republican Party. After that, even the corruption-challenged Republicans had had enough.

With the help of Chester Arthur, a newly reformed vice president turned president, Republicans surprised even themselves by passing the Magna Carta for civil-service reform, the *Pendleton Act* (1883). This law required people to have qualifications and pass tests to get government jobs. Extorting political "contributions" from government workers became illegal, even if the president *had* appointed them.

William McKinley got to preside over the Spanish-American War and the annexation of Hawaii at the turn of the 20th century. He rolled back civil service reforms to benefit his own Republican party. Civil-service reform was great, but it had two drawbacks:

✔ Politicians couldn't fire incompetent government employees who had slipped through the system.

✔ Because elected officials couldn't pay back political contributors with jobs, these politicians had to pay them back with legislation.

Grover Cleveland

The voters thanked the Republicans for finally getting honest by electing a Democrat for the first time since the Civil War. Grover Cleveland was no Progressive, but he was honest. He vetoed a bill to provide seeds to drought-stricken farmers. "Although the people support the government," he said, "the government should not support the people."

Cleveland lowered the tariff to save citizens money on imported goods and force American manufacturers to compete. The big industrialists didn't like competing. In the next election, they raised a war chest and managed to beat Cleveland by a few votes. It was the first big-business-money election in American history; many more would follow.

Benjamin Harrison

The businessmen got what they paid for. New Republican President Benjamin Harrison pushed through the highest tariff bill ever passed, the *McKinley Tariff Act* (1890). The McKinley bill set a record by taxing the average import almost 50 percent. As an example, this tax made an imported coffeepot worth $10 cost $15.

U.S. industrialists were delighted because they had less competition. U.S. manufacturers could raise their protected prices and make more profit. Regular people couldn't help noticing they were paying high prices for both imported *and* protected domestic goods.

The return of Grover Cleveland

Voters took most of the seats away from the Republicans in the House of Representatives and brought honest Grover Cleveland back again — the only president to win reelection after being out of office.

While Cleveland was making his comeback in the 1892 election, the new Populist Party managed to get more than 1 million votes. The party's platform called for a graduated income tax, government ownership of railroads and telephones, the direct election of U.S. senators, an eight-hour workday, and immigration reform. They never elected a president, but the Populists saw much of their program become law. The Populists also tried to help the Southern blacks, which made white Southerners angry. The whites tightened the Jim Crow laws so that almost no blacks got to vote in the South.

Cleveland had to face the Depression of 1893, the worst economic downturn of the 1800s. Strapped for cash to run the government, he turned to J.P. Morgan, the richest banker in the country. Morgan and his banker friends came up with the money, but they charged a commission of more than 10 percent. In the face of economic troubles, Cleveland couldn't get the tariff reductions he had promised through Congress, and the Republicans took control again in the next election.

Getting Down to Business

The United States went from also-ran to Number One among the manufacturing nations of the world in the 30 years after the Civil War. This amazing growth was based on *profits, people,* and *products:*

- ✔ The Civil War was terrible where the bullets were flying, but the North came through with almost no destruction and a lot of money earned by supplying the army. It invested much of that profit in new businesses.

- ✔ People kept coming to America. Many of them were hard workers willing to put in 12-hour days if that's what it took to move their families up the economic ladder.

- ✔ The United States almost burst with inventive ingenuity, creating new products like Alexander Bell's *telephone* (1876), the typewriter, the cash register, and the electric streetcar. Thomas Edison's *electric light* (1879), combined with the distribution system he designed to power it, changed the world. Before bright lights, people used to sleep at night. Edison also invented the phonograph (ancestor of the MP3 player) and the movies that led to DVDs.

The rise of the millionaire businessman

Ambitious businessmen learned how to take advantage of all this profit, people, and product innovation; that's how they became rich.

Andrew Carnegie

Andrew Carnegie (1890) ran a steelmaking operation that proved the power of *vertical integration* — controlling everything you need to make a product. Carnegie miners dug iron ore out of frozen northern Minnesota and loaded it onto Carnegie ships, which steamed across the Great Lakes to Carnegie trains, which took the ore to Carnegie blast furnaces running night and day in Pittsburgh.

Carnegie also helped fund thousands of public libraries, thus spreading "the poor people's university" all over the country. Carnegie wrote *The Gospel of Wealth*, a book that said rich people had a responsibility to spend their money in a way that would help poor people better themselves. By 1920, the United States had thousands of free public libraries — more than in the rest of the world combined — and half of them were built with help from Carnegie.

John D. Rockefeller

Using a different approach, *John D. Rockefeller* (1885) built Standard Oil into a company by using *horizontal integration* — controlling all the outlets for selling a product. Standard Oil drove retail and wholesale competitors out of business. Rockefeller said, "The day of combination is here to stay. Individualism has gone, never to return."

Rockefeller did whales an unexpected favor when he organized Standard Oil in 1870: The kerosene he made from petroleum gave much better light than the expensive whale oil that people had previously burned in lamps. Cans of kerosene from Standard Oil were invariably one of the first American products to arrive as U.S. commerce spread all over the world. Electric lights soon made kerosene obsolete, but freeways would lead to other uses for oil.

J.P. Morgan

J.P. Morgan (1895) controlled banks he didn't even own with interlocking directorates, using people who shared seats on many boards of directors. When a group of businesses conspired to fix prices, it was called a *trust*.

North versus South in manufacturing and tobacco

The South took a long time to do much manufacturing; it was farther behind the North in industrialization in 1900 than it had been before the war. Even making cloth from cotton lagged in the South; although Southerners had built a few textile mills by 1900, two-thirds of the cloth was still being made in the North.

The only good thing for the South was bad for people: The invention of the cigarette-manufacturing machine in the 1880s got Americans smoking in a big way. The machine meant more tobacco production and a cigarette-manufacturing industry for the South.

Breaking in against Northern firms on established products was tough. Birmingham, Alabama, just happened to have iron ore, coal, and limestone all close to town — perfect for making steel. Northern railroads slowed this competition on behalf of their Pittsburgh steel-making buddies by charging Birmingham steelmakers inflated shipping rates, as though they were sending their steel from Pittsburgh.

Private enterprise and antitrust laws

State governments tried to regulate the railroads but were pushed aside when the Supreme Court ruled in the *Wabash Cases* (1886) that states can't regulate interstate commerce, meaning that the states had to keep their hands off any business that worked between two or more states.

Congress knew it had to do something, so it passed the *Interstate Commerce Act* (1887). This legislation set up the Interstate Commerce Commission (ICC). Although the ICC didn't have much power to take on the powerful railroads, it at least established the principle that the public has an interest in private enterprise that the government has a duty to protect.

Besides the transportation companies, a number of other virtual monopoly trusts like steel and telephones took advantage of the public. To deal with companies so big that they stopped competition, Congress passed the *Sherman Anti-Trust Act* (1890). The term *antitrust law* has persisted in the United States as what the rest of the world calls competition laws, designed to make sure that consumers get fair prices based on competition, not price-fixing by businesses.

Attacking the victims, the Anti-Trust Act was even used against union organization in its early days, until the Clayton Act stopped it in 1914 (see Chapter 16). As with the ICC, the Anti-Trust Act took years to stand up to business.

Hard Times and Labor Unions

Even with some brave efforts, the working face of America wasn't what the founding fathers had imagined. The century started with Thomas Jefferson's dream of independent farmers creating a democratic utopia and ended with most of America working for other people.

During the last 20 years of the 1800s, several hundred thousand unskilled workers a year landed on America's shores, looking for work. This influx of workers made it easy for bosses to hire people at low wages — pay so low that whole families had to work, kids included.

Child labor went on until the 1930s, when photographs of children as young as 8 in dangerous jobs, taken by pioneering documentary photographer *Lewis Hine* (1910), finally made the government take action. Some employers took advantage of workers, charging them high prices in company stores and threatening them if they tried to organize.

Labor-union organizations grew as a result of bad treatment and low wages. The Knights of Labor (see Chapter 14) had close to 1 million members by 1886. Terence Powderly of the Knights denounced multimillionaire businessmen for "laying the foundation for their colossal fortunes on the bodies and souls of living men."

A demonstration in that year in Chicago's Haymarket Square turned to violence when a bomb was thrown, killing a policeman. Eight union leaders were arrested. Even though no evidence showed that any of the leaders had anything to do with the bomb, five were sentenced to death and three to stiff prison terms.

Association with violence, even though the Knights of Labor didn't cause it, cooled support for the organization. When a new organization of skilled workers called the American Federation of Labor (AFL) was formed later that year, it gradually took over the union fight from the Knights. AFL President Samuel Gompers concentrated only on skilled workers and knew how to work within the system to improve the position of working people gradually.

Question: What kind of labor unions made up the AFL?

Answer: Only skilled worker labor unions were admitted to the AFL.

Coxey's Army (1894), a small band of determined protestors, marched across the country to Washington, D.C., to demand jobs and federal help. During the *Pullman strike* (1894), in which workers blocked the railroad tracks to protest cuts in pay without cuts in company-housing rent, federal troops moved in against striking laborers for the first time. Union leader Eugene Debs, realizing that the system had to change, later ran for president.

For the time being, big business and big government appeared to have joined to keep poor people in their place. When William Jennings Bryan ran against William McKinley in 1896, the conservatives triumphed decisively. People with jobs and unmortgaged farms didn't want to take a chance of losing them to free silver and free trade. The *Dingley Tariff Bill* (1897) made imported goods cost more than ever, so that domestic industries could charge more without foreign competition. Gold stayed the standard, but new gold discoveries in Alaska, Canada, and elsewhere helped the money supply. The causes of women, workers, and blacks slowly edged toward acceptance in the public mind.

Question: What was the cause of the Pullman strike?

Answer: Pullman cut workers' pay without a corresponding cut in workers' rent.

Hard times for farmers, too

Major machinery became available to farmers in the 1880s. If you had a place big enough that you could afford it, a single machine could plow, plant, and work the seeds into the soil. The amazing combine coupled a machine that cut grain with another machine that threshed the grain off the stems and into bags, ready to sell. People don't become farmers because they like to do high finance, and a lot of landowners got caught in a financial squeeze by over-borrowing and overproduction.

Pushed by the banks and exploited by big business, farmers fought back in almost every way they could, trying to regulate railroads, organize cooperatives, form a political party, and even inflate the currency. But they never did what the trusts did every day: limited production to raise prices. That strategy would have taken more organization and trust than independent farmers could muster.

Question: What did farmers do to improve their financial situation?

Answer: They tried to lower railroad charges, organize production cooperatives, and get political help. Unlike monopoly capitalists, however, they never held down supply to increase demand and price.

Because more land and better farm equipment were available, the price that farmers got paid for a bushel of wheat fell from $1 at the time of the Civil War to 50 cents in 1890. Loans that farmers had taken out to grow more wheat cost twice as much wheat to repay.

Meanwhile, the nation got used to paying cheap prices for beautiful California produce, harvested by poorly paid Mexican and Chinese labor, and shipped east in the railroads' new refrigerator cars. Small family farmers went deeper into debt.

Question: How did farms change in size and equipment in the late 1800s?

Answer: More and bigger farms were available, with better equipment.

Farmers' "party" with laborers

Farmers joined with laborers to support cheap money and progressive causes through the *Greenback Labor Party* (1878) and the *Populist Party* (1892). Neither party won the presidency, but each polled as much as 10 percent of the votes and elected enough legislators to sway the Democrats in their direction.

Third parties have played a big part in American history; don't get them confused. Here's a rundown of major third parties in the 1800s:

- In 1832, the Anti-Masonic Party, seeking the eradication of the Freemasons and other secret societies from the United States, received a few votes.

- In 1848, the Free Soil Party, a precursor of the Republican Party, nominated former President Martin Van Buren as its presidential candidate, splitting the vote in New York and causing the election of Zachary Taylor.

- In 1856, parts of the disintegrating Whig Party teamed up with the Know-Nothing Party, which opposed foreign immigration. Even as a team, the parties came in third behind Democrat James Buchanan and John C. Fremont of the newly formed Republican Party.

- In 1860, four major candidates ran for president, including candidates from the breakaway Southern Democratic Party and the last-ditch-compromise Constitutional Union

Party. Republican Abraham Lincoln was elected with only 39 percent of the vote and wasn't even on the ballot in many states.

✔ In 1892, the Populist Party won 22 electoral votes and 8.6 percent of the popular vote. The Democratic Party eventually adopted many Populist Party positions, making this contest a good example of a delayed vote for change.

Settling the West: The End of Wide-Open Spaces?

Settlers rode the railroads to new homes in the West as American Indians were driven out of their wide-open country to try to survive on confined reservations. Said one American Indian, "The antelope have gone; the buffalo wallows are empty. . . . We are like birds with a broken wing."

James Earle Fraser's famous *End of the Trail* (1915), an image of an American Indian on horseback with bowed head and downcast lance, was reproduced so many times that it seemed to symbolize the end of wide-open-spaces freedom for urbanized settlers as well as the free life of Great Plains American Indians.

In one of the few times a professional historian actually made history, Frederick Turner gave a speech called "The Significance of the Frontier in the American History" at the Chicago World's Fair of 1893. Turner said that the American character was formed by the possibilities of the open frontier — a frontier, he announced, that was closing.

Maybe it was time to get powdered wigs and start dancing the minuet again. Actually, the frontier was as much a state of mind as a place. At the same time Turner was announcing the end of the West, the government was creating permanently open land with the world's first national parks in Yosemite, Yellowstone, and Sequoia. These preserves were the first of hundreds of national parks and forests.

Pressure on American Indians

Even American Indians' small reservations were threatened under the *Dawes Severalty Act* (1887), which tried to break up tribes and split up land for ownership by individual American Indian families. By 1900, American Indian tribes had lost more than half of the limited land onto which they'd been crowded 20 years before. Native families were forced to accept private allotments of poor land on which they'd be separated from their tribal culture. When this resulted in surplus land, the government sold it off at bargain prices to settlers.

The shortsighted policy of trying to make American Indians into settler farmers on land that wouldn't support crops lasted until the American Indian New Deal of the 1930s recognized American Indians as full U.S. citizens. One last American Indian massacre occurred in 1890, however, when federal troops opened fire with machine guns on American Indians gathering for a sacred dance at Wounded Knee, South Dakota, killing 200 men, women, and children.

From a low of fewer than 250,000 American Indians at the close of the Western frontier in 1890, the U.S. American Indian population rebounded to 1.5 million urban and rural American Indians by 2000.

Question: What was the main policy of the United States toward American Indians from 1877 to the New Deal?

Answer: To break up tribes and give individual American Indians their own land.

Helen Jackson's Ramona

People who fought for American Indian rights included Helen Jackson, who wrote the factual story of mistreatment in *A Century of Dishonor* (1881) and then the popular novel *Ramona* (1884).

Ramona is the story of a part-American Indian, part-Scottish girl in California. With black hair and blue eyes, Ramona is reared in a privileged ranch family until she falls in love with the poor son of an American Indian chief. The book sold 600,000 copies and spawned plays, movies, and even towns.

People loved the story so much that they named buildings for Ramona; localities competed with claims to be the inspiration for her homeland. Unfortunately, the story missed its immediate goal of winning widespread sympathy for the plight of American Indians; instead, it touched off the American love of Spanish mission architecture that lives on today in many Mexican restaurants. *Ramona* did encourage the trend toward thinking of the defeated American Indians as being somehow noble and worthy of humane treatment. Long after the story was forgotten, its meaning moved society.

Backing Paper Money with Precious Metals

After the California gold rush that began in 1849 and lasted into the 1850s came the Nevada Silver bonanza of the 1860s. Scattered gold and silver discoveries also popped up in other Western states. All this glittering metal allowed the U.S. Treasury to back paper money with gold by 1879 (see Chapter 14).

The many senators who represented the few people living in the low-population, high-treasure West pushed for the government to buy more precious metal. This push combined with the belief of debt-ridden workers and farmers that money based on silver would ease their woes by making loans easier to repay with inflated cheap money (see Chapter 14).

At the Democratic Party convention in 1896, presidential candidate William Jennings Bryan made his famous "cross of gold" speech, which emotionally compared the Republicans, who demanded money tied only to gold, to the Romans who crucified Jesus. Poor people were elated; rich people were horrified. Backed by middle-class fear and upper-class financing, the Republicans easily beat Bryan.

Question: What was William Jennings Bryan's "cross of gold" speech?

Answer: Delivered to the Democratic convention that nominated him for president, the speech called for the inflationary use of silver money to keep poor people from being crucified by golden hard money on the bankers' "cross of gold."

Being the Nicest Imperialist

As the 1800s drew to a close, America was bursting at the seams. It had been the longest time in U.S. history without a war, and the country needed something to distract itself from its economic troubles. The European powers were in a final imperialistic feeding frenzy, gobbling up bits of Africa and Asia they'd overlooked before.

Could the United States, founded on anticolonialism, stay out of the game? As the *Washington Post* editorialized, "The taste of Empire is in the mouth of the people even as the taste of blood is in the jungle." Some people believed social Darwinism proved that the United States *must* rule because it *could* rule.

The old Monroe Doctrine (see Chapter 11) got enforced in 1896 when the United States offered to mediate in a conflict between Venezuela and Britain on the border of British colony British Guiana in South America. After blowing America off at first, the British got all friendly and agreeable when they found themselves up to their knees in the Boer War in Africa. Score one for the United States.

Annexing Hawaii

Hawaii had been flirting with the United States since it became a whaling supply station in the early 1800s and the site of a major American missionary effort. Thanks to missionaries, Hawaii actually had the first printing press west of the Mississippi. Thanks to the king of Hawaii, John Sutter founded Sacramento (and touched off the gold rush) with the help of Hawaiian workers. The sons of the first missionaries planted sugar cane, and the Hawaiian government granted Pearl Harbor to the United States as a naval base.

When the McKinley Tariff made it more expensive to sell Hawaiian sugar in the United States, the American sugar planters in Hawaii had an easy solution. They deposed Queen Liliuokalani and asked to be admitted to the United States; Hawaii wouldn't be subject to the tariff if it were part of the United States. For five years, the United States held Hawaii off as a point of honor — it didn't want to be associated with land-grabbing. With the outbreak of the Spanish-American War, the United States got over the honor thing and annexed Hawaii.

Fighting the Spanish-American War

Sugar also made problems in Cuba when high U.S. import duties caused fewer sales and more hardship for the sugar workers. The workers rose in revolt against the Spanish colonial government, which suppressed them severely.

The United States was sympathetic to the workers' plight, and yellow journalists egged the country on toward war with Spain. Sensational newspaperman William Randolph Hearst sent famous Western artist Frederick Remington to Cuba to draw pictures of the atrocities. When Remington cabled that conditions weren't bad enough for a war, Hearst cabled back, "Please remain. You furnish the pictures and I'll furnish the war."

Losing the battleship Maine

At the worst possible time for the Spanish, the U.S. battleship *Maine,* which had been sent to Cuba on a goodwill visit, blew up in Havana harbor. Four independent investigations over the past 100 years have come to four different conclusions about what caused the explosion, but at the time everybody but the Spanish believed that Spain had torched it. Congress voted to invade Cuba, but also passed the *Teller Amendment* (1898), which promised to free Cuba after the island was free of the Spanish.

Using some tricky fighting, the United States first attacked the Spanish not in Cuba but in Spain's Philippine Islands colony, halfway around the world. The U.S. fleet sailed into Manila harbor, pulverized the Spanish fleet, and then sat around sweltering through the tropical summer, waiting for American troops to get there and take the islands. With the help of Filipino insurrectionists, the American army made short work of the Spanish troops.

Cuba was the same story. The American navy smashed the Spanish without losing a ship, and the American army, with Teddy Roosevelt leading the Rough Riders, quickly defeated the Spanish troops. The army still had a few Civil War veterans from 33 years before; Northerners and Southerners felt good about fighting on the same side.

Letting Cuba go but keeping the rest

To end the one-sided Spanish-American War, Spain agreed to give the United States control of Cuba, the Philippines, and Puerto Rico. The United States, feeling a little guilty, generously kicked in $20 million for the Philippines, because they were kind of a bonus for freeing Cuba. Puerto Rico came as a free bonus, which America decided to keep.

U.S. expansionism at the end of the 1800s is a natural stopping place for any essay discussion on Manifest Destiny you may have to undertake on AP U.S. History game day. Remember: *Imperialism* is keeping colonies; *expansionism* is adding land that becomes a real part of the mother country. With the Philippines free, Hawaii a territory, and Puerto Rico regularly voting to stay with the United States, the end of the United States' 1890s overseas adventures came out as expansionism.

The United States set Cuba free as promised, keeping only a naval base at Guantanamo Bay, which was a little bigger than Manhattan. Having cleaned its clock once, the United States felt free to intervene in Cuba any time it wanted until Fidel Castro took power in 1958.

Fighting in the Philippines

The Philippines were trickier. European countries, especially Germany, were still sniffing around the world for colonies. The United States decided to keep the Philippines for a few years to add some schools and roads and stuff. That meant fighting a bloody war against the same Filipino revolutionaries who had just finished helping America get rid of the Spanish.

The Philippines conflict lasted for five years and led to the deaths of thousands of soldiers on both sides and hundreds of thousands of civilians caught in the crossfire. The United States finally freed the Philippines in 1946, after World War II.

Rebelling against the idea of empire

The U.S. flirtation with empire, especially keeping the Philippines, was opposed by a lot of Americans, including Mark Twain, Andrew Carnegie, former President Grover Cleveland, Jane Addams, and the presidents of Harvard and Stanford universities.

Eventually, the imperialist eagle came to rest with the release of Cuba and the Philippines; Puerto Rico and Hawaii were mostly cool about staying part of the United States. As the United States increasingly became a Big Dog world power, the temptation to push smaller nations around never went away.

Question: What was the biggest controversy following the Spanish-American War?

Answer: Americans debated whether freedom-loving America had any right to keep the Philippine Islands unfree, as a colony.

Chapter 16

Into the World, Ready or Not: 1900–1919

In This Chapter

▶ Trying to be a good imperialist

▶ Following the Teddy Roosevelt, William Howard Taft, and Woodrow Wilson presidencies

▶ Sweeping America's shortcomings out from under the rug

▶ Making progress with the Progressives

▶ Marching into World War I

*A*t the beginning of the 20th century, the U.S. was all dressed up for a world party but not too sure about going into the dance. America's somewhat-reluctant empire extended halfway around the globe, so the country was beginning to look like an international player. But people still remembered the Founding Fathers' warnings to stay away from entangling foreign hassles, and they were more concerned with the economic and social work to do at home.

After years of holding off change, the U.S. shifted into high gear and went trucking down the road to major reform when the odometer of history flipped over to 1900. Just when the Progressives were looking for even more corruption to haul away, the U.S. got dragged into World War I. After tipping the balance toward victory in the war, the nation got so moral at the peace negotiations that it couldn't stand itself. By not quite agreeing to sign on for its own ideals, the U.S. unintentionally ensured that it would have to fight for them again. But World War II is a story for Chapter 18; this chapter is about what happened in the early 20th century leading up to World War I.

For the test, the way the political, economic, and social (PES) system works is to associate a PES topic *in italics* with a date (in parenthesis), like *Progressives* (1910). (See Chapter 1 for more on the PES system.) The big AP test doesn't care much about exact dates, but you do need to be able to keep the highlights in chronological order. If the PES topic is a law, the date is when it was passed, like the *Seventeenth Amendment* (1913). If the topic is an institution like *Hull House* (1889) or a person like *John D. Rockefeller* (1885), the date is just a representative year in what could be a long career. Remember, the date in parentheses is just an approximate time signal.

More Substitute Teacher than Cop: The U.S. in Asia

In 1899, the Americans and the Filipinos were standing side by side waving goodbye to the Spanish colonists when the native independence fighters realized something was wrong with this picture: The Yankees weren't leaving.

After five years of the U.S. Army slogging through the jungle led by ex-American-Indian-fighters from the Wild West, the Americans managed to knock out all the major rebel armies at a cost of thousands of soldiers and hundreds of thousands of civilian lives. The rewards to the U.S. were slight; it got a naval base and a jumping-off place for activity in Asia. The Filipinos learned some English in the schools Americans helped build but were quite happy to finally get their freedom on July 4th, 1946 — see Chapter 18.

China and the Open Door Policy

Colonialism made little European countries feel like big dogs, so they tried to nip off pieces such as Hong Kong from large-but-weak China. The U.S. didn't want to nab China, but the nation also didn't want other countries to set up permanent shop and exclude them from the party. So the U.S., consulting more or less with the other major players, issued the *Open Door Policy* (1899). All foreign nations in China were supposed to respect Chinese rights and let other countries bid fairly on commercial contracts. To the Chinese, it felt like an agreement among the bullies about how to fairly divide the lunch money they stole.

Question: What was the Open Door Policy?

Answer: A U.S.-sponsored agreement among Western nations to respect Chinese rights and let other countries bid fairly on commercial contracts.

The Boxer Rebellion

Chinese anti-Westerners called the Boxers murdered Western missionaries and besieged Western diplomats holed up in the capital of Beijing. Western governments quickly threw together an eight-nation rescue/invasion force of 20,000 soldiers to put down the *Boxer Rebellion* (1900).

The United States contributed a couple of thousand troops handily located in the Philippines. The Western diplomats barricaded their offices into one big fort and held out for 55 days with nothing but one old cannon until help arrived.

China had to pay a huge amount of money for the trouble some of their citizens had caused the Westerners. Shame over their weakness led the Chinese to get rid of the ancient Empress Dowager and start a more modern government. The U.S. used some of its share of the money to educate Chinese students in America.

Rough Riding with the Teddy Bear

A nation happy to be a world power without having to do much fighting overwhelmingly reelected William McKinley for a second term. This time, plump and popular McKinley was almost overshadowed by his rambunctious running mate, Theodore Roosevelt, hero of the Spanish-American War.

The political bosses in New York State were so happy to see their reform-minded energy-ball governor Roosevelt leave to run for vice president that they would have bought him the office if they could just to get rid of him.

Teddy toured with cowboys and cut into the rural and Western support for the Democratic nominee, good old cross-of-gold William Jennings Bryan. In the end, the election wasn't even close — McKinley and Roosevelt won because although a lot of people didn't like imperialism, they were more afraid of Bryan's crazy economic theories.

The U.S. didn't get long with safe and sane William McKinley; a crazy anarchist gunned him down at the 1901 world's fair in Buffalo. Although the fair displayed an early X-ray machine, doctors didn't know how to use it, so they never removed the bullet, which would have saved McKinley's life. Worse, they had to operate in a room without electric lights. Electricity was relatively new, and although the outside of the building had beautiful lights all over it, no one had thought to put one in the medical department on the inside. At 42, Rough Rider Teddy Roosevelt became the youngest president ever.

The rise of Teddy Roosevelt

Theodore Roosevelt was a whirlwind. One of the greatest and toughest presidents in American history, Roosevelt was so sickly as a child that he had to sleep sitting up to keep from dying of asthma. His father insisted that he exercise and take up boxing to keep from being beaten up by bullies. Even though a doctor told him that his heart condition would keep him at a desk job, Roosevelt just increased his activity.

Roosevelt was brilliant, graduating from Harvard magna cum laude. He wrote books about U.S. Navy battles in the War of 1812 and a four-volume history of the West, both of which scholars still cite today. Roosevelt's first presidency was as leader of the American Historical Association.

When his mother and his young wife both happened to die on the same day, Roosevelt headed west. He built a ranch in the Dakota Territory and learned shooting, riding, and roping. Elected deputy sheriff, he single handedly brought in three desperados, guarding them without sleeping for almost two days by reading Tolstoy to keep awake. He later married his childhood sweetheart and took her on a honeymoon to Europe, where he climbed Mont Blanc, the highest peak in the Alps.

Appointed to the Civil Service Commission, he served with such fairness that even after the Democrats won the White House, they kept Progressive Republican Roosevelt at his post. As the police commissioner of New York, he cleaned up the police department, often calling officers in the middle of the night to make sure they were on duty.

Roosevelt had always loved the Navy, so Republican President William McKinley appointed him Assistant Secretary of the Navy. Assistant was enough power for Roosevelt; he pretty much ran things over the head of his boss and modernized the Navy.

When the Spanish-American War broke out, Roosevelt quit his desk job and organized a regiment of volunteers called the Rough Riders: cowboys, American Indians, polo players, and policemen. Fighting alongside a black regiment, they did well in the key battles of the fight for Cuba. See Chapter 15 for more on the Spanish-American War.

The Big-Stick philosophy

When news of McKinley's assassination reached Roosevelt, he was camping in the mountains. Even before becoming president, he used to speak publicly in favor of speaking softly but carrying a big stick. Teddy worked to carry out McKinley's careful policies, but he began to use his famous Big Stick to support progressive laws as he became comfortable as president. Roosevelt charmed his opponents with talk and threatened them with the Big Stick of power. Roosevelt began the practice of busting up *trusts* (corporations that controlled whole industries so they could fix prices) to encourage competition and lower prices for customers. See Chapter 15 for more on trusts.

Don't get mesmerized by Theodore Roosevelt's Big-Stick philosophy and think that he made all the progress in the 1900s. Roosevelt's successor, William Taft, actually busted more trusts than Teddy. Roosevelt set the tone, but he was balanced and opportunistic in his politics.

Building the Panama Canal

One place Theodore Roosevelt didn't settle for incremental progress was in dealing with other nations. When the nation of Columbia wouldn't let the United States build a canal through its Panama district, Teddy helped set up a revolution in which Panama became an independent country. The new country was — big surprise — thrilled to have a U.S.-owned canal running through the middle of it.

Teddy became the first president to leave U.S. soil when he energetically dashed down to Panama to help with the digging. Health workers figured out how to protect people from yellow fever and malaria as the result of America's interest in surviving in both the canal and in Cuba. The *Panama Canal* (1914) was a big success, cutting sailing time between the Atlantic and Pacific by more than half. The U.S. finally turned the canal over to Panama in 1999 after owning it for almost 100 years.

The Roosevelt Corollary

Teddy also created the overreaching *Roosevelt Corollary to the Monroe Doctrine* (1905), also known as *preventive intervention*. The original *Monroe Doctrine* (1823) said that the United States would defend the New World from any further attempts at Old World colonization.

The Roosevelt Corollary said that to keep the little countries of South America from being taken over by bad Europeans, the U.S. would step in with good Americans but only to help them. Well, maybe also to help some big businessmen. U.S. troops invaded six Latin American countries but kept none of them as colonies.

Question: What was the Roosevelt Corollary to the Monroe Doctrine?

Answer: The U.S. would prevent the intervention of Old World powers in Latin America by intervening itself as necessary.

Nativism and the Great White Fleet

Still squabbling over the China situation, Japan and Russia fought a war in 1904. Roosevelt got them to a conference table in the U.S. and hammered out a peace agreement, for which he won a Nobel Peace Prize. Roosevelt sent the entire U.S. Navy, painted white, on an around-the-world cruise as *The Great White Fleet* (1908), symbolizing both American purity and strength.

In 1906, he made a secret deal with the Japanese to limit immigration, thus reassuring California, which was beginning to work up an Asian paranoia again after having previously excluded the Chinese. The movement to limit immigration, called *nativism*, grew in the early

1900s due to increases in the foreign-born population, competition for jobs, and paranoia about imported radicals.

Question: What influenced the rise of nativism in the early 1900s?

Answer: Increases in the foreign-born population, competition for jobs, and paranoia about imported radicals. California was a center of anti-Asian feeling.

Exposing the Shortcomings of Society

Although change sometimes begins slowly, it can be pretty rambunctious after it gets going. The U.S. had always had a Progressive movement, even as early as Abigail Adams's remember-the-ladies letter before the Revolution. Although "walrus" presidents (with their slow-moving politics and big business) seemed to dominate the post-Civil War 1800s, the Greenback Labor party of the 1870s and the Populist party of the 1890s also got in on the act. Progressive thinkers rejected the Social Darwinism of unregulated business and called for government action because concentrations of wealth were hurting, not improving, society.

Women and working people didn't win their crusades, but they also didn't give up. Upper-class suffragettes worked for the women's vote and improved living conditions through urban settlement houses like Jane Addams's *Hull House* (1889) in Chicago and Lillian Wald's *Henry Street Settlement* (1893) in New York. Women's clubs blossomed from 100,000 members in the 1890s to more than 1 million by World War I.

Question: Why did Progressives reject Social Darwinism?

Answer: Because the natural competition of unregulated business seemed to be hurting people, not helping society to evolve.

Muckraking becomes an art

Exposing the shortcomings of society became a major occupation with the increase in the circulation of newspapers, popular magazines, and books in the early 1900s. People seemed to be able to dredge up almost any hidden secret. *Lincoln Steffens* (1902) wrote *The Shame of the Cities,* detailing municipal corruption in leading towns. *Ida Tarbell* (1904) exposed the monopolistic practices of the Standard Oil Company that had ruined her father. *Thomas Lawson* (1905), himself a major stock manipulator, tattled on the trust scammers in *Frenzied Finance.* Other socially conscious authors examined legislative corruption in *The Treason of the Senate* (1906), the slow progress of the blacks in *Following the Color Line* (1908), and child labor in *The Bitter Cry of Children* (1906). Teddy Roosevelt called these reformers *muckrakers* (1904) because they insisted on cleaning up the country by looking down at the mucky mess.

Question: What helped muckrakers publicize their investigations?

Answer: The growth in the popular press, magazines, and books.

Clearing away bad food

Dr. Harvey Wiley worked from within the government with a Poison Squad to uncover enough bad food to lead to the *Pure Food and Drug Act* (1906), forcing manufacturers to use safe ingredients and honest labels.

The Jungle (1906) by muckraker *Upton Sinclair* sickened the public with its description of what went on inside the food industry and led to the *Meat Inspection Act of 1906*. Federal inspectors visited packing houses to work toward protecting people from being poisoned by their own food. Like the novel *Ramona* (see Chapter 15), which intended to save American Indians but ended up initially saving Mission architecture, *The Jungle* intended to save workers but ended up saving the food they processed.

Charting progress with the Progressives

Forward-thinking attempts to clean up politics became a cause for both political parties. The *Progressives* (1910) succeeded because they weren't marginalized as dangerous radicals: Progressives were middle- and even upper-class reformers working to fix the system from within.

> Question: Why were the Progressives so successful?
>
> Answer: They were respectable middle-class reformers with popular support.

To get around the influence of political bosses, Progressives introduced the *initiative* system so that voters could propose and vote on new laws without going through the legislature. The still-ongoing attempts to limit campaign contributions and the corruption they can bring began with the Progressives passing campaign financing laws in a few states in the early 1900s. Previously, voters had to mark ballots in public, and party bosses could see how people voted; the Progressives made the secret Australian ballot the national standard. Often-corrupt state legislatures elected Senators until Progressives passed the *Seventeenth Amendment* (1913), which mandated the election of Senators by the people.

In the key Supreme Court case of *Muller v. Oregon* (1908), Progressive attorney *Louis Brandeis* convinced the Court that states have a right to protect employees in the workplace; in this case, that meant protecting women from having to work more than 10 hours a day. Brandeis went on to become the first Jewish high official when he himself joined the Supreme Court.

The tragic industrial *Triangle Shirtwaist Fire* (1911) claimed the lives of almost 150 women workers but led to legal regulation of workplaces. By the time of World War I, more than half of the states had laws providing some worker's compensation to people injured on the job. Prohibition rode along with other causes; by 1914 more than half of the country had prohibited the sale of liquor.

Implementing Roosevelt's Square Deal

Theodore Roosevelt promised Americans a *Square Deal:* He would control the big corporations, protect consumers, and conserve the environment. When coal miners stayed on strike for almost half a year, it looked like a frozen winter for the many people who heated their homes with coal. Roosevelt called employers and workers into the White House and became the first president to hammer out a labor agreement. He threatened to use federal troops against the mine *owners* if they didn't compromise — a big change from previous government actions, when the troops were always ordered in against the workers. Congress created the *Department of Commerce and Labor* (1903) to oversee both business and workers.

> Question: How did President Roosevelt handle the coal strike?
>
> Answer: He became the first president to arbitrate a labor settlement.

The all-powerful railroads got slapped around a bit when the *Elkins Act* (1902) prohibited rebates that kept rates high for little shippers and the *Hepburn Act* (1906) ended the practice of giving free passes to anyone who could write or pass laws against the transportation companies. The heretofore wimpy Interstate Commerce Commission actually got the power to take action against fares that gouged the public.

Roosevelt busted his first big trust with the *Northern Securities Company* (1904). Famous rich guy J.P. Morgan and his friends were trying to monopolize railroads in the Northwest. Roosevelt slapped them down, and the Supreme Court backed him. Teddy Roosevelt didn't believe that big business was automatically bad. He was just against businesses that controlled a market so that they could unfairly make people pay high prices. He probably wouldn't have minded today's big-box stores as long as they allowed real competition.

Preserving the American Wilderness

Teddy Roosevelt went camping with the famous environmentalist John Muir and got really committed to saving land. Because the frontier was no longer limitless, the U.S. started locking up land for the future in parks and national forests.

Before Roosevelt, the U.S. had the *Forest Reserve Act* (1891), which set aside some land, but most of the country was open to exploitation by loggers, miners, ranchers, or anybody else with a profitable way to use it up.

First Roosevelt increased the value of Western land by supporting the *Newlands Reclamation Act* (1902), which resulted in damming nearly every river in the West to irrigate nearby fields. Then he set aside almost 200 million acres of land for national forests and parks — way more land than all the previous presidents combined.

Working with farsighted Forest Service head Gifford Pinchot, Roosevelt created 42 million acres of national forests, 53 national wildlife refuges, and 18 areas of special interest like the Grand Canyon. Americans responded by joining new outdoor organizations like the Boy Scouts, Girl Scouts, and Sierra Club (founded by Roosevelt's buddy Muir).

Roosevelt Gives Way to Taft and then Wilson

Roosevelt rode out a financial panic in 1907 by passing the *Aldrich-Vreeland Act* (1908), which provided for the issuance of emergency currency and paved the way for the *National Reserve Act* (1913) that's still responsible for dealing with national financial problems.

He easily won reelection in 1904 and supported William Howard Taft as his successor when his second term expired in 1908. Most of the nation wanted him to stay on as president, but he went hunting in Africa instead.

Trust-busting with William Howard Taft

President William Howard Taft had a hard act to follow. Fat and jovial, Taft tried to stick to Roosevelt's policies without Roosevelt's vision or charm. He took on the U.S. Steel trust and a number of other monopolies, carefully following laws passed under Roosevelt.

Taft and the trusts

The Supreme Court ordered that Standard Oil Company be broken up in 1911. At the same time, the Court issued a *rule of reason* that said the law applied only to companies that *unreasonably* restrain trade, thus making it harder to bust trusts. Even so, Taft went after twice as many monopolies as Teddy actually sued.

Republican businessmen generally liked high tariffs on imported goods; it made their products easier to sell at a profit. Problem was, the Progressive wing of their own party called high tariffs the Mother of All Trusts and vowed to substantially lower the charges. After lots of inner-party wrangling, Congress passed the *Payne-Aldrich Bill* (1909), which only lowered tariffs on the items people didn't want anyway.

Taft had failed to come through for the Progressive wing of his party. He did act to protect U.S. business interests in Latin America with a few invasions of little countries, but he got in even more trouble with Progressives for firing environmental hero Gifford Pinchot for criticizing the sale of public lands to corporate development. Taft did establish the Bureau of Mines to protect coal land and water supplies, but it was too little too late. The Republicans lost big in Congress and then, with Roosevelt running on a third-party ticket, lost even bigger in the presidential election of 1912 to Democrat Woodrow Wilson.

Injured in a perilous exploration in South America, Teddy Roosevelt died in his sleep in 1919. Said Wilson's vice president Thomas Marshall, "Death had to take him sleeping, for if Roosevelt had been awake, there would have been a fight." Roosevelt enlarged the Presidency and the nation in three ways: He civilized capitalism so that it could survive in a world where people as well as profit mattered; he began to make the environment a concern of government; and he introduced the U.S. to its growing responsibilities on the world stage. He is also associated with the introduction of the teddy bear, the model of a little bear he refused to shoot on a hunting trip. Actually, realist Roosevelt didn't like the idea of a bear being seen as cuddly.

Idealism with Woodrow Wilson

1912 was a campaign to remember. Roosevelt's name was put in nomination at the Progressive party convention by Hull House feminist Jane Addams. The convention exploded when Roosevelt declared, "We stand at Armageddon, and we battle for the Lord."

During the campaign, Roosevelt was shot in the chest in Milwaukee by John Schrank, a crazy person. Fortunately, the bullet went through Roosevelt's steel glasses case, but he was still wounded and bleeding. Roosevelt refused all help and went on to make an 80-minute speech after he had been shot. Doctors decided the bullet was too dangerous to remove, and he carried it with him for the rest of his life. He took a couple of weeks off and then was back on the campaign trail.

On election day, Democrat Woodrow Wilson won easily because Taft and Roosevelt split the Republican vote (although Teddy got more of the vote). The country's heart was clearly with the Progressives. Not counting the very unprogressive South, which voted for Democrats just because they weren't Republicans, Progressive votes would have easily won the election. Even the perennial Socialist candidate Eugene Debs racked up 900,000 votes. It was time for some changes.

Wilson sets out to teach America

Woodrow Wilson was only the second Democratic president since the Civil War and the first teacher ever elected president. He promised a program of *New Freedoms*, which included antitrust action, tariff revision, and reform in banking.

A man of serious purpose, he went after a clear program and got what he fought for on the domestic front. He was also, ahem, the second great president (after Teddy Roosevelt) to be a historian. Maybe we could all make history if we weren't so busy talking about it.

Wilson got real reductions in the cost of imported goods in the *Underwood Tariff Bill* (1913). By taking the unprecedented step of going to Congress himself and appealing to the American people to watch their representatives for last-minute special-interest tricks, Wilson got a bill that really reduced import fees. Because the passage of the *Sixteenth Amendment* (1913) allowed for an income tax, Congress slapped on a modest charge on all incomes over the equivalent of $65,000 in modern money ($3,000 back then). By 1917, income tax passed tariff receipts as the largest share of the federal income.

Question: When did taxes on imports stop being the largest share of federal income?

Answer: With the passage of the income tax in 1917.

Shoring up the banking system

Clearly, the banking system needed some help. The Roosevelt panic of 1907 had shown that the government could ease financial downturns if it had some extra cash to throw into the game when times got tough. Wilson went directly to Congress and got the *Federal Reserve Act* (1913), one of the most important economic landmarks in U.S. history and still the law of the land.

What the Federal Reserve Act did was establish a national system of 12 privately owned regional banks under the central authority of the Federal Reserve Board appointed by the president and Congress. In this best-of-both-worlds establishment, the regional banks can issue Federal Reserve Notes for private money backed by the government, but only under direction from the government-controlled Federal Reserve Board.

With the power of private enterprise and the control of central government policy, the government spaced the regional banks around the country to try to minimize the control of Wall Street New York money. Good luck; New York remained the financial capital no matter how many solid-looking bank buildings the rest of the country got.

The Trade Commission and Anti-Trust Act

In early 1914, Wilson made his third appearance before Congress. Moving on from the Roosevelt/Taft program of busting trusts, Wilson encouraged fair competition through the *Federal Trade Commission* (1914), which stopped monopolistic trade practices.

With the addition of the *Clayton Anti-Trust Act* (1914), the practices of price discrimination, agreements forbidding retailers from handling other companies' products, and interlocking directorate agreements to limit competition all became illegal. Even better, individual officers of corporations could be held responsible if their companies violated the laws.

The new business laws set out clear guidelines that corporations had to follow, much better than being thumped with no warning under previous, less clear legislation. As a plus for labor, the law ended the silly business of applying anti-trust laws to unions.

Victories for ordinary people

Wilson made himself even more popular with working people when, in 1916, he approved legislation (the *Adamson Act*) that increased wages and cut working hours of railroad employees, thus avoiding a strike.

Wilson was on a roll; the victories for ordinary people just kept coming.

> ✔ The *Federal Farm Loan Act* (1916) and the *Warehouse Act* (1916) let farmers get much-needed loans at low rates.
>
> ✔ The *La Follette Seamen's Act* (1915) guaranteed sailors on American merchant ships decent wages and treatment (and doomed the U.S. merchant fleet, which couldn't compete).
>
> ✔ The *Workingmen's Compensation Act* (1916) granted help to disabled federal employees.

Wilson's shortcoming: Government segregation

Wilson had a moral blind spot when it came to the treatment of blacks. A Southerner who fondly remembered seeing Robert E. Lee as a child, Wilson delivered for his racist South Democratic voters by segregating federal offices for the first time since the Civil War and dismissing many blacks from government work.

His segregation of government lasted until after World War II, when the Democrats under Harry Truman decided to do the right thing for civil rights even if it cost them the next election (which it did). Since that time, the South has moved into the Republican column in most elections.

The most important black leader to stand up to Wilson's segregationist tendencies during the Progressive Era was the eloquent W.E.B. Du Bois, founder of the NAACP. Du Bois fought for African American progress for most of his 95-year life. He carried the torch until the day he died, which just happened to be the day before Martin Luther King's "I have a dream" speech.

Question: Who was the most important black leader during the Progressive time period?

Answer: W.E.B. Du Bois, a founder of the NAACP.

Progressing Internationally

Wilson tried to apply morality to international relations, but it's hard to be idealistic when other people are shooting at you. He withdrew subsidies for U.S. companies investing abroad and stopped giving American ships free passage through the Panama Canal. He reluctantly continued the Roosevelt Corollary by sending Marines in to tame violence in Haiti and the Dominican Republic. Wilson bought the Virgin Islands in the Caribbean from Denmark, thus giving Americans another naval ship base and another navel tanning choice.

Wilson did his best to stay out of Mexican politics as factions maneuvered after a revolution. Standing up to pressure from American businessmen worried about their Mexican investments, Wilson declared that he wouldn't decide foreign policy "in the terms of material interest."

After innocent Americans had been killed on both sides of the border by Pancho Villa's soldiers, Wilson sent General "Black Jack" Pershing on a lightning cavalry raid into Mexico. Pershing chased Pancho's army and was swiftly pulled back. He may be needed elsewhere; the situation in Europe was looking grim.

World War 1 Begins

Germany and Austria-Hungary were locked in a war with Britain, France and Russia. The actual fighting started in 1914 after Franz Ferdinand, the prince who was set to become emperor of Austria-Hungary, was assassinated on a visit to Serbia. However, the endless fight to be top dog of Europe had been brewing for hundreds of years. This was exactly the kind of war the United States wanted to avoid.

The natural tendency of English-speaking America to side with England was helped along by careful propaganda coming over the only news wire from Europe, which conveniently ran through Britain. Plus, Germans looked like bad guys with their spiked helmets, upturned mustaches, and habit of tromping through neutral countries.

The millions of Americans with German heritage did little cheering for their old homeland; one of the reasons they left Germany in the first place was to avoid all that military bluster. Americans even changed the German names of foods: sauerkraut became victory cabbage, and more Americans started saying "hot dog" instead of wiener.

Germany paid a penalty for not ruling the waves. America proclaimed her neutral rights to the seas in hopes of continuing trade with the warring parties who were very much in need of supplies. Meanwhile, Germany and Britain both blockaded each other. Britain used surface ships that could gently force American cargo ships away from Germany and into British ports. Germany used submarines, which could only wave at passing ships or sink them; they weren't big enough to shepherd the American ships to distant German ports or even take on extra passengers if the ships sank. Because this war was the first with submarines, the whole game seemed like dirty pool to many Americans.

The sinking of the Lusitania

Germany said that it would try not to sink any neutral ships but that mistakes could easily happen. The first so-called mistake wasn't a neutral ship but the British liner *Lusitania* carrying ammunition as well as passengers. The Germans sunk it off Ireland in 1915, killing over a thousand people, more than a hundred of them Americans.

Germany agreed to stop sinking passenger liners but reasonably asked that Britain respond by lifting its blockade, which was starving the German people. Britain refused, so safety on the sea was definitely up in the air as the U.S. got ready to vote for president in 1916. Wilson barely squeaked through to reelection on a platform that said, "He kept us out of war," but he made no guarantees for the future.

America marches to the Great War

At the beginning of 1917, Wilson made one last, moving speech asking the fighting powers to come to the peace table. Meanwhile, the Germans made a whopping tactical decision. Figuring that it would take the U.S. longer to get to France than it would take Germany to win the war with full submarine warfare, the Germans announced that all bets were off. They were blockaded, and they intended to blockade Britain by sinking any ships headed that way. Then stupid got stupider.

The Germans sent a note called the *Zimmermann telegram* to Mexico, inviting them to invade the United States with the help of Japan. This harebrained scheme would never have worked, and the Mexicans knew it. Britain, who had been happily reading diplomatic mail from other countries that passed through their island along the transatlantic cable, intercepted the telegram and excitedly showed it to the United States. The Germans had already started sinking ships, and the telegram was the last straw for even peace-loving Wilson. The United States declared war on Germany.

Making war with noble intentions

Forced to resort to cold steel, Wilson turned fighting into an idealistic crusade. He declared that this was a "war to end all wars" and a "crusade to make the world safe for democracy." Wilson outlined the *14 Points* (1918) he felt should be the righteous aims of the Allies. In short form, they included:

- ✔ No secret treaties (like the spider webs of undercover alliances that started the war)
- ✔ Freedom of the seas
- ✔ Free trade
- ✔ Fewer weapons
- ✔ National *self-determination* (a people's right to choose its own form of government without interference)
- ✔ An international organization to keep the peace

A propaganda machine led by George Creel talked up America's peaceful war aims. Meanwhile, an ugly set of repressive laws, the *Espionage Act* (1917) and the *Sedition Act* (1918), led to the arrest of virtually anyone who spoke up against the war.

Most of the 2,000 prosecutions were against union leaders, including Socialist presidential candidate Eugene Debs, who had been putting up with persecution for 24 years since the Pullman Strike of 1894.

Question: What were the main issues in Wilson's 14 Points?

Answer: Open treaties, freedom of the seas, national self-determination and an international peace keeping organization.

Preparing for war

America never got into full production for World War I. The draft supplied lots of soldiers after the War Department issued a work or fight declaration. Labor was kept under control by the National War Labor Board chaired by roly-poly former President Taft. Unions made solid gains in membership, and pay improved with lots of wartime work.

For the first time, blacks (who had for years stayed in the South) began to move North to take wartime jobs; 500,000 made the move by 1920. This migration led to violence on the part of whites, especially when blacks helped break white labor actions like the great steel strike of 1919.

Question: When did blacks start to migrate to the North?

Answer: They made the move during and after World War I.

The role of women in the Great War

President Wilson learned how determined women were to get the vote when police arrested 20 suffragettes who were trying to storm the White House. During the war, he came out in favor of women's suffrage as "a vitally necessary war measure." Most Western states had given women the vote before 1914 (see Chapter 15). New York, Michigan, Oklahoma, and South Dakota jumped on board during the war, and after only 130 years of waiting, Abigail Adams' pre-Revolution wish finally came true. With the passage of the *Nineteenth Amendment* (1920), all American women got the right to vote.

With men gone to fight, some women took temporary so-called men's jobs in railroads and factories, but they quickly gave up their positions when the war was over. Still, by the end of the war, one out of four women had a job outside the home.

Food and drink (and Prohibition) at wartime

Food was no problem for America during the war; farm production increased by 20 percent. An effective humanitarian engineer named Herbert Hoover had already led a food drive to help Europe — now he headed the national effort.

People grew victory gardens and patriotically observed meatless Tuesdays and wheatless Wednesdays. *Liberty Loan* drives got ordinary citizens to buy government bonds and raised billions of dollars to finance the war.

Question: What was the Liberty Loan program?

Answer: Liberty Loan was a government bond program in which ordinary citizens helped raise money to finance the war.

Congress restricted the manufacture of alcohol, and that set the already half-dry country up for its national experiment with Prohibition. Lots of brewers were a little suspect anyway, what with all the German names like Budweiser, Schlitz, and Pabst. Progressives were under fire from prohibitionists to try a perfect boozeless society.

In 1919, the *Eighteenth Amendment* prohibited the legal sale of alcoholic beverages in the United States, thus opening the door for lots of profitable illegal sales. (In 1933, the *Twenty First Amendment* repealed Prohibition; see Chapter 17.)

Question: What led to the passage of Prohibition in 1919?

Answer: Years of Prohibition campaigning, war shortages, the belief that human beings could be perfected, plus the spreading passage of state anti-liquor laws.

Entering the fight — reluctantly

At first, the U.S. hoped to just send the Navy and let the Europeans do the ground fighting. The British and French quickly fessed up: They were almost out of men. The United States drafted a minimally trained army of 4 million men and began to ship them to Europe.

A year passed between the time America declared war and the time an effective U.S. fighting force assembled in Europe, and it was none too soon. Russia, which had been fighting on the Allied side, was swept by a Communist revolution and dropped out of the war.

Experienced German troops shifted to fight in France. By May of 1918, the Germans were within 40 miles of Paris. The first large American contingent was thrown right into a breach in the French line. By July, the German advance ground to a halt. By the fall, over a million American troops were helping to slowly push the Germans back.

Heroes came from the strangest places: Sergeant York, an American soldier raised in an anti-war church, singlehandedly killed 20 Germans and captured 132 more.

The Great War ends — sort of

In October, the Germans asked for peace based on Wilson's 14 Points. At 11:00 a.m. on the 11th day of the 11th month (November 11, 1918), the Great War was over.

The Allied forces won because Germany knew what was going to happen if it continued fighting; Socialist revolutions were going on back in Germany, and lots of German (and Allied) troops were dying from a worldwide flu epidemic. Germany had given up before it was completely defeated, something that would come to bother a hard-fighting, wounded German army corporal named Adolf Hitler.

The United States was far from the arsenal of democracy it would become in World War II; Britain and France actually supplied most of the planes, big guns, and transport ships used by American troops.

Leaders of the world hurried to Paris in January of 1919 to conclude a peace treaty while revolutions were tearing apart Russia and central Europe. Woodrow Wilson was the hero of the day. People expected freedom and peace from the 14 Points. Unfortunately, most of the points' good ideas didn't end up in the Treaty of Versailles, a compromise Wilson had to make with broke, tired, and angry European victors.

Wilson tried to move the world toward fairness, and he did succeed on getting a few new nations established and some more reasonable boundaries drawn. In the end, Wilson got a treaty with too much reparation money due to be paid by a too-poor Germany. He took what he could get to preserve his pet project, the *League of Nations*.

The peace that can't hold

Back in America, powerful conservative forces had taken over Congress. They refused to ratify the Treaty of Versailles as written, and Wilson refused to accept anything less. The misunderstood final warning from George Washington to "avoid foreign entanglements" hovered over the hall like an outdated ghost.

George had been speaking to a small, weak nation of farmers in a world where crossing the ocean took weeks and America didn't have to trade with anybody. Now the U.S. was the one nation with the strength and moral position to make the League of Nations work, but it wouldn't take the responsibility. Wilson's moral position worked against him — some senators had just *had* it with the do-gooder.

Wilson works to hold everything together

Wilson went on a speaking tour to try to get people to put pressure on the Congress to accept the treaty. In Pueblo, Colorado, with tears streaming down his cheeks, he pleaded for the League of Nations as the only way to avoid another war. That night he collapsed. Hit by a stroke, Wilson didn't make public appearances for months afterwards. The political strategy he followed from his sick bed was feverish.

Wilson's Democratic Party had lost control of Congress in the 1918 elections. Senator Henry Cabot Lodge, the great Republican enemy of the League of Nations, attached some reservations to the treaty that Wilson didn't like. Wilson ordered all the Democratic senators to vote against the treaty rather than compromise. Having been so successful in the past, Wilson seemed to think he could turn the upcoming presidential election of 1920 into a referendum on the treaty.

Question: How did President Wilson try to convince Congress to vote for the Treaty of Versailles?

Answer: He appealed directly to the people to put pressure on Congress.

The League of Nations falls

The Republicans nominated affable and empty-headed Warren Harding for president. He trounced the Democrats who supported the League of Nations by saying he would work for a vague Association of Nations and playing to the postwar atmosphere of relief. The Republicans got almost twice as many votes as the too-serious Democrats.

The failure of the United States to join the League of Nations led to World War II. The United States didn't create Hitler, Mussolini, or the poverty, greed, and hatred that sparked World War II and caused the deaths of 72 million people, including 418,000 Americans. But because of outmoded isolationism and an almost-adolescent snit between people who were too righteous to work together, the United States did nothing to stop it. As the saying goes, if you're not part of the solution, maybe you're part of the problem.

Chapter 17

Roaring, Soaring, and Fighting Depression: 1921–1939

In This Chapter

▶ Business gets bigger in the 1920s

▶ Dealing with attacks on minorities

▶ Weathering the Depression

▶ Meeting Franklin Roosevelt with new hope

*P*resident Warren G. Harding wasn't a bad man, but he was suspiciously lazy in his choice of political friends. When Republican Warren Harding took over as president in 1921, the nation was ready for happy days after all the preachiness of Woodrow Wilson. Harding's Cabinet members weren't about to preach; in fact, they included a den of thieves.

His Secretary of the Interior leased America's emergency *Teapot Dome* oil reserve to private businessmen in exchange for a $400,000 bribe ($4 million in modern money). His head of Veteran's Affairs ripped off the modern equivalent of $2 billion by allowing shady work on veterans' hospitals. His Attorney General — the guy who was supposed to, you know, enforce the laws — was charged with the sale of pardons and liquor permits. Harding didn't have to face the ugly scene his friends had created: He died of an illness in the middle of his administration.

That's the way it went in the Roaring '20s: high times with a big bill coming later. Kicking off the 1900s, activist presidents Theodore Roosevelt, William Howard Taft, and Woodrow Wilson had tackled serious problems with the belief that progressive reform would help America live up to its high ideals (see Chapter 16). After all that progressing and the trauma of World War I, people were tired of idealism — they just wanted to return to normal. Trouble is, you can never get in the same river twice — the current moves on without you. Normal in the 1920s was a whole new world. Unfortunately for the people of that era, the Great Depression was right around the corner. More on that in this chapter.

U.S. versus Communism: The Early Years

With the Communist revolution running wild throughout Russia, the United States had the terrorist jitters. President Wilson expanded the federal police with a new bureau headed by J. Edgar Hoover. Before the *Red Scare* (1920) was over, more than 10,000 people were arrested (some beaten up or held illegally).

Real terrorists did actually strike: A bomb in Washington D.C. just missed a young Franklin Delano Roosevelt, and another killed 38 people and wounded hundreds on Wall Street. The actual bombers escaped, and almost all of the people arrested were guilty of nothing more than being radical union members or recent immigrants. Immigrants suspected of trouble-making were deported.

Scared for their lives and property, most Americans supported the anti-Communist raids at first. But when the police issued a red alert for a Communist takeover on May 1 that never materialized, public support for police-state tactics started to fade. Factory owners kept the Communist issue going as long as possible by trying to link unions with Communists.

During the hysteria, five legally elected members of the New York legislature and one U.S. Congressman weren't allowed to take their seats because of their left-wing views. Two immigrant Italians, *Sacco and Vanzetti* (1921) were executed for murder on evidence that had more to do with their radical views and the fact that they were immigrants than proof of their alleged crime.

Question: What happened to immigrants suspected of being trouble makers during the *Red Scare* (1920)?

Answer: They were deported.

The Return of the Klan

The same Ku Klux Klan (KKK) that had terrorized blacks and their Reconstruction allies in the post-Civil-War South came back from the dead like a racist Dracula during the 1920s. This time, the Klan had more than blacks to hate: It was also against booze, international cooperation, evolution, gambling, immigrants, and sex.

The Birth of a Nation

The Birth of a Nation follows the family of Northern abolitionist Congressman Stoneman (based on real life Congressman Stevens, an abolitionist leader). His Northern family visits their Southern friends the Camerons, who live on the quintessential South Carolina plantation, complete with happy slaves.

When the Civil War breaks out, the children of the two families support their respective sides, but young Northern soldier Phil Stoneman can't forget his love for Southerner Margaret Cameron. The only other surviving son is Ben Cameron. Wounded while fighting bravely for the Confederates, Ben is recovering in a Northern hospital when a lovely young nurse comes by who is, oh my gosh, his childhood love Elsie Stoneman.

After the war, Ben creates the Ku Klux Klan when he sees white children dressing up like ghosts to scare black children. He does it just in time, too, because black ex-slaves are menacing white women, including Ben's sister Flora, who jumps off a cliff to escape. When Elsie is also threatened, Ben and the Klan arrive in the nick of time to save her. Phil Stoneman and his Union army friends realize they must work together with the Klan to save what the movie calls their "Aryan birthright."

A title slide has an authentic quote from Woodrow Wilson about "the great Ku Klux Klan." The movie ends with a double Cameron/Stoneman wedding as the world lives happily together under a picture of Christ.

Because it used lies to sell tickets and inflame hatred, *The Birth of a Nation* was boycotted in many cities and states.

Change always brings out reaction, and the 1920s version of the Klan had millions of aggressive and frightening hood-wearing members including senators, mayors, and, according to some sources, President Warren G. Harding. Although the original Klan died out some 20 years after the Civil War ended, the new Klan sprung out of the popularity of one of the first story movies: *The Birth of a Nation* (1915). Showing the power of popular culture, the movie made up different Klan traditions than those started by the original KKK. The new Klan organization followed the film, not the original group — basically, they learned it at the movies.

The reconstituted Klan fizzled out in the late 1920s when the corruption of their leaders and the shamefulness of their tactics became obvious even to people with sheets over their heads. Although the new Klan made lots of temporary converts among people frightened by change, the KKK also faced something it never had in the old South: stand-up opposition from progressive people who wouldn't let hate win.

Immigration Act of 1924

In the 1920s, new laws to slow immigration relieved the nativist fear of being overwhelmed by immigrants. (See Chapter 16 for more on nativism.) The *Immigration Act of 1924* capped the number of immigrants allowed in the U.S. each year at 2 percent of the number of a home nation's citizens already in the United States as of 1890. For example, if 3 million Americans of German descent lived in the U.S. in 1890, 60,000 Germans (2 percent of 3 million) could come to the country each year under the 1924 act. This quota barred the door to many hopeful immigrants from countries that didn't have a lot of people in the U.S. in 1890.

One such country was Italy. Lots of Italian people wanted to come to America, but the whole country was only able to send fewer than 6,000 people a year. This number still made the Italians better off than the Japanese, who were completely locked out by the act. The various groups that actually got into the U.S. tried to maintain their national cultures, but their children learned to speak English and made friends with kids from all over. Radio and movies accelerated the melting pot by teaching standardized language and culture. The number of immigrant children who were forced into child labor declined as individual states began to require school attendance and forbid underage employment.

Question: Why did fewer immigrants come to the United States in the 1920s?

Answer: The *Immigration Act of 1924* limited new Americans to a low quota of 2 percent of the number of citizens by national origin in the United States by 1890.

Question: What reduced child labor in the 1920s?

Answer: States passed laws that required children to attend school and prohibited underage labor.

Bathtub Gin and a Little Sin: The Jazz Age

During the 1920s, radios, record players, magazines, and movies began to bring the world to average working people who could never have afforded to go to plays, concerts, or college. Telephones, electricity, and indoor plumbing all made life more comfortable. More people had cars than bathtubs. (After all, you can't drive a bathtub to town.) Young people left the farm; for the first time in history, more people lived in cities than in the country. The 1920s were called the Jazz Age because popular music shared influences from big band, ragtime and rhythm, songs you could get up and dance to.

Prohibition: High demand and high crime

Prohibition, implemented by the *Volstead Act* after the passage of the *Eighteenth Amendment* (1919), may have cut down on drinking by 10 percent, but it increased crime by 50 percent. Because booze was illegal but in demand, liquor made great profits for organized crime. For every large saloon that closed, at least three small *speakeasies* (illicit pubs) opened.

Because low-alcohol beer and wine were bulky and hard to transport, potent hard liquor cocktails became the quick-acting drink of choice. Lots of hard liquor was smuggled, but desperate drinkers learned to make gin in their bathtubs or bought special grape juice that turned to wine with minimal effort.

Arrests for drunken driving and public intoxication went up more than 50 percent. The law made millions of otherwise-law-abiding Americans into criminals, and it gave real criminals so much money that they fought ugly wars over territory in big cities.

The king of the mobs in Chicago was Al Capone. After more than 500 deaths in the Windy City, Capone was finally sent to prison for tax evasion. At their height, illegal liquor mobs took in more money than the federal government. The *Twenty-First Amendment* (1933) finally repealed Prohibition.

Sex in the city

A lot of people had fun in the *Roaring '20s* (1925). People did crazy dances to the new music of the *Jazz Age*. Anything seemed possible with the new-found freedom provided by women's suffrage, cars, radio, movies, and — Prohibition be damned — plenty of booze. The scene also included well-known gay clubs, but they disappeared at the end of the 1920s and didn't reappear until the 1970s.

Because Sigmund Freud had explained sex drives as a natural part of being human, the subject of sex was less taboo. *Margaret Sanger* (1921) risked arrest to get birth control information to women.

Question: Who was Margaret Sanger?

Answer: Margaret Sanger was an early advocate who publicized information about birth control.

Mass production and mass consumption

Prosperity was the lion behind the '20s' roar. Mass production made new inventions and former luxuries available to almost everybody, especially with the financially dangerous new invention of time payments. Henry Ford lowered the price of his Model T to a few hundred dollars, cheap enough for most working people who could get a loan to buy their car on time. By the end of the decade, the U.S. had one car for every five Americans, far more than all the automobiles in the rest of the world.

Advertising got good at making people want things they didn't even need through the mass media of radio, billboards, and popular magazines. *Frederick Taylor* (1922), the father of scientific management, broke work assignments down into tasks and figured out the most efficient way to get jobs done. Unions lost membership as employers used government support and fear of radicals to break up strikes.

Question: What happened to the Progressive political movement in the 1920s?

Answer: Progressive reforms all but disappeared as conservative Republican government slowed immigration, relaxed the regulations on business, and weakened unions.

Cars and planes

Motor vehicles were good for more than just joy rides. Trucks moved goods to market more cheaply and quickly than trains; produce farmers made more money *and* city people got better fruit and vegetables. People didn't have to live right next to where they worked anymore; the first suburbs appeared. Buses allowed schools to consolidate and reach more students.

Women took to driving right from the start; it gave them freedom from dependence on men. Cars were so handy that people didn't even begin to notice the cost in dollars, accidents, and pollution until years later.

Automobiles were fast, but planes were faster. The Wright brothers flew the first plane in 1903. After that, it took 20 years and countless crashes for aviation to become practical. The first transcontinental airmail route began from San Francisco to New York in 1920. Few passengers flew in the 1920s; most airliners concentrated on carrying the mail.

After Charles Lindbergh became a hero by single-handedly flying his *Spirit of St. Louis* (1927) from New York to Paris, aviation was on everybody's mind. The first flight attendant stepped on board a regularly scheduled commercial flight in 1930.

Radio

The first radio breakthrough occurred when original station KDKA in Pittsburgh broadcasted the news of Warren Harding's election in 1920. As more and more families gathered around the early radios, commercials for products soon began popping up.

Radio broke down local accents by providing a national standard of speech. It also affected politics by carrying the words of candidates and the sound of their speaking voices, something only a small proportion of the population had ever heard before the 1920s. This development hurt squeaky-voiced politicians like Al Smith and helped great radio personalities like Franklin Roosevelt.

The Harlem Renaissance

The *Harlem Renaissance* (1926) expanded the urban culture of black Americans with writers like Langston Hughes and Zora Neale Hurston, plus musicians like Louis Armstrong and Duke Ellington.

William Haines

The most famous movie actor of 1925 was William Haines, who lived openly with his gay lover. Pushed to cover up by the studios, they switched to interior decoration and lived together the rest of their lives, more than 50 years — in the words of Joan Crawford, "the happiest married couple in Hollywood." They decorated the houses of the stars, including Ronald Reagan's Governor's Mansion.

Marcus Garvey (1921) tried to raise money for black-owned businesses and an African American colony in Liberia. He galvanized black pride but was set up by the first black employees of the FBI and deported. For the first time, blacks and whites mingled in the nightspots. The Harlem Renaissance basketball team was the best in the world.

Question: Who was Marcus Garvey?

Answer: Garvey was an organizer who raised African American pride with plans for black owned businesses and an African colony.

Movies and their influence

Movies changed history during this period, whether it was through an overt message like *The Birth of a Nation* or the shared experience of just going to the movies together.

As one of the first feature films, *The Great Train Robbery* (1903) excited the audience so much that some of them ducked when the train went by. The earliest movies were silent and included explanation signs; the cowboys would be galloping silently away and suddenly everything would stop for what looked like a PowerPoint slide. That kept people reading, but it didn't survive the 1920s.

In 1927, *The Jazz Singer* contained the first synchronized dialogue (and singing) in a feature film. After sound was possible, nobody wanted to read written explanations in films again (except for maybe the beginning of *Star Wars*), and from then on movies could talk. About the same time, color movies began to appear. Films largely replaced ethnic theater and united the country in shared dramatic experiences. Movies helped ethnicities become regular Americans.

Flappers

The most beautiful woman in films was The It-girl, Clara Bow, whose brassy personality was a model for the *flapper*s (1925), newly liberated women who made up their own rules about clothes (including short dresses and hair) and behavior. Females could afford to be more independent because the number of women with jobs increased by 25 percent in the 1920s. People called them wild, but flappers didn't care what people thought.

Question: Who were the flappers in the 1920s?

Answer: The flappers were women who felt liberated to make up their own minds about appearance and behavior. Their style was short hair, short dresses, independence, and wild dancing.

Monkeying around with evolution

The idea of evolution scared a lot of conservative religious people who thought that it didn't fit with their idea of God. The state of Tennessee banned the teaching of evolution, but a young high-school football coach named John Scopes taught it anyway and landed in court in the *Scopes Monkey Trial* (1925).

The trial starred famous defense attorney Clarence Darrow as Scopes' lawyer and former presidential candidate William Jennings Bryan as the prosecutor. Bryan took the stand to explain why the Bible was right, and Darrow made him look foolish.

Laws against teaching evolution stayed around until the 1960s, when the Supreme Court ruled that such bans violate the First Amendment because their primary purpose is religious. Fundamentalists still try to get what they call intelligent design recognized in schools, but now they're trying to get into the classroom instead of keeping science out.

Even though the *Scopes Trial* didn't immediately repeal the law, it began to change the way most people thought, which eventually changed the law.

Question: Who were the key attorneys in the Scopes Trial?

Answer: William Jennings Bryan and Clarence Darrow.

The power of the pen

The sharpest pen of the 1920s belonged to H.L. Mencken, who was the Jon Stewart of his generation. As a Baltimore newspaperman and editor of the *American Mercury* magazine, Mencken took on the backward establishment of America. He defined a puritan as someone with "the haunting fear that someone, somewhere, might be happy."

Other writers stirred the dark coals of the happily roaring '20s:

- F. Scott Fitzgerald wrote *The Great Gatsby* (1925) about the hopeless social climbing of an also-ran who could never reach success because glamor isn't life.

- Theodore Dreiser went even sadder in *An American Tragedy* (1925), a novel about the murder of a pregnant girl by her social-climbing boyfriend.

- The poet e.e. cummings wrote verse so direct that it didn't need capitalization.

- Ernest Hemingway stripped away all the Victorian prose and wrote in simple English. His *A Farewell to Arms* (1929), a novel paralleling his own experience in World War I, combined toughness with feeling.

- Sherwood Anderson's *Winesburg, Ohio* (1919) contained the touchingly pathetic stories of small-town Americans lost in their own private suffering.

- Sinclair Lewis wrote *Main Street* (1920) and *Babbitt* (1922) about the limits of sophistication in early 1900s America. The character Babbitt became a synonym for the short-sighted, self-serving boosterism encountered in any club or city.

- William Faulkner described the South, prejudices and all, in *The Sound and the Fury* (1929).

On the whole, the writers of the 1920s were surprisingly gloomy for a roaring decade. Maybe they saw trouble coming, or perhaps they just valued honesty more than uplift. So did the many Americans who chose to read their books. In that sense, the writers of the '20s were the worthy successors to the early-1900s muckrakers. Unlike the early muckrakers, however, these writers were living in a political world that, for the time being, valued wealth more than progress.

Question: What was the spirit of critically acclaimed writers of the 1920s?

Answer: Writers generally reflected a gloomy questioning of society.

Architecture

Frank Lloyd Wright (1928) was something of an architectural poet. If architecture is frozen music, he made that music new, stripping off tired classical references to build for a new world.

The soaring Chrysler Building and Empire State Building in New York were further proof of late-1920s architectural exuberance. The International style began to emphasize glass and light as modern building techniques allowed more openness.

Major Money Shift: Signs of Trouble Ahead

Even as the 1920s roared, signs that America's fast growth was running on empty began to appear.

- ✔ U.S. manufacturing output rose by 50 percent, but even in good times, hundreds of banks failed every year.

- ✔ Buying on credit was rare at the beginning of the decade, but by the end of the 1920s, more than half of the purchases for cars and appliances were on time payments.

- ✔ A Florida land boom so hot that people even bought lots that were under water turned to bust in one 1925 hurricane.

The stock market went up for so long that everybody forgot it could go down. Ordinary working people bet their life savings on stocks, buying them *on margin* — a kind of time payment, just like the financing scheme they used for their cars.

The Republican-controlled Congress cut the taxes on rich people: What was three dollars in tax for the rich in 1920 became only one dollar. Wealth-friendly politicians said this money would trickle down to the poorer people.

Question: What was the Republican position on taxes for the rich?

Answer: Republicans cut taxes on the rich, claiming benefits would trickle down to poorer people.

A little trickling down would have been good, because 40 percent of the whole nation (and a much higher percentage of farmers and blacks) lived below the poverty line. While the poor people lived without government help, cheap taxes for the rich made the economy blow up like a big balloon.

Question: Which groups had it hardest during the 1920s?

Answer: The most-economically-depressed groups were farmers and blacks. They didn't share much in the 1920s boom times.

Politics Lead to Depression

The three Republican presidents in the 1920s really thought people should take care of themselves. Even after the stock market crashed in 1929, Herbert Hoover quoted the cold-hearted words of President Cleveland from 50 years before: ". . . though the people support the Government, the Government should not support the people."

The same hands-off governmental philosophy guided the Republican presidential trio in international affairs; the U.S. was isolationist and unprepared for war. Antitrust laws passed by Progressive presidents went unenforced, and businesses soon learned that they could get away with forming trade associations that limited competition:

- ✔ The *Esch-Cummins Transportation Act* (1920) allowed the private combination of the railroads and committed the Interstate Commerce Commission to help them make a profit.

- ✔ The *Merchant Marine Act* (1920) sold off ships built by the government at bargain prices to big businessmen. A railroad strike protesting a 12 percent pay cut during boom times was put down with harsh measures by the government in 1922.

International efforts were mostly symbolic:

- ✔ The U.S. called the leading powers together to sign the *Washington Naval Treaty* (1922) where they agreed to limit warship construction at a nice high level.

- ✔ Harding helped American companies grab *oil concessions* (1923) in the Middle East that would eventually become habit-forming.

- ✔ The *Nine-Power Treaty* (1922) made an Open Door policy to China look official, but it didn't keep Japan and Russia from trying to sneak in that door to grab some territory for themselves.

- ✔ The *Kellogg-Briand Pact* (1928) proved how easy it is to say good words by "outlawing war."

All these agreements sounded good, but with only a weak League of Nations, they didn't have any power to enforce them.

Republicans hiked the tariffs, like they always did, under the *Fordney-McCumber Tariff Law* (1922), which also gave the president the power to raise or lower tariffs by himself. No surprise, the Republican presidents sent the tariffs even higher on 32 important commodities like dairy products and iron. They lowered taxes on only five items nobody wanted anyway, including paintbrush handles and bobwhite quail.

Calvin Coolidge: "Silent Cal" stands by

After President Harding escaped facing his administration's corruption through the clever tactic of dying, Calvin Coolidge took over and cooled the situation down. Coolidge specialized in keeping his remarks simple. A famous story tells of a dinner guest who said, "Mr. Coolidge, I've made a bet against a fellow who said it was impossible to get more than two words out of you." Coolidge's reply: "You lose."

Although Coolidge had little to say, he supported business like it was a religion. In fact, he believed that "the man who builds a factory builds a temple" and "the man who works there worships there." He'd obviously never worked in a factory.

Although Coolidge came from a New England farm family, he stood by and did nothing as one out of four families lost their farms to debt in the 1920s. He just said that farming had never paid much and that the government couldn't do anything about it. Coolidge got elected once in his own right and then ran out of energy to try it again.

Herbert Hoover: Good intentions, bad mistakes

Herbert Hoover had a great reputation as a humanitarian and a problem-solver for three earlier administrations. Then he actually became president and blew it all away in the Great Depression. Elected in a landslide in 1928, he started by actually trying to do something for the desperate farmers.

The *Agricultural Marketing Act* (1929) lent money to farmers' organizations to manage their crops for maximum profit. It didn't work very well; prices for grain and cotton just kept dropping because farmers kept growing an oversupply of crops.

The Stock Market Crash of 1929

On *Black Tuesday* (1929) in October 1929, the stock market crashed. Stocks kept sliding until they reached a point in 1932 when they were down 89 percent, lower than they'd been since the 1800s. Prudent investors who bought slowly over their lifetime would have been protected from the worst market fluctuations by the law of averages. However, anyone who bought stocks only at the highest and therefore worst time in mid-1929 and held on to them saw most of his adult life pass by before finally breaking even in 1954.

Responding to business pressure, Hoover did exactly the wrong thing by signing the terrible *Smoot-Hawley Tariff* (1930). A world economy teetering on the brink of economic collapse certainly didn't need the highest peacetime tariff in U.S. history; the rest of the world viewed the tariff as a kind of giant "screw you," and economic walls went up all over the world.

Tariffs certainly didn't help the United States get over the crisis that started with the Wall Street meltdown in 1929. Unemployment was at 9 percent in 1930 when the Smoot-Hawley tariff passed, but it jumped to 16 percent the next year and 25 percent two years after that.

Bad news hits hard

As people's jobs evaporated and families started to go hungry, Hoover's response was to assist businesses so that their wealth would trickle down to the poor.

After the Depression had gone on for three years, Congress finally passed the *Reconstruction Finance Corporation (RFC) Act* (1932). The RFC lent money to businesses, agricultural organizations, and local governments. Many called it *the millionaires' dole*.

Actually, Hoover had come a long way from the take-care-of-yourself position of earlier 1920s Republicans, including himself. Realizing that they would have to do something for worried laborers whose union membership had gone down by a third in the union-busting 1920s, Congress passed the *Norris-La Guardia Anti-Injunction Act* (1932), which forbade court interference in peaceful strikes and stopped management from forcing workers to sign anti-union pledges.

Question: What national program did Herbert Hoover establish to help fight the Depression?

Answer: Hoover established the Reconstruction Finance Corporation (RFC) at the end of his term in 1932 to loan money to businesses, organizations, and state and local governments.

A march on Washington by 20,000 hungry veterans called the *Bonus Expeditionary Force* (1932) asked for the bonus ($15,000 in modern money) promised them in the *Adjusted Compensaton Act* (1924) when they really needed it, which was *right now*. General Douglas MacArthur broke up the march with force, but that didn't make Hoover any more popular.

Meanwhile, Japan used the economic troubles of the U.S. as a good time to brutally attack China. The United States did nothing but shake its finger.

While his own country was slipping down the economic drain, Hoover did manage to make some conciliatory gestures in Latin America that later formed the basis of the *Good Neighbor Policy* (1933) under Franklin Roosevelt. At home under Hoover, the situation just kept getting worse.

Question: What did the government do when the Bonus Expeditionary Force marched on Washington during the Great Depression?

Answer: The government used the army to break up the march and sent the marchers home.

Hoover is left holding the bag

1932 wasn't a good time to be Herbert Hoover running for re-election. One in four Americans — more than 11 million people — had no job. The people didn't want to hear any more Republican philosophy about how it was good for the poor to have to struggle on their own. As people pointed out, Hoover's RFC could pay to feed a pig but not a human child.

Shantytowns of displaced people called *Hoovervilles* sprung up near big cities. The Depression was cause for a great internal migration of transient people traveling from town to town looking for work; 2,000 applicants would show up for a single job interview.

Question: What was the impact of the Depression on where people lived?

Answer: Transient people travelled from town to town in a great internal migration around the United States looking for work.

Franklin D. Roosevelt: Helping the Country to a New Deal

Franklin Delano Roosevelt (FDR) was the Democratic candidate for president. Roosevelt was a distant cousin of Teddy Roosevelt, and his wife was Teddy's niece Eleanor. FDR had been the Democratic nominee for vice president in 1920 — tall, athletic and maybe just a little stuck up. Beaten for vice president in the Harding landslide, in 1921 he was struck by a disease that paralyzed his legs for life. He didn't give up, but he did begin to see what a struggle life could be for what he called the *forgotten man*.

FDR was governor of New York when the Depression hit, and he immediately launched relief programs that reached worried people. His campaign song is still a theme for the Democratic party: "Happy Days Are Here Again." People believed in his hope and determination, and Roosevelt beat Hoover in a landslide.

His inaugural address contained now-famous words, quoted here in a slightly extended version to show their serious context: "The only thing we have to fear is fear itself —nameless, unreasoning, unjustified terror which paralyzes needed efforts to convert retreat into advance."

Roosevelt's *New Deal* (1933) program centered on three *R*'s: relief, recovery, and reform:

✔ First, FDR wanted to provide immediate relief from hunger and homelessness, very real problems in 1933, when one out of four Americans were unemployed.

✔ Second, the New Deal hoped to help the economy recover so that people would have stable jobs and businesses with which to support themselves.

✔ Third, the Democrats planned to reform the system so that no American would have to suffer another Great Depression again.

A newly elected, heavily Democratic Congress passed a slew of legislation so quickly that it became known as the *Hundred Days* (1933) of the new administration. Roosevelt wanted to fix agriculture, banks, and jobs without nationalizing basic industries.

Question: What were Roosevelt's key aims with the New Deal?

Answer: FDR wanted to save the country and the capitalist system by reforming banks, agriculture, and jobs without nationalizing major industries.

Healing with an alphabet soup of agencies

The first step was to stop the run on the banks that had people desperately trying to withdraw their savings, thus making bank collapse a self-fulfilling prophecy. Roosevelt temporarily closed all the banks, then reopened them under the Emergency Banking Act, which took all of eight hours to pass.

Congress created the *Federal Deposit Insurance Corporation* (FDIC) (1933), guaranteeing bank deposits and thus helping stop the panic. To create more money, FDR purposely caused inflation by increasing the price of gold.

For direct help to starving people, Congress passed the *Federal Emergency Relief Administration* (1933), which handed out billions of dollars in grants and jobs through the states. More help was on the way.

Civilian Conservation Corps (CCC)

The *Civilian Conservation Corps* (CCC) (1933) created more than 3 million jobs in the nine years of its life, hiring mostly young men from poor families. Civilian Conservation Corps camps were run by the Army in every state in the nation.

The CCC constructed buildings and trails in city, state, and national parks that still exist today. The first CCC recruit was ready for training little more than a month after Roosevelt took office; the program continued until World War II gave young men something else to do.

Most Americans happily endorsed the CCC as a combination of good work and necessary economic support — most of a CCC recruit's small-but-regular pay went home to help his family. Although the national CCC ended, over a hundred state and local work programs still exist today modeled on the Conservation Corps.

WPA, CWA, and PWA

More jobs were created by the *Works Progress Administration* (WPA), the *Civil Works Administration* (CWA) and the *Public Works Administration* (PWA). A regular alphabet soup of well-meaning agencies tried to help America keep working through the nightmare of the Depression.

Trails and roads weren't the only major projects; the PWA built the Grand Coulee Dam on the Columbia River, the largest structure in the world that had been built up to that time since the Great Wall of China. To keep people cheerful and raise a little tax revenue, the nation got rid of Prohibition with the *Twenty-first Amendment* (1933).

Tennessee Valley Authority (TVA)

The federal government got into the electricity business with the construction of the nine dams of the *Tennessee Valley Authority* (TVA) (1933). Even by Depression standards, the Tennessee Valley area was in bad shape, with exhausted soil, epidemic malaria, and wide-spread poverty. The TVA brought jobs and low-cost power with what was to become one of the largest electrical utilities in the world. At the same time, state public utility commissions began to control abuses by private power companies.

Help for agriculture

The *Agricultural Adjustment Act* (1933) helped improve farm income by limiting supply, but the Supreme Court overturned it. The *Soil Conservation and Domestic Allotment Act* (1936) and a reformed second *Agricultural Adjustment Act* (1938) passed Court tests to become the beginning of the national farm support program that continues to this day.

> Question: What was the *Agricultural Adjustment Act* (1933)?

> Answer: This act was the first attempt at a national farm policy that included limiting supply to raise farm income.

Securities and Exchange Commission (SEC)

Because Wall Street represented as a bad guy in the Great Depression, the Roosevelt government started the first fair trading rules for stocks with the *Securities and Exchange Commission* (SEC) (1934). The SEC is still around and gets regularly strengthened when corporations devise new ways to fool investors.

Federal Housing Administration (FHA)

To increase the number of construction jobs and homes, the *Federal Housing Administration* (FHA) (1934) began to back small loans for remodeling and new home construction.

When the FHA started, most home mortgages were short-term, three-to-five-year interest-only loans, with a huge balloon payment for the entire value of the loan at the end of three or five years. Buyers had to come up with at least 40 percent of the value of the home as a down payment. With the Depression, people couldn't make big balloon payments *or* find 40 percent for a down payment. Banks were stuck with houses nobody could afford to buy, and the housing market tanked. With the FHA, home ownership has increased from 40 percent in the 1930s to nearly 70 percent today.

Social Security

Certainly the largest, lasting change in life for older people was the creation of the *Social Security Administration* (1935), which guaranteed small pensions for the elderly and the handicapped by taxing the income of current workers. In the presidential election of 1936, Roosevelt tromped his Republican opponent. The Democrats controlled two thirds of the votes in both the House and the Senate. No political party had enjoyed this much public support since the Era of Good Feelings (see Chapter 10) more than 100 years before.

Question: How was the Social Security Administration funded?

Answer: Social Security taxed current workers to pay for retirement benefits.

One not-so-perfect new deal

The New Deal made mistakes. To create more jobs, the government created the *National Recovery Administration* (NRA), in which participating industries agreed to job sharing and wage and price controls to make more work. It was an administrative nightmare and was soon declared unconstitutional.

Roosevelt went too far when he tried to add more justices to the Supreme Court to keep it from blocking his legislation. Even his supporters couldn't go along with this manipulation of the Constitution.

Wrapping up the New Deal agencies

The Indian New Deal, officially named the *Indian Reorganization Act of 1934,* encouraged tribes to organize their own governments and stopped the breakup of American Indian lands.

A change in government treatment of unions was signaled by the *National Labor Relations Board* (NLRB) (1935), which allowed workers a fair hearing when organizing unions. Even with a more sympathetic government, strikers were killed in San Francisco (1934) and Chicago (1937). The *Congress of Industrial Organizations* (CIO) (1937) later formed to organize whole industries, including unskilled workers and blacks who hadn't been part of the older AFL confederation (see Chapter 15). By 1938, the CIO had 4 million members.

To keep enthusiastic government employees from campaigning for their boss, the *Hatch Act* (1939) barred political work by government employees.

Question: What did the *Congress of Industrial Organizations* (CIO) add to the labor-organizing movement?

Answer: The CIO offered representation to unskilled workers and blacks across whole industries, going beyond the AFL's push for skilled workers by trade.

The legacy of the New Deal

Fighting the Depression before World War II closed in, Roosevelt managed to cut unemployment from 25 percent to 12 percent. He literally kept people all over the country from starving. The New Deal also started programs that prevented something as horrible as the Great Depression from happening again. Millions of people got a chance to improve their lives, and the spirit of the New Deal put a safety net under the American people that no President — no matter how conservative — has ever seriously tried to take away.

You don't really have to memorize all the New Deal alphabet letters, but be ready for questions on the Depression. For essay answers, an understanding of the scope of Roosevelt's recovery program and some specific agencies is important. At minimum, you want to know the agencies started in the New Deal that are still part of America: FDIC, TVA, SEC, FHA, NLRB, and Social Security. If you can figure out what the letters mean, the agencies pretty well explain themselves.

The Grapes of Wrath

John Steinbeck's *The Grapes of Wrath* (1939) tells the story of the Joad family's trip from barren Oklahoma to California in search of a new life. Enduring death and the desertion of family members, the Joads push on, learning that their only hope lies in solidarity with other poor people. A New Deal relief program tries to help, but in the end their daughter Rose gives up the milk she had for her stillborn baby to save a starving man.

Steinbeck won the Pulitzer Prize and the Nobel Prize for Literature, and the film version won two Academy Awards. *The Grapes of Wrath* showed rural poverty up close and put a face on the bravery it took to confront Depression homelessness. The story built solid support for social programs in the United States, a country that only a few years before had elected presidents who said the government shouldn't help the people.

Toughing It Out in the Dust Bowl

The New Deal tried to give long-suffering farmers a break by paying them not to grow crops, thus limiting supply, conserving land, and raising prices of now more moderately produced food. When things were already bad out on the land, overplowed dry land blew away in the *Dust Bowl* (1935) centered in Kansas and Oklahoma. This led to an exodus of poor farmers headed west to look for work and food.

Depression-era Demagoguery

Whenever there is a shortage of money, there is a surplus of people with good sounding schemes about how to change things. The 1930s had its share of demagogues ready to fool the people with big talk:

- ✔ *Huey P. "Kingfish" Long* (1934) promised fat money bonuses for everyone in his native Louisiana in order to get almost-dictatorial power as governor and senator.

- ✔ *Father Charles Coughlin* (1935) was a thorn in the side of the Roosevelt administration, preaching unchristian hatred and isolationism over a national radio network.

- ✔ *Francis Townsend* (1936) had a plan for old age assistance (aptly named the *Townsend Plan*), which wasn't practical itself but did help spur the Social Security Act.

Question: What was the contribution of Francis Townsend in the 1930s?

Answer: His Townsend Plan helped encourage the development of Social Security.

Chapter 18

Fighting for Good in World War II: 1940–1945

America's self-absorbed it's-all-about-me attitude in the 1920s contributed to the nation getting kicked in the butt by the Great Depression (see Chapter 17). As if that wasn't bad enough, the same kind of me-first isolationist impulse on an international scale helped get the country socked in the kisser by World War II. The U.S. came out of this two-ended attack stronger than ever because Americans learned to fight back together and take the lead in solving world problems that they couldn't escape.

True to the modern social history approach, the big AP exam won't expect you to know all the battles, generals, and airplane names. You do need to understand what led up to the biggest war in history, plus the course of the conflict and its main high points and outcomes. Because of their age, the Test Masters who put the finishing touches on the AP History Challenge almost certainly know people who lived through World War II. They'll expect you to take this chapter's topic as seriously as they do.

Backpedaling from the Brink of War

After World War I, Americans tried to crawl back into bed and pull the isolationist covers over their heads. With the nightmare of the Great Depression already disturbing their sleep, the last thing they wanted was to get out of bed to see what all that international yelling was about. The U.S. wasn't looking for trouble, but no matter how hard the country covered its ears, trouble seemed to be looking for them from overseas.

Conferring with words, deferring with action

At first, President Franklin Roosevelt was all in favor of the *London Economic Conference* (1933), which convened to get the nations of the world working together on solutions to the Depression. Maybe he thought they were going to send him some money.

When he discovered the Conference just wanted to fix the value of gold, Roosevelt backpedaled fast. He had been lowering the value of gold in the U.S. to get more dollars in circulation; the last thing he wanted was an agreement that would fix the dollar-to-gold ratio and take away his money-juggling trick. Even though the Conference may have helped the rest of the world, Roosevelt blew it off because it didn't help the United States.

Other nations noticed the selfish stance of the U.S. and started to act like little brats, too. Not only did the London Economic Conference fall apart without the United States, but it also made countries that much more determined to go it alone and shoot anybody who got in their way.

Getting along with Latin America

The U.S. was a little chummier with Latin America. Roosevelt initiated a *Good Neighbor Policy* (1933) that pledged the United States to work with Central and South American nations to protect the hemisphere.

The idea of working together peacefully was a marked departure from previous U.S. policy, which had usually involved the Marines' polite invitations to cooperate, delivered on the point of a bayonet. In the 1930s, the U.S. removed troops from Haiti, Panama, and Cuba, holding on to the base at Guantanamo, Cuba, as a naval keepsake. When Mexico grabbed American-owned oil wells in their country, the U.S. gritted its teeth but didn't intervene.

Franklin Roosevelt flew down to Argentina for the *Inter-American Conference* (1936) and received cheers as he announced friendly aid and cooperation. With the beginnings of World War II thundering in Europe, the United States agreed to share responsibility for the Monroe doctrine with Latin American countries in the *Havana Conference* (1940).

Japan eyes the Philippines

Following through on the promise the U.S. made when they took the Philippines from Spain, Congress passed the *Tydings-McDuffie Act* (1934), which promised the islands their freedom in 1946 after a final 12-year tune-up. Despite the fact that World War II filled up a large chunk of that time with a Japanese military occupation of the Philippines, the U.S. kept its promise.

In the meantime, the United States' willingness to free the Philippines made Japan think the U.S. really didn't care that much about the islands. By promising to be nice later, the U.S. unintentionally let Japan believe that America may be easy to push around.

Reciprocal Trade Agreement Act

In another make-nice bid, Congress let the president set tariff-lowering deals with other countries under the *Reciprocal Trade Agreements Act* (1934). This measure reversed some of the self-absorbed damage of the *Hawley-Smoot* law and started the U.S. and the world on a decreasing-tariff trend that led to the free trade policies that most nations enjoy today.

Although reciprocal trade was hardly enough to make the world peaceful, it was a step in the right direction. Over the protests of vehement anti-communists, Roosevelt recognized the Soviet Union in 1933, something that would come in handy later when the U.S. needed allies in World War II.

Hitler and Mussolini (and sometimes Franco)

Meanwhile in Europe, bad guys were moving into the neighborhood. Benito Mussolini, the strutting proponent of Fascism, had taken over Italy in 1922. Looking for something strong and glorious to do, Mussolini invaded the independent African kingdom of Ethiopia in 1935, sending Italian soldiers in tanks and planes to fight people armed with spears. The League of Nations, without American support, did little but bluster to stop Mussolini.

Adolf Hitler, the 20th century's worst bad guy, took over Germany in 1933. After quickly getting rid of his country's struggling democracy, Hitler revived the German economy with dictatorial control and projects like the world's first national freeway system (the *autobahn*) and commissioning the world's first specially created "people's car" (the *Volkswagen*). Ominously, he also began an ever-tightening persecution of Jewish people and other minorities. Western democracies tried to overlook Hitler's crimes because they thought he would fight Communism.

In 1936, Hitler and Mussolini aligned themselves as the Axis powers. Soon they had a joint project. The democratic government of Spain was fighting a civil war with would-be dictator General Franco. Germany and Italy jumped in on Franco's side, sending troops, planes and tanks. The elected democratic government got some help from the Soviet Union and individual volunteers from many countries including the United States. The governments of France, Britain, and the United States refused to get involved to save the Spanish government, but Germany and Italy had no such hesitation about destroying it. After three years of brutal fighting — including the bombing of civilians by Germany and Italy — Franco won.

The Neutrality Acts

As the dictators increased their power, the United States increased its effort to build itself a better shell. Congress passed separate *Neutrality Acts* for three years in a row starting in 1935, in an attempt to avoid the kind of economic entanglement that had led to the U.S. being drawn in to World War I.

These neutrality acts said that when the president proclaimed the existence of a foreign war, no American could loan money, sell weapons, or even sail on a ship belonging to one of the fighting sides. These rules were a step back from the freedom of the seas for which the U.S. had fought major wars in the past. The Neutrality Acts made no distinction between good guys and bad guys; the United States wasn't going to help anybody.

By not working for good, the neutrality acts gave the advantage to dictatorships. The United States' hideout also included a refusal to prepare for any possible war. Throughout most of the 1930s, the American army contained fewer than 200,000 men, smaller than the armies of Poland or Turkey.

Watching the Flames of War Grow Higher

The military leadership of Japan wanted to control China, and it launched an invasion of that country in 1937. The United States forgave Japan after the Japanese apologized for sinking an American gunboat on a Chinese river. In 1940, Japan became a formal ally of Nazi Germany and Italy.

Meanwhile in Europe, Adolf Hitler gobbled up territory from countries on both sides of Germany. At first, his moves were tentative. When Hitler's troops marched into the demilitarized Rhineland region of Germany in 1936, they had orders to turn right around and go home if anybody stood up to them. Nobody did.

In March of 1938, the German army took over Austria without a fight. At the *Munich Conference* in September of that year, England and France agreed to let Hitler take over the German-speaking part of Czechoslovakia. This sellout by the democracies only bought peace for a few months. Negotiating with Hitler was like trying to stop a wolf by throwing meat. In August of 1939, anti-Communist Hitler stunned the world by signing a treaty with Joseph Stalin, leader of the big Communist Soviet Union. One week later, Hitler invaded Poland.

Britain and France take a stand

Finally England and France had had enough; they declared war on Germany, and the greatest conflict in history was under way. After several months of preparation, Hitler's well-organized forces swept across Holland and Belgium into France. By the summer of 1940, Hitler and his Italian buddy Mussolini controlled all of Europe except for the home islands of Britain 35 miles across the English Channel.

Hitler pounded Britain with planes to destroy the British Royal Air Force (RAF) and prepare the islands for German invasion. In the *Battle of Britain* (1940), the RAF, down to its last few planes, heroically defended its island nation. As the bombs fell, bulldog Prime Minister Winston Churchill told the British people to conduct themselves so that if Britain "lasts for a thousand years, men will still say, 'This was their finest hour.'" It was.

The U.S. takes a tentative step toward war

By 1938, the United States finally acknowledged that trouble may be coming its way, so it started to build up the Navy to sink any bad guys before they could get to American shores. With Europe under Nazi control and America's mother country Britain fighting for its life, the U.S. passed its first peacetime draft in September of 1940, beginning a slow process to bring millions of men into the armed forces.

"Any aid short of war"

Also in September, President Roosevelt took the dramatic step of sending 50 old destroyers to Britain in exchange for some defensive bases in the Atlantic. He didn't wait for Congress: His old friend Churchill had asked him to act *now*. Aid wasn't that easy; an *America First* (1940) organization led by aviation hero Charles Lindbergh opposed any help for Britain that may draw America into the war. A law to continue the draft passed by only one vote. Despite Lindbergh's popularity, a majority of Americans now favored helping the fight with "any aid short of war."

In the middle of the drama came a presidential election. Franklin Roosevelt decided he had to run again for an unprecedented third term. He won easily despite some uneasiness about electing anybody three times; the Democrats also maintained their majority in Congress.

Lend-Lease Bill

Britain was running out of money as well as supplies. A newly reelected Roosevelt introduced the *Lend-Lease Bill* (1941), which allowed the U.S. to lend or lease military supplies to Britain and other countries America supported without payment. This move was as close to declaring war as the nation could come without actually pulling the trigger; the hope was that other democracies would do the fighting for America. Lend-Lease had the additional advantage of tooling up U.S. defense plants to operate at full production before the country eventually ended up in the war.

Question: What was the purpose of the *Lend-Lease Bill* (1941)?

Answer: The purpose of Lend-Lease was to get desperately needed supplies to the Allies without payment in advance.

Hitler invades the Soviet Union

In June of 1941, less than two years after he had shocked the world by signing a peace treaty with his Communist enemy the Soviet Union, Hitler shocked the world again by invading his Soviet treaty buddies with a huge army. Having conquered most of Europe, Hitler thought he could get away with anything. In addition, he sincerely hated Communists (and basically anyone who got in his way).

Hitler was sure his genius planning would have the German army safely in Moscow before the first snows fell. During the first weeks of the invasion, the Germans won so much terri-tory that it looked like those dreams may come true. The Soviet Union seemed to be on the brink of collapse.

Against the nightmare scenario of the Soviet Union folding like it did in World War I, Churchill met with Roosevelt on a battleship off Canada. They weren't supposed to be allies; after all, the U.S. was still officially neutral and not at war. The two took the unusual step as unofficial buddies of drafting the *Atlantic Charter* (1941). The Charter said that all people had the right to choose their own government, especially to reinstate the democratic governments that dictators had taken away. It also called for disarmament and peace overseen by an interna-tional organization.

When they had time to catch their breath, the leaders of the Soviet Union signed on to the Charter later in 1941. The United States was in the interesting position of dictating war aims for a conflict it was not fighting. The charade got even thinner when America started to convoy supplies as far as Iceland through the German submarine packs with a shoot-to-kill order against attacking U-boats.

Japan attacks Pearl Harbor

In the Pacific, the U.S. also managed to twist the imperial tail of Japan without actually attack-ing. In late 1940, the United States cut off the shipment of scrap iron and other industrial sup-plies to Japan; in mid-1941, America froze Japan's investments in the U.S. and cut off all gas and military supplies. The Japanese war machine was going to grind to a halt without either buying supplies from the U.S. or stealing them from the lightly guarded Dutch West Indies.

America said it would turn on the supplies again if Japan backed out of China, but that would be a loss of both honor and hard-won territory. Japan pretended to negotiate and got ready for a surprise attack against the United States.

Early on the morning of Sunday, December 7, 1941, with most of the U.S. Pacific Naval Fleet rocking gently at anchor in the tropical breezes of Pearl Harbor, Hawaii, Japanese carrier planes flew in low to drop bombs that sank or disabled almost the whole fleet and killed 2,500 Americans. Unfortunately for the Japanese, they missed sinking the most valuable ships in the Pacific navy, three aircraft carriers that weren't in the harbor at the time. In months to come, these ships would come looking for the Japanese. Given that the U.S. had had no experience at being invaded for the last 125 years, the attack on Pearl Harbor came as a shocking surprise. Within days, the United States was at war with Japan, Germany, and Italy.

Having trouble remembering who's on what side? The major players in World War II were *JIG* versus *SUB*. The Axis Powers were *J*apan, *I*taly, and *G*ermany against the Allies, who were the *S*oviet Union, the *U*nited States, and *B*ritain. Hokey but useful.

Fighting to Win on the Home Front

Having had a couple of years to contemplate, Britain and the U.S. had already agreed to put most of their efforts into beating Germany first. Although you may be inclined to chase the wasp that has just stung you, you're better off to go after the biggest hive first. Plus, little Britain and the almost-overwhelmed Soviets were politely saying, "Hey, can we get some help over here?" Sure, but first the Unites States had to figure out how to feed and equip all three countries, plus ship its fighting forces and supplies half way around the world in two directions.

The treatment of Japanese Americans

The American mainland home front was pretty steady, with no real challenge from enemy bombs or sabotage. However, out of paranoia and racism, the U.S. government herded over 100,000 Japanese Americans into internment camps just to be safe. Most of them were American citizens; none of them were ever proven to be a real danger to the United States. They were politely treated for the most part, but many of them lost the small farms they had managed to buy before the war, when they had grown most of the West Coast's green beans, tomatoes, and strawberries. They appealed their internment to the Supreme Court in the case of *Korematsu v. United States* (1944), and the Court ruled that the internment was legal.

Despite their harsh treatment, thousands of Japanese Americans volunteered for the army and fought bravely in Europe. After the war, they went back to their normal lives. Thirty years after the War, the United States apologized and paid the Japanese Americans who were still around a small compensation.

Question: What was the Supreme Court decision in *Korematsu v. United States*?

Answer: The Supreme Court held that the internment of Japanese Americans on the West Coast of the United States during World War II was legal.

Production kicks off

Production of war material made the United States what President Roosevelt called the "arsenal of democracy." For starters, the U.S. launched almost 3,000 Liberty Ships, each capable of carrying 10,000 tons of cargo anywhere in the world. On those ships went more than 2 million machine guns, billions of bullets, four times as many tanks as the dictators produced, twice as many fighter planes, four times as many bombers, and five times as many heavy guns and trucks.

Farmers hauled in record billion-bushel wheat crops by using machinery to replace manpower. Rationing held down domestic consumption to speed food to American soldiers and their allies. Government agencies worked to keep a lid on wages and prices. Labor unions grew, but their leaders mostly kept their men off the picket lines and on the job. To encourage worker cooperation, Congress passed the *Smith-Connally Anti-Strike Act* (1943), which allowed the government to take over industries tied up by strikes.

The federal government took over the coal mines and for a short period even ran the railroads. Most of the time, the federal government did not need to step in: business and labor worked together for the war effort. Over all, American workers cooperated with the war effort by having even fewer work stoppages than laborers in besieged Britain.

During the war, thousands of Mexican farm workers entered the United States, partly as a replacement for the interned Japanese. They never left.

Workers built liberty ships cheaply and quickly. In a break with tradition, they welded the ships together instead of riveting them. Ship building used to take months, but Liberty ships were ready in six weeks.

Women made up a third of the civilian work force; most of these women had never held a job outside their homes before. They welded the Liberty ships that supplied the armies of democracy. After the war, two thirds of the women quit their jobs to return to housework, but they didn't forget their successful employment. Working women became a natural part of the United States' economy in the 1960s, about the time the daughters of the women who helped win World War II came of age.

The U.S. fights discrimination in defense industries

Despite massive federal investment for industrial plants in the Southeast, millions of blacks left the land of their former enslavement to take new manufacturing jobs in the North and California.

Cotton-picking was over as an occupation in the South after the invention of a machine to do the work. Within a generation, a majority of Southern blacks gave up their rural homes and gravitated toward the city. This migration was so large that it rivaled the influx of immigrants at the beginning of the 1900s.

Under pressure from the nation's only black union, the Roosevelt administration forbade discrimination in defense industries. This was the first time black workers had been given a fair shake in major industries, and they responded by going to work in record numbers.

Minorities contribute in the armed forces

The American record on discrimination was not as good in the armed forces. Blacks fought in segregated units, often in service rather than combat jobs; however, they did have a limited but proud record as fighter pilots, soldiers, and sailors. In 1948, three years after the end of the war, the armed forces became the first major institution in the United States to be officially desegregated.

More than 25,000 American Indians served in the armed forces during World War II. In both Europe and the Pacific, they made special contributions as *code talkers* who relayed radio messages in Indian languages that enemy troops couldn't understand. After the war, American Indians migrated from reservations to cities in record numbers.

Hundreds of thousands of Mexican Americans served in the armed forces, making up around 3 percent of the army. Although they faced discrimination in housing, education, and even veterans services after the war, they fought back through legal defense organizations.

Mexican American school children had to attend so-called Mexican schools in California. In 1947, the *Mendez v. Westminster* court ruling declared that segregating children of "Mexican and Latin descent" in the state of California was unconstitutional. This ruling helped lay the foundation for the landmark *Brown v. Board of Education* (1954) case that ended official racial segregation for all minorities in the United States public school system.

America finally recovers from the Depression

The United States *gross national product* (the value of its output of goods and services) doubled during World War II. Although the Depression had hit the U.S. harder than most countries, America recovered strongly during the war. People were working decent jobs and had money to spend; average pay by the end of the war was almost twice as much as it was at the beginning.

As the only industrialized nation not being bombed, the U.S. outproduced the rest of the world. Millions of people were either in the armed forces or employed by defense industries supported by federal contracts. The federal *Office of Scientific Research and Development* (1941) spent billions of dollars on university research and technical innovation, including the top secret *Manhattan Project* (1941) to develop the atomic bomb.

This flood of war spending, not the modest streams of help from New Deal programs, was what finally brought a complete end to the Great Depression. The war cost more than the total of every penny the government had ever spent since the American Revolution. As terrible as it was, World War II lifted up the United States both as an international power and as the world's richest economy. The same people who started the New Deal in the face of the Depression ran America during World War II.

The optimistic can-do attitude the United States gained from its trials in war and the Depression buoyed the nation for the rest of the century.

Question: What was the economic condition of the U.S. home front during World War II?

Answer: The U.S. home front economy completely recovered from the Great Depression and boomed during World War II.

Following the Fight in the Pacific

After Pearl Harbor, the situation looked bleak for the Allies. Japan had conquered most of the East Asia, including the American possessions of the Philippines, Guam, and the Wake Islands and the European possessions of Hong Kong, Singapore, the East Indies, and Indochina. The Japanese said they wanted to start an Asian commonwealth run by Asians, but in fact their rule was often more brutal to the natives than that of the Europeans they replaced.

The Philippines fell to Japan in 1942 after five months of resistance; General Douglas MacArthur was relocated at the last minute to lead the U.S. Pacific forces in Australia. The Japanese fought their way to islands just off Australia before they ran in to the slowly growing strength of the Allied forces.

In the naval battle of the *Coral Sea* (May, 1942), the first battle in history in which the ships never saw each other and all the fighting was done by planes, the combined U.S. and Australian forces fought the Japanese to a standstill and prevented an invasion of southern New Guinea that would have threatened Australia.

Midway

The tide began to turn for real in the *Battle of Midway* (1942). In this second all-carrier battle, the U.S. defended an island outpost west of Hawaii with everything that could float. The Japanese lost four aircraft carriers and many of their carefully trained pilots; the Americans lost just one carrier. With its greater population and production power, America was on the offensive in the Pacific from Midway on.

Guadalcanal

The first real land fighting was an American attack on the small island of *Guadalcanal* (1942) that threatened the shipping of supplies to Australia. It took months, but the Americans finally drove the Japanese off the island. The U.S. hopped from island to island across the South Pacific, refusing to back down from the fight-to-the-death resistance by the Japanese, but never backing off. By the end of 1944, the U.S. had won islands close enough to the Japanese homeland to serve as launching fields for around the clock bombing of Japan itself. American submarines and planes sunk Japanese supply ships at a rapid rate.

Hunting Hitler in Europe

The first challenge the U.S. faced in fighting for Europe was getting supplies through the well-armed wolf packs of German submarines. In the first months of the war, the Germans sunk more than 500 American merchant ships faster than the U.S. could rebuild them. Without supplies, Britain couldn't continue fighting.

Faced with a high tech sub threat, the U.S. and Britain devised cutting-edge solutions. The British broke the German codes so the Allies had an idea of where the German submarine packs were hiding. Patrol planes and convoys equipped with sonar attacked the subs.

Over a year, the tables turned. The German subs had to draw back as the Allies sunk more than a hundred of their undersea boats, in some months at the rate of almost one a day. With fewer German subs, Allied supply ships were safer; their losses decreased from the equivalent of 75 Liberty ships sunk a month to fewer than 20. Although the Germans kept up their submarine attacks at a low level for the rest of the war, the time for subs to make a real difference had passed.

The British attack from the air

The British believed that heavily bombing German cities would break the German will to fight (even though when the Germans bombed Britain, it only made the British tougher). Britain sent more than 1,000 bombers to attack the German city of Cologne.

Now that America was in the war, the Germans were under constant attack from the British at night and the Americans by day. Heavy conventional bombing didn't break the Germans' will to fight or even stop production; the Germans made planes and submarines until the end of the conflict. What bombing did do was open up a second front in the air before the Allies invaded Europe while only Soviet troops were fighting on the ground in the first front against the Germans.

Allied strategic air attacks forced the Germans to spend limited resources on protecting civilians with their guns and fighter planes. Domination of the air over the battlefield by Allied tactical planes meant the Germans had to give up lightning raids in the open and settle down to trench warfare, much like in World War I. The Allies remained free to move.

The Soviets fight back

After giving ground to early German attacks, the Soviets caught a break by way of intensely harsh weather. One of the earliest, coldest, and snowiest winters in Soviet memory broke over German troops, who didn't have winter equipment because Hitler had expected them to win long before the weather got cold. When the snows hit, the Germans were so close to taking Moscow that they actually stole tickets from the end of the Moscow tram line, but the Soviets threw their last fresh troops (who just happened to include Cossack ski troops) into the battle and pushed the Germans away from their capital.

The Germans held on deep in the Soviet Union for another year, but after a heroic defense the Soviets launched a counterattack late in 1942. From then on, it was a slow and costly three year fight to Berlin. The Soviets lost 27 million people in World War II, more than 50 times as many people as the U.S. lost. Through 1943, Britain and the United States had lost only a few thousand soldiers in Europe. The Soviets pleaded for a second front in Europe to take some of the pressure off their army.

The Allies advance: D-day and Normandy

The Western allies took two and a half years to launch their D-day invasion; meanwhile they nipped away at the outskirts of Europe. The Allies invaded North Africa in November of 1942, and by the following summer they'd defeated the German and Italian armies there. Churchill and Roosevelt met in the newly liberated city of Casablanca to plan the rest of the war. The Allies next invaded Italy. Although the Italians were happy to get rid of Mussolini and called it quits by September of 1943, the Germans fought on in Italy until almost the end of the war.

In June of 1944, the Allies launched a massive invasion of Normandy in France. Over 3 million men had assembled in Britain for the cross-channel push. Thousands died on the beaches, but the Allies pushed inland. A second, smaller invasion came from the south of France. Paris was liberated in August of 1944, and the first major German city fell to the Allies in October.

In the U.S., Franklin Roosevelt won reelection for an unprecedented fourth term as the Allied armies rolled toward victory. Hitler counterattacked at the *Battle of the Bulge* (1944) in December, but this move merely hastened the end of the war by using up his reserves. By April of 1945, the Soviets and their Western allies were in Berlin, and Hitler had committed suicide. Franklin Roosevelt had died of a stroke a few days before.

Revealing the Horror of the Holocaust

After Hitler's death, the world began to face the terrible crime of the Holocaust. Almost every Jew the Nazis could find in Europe had been murdered in cold blood, 6 million people in all.

In addition, Hitler and his willing German and European accomplices had murdered another 5 million political opponents, prisoners of war, Gypsies, Freemasons, disabled children, and Jehovah's Witnesses, among others. The United States struggled with the fact that the country had been unwilling to allow refugees from Europe to seek safety in the U.S. before the war. After they knew about the death camps and the killing of families and children, many Americans made a simple pledge: never again. The experience of World War II influences America's international policy to this day.

The Japanese fight on

By the summer of 1945, the Allies had defeated Germany, and U.S. forces were within bombing range of Japan. Authorities as diverse as future Nobel Prize winner William Shockley and ex-President Herbert Hoover estimated that the planned U.S. land invasion of Japan would cost 1 million U.S. casualties and up to 10 million Japanese lives. The Japanese military was training all civilians — including children — to fight to the death.

The United States had just completed the first test of the new atomic bomb. The Soviet Union was attacking the Japanese army through China, and the U.S. didn't want to give the Soviets time to make territorial claims. After dropping warning leaflets, the U.S. exploded an atomic bomb over the Japanese city of Hiroshima, killing around 130,000 people. The Japanese still didn't surrender. Three days later, the Americans dropped another bomb over Nagasaki that killed an additional 60,000 people.

Question: Why did the United States drop the atomic bomb on Japan?

Answer: To end the war, stop Soviet expansion, and ultimately save lives.

The ending was deadly, but at least it was actually the end to years of global suffering during World War II. The dictators' threat to democracy was so serious that some have called the Allies' defense of international freedom the Good War.

Before World War II, only a handful of democracies existed throughout the world. Now, most of the countries in the world hold democratic elections (or at least pretend to). Before World War II, the world was an international jungle — every nation for itself. Now, although pain and conflict are certainly still plentiful, the United Nations and other international organizations at least try to call attention to abuses and occasionally take real action.

The United States was changed as much as any part of the globe by World War II. Thrust into world leadership, America could never go back to the dream of isolationism.

Chapter 19

Cold War Wind at the Victory Dance: 1946–1960

*F*rom the outside, the United States seemed like the place to be in the autumn of 1945. With the help of its allies, the nation had won a stunning victory in battles beyond both its oceans' shores (see Chapter 18).

Unlike every other industrialized nation in the world, the U.S. suffered little damage to its cities. American farms and factories were in full production, and labor had never been so highly paid. People finally felt safe. The bad guys from overseas had been vanquished, and the U.S. was the only country with the biggest bat in history: the atomic bomb. Prosperity continued, but the feeling of safety didn't last for long. This chapter covers the years after World War II, particularly the Cold War and its effects on the nation and the rest of the world.

Doing Well but Feeling Nervous

World War II had been a four-year roller coaster ride of war for the U.S. As exciting and wonderful as it felt to be victorious, however, Americans couldn't forget that before those four years had come more than ten years of economic uncertainty in the Great Depression. With no more wartime jobs, folks had to wonder whether hard times were going to return.

President Harry S Truman had taken over when Franklin Roosevelt died just as the war with Germany was ending; nobody knew whether he could fill Roosevelt's shoes. Even more worrisome was the Soviet Union; that country seemed to be going from ally to enemy even before the last round of toasts at the victory party.

Enjoying a victory bonus

The baby boom started after World War II — war families were reunited, and people felt optimistic enough about the future to want to bring more children into the world. During the Depression years before the War, birth rates had been down and suicide rates were up (because the economic depression made people emotionally depressed).

After victory and years of good pay, people felt much better. The postwar baby boom formed a ten-year population bulge that helped invent '50s rock-and-roll, '60s protest, '70s attitude, '80s yuppies, and at the beginning of the 21st century the baby boomers were poised to make retirement an active sport.

After the removal of wartime government price management, costs shot up to match higher wages. The annual inflation rate went from 2 percent in 1945 to 9 percent in 1946 and 14 percent in 1947 before it started to level off. Higher costs meant wages bought less, and that led to strikes: More work stoppages occurred in 1946 than during all of World War II.

The Taft-Hartley Act

Although the country still had a Democratic president, it had elected the first Republican-controlled Congress since Herbert Hoover. Those Republicans managed to pass a bill over President Truman's veto that they said would get strikes under control.

The *Taft-Hartley Act* (1947) prohibited unions from putting pressure on their employers by picketing other companies that did business with their own company. The act also forbid unions from requiring that an employer hire only union members (called a *closed shop*) but allowed *union shops,* in which everybody had to join the union after they were hired.

The Taft-Hartley Act is still in effect. It allows states to forbid union shops: Several states have established *right to work* laws that prohibit all workers from having to join a union. Additionally, unions have to give 60 days' notice when they're threatening to strike, and the president can put a hold on strikes that he feels will cause a national emergency.

Switching blue collars to white

At the high point of union membership in the early '50s, a third of the population was involved in some sort of union; by the early 21st century, that number had declined to less than 15 percent. The Taft-Hartley Act itself didn't cause unions to lose membership — a change in the kind of work Americans were doing did.

In the 1950s, America experienced a decrease in the number of blue-collar manual laborers and an increase in the number white-collar service workers; for the first time, the white-collar workers outnumbered the manual laborers. This abundance of service workers has increased over the years, and the number of union members has decreased accordingly.

One obstacle for unions is the fact that service workers stay in jobs for a shorter period of time than they used to; the average American now spends less than four years at one job. This rapid turnover makes union organizing difficult.

In addition, unions are victims of their own success. Employment practices and wages have improved so much that many workers don't think they need the kind of protection unions can bring.

The Employment Act

After the war, the Truman administration sold unneeded defense plants and equipment at bargain prices to help employers grow civilian businesses. Congress passed the *Employment Act* (1946), which set a goal of maintaining full employment and required the president to submit an annual economic report along with the federal budget. The act established the Council of Economic Advisers, who was responsible for supplying the smarts to keep the economy and the job market rolling.

Roosevelt's final New Deal: The GI Bill

A bigger, more immediate payoff than the theories of the Economic Advisers was the benefits of the Servicemen's Readjustment Act of 1944, better known as the *GI Bill* (1944). The GI Bill provided for college or vocational education as well as one year of unemployment compensation for returning World War II veterans, whom everybody called GIs (short for Government Issue). It also provided loans for returning veterans to buy homes and start businesses.

The GI Bill was the last piece of New Deal legislation endorsed and signed by Franklin Roosevelt. (See Chapter 17 for more on the New Deal.) Ex-soldiers couldn't believe their good fortune: The bill paid for education and offered low-interest loans. Although most veterans attended vocational schools to learn a trade, enough GIs opted for college that many universities doubled in size. The proportion of the population with a college degree grew from 5 percent before the war to more than 25 percent in the early 21st century.

Question: What most influenced the number of men going to college in the United States during the 20th century?

Answer: The GI Bill, which paid for the education of veterans.

Millions of young American families moved to small houses in the suburbs thanks to zero-down-payment loans from the GI Bill. This started a housing revolution that took home ownership from 44 percent in 1940 to almost 70 percent in the early 21st century. All this education and house-building also helped stimulate the economy by making more jobs. The GI Bill provided up to one year of unemployment coverage, but few ex-soldiers could resist getting one of the plentiful jobs before that year was up.

Truman, the Unexpected President

Nobody expected Harry S Truman to be president, least of all Truman. A last-minute compromise candidate as Franklin Roosevelt's third vice president, Truman had only a few months on the job when Roosevelt died. Truman said to reporters: "Boys, if you ever pray, pray for me now. I don't know if you fellas ever had a load of hay fall on you, but when they told me what happened yesterday, I felt like the moon, the stars, and all the planets had fallen on me."

Truman was an honest man elected by a political machine, a failed men's clothing store owner who joined George Washington, Abraham Lincoln, and Andrew Jackson as a president who never went to college. When the love of his life turned him down when he first asked her to marry him, Truman went off, earned some money, fought in World War I, came back, asked her again, and she said yes.

As a senator before World War II, Truman took it upon himself to visit defense plants and push them to be more productive. The sign on his desk said, "The buck stops here"; Truman wouldn't stand for blame-passing. Counted out politically, he ran a give-'em-hell campaign and surprised everybody by winning the presidential election in his own right in 1948.

In his second term, Truman faced an icy freeze of relationships with the Soviet Union, who had still been America's warm wartime allies when he first took office. More on those relationships in the following section.

Stepping into Icy Waters: Beginning the Cold War

The division of the world into Soviet Union Communist buddies against the United States capitalist team happened seemingly overnight at the end of World War II. People called it the *Cold War* (1950), although it got pretty hot in Korea and Vietnam.

World War II ended with the Soviet Union in control of Eastern Europe. The Soviets established Communist governments backed by Soviet troops in Poland, Czechoslovakia, Hungary, and other Eastern European nations. Westerners on the capitalist side said that an iron curtain had descended across Europe, dividing the free countries that had real elections from the Communist countries ruled by party officials.

Don't get all confused when countries change names. The Soviet Union, also known as the Union of Soviet Socialist Republics, also known as the U.S.S.R., was really just the big old Russian bear with a few captive cubs. When Russia went Communist after World War I, it took a few (sometimes independent) provinces or countries with it and became the Soviet Union. When it got over the Communist thing in the 1990s, it let the provinces go and went back to just being Russia.

Shifting from Allies to enemies

Paranoia struck deep after World War II. The Soviet Union was torn apart by German troops and had lost millions of people fighting alone in Europe for three long years before Britain and the U.S. finally got around to the D-day invasion.

The Soviets saw the world as an anti-Communist conspiracy, and they were on a self-protective and ideological crusade to turn other countries Communist. They especially wanted a protective barrier of Communist satellite countries between themselves and Germany, a country that had torn into Russia twice in 25 years.

The Soviets knew that the West had put up with Hitler for years partly because Western countries thought Hitler could kill off Communism. During the War (before he was vice president), Truman had said the U.S. should let the Germans and the Soviets kill each other off and help whichever side seemed to be losing to keep the bloody fight going. Having lost 27 million people (and almost their country) in World War II, the Soviets had reasons to worry.

So did the United States. Not only did its so-called Soviet allies become increasingly hostile, but within a few years the Soviets also got the atomic bomb, and lots of countries, especially China, went Communist. To people in the U.S., it looked like a conspiracy was afoot in the world; how else could the Communists become so powerful?

Renewing the sport of distrusting Communists

Like any argument, push came to shove pretty fast between the U.S. and the U.S.S.R. because each side was sure that it was right and the other side was cheating. The United States shut off Lend-Lease aid to the Soviets and refused to include the Communist countries of Eastern Europe in the Marshall Plan to rebuild Europe. The Soviets refused the rebuilding aid that was offered by the U.S.

The Soviets clamped a lid on Eastern Europe and supported any country who said it was Communist. In response, the United States supported all countries who said they were anti-Communist. The showdown lead to a dangerous arms race, plus a showdown in jointly controlled Germany and shooting wars (sorry, officially *conflicts*) in Korea and Vietnam.

A diplomat named George Kennan saw it coming. In his influential 1947 paper "The Sources of Soviet Conduct," he maintained that Russian policy, whether from the tsar or from the Communist Party is relentlessly expansionistic but cautious, and he recommended a policy of firm and vigilant containment. The United States followed Kennan's policy.

> Question: What was George Kennan's 1947 policy recommendation?
>
> Answer: Kennan recommended a policy of firm containment of Soviet Communist expansion.

Starting the United Nations

Despite the postwar tensions, at least one peaceful organization popped up. The *United Nations* (1945) got going at the end of the war; President Roosevelt was getting ready to speak to the first U.N. session when he died.

Unlike the similarly themed League of Nations (see Chapter 16), the U.N. began with the full support of the United States. The U.N. has a Security Council controlled by the big powers and a General Assembly of all nations. Able to act only when the big powers agree, the U.N. has become an organizing center for peacekeeping missions around the world.

The International Monetary Fund

In other international news, the Western Allies established the *International Monetary Fund* (IMF) (1944) during a meeting at Bretton Woods, New Hampshire, toward the end of the War. The IMF is an international organization consisting of just about every country in the world. The IMF oversees the global financial system by controlling exchange rates and making loans.

Although IMF international policy has its critics, cooperation tied a more prosperous world together and helped to lift countries out of poverty to some extent.

Putting the final wraps on World War II

The Allies wrapped up World War II by occupying Japan and Germany. They divided Germany into zones controlled by Britain, France, the U.S., and the U.S.S.R. Although Berlin was technically in the Soviet zone, the parties divided it separately; the Soviets got East Berlin, and the West took West Berlin (go figure). Japan was an all-American show, with General Douglas MacArthur dictating a democratic constitution.

The Nuremberg trials

In both Japan and Germany, 20 or so major war criminals went on trial, and a few were executed. In Germany, these postwar hearings were called the *Nuremberg trials* (1946), and they established the principle that people have the responsibility not to follow orders if those orders violate international law.

The Berlin Airlift

As Cold War tensions rose, the Soviets cut off Western ground access to the West's part of Berlin by closing the road that ran across the Soviet governed part of Germany. The Americans responded with a giant airlift of supplies that kept Berlin alive for almost a year until the Soviets relented and allowed ground access again. The *Berlin Airlift* (1949) landed a plane every minute, using some of the same aircraft that had recently been trying to kill Berliners.

The Truman Doctrine

President Truman got Congress to approve loans to Greece and Turkey to counter Soviet moves to turn those countries Communist. He launched the *Truman Doctrine* (1947) of containing Communism by supporting capitalist countries with money and arms if necessary.

The Marshall Plan

The U.S. supplied a much bigger financial support package to Europe through the *Marshall Plan* (1947), which lent billions of dollars to rebuild Western Europe. It worked. By the end of the 1950s, Western European economies were well on the way to recovery, and the region had begun plans for the European Community.

Truman also threw American support behind the creation of the state of Israel in 1948.

The National Security Act and NATO

America's anti-Communist jitters led to the creation of super agencies to fight the Cold War. The *National Security Act* (1947) established the *Joint Chiefs of Staff,* which brought together top military leaders, and the *National Security Council,* which brought together intelligence information gathered by the new *Central Intelligence Agency* (CIA). The next year, Congress reinstituted the peacetime draft, and in 1949 the nation swallowed hard and entered into the very kind of "entangling alliance" George Washington had warned about.

With the birth of the *North Atlantic Treaty Organization* (NATO) (1949), the U.S. allied itself with European nations and pledged to respond to an attack on any one of them as an attack on all. NATO kept a wary eye on the Soviet Union and its Warsaw Pact treaty buddies. The Warsaw Pact was the Soviet equivalent of NATO, made up of Eastern European nations under the control of Moscow.

Fretting over China

While MacArthur helped Japan turn into a peaceful and prosperous democracy, the Chinese were fighting among themselves. In 1949, Communist leader Mao Tse-tung was triumphant, pushing the non-Communist Chinese off the mainland and on to the island of Formosa.

The Republicans roundly blamed Truman for "losing" China, but in fact the huge country had never had a democratic government to defend. The Soviet Union's detonation of its first atomic bomb around this same time didn't really help America's nervous feelings, either.

Growing Communist paranoia in the U.S.

President Truman actually launched the anti-Communist hysteria in the United States by appointing a Loyalty Review Board in 1947 that checked to see whether any of the 3 million federal employees were members of supposedly subversive organizations. About 3,000 federal workers resigned under pressure, although none of them was charged with a crime.

By 1949, supporting those so-called subversive groups *was* a crime, and members of the U.S. Communist Party went to jail for supposedly advocating the overthrow of the U.S. government. The House Committee on Un-American Activities (HUAC) had a field day uncovering suspected Communists everywhere, led by an ambitious young congressman named Richard Nixon who didn't mind calling anyone who got in his way a Communist sympathizer.

In 1950, Truman vetoed a bill that would have given the president power to arrest and lock up any suspicious person during a security emergency because it sounded too much like a police state.

In the midst of paranoia, however, Truman did manage to build some public housing, raise the minimum wage, and extend Social Security. Any further social programs were held hostage by the Cold War.

Senator Joseph McCarthy and McCarthyism

Senator Joseph McCarthy made outrageous claims that Communists had infiltrated the federal government. He said that hundreds of known Communists worked in the State Department, and he pretended to have a list of their names. He accused respected officials of being "fellow travelers" with Communists, even picking on former army chief of staff George Marshall (author of the Marshall Plan) and President Eisenhower.

Communist actions in China and Korea and the speed with which the Soviets had gotten the atomic bomb scared Americans enough that they supported McCarthy's wild accusations. Every time he made a charge that proved false, he simply came up with a new charge. His witch hunt was called *McCarthyism* (1952).

McCarthy finally went overboard when he attacked the United States Army. In the great tradition of journalists who would not be frightened away from telling the truth, television's Edward R. Murrow took on McCarthy while politicians were afraid to act. After 35 days of televised hearings, many Americans saw who McCarthy really was: a mean-spirited liar who twisted the people's worries to get power. He was censured by the Senate and died of chronic alcoholism three years later.

McCarthyism showed the power of fear connected to conspiracy theory; it still serves as a useful example of the danger of hysteric leadership.

Fighting in Korea

Korea was divided between Communist North Korea and capitalist South Korea after World War II. In 1950, the North invaded the South and the *Korean War* (1952) was underway. The United States called the fighting a "conflict" since war was not officially declared, but it certainly seemed like a war to the people who were getting shot. The Communist North, armed with Soviet weapons, pushed the South Koreans back to a small pocket on the edge of the peninsula.

Taking command from Japan, Douglas MacArthur engineered a brilliant landing way behind Communist lines and pushed the North Koreans back across their border. The U.S. then made the mistake of taking over all of Korea, right up to its border with Communist China.

The Chinese sent in huge waves of soldiers and pushed the Americans and South Koreans back to the South's border.

After years of sniping, both Koreas signed a peace treaty, putting things back the way they were before the invasion.

The Korean War got a U.S. military buildup going that eventually ate up 10 percent of the gross national product. With Communism in the past, the U.S. defense figure is now less than 5 percent of the GNP.

In the 1950s, the U.S. spent money and lives to defend its democratic capitalist system, but it avoided touching off a nuclear war that could destroy the world. When Chinese Communist troops stormed into Korea, General MacArthur wanted to use atomic bombs and risk a global meltdown. President Truman fired him.

Truman was aggressive in Korea in part to answer critics that his administration had been soft in letting China go Communist. Nonetheless, he wasn't going to let Korea lead to World War III. Paranoia of both sides caused the Cold War, but when the war turned hot in both Korea and Vietnam, the U.S. took hits rather than use weapons that could destroy the world.

Question: What influenced President Truman in responding with toughness to Communist aggression in Korea?

Answer: Truman wanted to correct the impression that his administration had turned soft on Communism because it had watched the Communists take over China without launching military opposition.

Stepping into the fray: Dwight D. Eisenhower

The Democrats had a five-term run in the White House; now it was time for a Republican. Actually, the Democrats were thinking of nominating Eisenhower themselves, but after some reflection he decided he was a Republican. To give Ike a tough anti-Communist ticket, the Republicans ran Richard Nixon as vice president.

When there was some controversy about Nixon, Ike almost dumped him. Nixon made the first dramatic use of national television as a political tool by going on the air to speak about how his wife had only a respectable Republican cloth coat (no minks for her) and how next the Communist sympathizers would attack the fact that his kids had been given a dog named Checkers. The Checkers speech saved his nomination, and Eisenhower won the election by an overwhelming majority.

Eisenhower had been a mediator of often-contentious military units as the overall head of the Allied forces in Europe in World War II. He used these talents to lead by consensus during the 1950s. This knack meant that although he was seldom in the forefront on important issues, he usually came through with reasonable compromise solutions.

Ending the Korean War

The Korean War finally ended after Ike visited the front and threatened to use atomic weapons. Korea had cost more than 30,000 U.S. lives and hundreds of thousands of Korean and Chinese deaths. Troops still guard the border to this day.

Liking Ike in the Prosperous 1950s

Americans were ready for some grandfatherly reassurance. The Depression and World War II had been a strain, and the Communists, Korea, and the Cold War didn't give anybody much of a chance to relax. Electing Dwight "Ike" Eisenhower, a balding, kindly leading general from World War II, as president in 1952 was a relief.

Real income grew at a rapid rate in the 1950s and beyond. Americans — only 5 percent of the world's population — controlled almost 40 percent of the world's wealth. Money was the biggest story in the history of the United States since World War II.

Not all Americans profited equally from the affluence of their country, and the nation experienced both recession and inflation, but overall the economic course was up for most of the people most of the time.

The seeds of future trouble were contained in some aspects of American affluence. Defense spending stayed high, fully 10 percent of the *gross national product* (GNP) (value of goods and services) during the 1950s. President Eisenhower also warned about the bad influence of the military industrial complex on U.S. society.

Doubling the middle class

Cars, houses, and too many stomachs got bigger. The proportion of the population in the middle class doubled from the Roaring '20s; by the end of the 1950s, two-thirds of Americans were comfortably middle class. Prosperity gave people the space to improve education, civil rights, and medical care. It also gave the country the income necessary to outspend the Soviet Union in the arms race and Cold War.

By 1960, one out of four homes in America was less than 10 years old. People could afford new homes because their jobs were better — more than likely white collar or sales. The first 707 jet passenger planes launched the travel revolution; before the 1950s, most people had never been on a plane.

Television takes over American households

The 1950s saw the birth of television and fast food. Many now look down on both, but both provided a rich option of experience and convenience that people wanted. Only 3 million people in the country had televisions in 1950; by the end of the decade, they were in nearly every home. In the 1950s, TVs got only three channels; people had to choose from one of the three shows broadcast by the major networks. Originally, television was only black and white on tiny screens — color television was a big deal when it came out in the mid-'50s — and a 21-inch picture tube was considered large.

Rocking in the U.S.A.

Rock-and-roll changed music and culture starting in 1954. Elvis Presley may not have had the first rock record, but he was there at the beginning with Little Richard, Ike Turner, Buddy Holly, and Jerry Lee Lewis. Rock-and-roll spread like wildfire, bridging the gap between black rhythm and white melody. The open sexuality didn't hurt, either; rock was in the sexy company of Marilyn Monroe, Playboy magazine, and the Kinsey report, which detailed how normal lust could be. Victorian times were gone forever.

Examining alienation and conformity in literature

Literature was actually more dramatic and upbeat in the happy 1950s than in the roaring 1920s. Early-decade social critics like David Riesman in *The Lonely Crowd,* William Whyte in *The Organization Man,* and Sloan Wilson in *The Man in the Gray Flannel Suit* saw the future in alienation and conformity. Later, the 1960s would show them how wrong they could be.

Hemingway and Steinbeck turned out career-capping work and won well-deserved Nobel prizes. Tennessee Williams *(Cat on a Hot Tin Roof)* and Arthur Miller *(Death of a Salesman)* wrote searing drama. J.D. Salinger captured adolescent angst and its answer forever in *Catcher in the Rye.*

People like Joseph Heller *(Catch-22),* Kurt Vonnegut *(Slaughterhouse Five),* and Philip Roth *(Goodbye, Columbus)* wrote wittily and meaningfully at the same time. Television wasn't killing off culture, at least not yet.

> Question: What did social critics like David Riesman warn was a coming social problem?
>
> Answer: Social critics in the 1950s often warned about conformity and alienation from community.

Women in the workforce

Of the 40 million new jobs that started between 1950 and 1980, 30 million were in clerical and service work — jobs that women often filled. Women didn't displace men in the job market; they just found jobs that were never there before. Working women were nothing new — women had worked as hard as men on the farm for years. The real anomaly in history was the first hundred years of the Industrial Revolution, during which time middle-class women were supposed to just stay home and be domestic goddesses.

Women moved from being less than one quarter of the work force at the end of World War II to being about half the workers in the early 21st century. This change allowed families to stretch their incomes, but it caused some wrenching readjustments at first as women tried to cover being wife, mother, and full-time worker all at the same time (and men learned some parenting skills to take up the slack).

At least the children were in school; in 1950s America, most kids finished high school. This number contrasts with the time before World War I, when only half of school-age children regularly attended classes.

Getting addicted to energy

America began its energy addiction in the 1950s; oil consumption doubled and electric energy usage increased 600 percent in the two decades after World War II. Big cars burned more gas and commutes got longer as people moved out to the suburbs, which were home to 25 percent of the population by the end of the 1950s and more than 50 percent of the people by the 21st century.

The growth of Sunbelt living in the warm Southern climate made air conditioning a regular part of many people's lives. Productivity increased with energy usage on the farm: using petroleum based fertilizers, hybrid crops and gasoline powered harvesters allowed one farmer to feed ten times as many people at the turn of the 21st century as his grandfather could at the turn of the 20th century.

The first computer

The first commercial computer appeared in the United States in 1951. The UNIVAC (for *universal automatic computer*) was the size of a small house and used 5,200 vacuum tubes and 125 kilowatts of power to store its full capacity of 1,000 words. With less computing power than a cheap digital watch, the UNIVAC sold for a nice even $1 million.

The ultimate cost of affluence

One downside of affluence was distance. People moved every few years; adult children often lived thousands of miles from their parents, grandparents, sisters, and brothers. Airplanes could bring people together for a few hours at the holidays, but the sense of extended family was gone. Self-help advice books and psychological counseling barely filled in the gaps. Affluence could cost a lot in isolation and loneliness.

Because people were cut off from their family roots anyway, they chose to live where it was sunny; Florida boomed and one out of eight Americans ended up in California. Every elected President for the last 40 years has come from the Sunbelt.

Changing politics under Ike

Eisenhower's legislative record was mild like his personality. He often worked with a Congress controlled by Democrats, and he had to put up with some boneheads in his own administration. When scientists invented a drug to prevent the horrible childhood disease of polio, Eisenhower's secretary of the federal department of health, education, and welfare condemned the free distribution of the vaccine as "socialized medicine."

Old soldier that he was, Eisenhower knew the waste that goes with military spending. He reduced Truman's military buildup, although costs remained high during the tense Cold War years.

The administration participated in a major roundup of illegal aliens called Operation Wetback and tried to set back the cause of American Indian identity by temporarily revoking the tribal rights of the Indian New Deal. Otherwise, Eisenhower kept the programs from the New Deal without trying to dismantle or change them. By continuing these programs in a Republican administration, he helped make them a permanent part of American society.

Ike made his biggest change to the American landscape by starting the huge freeway-building program that linked the whole country together under the *Interstate Highway Act* (1956). With climate change and oil politics, those smooth roads that make people slaves to their cars now look dangerous, but when Ike started to build them they were just practical.

Continuing tensions with the U.S.S.R.

Eisenhower tried to start peace talks, but the timing just wasn't right. In 1955, the Soviet Union rejected Ike's proposal at a summit conference for open skies over both countries as an obvious espionage trick. The open skies idea got embarrassing when the Soviets shot down a U.S. spy plane over the U.S.S.R. in 1960, just in time to shoot down another summit conference. The U.S. also had to stand by and watch as the Soviet Union brutally crushed a 1956 uprising in Hungary.

Worst of all, Vietnam was on the horizon. The U.S. tried funding the French fight against Vietnamese Communist rebels, but the French lost. After the French left, Vietnam was divided, and the U.S. supported South Vietnam because although it was a dictatorship, it wasn't Communist. America made the same mistake in Iran, using the CIA to put the brutal Shah in power. Both cynical moves would later come back to haunt the U.S.; I discuss that further in Chapter 20.

Question: Why did the U.S. increase its involvement in Vietnam?

Answer: When the French left Vietnam, the U.S. tried to shore up the anti-Communist South Vietnamese regime.

On the friendly side, Ike proclaimed the *Eisenhower Doctrine* (1957), which offered aid to Middle Eastern nations. (Because everybody since Monroe had to have their own doctrine.) Under Eisenhower, the U.S. put a stop to the joint Israeli, British, and French takeover of the Suez Canal, winning some thanks from the Egyptians. Ike landed troops to help the government of Lebanon and got out without a single U.S. death. With the GNP and economy up, sunny Ike carried almost the whole country in his 1956 reelection.

Working for Civil Rights

Although many blacks had migrated North for better jobs during World War II, more than half still lived in the South under Jim Crow laws that kept them prisoners of segregated schools, trains, parks, and hotels.

African Americans died because they couldn't be treated at whites-only hospitals. The only place for Martin Luther King Jr. to stay with his bride on their honeymoon was a blacks-only funeral parlor. Only a few African Americans were registered to vote in the South; the rest were disenfranchised by poll taxes, rigged literacy tests, and flat-out threats. The lives of blacks in the South in the 1940s and 1950s weren't much better than they had been in 1880.

The Democratic Party helped poor people, but it had trouble letting go of its historic base of support among white Southern racists — ugly, but handy for winning close elections. This support dated all the way back to the fact that the Democrats were *not* the party that led the North in the Civil War.

Dixiecrats

Franklin Roosevelt had made the first move for fairness when he ordered an end to discrimination in defense employment during the War. In 1944, the Supreme Court ruled that whites-only primary elections in the South were illegal.

When Harry Truman, a Democratic president from a Southern state, heard about the murder of six black servicemen returning from the war, he was outraged. Truman supported the first civil rights legislation in years and desegregated the federal civil service.

Southerners opposed to civil rights walked out of the Democratic Party in 1948 to start the short lived Dixiecrat Party, but Truman won reelection anyway. Because millions of blacks had moved to the North and West where they could vote, their voices began to be heard. Jackie Robinson became the first black player in professional sports in 1947.

Question: Why did some Southerners form the Dixiecrat Party in 1948?

Answer: Dixiecrats opposed President Truman's civil rights legislation.

Rosa Parks

On a cold day in the winter of 1955, *Rosa Parks* (1955), a college-educated 42-year-old black seamstress, refused to get up from her seat near the front of a Montgomery city bus to make way for a white man, and she was arrested. The protests that began with that arrest started the modern civil rights movement. An early leader of the Montgomery movement was a young Christian minister named *Martin Luther King Jr.* (1960).

Brown versus the Board of Education

The civil rights movement had legal and social support. In 1954, the Supreme Court ruled in *Brown v. Board of Education* (1954) that segregated schools are "inherently unequal" and that desegregation must proceed with "all deliberate speed."

Although Southern representatives initially resisted, desegregation has moved ahead with the deliberate speed of any major social change, which means it's taken generations. Legal forms of discrimination were abolished one by one in the decade after the civil rights movement began in the mid-1950s. These cases were the legal decisions that had the most impact on American society.

Question: What kind of legal decisions had the most impact following the Second World War?

Answer: Court cases involving civil rights were the most important in changing society.

The Civil Rights Commission

Dwight Eisenhower wasn't a revolutionary. He had grown up in the white Midwest and spent his career in the segregated army. But Eisenhower knew his duty. When the governor of Arkansas threatened to use force to keep black students from enrolling in Little Rock, Arkansas's *Central High School* (1957), Ike called out the army to protect the *Little Rock Nine* as they walked into class. Eisenhower also supported legislation to establish a permanent *Civil Rights Commission* (1957) to investigate and report on discrimination.

Question: What is the main purpose of the Civil Rights Commission?

Answer: The Civil Rights Commission is responsible for investigating and reporting on discrimination in the United States.

Sit-in demonstrations

In 1960, four black college students sat down to have lunch in a North Carolina store. Under orders, the servers refused to wait on them. The students refused to leave, starting the first *sit-in demonstration* (1960). The next day, they came back with 19 classmates, the day after, 85 — by the end of the week, a thousand protestors had converged on the store.

Sit-ins spread to segregated lunch counters all over the country; although the protestors often met with violence, they kept coming. Eventually, national laws outlawed public discrimination.

Question: What are some of the major domestic events during the Eisenhower administration?

Answer: During Ike's terms the gross national product (GNP) was up, the baby boom continued to increase population, black families moved from the rural South to the North and West, the civil rights movement got started, and the interstate freeway system was begun.

Firing Up the Space Race with Sputnik

In 1957, the nation got its second technological shock from the Soviet Union. Just eight years after the Soviets developed an atomic bomb, they launched *Sputnik* (1957), the world's first satellite. The supposedly backward and politically challenged Soviets now seemed dangerously ahead of the U.S. Although an early attempt to loft a tiny American satellite blew up on the launching pad, the Soviets brazenly sent up another tin moon; this one contained a dog astronaut named Laika.

Science fever swept the U.S.; the nation *had* to catch up. Eisenhower established the *National Aeronautics and Space Administration* (NASA) (1958) to coordinate a program that would take the U.S. from launching pad zero to moon walking hero in just over ten years. In addition, the *National Defense Education Act* (1958) offered almost a billion dollars in science and other scholarships.

Castro: Communism Comes Closer to Home

The Yankees got another bad surprise when *Fidel Castro* (1959) took over as head of Cuba from a corrupt, U.S.-supported dictator. Castro was a Communist who allied himself with the Soviet Union, and the Soviets threatened a missile attack if the U.S. messed with Castro.

Almost a million Cubans left their island for the United States, where many of them worked without end to keep American policy vehemently anti-Castro.

Ushering in the 1960s with Kennedy

Despite the Cold War and other problems during his administration, Eisenhower tried to stay positive. In his eight years as president, the country enjoyed unprecedented prosperity and a national unity of purpose that's hard to imagine in the 21st century. Eisenhower was a successful old soldier who as president ended one war and avoided all the others. He left trouble on the horizon, but there was peace on his watch.

The 1960 Presidential election featured Ike's Vice President Richard Nixon against dashing young Senator John F. Kennedy. The nation picked Kennedy in a close race, showing that it had become unprejudiced enough to elect an Irish Catholic. Television, the medium that had saved Nixon through his Checkers speech eight years before, now did him in. In the first televised presidential debates, Kennedy looked fresh and Nixon looked jowly. The visual was enough to swing a few thousand votes, and that swung the election.

Chapter 20

Rockin' with the '60s, Rollin' with the '70s: 1961–1979

In This Chapter

▶ Navigating the Cold War with JFK

▶ Fighting for civil rights

▶ Storming into (and crawling out of) Vietnam

▶ Surviving social unrest and protest

Contrary to what you may have heard from your elders, the 1960s and 1970s were neither the dawn of a hippie age of Aquarius nor the beginning of the downfall of society. America changed, but then if you've read the other chapters in Parts III and IV of this book, you know that America had always been changing.

The youth counterculture hippie movement often associated with the 1960s lasted from the arrival of the Beatles in 1963 until the departure of Richard Nixon in 1974. Actually, the hippies never really left; they just settled down with mortgages and kids, much like their GI fathers and flapper grandmothers had done.

The 1960s and 1970s pushed social changes into the lives of everyone — changes that had been on the way for a century. These social updates included further expansion of the role of women, more-equal treatment for African Americans and other minorities, and social freedom in dress and behavior. America got more choices and managed to roll over the rocky ground of Vietnam, assassinations, demonstrations, Woodstock, riots, peace, love, and Watergate. What a trip!

Although the AP test doesn't cover current events, questions from several decades ago are common.

Kennedy: Progressing Under Cold War Clouds

John F. Kennedy (1960) was only 43 years old when he was sworn in as the youngest elected president in American history. To add to the movie-star freshness of his administration, he appointed his 35-year-old brother, Bobby, as attorney general and surrounded himself with a cabinet of the best and brightest advisers. This strategy was quite a change from the grandfatherly President Eisenhower.

Kennedy was handsome and eloquent; at his inauguration, he uttered still-famous lines like "Ask not what your country can do for you — ask what you can do for your country" and "Whether you are citizens of America or citizens of the world, ask of us the same high standards of strength and sacrifice which we ask of you."

Trouble in Cuba

It was a good start, but within weeks of his inauguration, Kennedy was embarrassed by the failed *Bay of Pigs* (1961) invasion of Cuba, which the Eisenhower administration had planned.

Ever since Communist Fidel Castro had taken over Cuba two years before, the American CIA and right-wing Cuban exiles had wanted to kick him out. The exiles stormed ashore, but their invasion was stopped on the beach. It was an international black eye for the U.S., and Kennedy took full responsibility.

Round Two of the Cuban standoff took place a year and a half later with the *Cuban Missile Crisis* (1962). The Soviets had taken advantage of their alliance with Communist Cuba to install nuclear missiles on the island that could hit the United States (only 90 miles away) in the blink of an eye.

When Kennedy found out about the missiles, he ordered the U.S. Navy to blockade all shipments to Cuba. After a tense standoff on the high seas, Soviet ships turned around. Kennedy reached an agreement with the Soviets that they would remove the Cuban missiles if the U.S. publicly promised never to invade Cuba and quietly packed up U.S. rockets stationed in Turkey.

The Cuban Missile Crisis brought the world closer to nuclear war than it had been at any time before or since — one false move on either side could have touched off the bombs. After the crisis, both sides in the Cold War were more cautious about stirring up surprise threats.

Peace Corps

Kennedy had a small Democratic majority in Congress, but given that the Southern Democrats were about as loyal as the South had been during the Civil War, he couldn't get much legislation passed. Kennedy did manage to start the *Peace Corps* (1961), which began within months to send American volunteers overseas to help developing nations.

The Peace Corps still has about 10,000 volunteers (far less than the U.S. military of more than a million), but it continues its humanitarian work in countries around the world. Kennedy-proposed programs for civil rights, health care, and tax reform stalled but would later pass after his death.

The Space Race

Continuing the U.S. response to earlier Soviet space launches, Kennedy declared that America would land a man on the moon before the end of the 1960s. With focused scientific research and billions of dollars, the U.S. sent the first astronauts to the moon in 1969, faster than anybody thought possible before Kennedy became president.

Kennedy in Berlin

Back on Earth, the Soviets wanted the Western allies out of the democratic outpost of West Berlin because people kept defecting from Communist East Germany through Berlin, and it made the Communists look as bad as they really were. The Berlin Airlift had foiled the Soviets' plan to starve the West out of the city (see Chapter 19), so the Communists built the *Berlin Wall* (1961), a jagged fence through the middle of the city.

"Ich bin ein Berliner"

The story that Kennedy's words unintentionally meant that he was a Berliner jelly donut is an urban legend — funny, but untrue. Nobody misunderstood President Kennedy during his dramatic speech face-to-face with Communist repression in 1963; he was speaking in German, which he didn't understand, but he said the words correctly.

A too-fancy false reading by a non-German-speaking *New York Times* reporter in the 1980s led to the jelly donut story being later repeated by the BBC, *The Guardian*, MSNBC, CNN, and *Time* magazine. It will remain false, as any German-speaker knows, no matter how many times it gets repeated by journalists who don't bother to check their sources.

The same is true for legends that the U.S. somehow faked the moon landings. Few people believe that now, but a new urban legend pops up whenever any wild but unsubstantiated rumor comes along. Usually, these rumors involve what a mysterious group called "they" are up to; people love conspiracy theories. As with urban legends about 9/11, it's worth doing real research before passing along a rumor that only proves how gullible some people can be. For more information, check out *Conspiracy Theories & Secret Societies For Dummies* (Wiley).

Kennedy flew to Berlin in 1963 and declared that he stood so firmly behind the freedom of West Berlin that *"Ich bin ein Berliner"* ("I am a Berliner"). Kennedy's speech electrified the surrounded Berliners; almost the whole population was in the streets to cheer him.

First Steps Toward a European Union

Europe was getting itself together on its way to becoming the *European Union* (1993), an international European country with common laws and currency.

Congress took a positive step to back European togetherness and free trade throughout the world with the *Trade Expansion Act* (1962). The act allowed import tariffs to be lowered if reciprocal agreements could be reached with other nations. International negotiations under the *Trade Expansion Act* were called the *Kennedy round* in honor of President Kennedy.

The lowering of tariffs was part of the decades long *General Agreement on Tariffs and Trade* (abbreviated GATT) originally created by the *Bretton Woods Conference* (1944) as part of a larger plan for economic recovery after World War II. The GATT's main objective was the reduction of barriers to international trade.

The functions of the GATT were taken over by the *World Trade Organization* (1995), which was established during the final round of international tariff-lowering in the 1990s.

The United States' Role as World Cop

The U.S. under Eisenhower had been leaning on its huge nuclear arsenal in eye-to-eye confrontations with the Soviet Union, under the horrifying doctrine of *Mutually Assured Destruction* (aptly known as MAD). The MAD idea was that neither side could start a war because they knew both sides would be destroyed.

Under Kennedy, the United States started to play the role of world policeman, even if nobody had actually called the cops. America largely paid for a U.N. force to police violence in the newly independent Congo and helped work out an international agreement to prop up a shaky truce in Laos. These peacekeeping actions called into question the limited military options of the United States; the U.S. military was set up more to shoot other armies than to keep the peace.

Non-nuclear brushfire wars demanded a more flexible response, so Kennedy began to build up elite combat forces such as the Green Berets. These soldiers were supposed to be tough enough to fight anywhere at a moment's notice. They were, but that didn't mean they could control other countries. In the end, having a ready army and a belief that America could do anything led to no-win wars like Vietnam.

American troops could go anywhere, but it was just a waste of life to have them stay if the local government they supported couldn't win the backing of its own people.

Trouble brewing in Vietnam

Bad local government number one in a parade of anti-Communist losers supported by the United States was the corrupt Diem regime in South Vietnam. Kennedy ordered increasing numbers of U.S. advisers to South Vietnam. By the time of his death, more than 15,000 U.S. troops were in South Vietnam, too many to advise but not enough to fight.

Kennedy's successor, President Lyndon B. Johnson, upped the ante to more than 500,000 troops, enough to fight, but not nearly enough to win against a popular revolution.

If the Big AP has an essay question about Vietnam, it may be looking for trends in U.S. foreign involvement. The U.S. has had a hard time learning the same lesson it taught the British during America's own fight for independence: The very presence of a foreign army creates a cause for local rebels. Modern armies can go anywhere, but their weapons let them control only the ground they're standing on, not the minds of the people who live there.

The Alliance for Progress

Along with chest-beating confrontation, however, the U.S. under Kennedy also tried some peacemaking moves. The *Alliance for Progress* (1961) was an ambitious attempt to offer Marshall Program-like support to Latin American governments. It failed to transform the area because unlike Europe, Latin America contained rich elites (including U.S. companies) unwilling to make room for progress by poorer citizens.

Dictatorships took over 13 Latin American countries during the 1960s, and the *Alliance for Progress* was later forgotten under President Nixon. Only in the 1990s did Latin America see the rise of democratic governments able to remain in power despite the opposition of economic interests in their own countries and the United States.

Linking up with the Soviet Union

President Kennedy signed the first *Nuclear Test Ban Treaty* (1963) with the Soviet Union that stopped polluting bomb tests. A Comprehensive Nuclear Test Ban Treaty was signed in 1996, although several nations still don't go along with the agreement.

Kennedy pushed for a live-and-let-live approach to the Soviet Union and Communist China, a policy that would later be called *détente* (1975), a French word that means "relaxation of tensions." In another move for peace, Kennedy installed a *hot line* between the White House and the Soviet Kremlin, so that the leaders could talk directly to defuse dangerous confrontations.

The Supreme Court: Expanding Freedom and Responsibility

Throughout the 1960s, the Supreme Court was active in the changes that brought about more American freedom and responsibility:

✔ In *Engel v. Vitale* (1962), the Court ruled that officials can't require prayers and Bible-reading in public schools because they may go against the beliefs of some of the students.

✔ In the *New York Times v. Sullivan* (1964), the Court held that news media could be sued for libel only if they wrongly attacked a public official out of malice, thus completing a long chain of free-press decisions that went back to the Peter Zenger case before the American Revolution.

✔ With *Griswold v. Connecticut* (1965) and *Roe v. Wade* (1973), the Court made birth control and abortion legal.

✔ In the case of *Reynolds v. Sims* (1964), the Court ordered that state legislatures regularly redraw their voting districts to reflect changes in population, thus taking power away from rural counties and giving it to the places where people actually lived.

✔ In *Miranda v. Arizona* (1966), the Court ordered police departments to read defendants their rights to remain silent and be represented by an attorney when they're arrested.

Widespread quoting of the *Miranda* warning in police TV shows and movies has led people in other countries to demand to be read their rights when they're arrested. They find out the hard way that they don't have American rights yet, but what other countries see in the widespread U.S. media helps spread social ideas.

The Assassination of JFK

President and Mrs. Kennedy were riding in a 1963 motorcade in Dallas when an assassin named Lee Harvey Oswald shot him in the head from an office building window.

Oswald was a 24-year-old mentally unbalanced former Marine who defected to the Soviet Union and later returned to the United States. He never stood trial for the assassination because he himself was shot by an enraged night club owner while in custody. President Kennedy was so respected and his death was so sudden that most people believed the shooting must have been a conspiracy to get rid of him.

After more than 40 years, during which hundreds of honest and intelligent people have devoted lifetimes' worth of research and scientific investigation to Kennedy's assassination, no credible proof of a conspiracy has ever surfaced. Although human nature impels people to look for a conspiracy to explain any major tragedy, sometimes the explanation is just that tragedy happens when scared or angry individuals think they can change history by killing a leader.

Although it's tempting to rely on conspiracy rumors to explain tragic events, it's up to people to make sad events meaningful by the work they do in memory of those who die. That's what Vice President Lyndon Johnson set out to do after he was sworn in as president; I discuss LBJ later in this chapter.

The Civil Rights Movement Hits a Crescendo

The fight for civil rights that started with Rosa Parks and the Montgomery bus boycott in the Eisenhower administration kept rolling with *sit-in demonstrations* (1960) (see Chapter 19). Civil rights activists called *Freedom Riders* (1961) risked a trip on interstate buses into the segregated South to test the Supreme Court decision *Boynton v. Virginia* (1960), which made it illegal to discriminate on transportation that crossed state lines.

Near the beginning of the Kennedy Administration, buses of Freedom Riders were attacked in the South and riders beaten. Although Kennedy couldn't get the civil rights legislation he wanted through Congress, he used his personal clout to support black rights and voter registration. When a 29-year-old African American air force veteran faced violent mobs when he tried to register to attend the then-all-white University of Mississippi, Kennedy ordered out the National Guard to protect him.

Taking a stand in Birmingham

Martin Luther King Jr. led a series of demonstrations in segregated Birmingham, Alabama, in the spring of 1963. After King and other peacefully demonstrating citizens were beaten and thrown in jail, thousands of students left school to join the protests.

With the news full of pictures of children being blasted with high-pressure hoses and attacked by police dogs, the white leaders of Birmingham decided they'd better grant blacks some rights.

A few weeks later, President Kennedy had to use troops again to move Alabama Governor George Wallace, who was personally blocking the door of the University of Alabama against two black students. That evening, Kennedy went on national television to talk about civil rights, a cause he said was "as old as the Scriptures" and "as clear as the American Constitution."

The next day, civil rights worker Medgar Evers was murdered in Mississippi. A few months later, Ku Klux Klan members bombed the Sixteenth Street Baptist Church in Birmingham, killing four little black girls.

Speaking for peace: Martin Luther King Jr.

In August of 1963, Martin Luther King Jr. spoke to a peaceful demonstration of 200,000 black and white Americans in Washington, D.C.: "I have a dream that one day this nation will rise up and live out the true meaning of its creed: 'We hold these truths to be self-evident that all men are created equal.'"

Separation versus integration

Both black and white people were beaten and killed in the South as they worked to register voters and integrate services. With the rise of the *Black Power* separatist movement in the mid-1960s and riots in black urban neighborhoods, whites became less interested in pushing for civil rights for blacks — they seemed to be pushing hard enough on their own. The fiery Black Muslim leader Malcolm X called for blacks to separate themselves from whites; he was assassinated by a black man from another sect. Other separatist leaders included Black

Panther Huey Newton and Student Nonviolent Coordinating Committee leader Stokely Carmichael. Working for integration, not separation was the National Association for the Advancement of Colored People (NAACP), chaired by Roy Wilkins.

Question: What was the Black Power movement?

Answer: The Black Power movement of the '60s was some African Americans' rejection of integration in favor of black control over their own communities.

Martin Luther King Jr.'s legacy

In 1968, a white racist assassin killed Martin Luther King Jr. King left a legacy of inspiration and solid progress that is now as much a part of the U.S. as freedom and independence.

In the time since King's death, black income, education, and community participation has risen steadily. After 200 years of slavery and another hundred years of racist discrimination, America still has miles to go, but Martin Luther King Jr. showed the way.

Question: What were the leading black organizations (and their leaders) of the civil rights movement?

Answer: Important black civil rights organizations include the Southern Christian Leadership Conference (led by Martin Luther King Jr.), the Student Nonviolent Coordinating Committee (headed by Stokely Carmichael), the National Association for the Advancement of Colored People (chaired by Roy Wilkins), the Black Muslims (led by Malcolm X) and the Black Panthers (led by Huey Newton).

From Reform to Quagmire with LBJ

Lyndon B. Johnson took the oath of office on a plane back to Washington while standing next to the wife of just-murdered President Kennedy. He had been only two cars behind in the motorcade when Kennedy was shot.

As soon as he could, President Johnson began to work to pass legislation. He told Congress that he knew no better way to "honor President Kennedy's memory than the earliest possible passage of the Civil Rights Bill for which he fought so long."

Over continuing Southern opposition, Congress passed the landmark *Civil Rights Act of 1964*. The act prohibited discrimination in public facilities, in government, and in employment, invalidating the Jim Crow laws in the South. Forcing segregation of the races in schools, housing, or hiring became illegal. Opponents argued that the government couldn't legislate morality on the race issue; supporters countered that they didn't care what people thought in their minds as long as what they did was fair.

Legislating for the Great Society

A year after Kennedy's assassination, Johnson ran for president against the conservative Republican Barry Goldwater. When Johnson pushed through the Civil Rights Act, he said that it would cost the Democrats the votes of the South for a generation. Five states from the old South did vote for Goldwater, but except for his home state of Arizona, that was all Goldwater won; the rest of the country was for LBJ. Johnson's landslide helped sweep the Democrats to a two-to-one majority over the Republicans in both houses of Congress.

Johnson lacked Kennedy's charm, but he knew how to get things done; he may have been the most successful legislative president in U.S. history. When he was really rolling after his reelection, he got almost all of the bills he wanted passed by Congress. These laws included the *Voting Rights Act of 1965,* which outlawed unfair qualifications tests that kept minorities from the polls, and the *Economic Opportunity Act of 1964,* which created programs to help poor people. The road seemed opened to creating what Johnson called the *Great Society* (1965). Great Society programs still in effect today include the *Job Corps* (1965), *Head Start* (1965), and *Food Stamps* (1964). These and other *War on Poverty* (1965) programs were designed to help lower the poverty rate in the United States. During the Great Depression, the poverty rate was 40 percent; when Johnson became President it was 15 percent, and it's now about 12 percent.

Women's liberation

The 1960s saw a progressive tide that included a second wave of women's rights often called women's liberation. Betty Friedan wrote *The Feminine Mystique* (1963) about unfulfilled women, and helped found the *National Organization of Women* (NOW) in 1966.

Question: What was the second wave of women's liberation?

Answer: The second wave focused on equal rights for women in the workplace and home and was supported by author Betty Friedan and the National Organization of Women (NOW).

Medicare, Medicaid, and the 24th Amendment

The most extensive benefit program passed by Johnson was the *Medicare Program* (1965), which pays for health care for older people, and the *Medicaid Program* (1965), which covers health care for poor people. These programs faced diehard opposition from both Republicans and the American Medical Association, but Johnson maneuvered around the foes of government-sponsored medical care to bring coverage to millions of people.

Question: What was LBJ's Great Society plan?

Answer: A set of training and social assistance programs designed to lower the poverty rate in the U.S.

Johnson appointed the first black Supreme Court justice and the first black Cabinet member. He guided the ratification of the *Twenty-fourth Amendment* (1964), which banned the use of a poll tax to limit voting in federal elections. The *Immigration and Nationality Act* (1965) abolished the national origins qualifications for immigrants and doubled the number of new Americans admitted to the country.

Vietnam Explodes into Full-Scale War

As President Johnson was winning battles to control domestic legislation, he was losing battles to control Vietnam. Kennedy had limited U.S. involvement to a few thousand so-called advisers, but all the advice in the world couldn't get the corrupt South Vietnamese regime to defeat a dedicated group of South Vietnamese Communist rebels and their North Vietnamese allies.

Just before the 1964 election (which Johnson won by playing a peacemaker), the U.S. Navy had traded a few shots with North Vietnamese patrol boats when the U.S. ships pushed too close to the North Vietnamese shore. This *Gulf of Tonkin* (1964) attack got Congress to pass the *Gulf of Tonkin Resolution* (1964), authorizing the use of direct American force in Vietnam. When the Vietnamese rebels attacked an American adviser base after the elections, Johnson declared war.

By the end of 1965, almost 200,000 U.S. troops were in Vietnam, and Johnson was in a major macho-off with the Communist leaders. Over Johnson's presidency, the troop levels grew: 200,000 became 300,000, which grew to 400,000 and finally 500,000 soldiers. It always seemed like just a few more troops ought to be enough to win, but it never was.

Question: What was the Gulf of Tonkin resolution?

Answer: In response to a minor naval confrontation, LBJ got Congress to authorize the use of direct U.S. force in Vietnam.

Hard fighting in Vietnam

The battle in Vietnam was like a war between an elephant and a fly: The fly couldn't kill the elephant, but the elephant couldn't fly. American soldiers had a hard time fighting with no front line, in steaming jungles where the enemy could be anywhere. A young man in street clothes could shoot you in the back and then hide in a group of civilians.

Vietnamese farmers and their wives and kids were in the middle of the war — millions of them got killed, both by the rebels and the U.S. side. Desperate to stop the rebels, the U.S. dropped thousands of tons of bombs, some with chemicals to kill the trees the Vietnamese hid under.

Protesting against the war

With the draft hanging over their heads, hundreds of thousands of students marched in protest demonstrations against the war. Demonstrators showed up wherever President Johnson tried to speak, chanting "Hey, hey, LBJ, how many kids did you kill today?" They ignored his attempts to change the subject to the War on Poverty and instead shouted against the real war in Vietnam that was killing the people of their generation at a rate of more than 20 deaths a day.

LBJ's Vietnam was eating up LBJ's Great Society. In violation of the law, Johnson used the CIA and the FBI to spy on antiwar protestors.

Question: How did the war in Vietnam affect LBJ's domestic Great Society program?

Answer: By taking money and political support, the war made Johnson's Great Society program less effective.

Losing heart after the Tet Offensive

Believers in the war kept saying that they could see the light at the end of the tunnel; they believed that the U.S. had almost won. The light at the end of the tunnel went out during the huge Vietnamese Tet offensive in early 1968.

Although the U.S. was hoping that the rebels were almost beaten, the Communists launched a simultaneous attack on most major South Vietnamese cities beginning during the New Year's holiday Tet. The rebels penetrated the South Vietnamese capital of Saigon; a few of them even made it to the grounds of the U.S. embassy.

Although the rebels were pushed back with heavy losses, the very fact that they could mount such a wide attack destroyed American confidence. The long road to a negotiated peace began.

Question: What was the Tet Offensive?

Answer: Widespread rebel attacks during the Vietnamese new year that led to increased U.S. opposition to the war.

LBJ bows out; Robert Kennedy is assassinated

With the U.S. population turning against the war, LBJ knew he stood little chance of reelection. Even though he had won by a huge landslide in 1964 and had passed the most legislation, he hardly beat an obscure challenger from his own party in an early primary.

What was worse, he was finally opposed by Robert Kennedy, the younger brother of the now-sainted President Kennedy. In a surprise announcement, LBJ declared he wouldn't run again. Vietnam had ruined him.

Robert Kennedy swept the primaries but was assassinated by an Arab immigrant only a month after Martin Luther King died.

As with the JFK assassination, no real evidence of a conspiracy in the second Kennedy killing has ever come to light.

In the midst of demonstrations and police violence a few weeks later, the Democrats nominated Johnson's loyal Vice President Hubert Humphrey. With a Southern segregationist running as a third-party candidate, Humphrey narrowly lost the presidential election to Republican former Vice President Richard Nixon.

Nixon, the Experienced One

Richard Nixon was elected on the promise that he was the experienced one who could bring an honorable peace both to Vietnam and to the demonstration-thronged streets of America.

The U.S. was deeply divided between the established order and a counterculture of mostly younger people who opposed the war and supported a rights revolution of liberation for women, blacks, and other minorities, as well as free personal behavior and expression. The counterculture included a small violent fringe of Black Panthers who advocated armed defense of African American interests and mostly white radical Weathermen who were willing to be violent because they thought the times demanded force. The Weathermen took their name from the words of a Bob Dylan song that went: "You don't need a weatherman to tell which way the wind blows . . ." Most of the counterculture was a large peaceful tribe of flower-wearing hippies.

The U.S. actually has an unbroken and under-reported tradition of small group opposition to established power that limits any of the rights outlined in the Declaration of Independence. During the 1960s and '70s, the opposition got bigger; a lot of changes that had been in the works for hundreds of years came to the forefront. After much conflict, the social revolutionaries settled down to work in a new order that was freer than the old.

During the height of the demonstrations, Richard Nixon's Vice President Spiro Agnew called the youthful protestors "nattering nabobs of negativism." Several of the young people cut off their easily identified long hair and sent it to Agnew in a pillow, neatly embroidered with the words "Now we could be anywhere."

Increasing the fight for peace

The rapid economic growth of the 1950s slowed in the 1960s and '70s. As the U.S. spent more money on military campaigns, it had less to invest in business growth and social programs. More research and development went into bombs, not cars and other consumer products. Unburdened with big military expenses, the World War II losers Japan and Germany became economic winners by producing products people wanted to buy. The U.S. economy slid into inflation and slow growth.

Richard Nixon said he would end the war in Vietnam, but he didn't. As the war dragged on and deaths mounted, antiwar demonstrations increased. Frustrated young soldiers in Vietnam became more disorderly, sometimes attacking their own officers. Desperate to win, Nixon expanded the war to neighboring Cambodia.

Protests get violent

In the United States, hard-pressed National Guard troops killed four student demonstrators at Kent State University in 1970; police got into shootouts with black nationalists. Young war protestors got some official reprieve as military draft calls were reduced, and the *Twenty-sixth Amendment* (1971) allowed young people to vote starting at age eighteen.

Question: What happened at Kent State University?

Answer: Protesting students were shot by the National Guard in 1970.

China and the SALT talks

President Nixon's 20 years of experience in international affairs finally began to pay off with visits to China and the Soviet Union. Nixon normalized previously frozen U.S. relations with China and set the stage for further *détente*. Nixon arranged the sale of much-needed American food to the U.S.S.R, and started U.S.-Soviet *SALT (Strategic Arms Limitation Talks)* (1972) that limited missile deployment.

Question: What are some examples of *détente* in Nixon's foreign relations policies?

Answer: Nixon reestablished relations with China, sent food to the Soviet Union, and initiated the SALT talks.

Nixon's social programs

Conservative Nixon was surprisingly liberal with social programs. He expanded welfare, Medicaid, and Food Stamps and created a new *Supplemental Security Income (SSI)* program (1974) to help the disabled. In addition, he indexed Social Security payments to rise with inflation. As the U.S. moved toward being a modern welfare state, the portion of the national budget tied up in entitlement programs to pay for benefits rose. Nixon supported affirmative action for the hiring of minorities but opposed busing to achieve racial balance in schools. He actively managed the economy by briefly imposing a wage and price freeze and taking the U.S. off the gold standard.

Perhaps most important in the long run, Nixon established the *Environmental Protection Agency* (1970) to attempt to clean up damage to the natural world. The need for urgent action was first made clear by author Rachel Carson in the book *Silent Spring,* which warned that pesticides and pollution were poisoning song birds and other animals. The *Clean Air Act* (1970) and the *Endangered Species Act* (1973) began to set environmental standards for the country.

Pulling out of Vietnam

Nixon, who had managed to get 95 percent of the troops out of Vietnam, won reelection in a landslide over the Democratic antiwar candidate George McGovern. He ended the war with a face-saving peace treaty in 1973; by 1975 the Communists had overrun the South Vietnamese government supported by the United States.

A murderous Communist tyrant called Pol Pot seized power during the postwar instability in Cambodia and ended up killing a quarter of his own people. He was finally stopped by the very Communists the U.S. had been fighting.

The War Powers Act

The controversy over the war also led to the *War Powers Act* (1973), which limited the president's ability to send troops into combat without Congressional approval. If the long war with its 56,000 American and millions of Vietnamese deaths proved anything, it showed Communists that the U.S. was willing to fight and die to oppose Communist beliefs. Twenty years later, militant Communism was all but gone from the world.

Question: Who ended active U.S. participation in the war in Vietnam?

Answer: President Richard Nixon signed a treaty and withdrew U.S. troops.

Watergate

Richard Nixon got caught in dirty tricks that cost him his job only months after a landslide reelection. Back in 1972, burglars hired by the president's associates had broken into a local Democratic office in the *Watergate* apartment complex in Washington. A long investigation proved that Nixon had been involved in this and a number of other illegal actions against political opponents.

Meanwhile, Vice President Spiro Agnew was forced to resign in 1973 after being caught taking bribes. When Agnew went off to repay some of the money he stole, the *Twenty-fifth Amendment* (1967) handily provided for a replacement vice president. Congress gave the deeply-in-trouble Nixon only one choice: good old reliable Gerald Ford. Ford would assume the presidency when Nixon, faced with impeachment, resigned it in 1974.

Gerald Ford Steps In

Gerald Ford had been a congressman for 25 years without ticking people off (or even writing any legislation). Ford barely had time to warm up his vice president's chair before he became president upon Nixon's resignation.

Ford pardoned the departing Nixon, which made him almost as unpopular as Tricky Dick himself. He also signed the Helsinki Accords, marking a move toward détente in the Cold War, and supported women's rights and education for handicapped children. Despite President Ford's support, a proposed Equal Rights Amendment to the Constitution that would have legally prohibited discrimination against women fell three states short of passing.

Ford stood by without intervening as South Vietnam finally fell to the Communists; eventually half a million Vietnamese would escape to live in the U.S. Even though he was the sitting president, Ford barely won re-nomination in 1976.

During the Ford era, Congress passed *Title IX* (1972), making colleges give money to support women as well as men in sports. In *Milliken v. Bradley* (1974), the Court put a cap on the very school integration they had started 30 years before by holding that students couldn't be bused across school district lines to meet integration goals.

A few years later, in *University of California v. Bakke* (1978), the Court found that universities can't have separate, easier admissions programs for minorities; race and underprivileged status can be a factor but not the only factor for getting into school.

Too-Good President Carter

Jimmy Carter won the presidency in America's bicentennial year of 1976 by promising to be a good and honest leader. He may have been too good. Carter was a peanut farmer who had served a term as governor of Georgia. With no Washington political experience, he ruffled the feathers of congressmen used to feathering their own nests.

Carter tried to get America to cut down on its energy gulping habit by turning the thermostat down in federal buildings and even requesting a ban on Christmas lights. He signed the *SALT II* (1979) arms limitation treaty and patched up Social Security. Carter brokered a peace treaty between Israel and Egypt in the *Camp David Agreement* (1978). Putting human rights at the forefront of American policy, Carter began to withdraw support for brutal dictators, even if they were friendly to the U.S. The Soviet invasion of Afghanistan in late 1979 led to an American boycott of the 1980 Olympics in Moscow.

The Iranian hostage crisis

One repressive guy Carter continued to support came back to haunt him. The United States' buddy, the Shah of Iran, was overthrown by Muslim fundamentalists, who seized the U.S. embassy and held its staff hostage for over a year. Faced with an unhappy American public, Carter decided to tell the truth: "We've learned that piling up material goods cannot fill the emptiness of lives which have no confidence or purpose." That made Americans feel guilty; they weren't willing to stop piling up the goods just yet.

Carter's problems mount

The mood of the people wasn't improved when the *Three Mile Island* (1979) nuclear power plant experienced a near meltdown, and opposition to nuclear power increased. Carter's bad luck got worse when a swimming rabbit actually attacked him while he was out fishing. Americans were beginning to feel like maybe a tough-guy action hero would be a better choice than their good-guy President Carter.

Question: What was the result of trouble at Three Mile Island?

Answer: Opposition increased to the development of nuclear power plants.

Carter lost the 1980 election to Ronald Reagan, a former actor who did a much better job looking the part of a president than Jimmy Carter (more on that in Chapter 21). Jimmy Carter went on to win the Nobel Peace Prize, working tirelessly for peace and democracy. America took a turn toward conservative politics and an uncertain future as world leader.

Chapter 21

Leading in the Modern World: 1980–Now

In This Chapter:

▶ Riding forward into the past with Ronald Reagan

▶ Ending the Cold War once and for all

▶ Overcoming controversy with Bill Clinton

▶ Fighting terror with George W. Bush

▶ Finding the future of freedom

The U.S. took a turn to the right under Ronald Reagan in the 1980s. Reagan helped end the Cold War with a little help from the tapped out Communists. He also instituted a tax shift that let the rich get richer and the middle class get a little poorer.

Reagan talked against government but spent so much money on the military that by the end of his term he had tripled the debt of the country. But by energetically following the policy of containment of Communism started under Democratic President Truman after World War II and followed by every president, Republican or Democrat, since that time, Reagan got the honor of presiding over the end of the Cold War. The presidents who came after him got the dubious honor of facing a rising national debt.

As the U.S. sailed toward the 21st century, it seemed for a while that the entire world just wanted to live free and easy like the Americans they saw in movies.

When the 9/11 buildings came crashing to the ground, the U.S. discovered that the America-is-cool sentiment wasn't exactly unanimous. Some people hated American lifestyle, attitude, and foreign policy so much they were ready to explode themselves to get even. These people included both home-grown bombers and foreign militants.

Although the AP U.S. History exam has few questions on modern times, an understanding of how themes and topics apply to recent issues helps show good analysis in essay writing.

Ronald Reagan and Reaganomics

All the hippy-dippy demonstrating, impeachment, moralizing, and rabbit attacks of the 1970s had left Americans longing for a simpler life. They found their leader in Ronald Reagan, who handily defeated Jimmy Carter in the 1980 Presidential election.

Reagan believed in small government and lower taxes. He was a champion of the *antis*: Reagan was anti-gay, anti-abortion, anti-feminism, and especially anti-special programs to help minorities. He was especially supported by right-wing religious people who called themselves the *Moral Majority* (1980) and believed that their Christianity was right and that anyone who believed differently was a tool of the devil.

In a strange way, Reagan's appeal was a reverse copy of FDR's crusade for the so-called forgotten man; Ronald Reagan defended hardworking regular people that modern society seemed to have forgotten. The only difference was that Reagan defended their feelings, and FDR defended their income. Reagan's tax breaks ended up helping the rich far more than the poor.

Returning to the good old days with the neocons

Ronald Reagan had the support of thinkers who called themselves new conservatives or *neoconservatives* (1985). This small group of writers, known as *neocons* for short, believed in the counterintuitive proposition that if Reagan cut taxes, tax income to the government would actually rise because people would have more money to spend and the economy would grow. It didn't work for Reagan; he managed to pass a large tax decrease, but the economy just sputtered along during much of his administration.

Tax policy alone isn't the key to economic growth. High-tax Europe and Japan grew rapidly in the late 20th century. The low-tax United States slipped into the Great Depression in the 1920s. How much money people have isn't the issue — how they spend it controls the economy.

Supporting military buildup

Neocons also believed that aggressive military intervention would increase America's power in the world. They supported a large military buildup (difficult to do with lower tax revenues) and confrontation with Communists around the world.

Military power seemed to work best when it was restrained; America's potential for destruction helped force the U.S.S.R. to send Communism into a timely grave. When Reagan actually unleashed U.S. military might, the results were often unfortunate, like the U.S. intervention in Lebanon that ended with Marines being bombed in their barracks, or successful but overblown, like the large American invasion of the tiny island of Grenada.

Turning back the clock on government regulation

As far as domestic government policy goes, Reagan was against it, saying that "Government is not the solution to our problem. Government is the problem." Although he didn't succeed in making the federal government much smaller, he did what he could to turn back the clock on government regulations.

Reagan's first Secretary of the Interior eased environmental regulations on polluting industries and favored opening wilderness areas and shorelines for oil and gas leases. When air-traffic controllers went on strike, Reagan fired them.

His economic policies were called *Reaganomics* (1982) or *supply-side economics;* less government was supposed to mean more growth in the economy and, almost magically, more tax revenue. Tax cuts under Reaganomics mostly succeeded in making more money for the wealthy. The economy actually grew at a slower rate during the Reagan administration than the post-World War II average. Reaganomics simply didn't work when it came to creating growth or increasing government revenue.

To the credit of Reagan's administration, the interest rate policy of the economists he appointed helped bring inflation, which had soared under Nixon and Carter, back under control. Reagan also won applause by appointing the first woman to the Supreme Court.

Question: What was the most noticeable effect of Reaganomics?

Answer: It got more money for rich people.

Running up the trade deficit

During the Reagan administration, the U.S. went heavily into debt and ran an international trade deficit of billions of dollars a year. Neither of these trends has stopped since the Reagan period; addiction to foreign oil and imported consumer products has made the U.S. spend far more overseas than it takes in from exports.

This discrepancy is called the *balance of payments* (1986) problem. The U.S., which in the first half of the 20th century was the master of international business, became the world's largest debtor nation beginning in the 1980s.

Checkmating Communism

Reagan took an aggressive stance against Communism, which he called "the evil empire." He built up American military might and announced his intention to deploy a *Strategic Defense Initiative* (1983), better known as Star Wars, to shoot down Soviet missiles before they could get to the United States.

This plan apparently impressed the Soviets more than it did U.S. scientists; Star Wars was cited as one of the reasons the Soviet Union gave up the military race with the United States and began to dismantle their Communist economic system. The U.S. military was never able to deploy a large-scale missile defense system, but the bluff worked.

The Cold War reaches the freezing point

The Soviets clamped down on a freedom movement called *Solidarity* (1981) in the government of Poland (which they controlled). The U.S. responded with tough words and an economic embargo.

When the U.S.S.R. shot down a Korean passenger plane that had strayed into Soviet airspace in 1983, Reagan called it an act of barbarism. By the end of 1983, all arms-control negotiations had broken down. The Soviet Union almost launched nuclear weapons against the U.S. when they briefly mistook a Western military exercise for a nuclear attack. They also boycotted the 1984 Olympic Games held in Los Angeles. The Cold War was reaching the freezing point.

The U.S. flexes its military muscles

In the 1980s, Iran and Iraq were fighting a war that the United States didn't mind watching; America had little love for the leaders of either country. The U.S. supplied arms to Iraq in the early 1980s as payback against Iran for holding American embassy people hostage up to the first hour of the Reagan administration. This arms deal was one reason that Iran may have been behind the Marine barracks bombing in Lebanon.

In 1983, Reagan sent troops into Lebanon to try to calm endless Middle East conflicts. More than 200 Marines died when an Arab extremist suicide bomber blew up their barracks. U.S. troops, who never had a clear mission to begin with, withdrew a few months later.

In the same month, Reagan sent a heavily armed invasion party to the tiny Caribbean island of Grenada to wipe out some Communist troublemakers. They succeeded in restoring democratic government in a move that would have made Teddy Roosevelt proud.

Reagan cruised to reelection against a Democratic ticket that included, for the first time in history, a woman as vice presidential nominee.

Mikhail Gorbechev

The Soviet Union had a new leader: Mikhail Gorbachev promised *glasnost* and *perestroika* (1986), which mean openness and restructuring. The Soviets began to shrink their military spending and concentrate on long-overdue civilian improvements.

In 1987, Ronald Reagan stood in front of the divisive Berlin Wall and said, "General Secretary Gorbachev, if you seek peace . . . open this gate. Mr. Gorbachev, tear down this wall!" Late in the year, the two leaders signed the *INF Treaty* (1987) banning all intermediate-range nuclear weapons from Europe. Two years later, the Berlin Wall came tumbling down.

Iran-Contra and other problems

In an illegal and morally challenged international trick, Reagan administration officials later agreed to sell arms to the desperate Iranians in return for secret payments that these officials channeled to anti-Communist rebel forces in Nicaragua that Congress had officially rejected American aid to.

In making their secret deal, the Reagan administration officials weren't only helping a regime that had kidnapped Americans; they were also acting against the expressed direction of Congress. This kind of action is grounds on which Congress can impeach a president. Reagan pleaded ignorance of the plot; his secretary of defense was charged with criminal behavior. An investigation found that Reagan knew or should have known about the bad deal.

Other holes appeared in the ethical shell of the administration elected with the support of the Moral Majority. Environmental Protection Agency officials resigned in disgrace after they misused staff and gave special deals to polluters. Three of Reagan's cabinet members, including the attorney general, were investigated for lying and stealing; Reagan's personal White House aide was convicted of perjury.

His last days in office were clouded by a stock market crash, but he remained sunny and optimistic. When he died in the early 21st century, his burial site was inscribed with his own words: "I know in my heart that man is good. That what is right will always eventually triumph. And there's purpose and worth to each and every life."

One Term of George H.W. Bush

George Herbert Walker Bush came as close as you can to inheriting the presidency. His grandpa was a presidential advisor to Hoover, and his dad was a U.S. Senator. He himself already had a White House office as vice president to Ronald Reagan.

Family legacies in U.S. politics

In a large and diverse nation, some families just seem to pop up again and again in leadership roles. George H.W. Bush wasn't the first president to see his son take the office. That would be the father and son team of second President John Adams and sixth President John Quincy Adams.

William Henry Harrison, ninth president, was the grandfather of 23rd President Benjamin Harrison.

The Kennedy dynasty includes (but isn't limited to) 35th President John, his ambassador father Joseph, and his senator brothers Bobby and Ted, not to mention his niece Maria Shriver (who's married to California's best-built governor, Arnold Schwarzenegger).

Family legacies extend beyond bloodlines, too. Husband-and-wife team Bill and Hillary Clinton have held the offices of president, governor, and senator between them.

Even though Bush had once called Reaganomics "voodoo economics," he was happy enough being Reagan's vice president and was easily elected president in 1988. Although he was a former representative to China and head of the CIA, Bush stood by without even proposing economic sanctions in 1989 when Chinese tanks crushed democracy demonstrations in Beijing's Tiananmen Square. Democracy had more luck in Europe.

The fall of the Soviet Union

In 1989, the former Soviet puppet governments fell, as did the Berlin Wall. Eastern European nations were now free to govern themselves. What had been the Soviet Union split into the Commonwealth of Independent States, the largest of which was Russia. A hero for helping the Communist empire open toward freedom, Mikhail Gorbachev fought off a coup attempt from party hardliners and then retired, leaving behind a small world of independent nations struggling toward democracy.

Bush signed the *START II Treaty* (1993) with Russia, pledging both nations to reduce their long-range nuclear weapons by two-thirds. The U.S. military scaled back with the end of the Cold War.

In additional good news, Nelson Mandela gained freedom from prison and became president of a democratic interracial South Africa. Free elections in Nicaragua ousted the leftist government there without the necessity of the Iran-Contra plotting of the Reagan administration. The U.S. tossed a drug-lord dictator of Panama out by force.

Operation Desert Storm

Saddam Hussein, the leader of Iraq, invaded the neighboring oil-rich country of Kuwait in 1990. Working through the United Nations, President Bush skillfully put together a coalition of the United States and 28 other nations to kick Saddam out. Although the U.S. contributed more than half a million troops, the other nations added 250,000 more on their own.

Operation Desert Storm tore through opposition forces like a hurricane; U.S. and coalition forces rolled over Hussein's army in four days. Kuwait was free; the only problem was that Saddam Hussein was left in power in his capital of Baghdad.

Legislation under the elder Bush

On the domestic front, Bush signed the *Americans with Disabilities Act* (ADA) (1990), which prohibited discrimination against the one in seven people who have some form of physical or mental handicap. (Bush managed to appoint a conservative African American to the Supreme Court.)

Bush grudgingly accepted some improvements in environmental water usage and civil rights, but the only controversial legislation he proposed was the tax increase that cost him the presidency.

Campaigning in 1988, Bush had dramatically said, "Read my lips: No new taxes." Faced with huge budget deficits, he was forced to go back on his word and raise taxes in 1990. The Democrats wouldn't let people forget that mistake.

Modern Democracy with Bill Clinton

The Democrats hadn't elected a two-term president since World War II, but they had a charming centrist in Arkansan William Jefferson Clinton. Bill Clinton defeated Bush's reelection bid by emphasizing the paycheck of the average American, which had actually grown smaller during the Bush administration. A sign in Clinton's headquarters said, "It's the economy, stupid."

Clinton ran a positive campaign based on pro-growth, strong defense, and anti-crime platforms that almost sounded like the Republicans. He promised to overhaul the creaky welfare and health care systems. He admitted (as indirectly as possible) to "causing pain" in his marriage and smoking marijuana. He was the perfect candidate for the baby boom generation, which made up most of the U.S. voting population.

The new rainbow America

While Clinton won the presidency, the nation was undergoing a radical change in elected officials. The new House of Representatives included 1 American Indian, 7 Asian Americans, 19 Hispanic Americans, and 39 African Americans; 48 of the representatives were women. That was more women and minorities than had ever been elected before, and the numbers continued to grow into the 21st century.

At the beginning of the Clinton administration, the nation wasn't willing to accept just how broad the rainbow was becoming; a bid by Clinton to allow homosexuals to serve openly in the armed forces was rejected for a don't-ask-don't-tell halfway measure.

Clinton appointed his wife Hillary to come up with a national health plan. Industries making big money off a piecemeal non-system that left one out of six Americans with no insurance managed to convince people that Hillary's reform proposals were scary. Health care reform took a back seat until the 21st century.

Although Republicans often accuse Democrats of being tax-and-spend crazies, Clinton managed to turn the huge budget deficits run up by 12 years of Republican administrations into modest budget surpluses. He passed anti-crime bills that also contained some gun control provisions.

Battling extremism

Clinton was just in time with the anti-crime — in 1993 Muslim extremists took their first shot at the World Trade Center in New York with a bomb that killed six people. A couple of years later, home-grown terrorists blew up 168 people along with the federal building in Oklahoma City. Shootouts with extremists and in schools shocked the nation. Although the hundreds of deaths involved in these events were better than the thousands that happen in a war, domestic violence showed that Americans weren't all happy campers.

Contract with America

Especially unhappy were the members of the old Moral Majority, who saw the country being swept by the devil's work of abortion, drugs, welfare, and religious apathy. They joined a Republican counterattack called the *Contract with America* (1994), which promised welfare and budget reform. The Republicans swept to victory, controlling both the House and the Senate for the first time in 40 years.

Reforming Welfare

Now Bill Clinton got to see what it had felt like to be a president with an opposing Congress, something that Republican presidents had put up with for years. Clinton survived by working with the Republicans; after all, he was a conservative Democrat. Clinton signed the *Welfare Reform Bill* (1996). Over the wails of old-school Democrats, the bill forced welfare recipients to work when they could and restricted benefits for new immigrants. Despite angry opposition from social conservatives and Republicans, Clinton had most of the country with him when he breezed to reelection in 1996.

Politics of the possible

Clinton was unable to expand health care, but he added loans for college students and modest tax breaks for poor people and raised the minimum wage. His greatest political advantage was a robust U.S. economy that enjoyed the longest period of sustained growth in American history. Clinton supported international trade with the *North American Free Trade Agreement* (NAFTA) (1993) and the *World Trade Organization* (WTO) (1994); these agreements made exporting American manufacturing jobs easier but brought down the cost of goods in the United States to bargain levels. Clinton fought against tobacco and guns, both of which caused a lot of deaths.

In international affairs, Clinton intervened without getting America stuck in any big wars. He failed to offer effective help when millions of people died in tribal violence in Africa, but he sent in troops to stabilize Haiti and to stop years of ethnic cleansing in the former Yugoslavia. Clinton took some missile shots at terrorists in Afghanistan and Sudan, but limited U.S. involvement in the Middle East to the ever-elusive goal of encouraging peace talks between Israel and its Palestinian neighbors.

Dogged by controversy

Like most presidents, Clinton's administration wasn't without controversy. He staunchly denied having an affair with a 20-something White House intern, but DNA evidence later forced him to backpedal. The Republican-controlled Congress brought Clinton up on impeachment charges for lying to a grand jury about his involvement, invoking that extreme Constitutional mechanism for only the second time in U.S. history.

They clearly took it more seriously than the American people; the Democrats actually gained seats in Congress during the run-up to the Congressional trial. Impeachment requires a two-thirds vote to pass; Clinton's charges couldn't even get a majority vote. Clinton's wife, Hillary, said that ongoing investigations of the Clintons during most of their time in the White House were a right-wing tactic to stall social legislation. After years of public investigation, the Clintons were never convicted of anything, and Clinton left office with the highest approval ratings of any post-World War II president.

Clinton held off Republican attacks on most social programs and modestly improved the lives of regular people by protecting wilderness land, hiring new teachers, and increasing opportunities for higher education through grants and loans. The economy offered nearly full employment, and real income for working people crept up after decades of inflation-adjusted doldrums. As he was leaving office, the issue of global warming was heating up, and Clinton's vice president, Al Gore, promised to do something about it if only he could get elected president.

George W. Bush, Terrorism, and War

As the world faces the threats of climate change, it's tempting to think what would have happened if an environmentalist had won the most votes in the 2000 presidential election. Oh, wait a minute; Al Gore did win the most votes. He just didn't win the election because of a fluke in the way the Constitution structures the presidential election: indirect election through an electoral college.

Due to the state-by-state, winner-takes-all *Electoral College,* a candidate who narrowly wins more states can win with a minority of the votes. You can't get any narrower than George W. Bush's election in Florida: He won by 500 votes out of 5 million. Voting along party lines, the Supreme Court stopped the Florida recounts, and Bush was declared the winner of the election.

Ironically enough, under the recount rules Gore initially requested, Bush would have won, and under the rules Bush requested, Gore would have won. The election was that close. In a further irony, Ralph Nader's Green Party bid had siphoned off enough votes to deny environmentalist Gore a clear victory.

Texas governor to U.S. President

George Bush grew up around the White House while his dad was Reagan's vice president and then a one-term president on his own. Young Bush had been a popular governor of Texas and cultivated a close relationship with Moral Majority Christians based on his own story of being born again to true religion after a wild youth.

Without trying to turn the clock back on New Deal social reforms, Bush campaigned on social issues like being against abortion and in favor of business growth. His faith-based social services distributed billions of dollars through Christian religious organizations that were supposed to provide social help, not religious preaching, to stay clear of the First Amendment's prohibition of the establishment of a government-supported religion.

Facing increasing economic problems

If the key to being president is really, as Clinton felt, about "the economy, stupid," then the Bush administration could be judged on its economic numbers. The *gross domestic product* (value of the output of goods and services produced within the nation's borders) grew at an average annual rate considerably slower than the average for the post-World War II period. Unemployment stayed low. Budget deficits rose rapidly, a change from the budget surplus in the last year of the Clinton administration. Inflation-adjusted median household income was almost flat, and the nation's poverty rate increased slightly.

The national debt went up by trillions of dollars during Bush's presidency, adding more than a third to the burden future generations would have to pay off. With the low cost of imported manufactured goods, living was easy for most Americans, but the bulk of income gains went to people earning more than $250,000 a year.

Health care and children: Hot-button issues

President Bush signed the *No Child Left Behind Act* (2001), which improved educational standards but failed to provide much funding for schools. He vetoed the *State Children's Health Insurance Program* (SCHIP), which would have expanded health care for poor children, because he said he was against socialized medicine.

He may not have supported children's health, but Bush took a turn toward government health care for older people when he signed the Medicare Prescription Drug Improvement and Modernization Act, which added prescription drug coverage to Medicare (though people pay extra for it).

Bush also vetoed a bill that would have allowed for stem cell research to find cures for disease; some religious conservatives opposed the controversial research.

Climate change and global warming

Upon arriving in office in 2001, Bush withdrew United States support for the Kyoto Protocol, an amendment to the United Nations Convention on Climate Change trying to control global warming; as a major world polluter, the U.S. was the only leading country not to sign.

Bush administration officials censored the reports of government officials on global warming, and Bush said he didn't take action on the problem because of "debate over whether it's man-made or naturally caused."

Bush did set aside the Northwestern Hawaiian Islands as a national monument, creating the largest marine reserve in the world.

Hurricane Katrina

One of the worst natural disasters in U.S. history, Hurricane Katrina, struck early in Bush's second term. The storm destroyed much of the city of New Orleans and the surrounding north-central Gulf Coast of the United States. Many thought Bush was slow in getting aid to the region; his director of emergency management eventually resigned. To his credit, Bush took full responsibility for the problems.

9/11 and living in a terrorist world

After his minority election, Bush wasn't very popular, but the country came together to back him after the 9/11 terrorist attacks on the World Trade Towers and the Pentagon in Washington. As he stood in the smoking ruins of the towers and promised justice and protection, over 90 percent of the American people said they approved of his actions.

After the 9/11 attacks, in which hijacked planes destroyed the twin 110-story World Trade Center buildings in New York and damaged the Pentagon in Washington, Bush condemned Osama bin Laden and his organization *Al Qaeda* (2001) (which means "the base"). Bush announced that the United States would attack other countries (even though they weren't directly threatening the U.S.) if those countries harbored terrorists.

President Bush gave the Taliban regime in Afghanistan, where bin Laden was operating, a warning to "hand over the terrorists, or . . . share in their fate." Bush announced a global War on Terrorism, and after the Afghan Taliban regime wasn't forthcoming with Osama bin Laden, he ordered an invasion of Afghanistan to overthrow the Taliban regime.

In 2003, he also invaded Iraq, whose connection to 9/11 was vague at best. Unlike his father's 1991 Iraq war, this time only a few thousand outside troops joined the largely American effort as the U.S. Army pushed into Iraq. The U.S. military was bogged down for years in both Iraq and Afghanistan. With chances for a clear victory dwindling, the American public got tired of the news of bombs and casualties.

Following the 9/11 attacks, Bush signed an executive order authorizing wiretaps without a court order. The American Bar Association said that move was illegal, and after years of wrangling, Bush agreed to abide by the law. Although President Bush felt he was standing tough in the cause of freedom, his popularity sunk to historic lows.

At the end of his administration — as conflicts in Iraq and Afghanistan dragged on with no end in sight — Bush's approval rating had sunk to just 24 percent, the lowest since Nixon resigned in disgrace 35 years earlier.

Adjusting to the 21st Century

As the 21st century rolled in, the old school world was clearly gone for good. The United States was the senior modern democratic government in the world and the newest source of social innovation. In a sense, the U.S. was the U.N.; all the nations of the world were represented in its population.

If the world could ever find a way to live together, it would have to start in the United States of America. The U.S. moved closer to fulfilling the democratic dream of its founders as minorities and women were increasingly freer to express themselves and leadership looked more like the pluralistic society it represented.

Business changes with society

Business showed how society had changed. At the time of the Revolution in the 1700s, most people lived on farms and produced what they needed in isolation, except for a Sunday trip to church and maybe a little salt, sugar, and coffee from the country store. In the 1800s, canals and railroads stitched the states together. Buying or selling over distances as great as several hundred miles suddenly became possible. People got to know a wider world and formed associations that eventually changed women's rights, slavery, and government.

Large stores like Sears started out sending orders through the mail. With the growth of cities in the 1900s, stores built big buildings. As airplanes and telephones brought the world together, international trade made products cheaper, and world travel allowed people to appreciate both what was different and what was comfortably human about foreign lands.

In the early 2000s, the *Internet (2000)* brought general store sites like Amazon and the ability to trade pictures and text instantly anywhere in the world. Second-generation sites like Google, Wikipedia, YouTube, and Facebook allowed direct links to people, products, and ideas that the searcher may not have known even existed before. To the democracy of politics was added the democracy of culture and communication.

Because people could download any music for free (legally or otherwise), the economics of the recording industry changed dramatically. Movies had to go to immediate release before someone could copy them and pass them around. People longing to communicate churned out even more writing, music, and videos. Computer games allowed people to play with folks they had never met. MP3 players let everybody travel to her own soundtrack.

A continuing trend: The rich get richer, the poor get poorer

The United States wasn't a democracy of economics; America had in fact one of the largest gaps between rich and poor in the developed world. Moving toward the second decade of the 21st century, people who made more than $120,000 a year saw their share of the national income grow from 15 to 20 percent.

Part of this discrepancy was due to tax breaks passed by a Congress well funded by business contributions, and part of it was the natural rewards of educated workers in high tech industries. The virtual absence of well-paid union jobs for people with less education didn't help, either. Although the rich got richer, the middle class and most of the poor still had enough money to get by.

Breaking family ties

Family ties broke down, and people established new families of friends. One out of two marriages ended in divorce, and more and more people lived alone or in single parent households. Chat sites replaced front porches, and surfing the Internet largely replaced newspaper-reading.

Living longer, but at a price

More people exercised and fewer people smoked. After waddling into the 21st century due to the yummy presence of cheap fast food everywhere, Americans started to get a grip on their waistlines.

Most elderly people lived comfortably into advanced age with Social Security and Medicare. Because Social Security was a pay-as-you-go system, the number of young workers available to pay taxes that supported retirees was critical. In the early 21st century, there were seven young workers for every retiree; by the year 2050 there may be only four. Because people lived longer, the need for new sources of funding threatened old-age benefits. Social Security already cost more than regular taxes for most working people.

Question: As more Americans became older, what system became threatened?

Answer: The Social Security system needed an overhaul to maintain benefits.

Shifting minority demographics

Latinos replaced African Americans as the second most populous group in the United States. More and more places, like the state of California, were *majority minority:* no single group made up more than 50 percent of the population.

The U.S. took in more immigrants than ever before — almost a million a year. These new legal residents kept the United States growing and full of new ideas. Illegal immigration was a real problem for social service providers; at least 10 million undocumented people from other countries flooded the educational and health care systems. Illegal immigrants also paid taxes and seldom collected long-term benefits. Estimates indicated that one of every hundred dollars paid into the Social Security system came from an illegal immigrant who would never be eligible to collect benefits.

In the early 21st century, Asian Americans families made 20 percent more money than the average white household. Two and a half million American Indians and others who were part American Indian made up as big a population as was present when Columbus arrived. American Indian income went up as tribes operated gambling casinos in 29 states and took in billions of dollars a year in revenue.

More Americans in prison

Americans in the land of the free kept more of their citizens in prison than any other advanced society. The number of people in prison went up from less than 400,000 in 1980 to more than 2 million in the early 21st century. This increase was part of a great U.S. experiment to see if locking up perpetrators actually held down crime. It seemed to work; major crime was down in the U.S. in the early 21st century.

Venturing farther into the 21st Century

Escaping urban problems, most Americans lived in the suburbs. With air conditioning, more and more people lived comfortably in the South's hot climates. Both of these trends increased energy demands and made coping with global warming that much more challenging.

Americans were used to being distrusted for their affluence and feared for their easygoing cultural influence around the world. They were often seen by those who didn't like them as soft, yet Americans had stood up to frontier wars, militarism, Nazism, Communism, discrimination, and terrorism. They still welcomed the world. For better or for worse, the U.S. was more than just its past; the United States of America was the future.

Part V

Practice Makes Perfect: Two Tests Plus the Answers

The 5th Wave   By Rich Tennant

The 5th Wave   By Rich Tennant

"I always get a good night's sleep the day before a test so I'm relaxed and alert the next morning. Then I grab my pen, eat a banana, and I'm on my way."

In this part...

Because even the fastest NASCAR jockey needs a couple of turns around the track to get in shape, get ready to take some warm up laps. You know more than you think you know about U.S. History; now's the time to roll your brain out of the study tune-up garage and take it for a test drive.

Practice Test 1 covers the earliest times to the Civil War. Practice Test 2 takes you from the Civil War to the present.

You're going to win three ways on these realistic practice cruises:

1. Because these exams have the same types of questions and cover the same areas as the real tests, you'll get good at cutting through the kind of traffic you'll see on Test Day.

2. If you do less-than-spectacularly with one kind of question or one period in U.S. History, you still have time to make some final adjustments to your high-performance engine.

3. This is the kind of exam race everyone dreams of, with the answers right in the book. Because you've got all the answers and explanations with the exams, you'll be reinforcing your knowledge of history as you cruise through the practice tests. Racers, start your engines, and may the history force be with you.

Answer Sheet for Multiple Choice

Use this bubble sheet to mark your answers for Section I of the exam.

1. Ⓐ Ⓑ Ⓒ Ⓓ Ⓔ	41. Ⓐ Ⓑ Ⓒ Ⓓ Ⓔ
2. Ⓐ Ⓑ Ⓒ Ⓓ Ⓔ	42. Ⓐ Ⓑ Ⓒ Ⓓ Ⓔ
3. Ⓐ Ⓑ Ⓒ Ⓓ Ⓔ	43. Ⓐ Ⓑ Ⓒ Ⓓ Ⓔ
4. Ⓐ Ⓑ Ⓒ Ⓓ Ⓔ	44. Ⓐ Ⓑ Ⓒ Ⓓ Ⓔ
5. Ⓐ Ⓑ Ⓒ Ⓓ Ⓔ	45. Ⓐ Ⓑ Ⓒ Ⓓ Ⓔ
6. Ⓐ Ⓑ Ⓒ Ⓓ Ⓔ	46. Ⓐ Ⓑ Ⓒ Ⓓ Ⓔ
7. Ⓐ Ⓑ Ⓒ Ⓓ Ⓔ	47. Ⓐ Ⓑ Ⓒ Ⓓ Ⓔ
8. Ⓐ Ⓑ Ⓒ Ⓓ Ⓔ	48. Ⓐ Ⓑ Ⓒ Ⓓ Ⓔ
9. Ⓐ Ⓑ Ⓒ Ⓓ Ⓔ	49. Ⓐ Ⓑ Ⓒ Ⓓ Ⓔ
10. Ⓐ Ⓑ Ⓒ Ⓓ Ⓔ	50. Ⓐ Ⓑ Ⓒ Ⓓ Ⓔ
11. Ⓐ Ⓑ Ⓒ Ⓓ Ⓔ	51. Ⓐ Ⓑ Ⓒ Ⓓ Ⓔ
12. Ⓐ Ⓑ Ⓒ Ⓓ Ⓔ	52. Ⓐ Ⓑ Ⓒ Ⓓ Ⓔ
13. Ⓐ Ⓑ Ⓒ Ⓓ Ⓔ	53. Ⓐ Ⓑ Ⓒ Ⓓ Ⓔ
14. Ⓐ Ⓑ Ⓒ Ⓓ Ⓔ	54. Ⓐ Ⓑ Ⓒ Ⓓ Ⓔ
15. Ⓐ Ⓑ Ⓒ Ⓓ Ⓔ	55. Ⓐ Ⓑ Ⓒ Ⓓ Ⓔ
16. Ⓐ Ⓑ Ⓒ Ⓓ Ⓔ	56. Ⓐ Ⓑ Ⓒ Ⓓ Ⓔ
17. Ⓐ Ⓑ Ⓒ Ⓓ Ⓔ	57. Ⓐ Ⓑ Ⓒ Ⓓ Ⓔ
18. Ⓐ Ⓑ Ⓒ Ⓓ Ⓔ	58. Ⓐ Ⓑ Ⓒ Ⓓ Ⓔ
19. Ⓐ Ⓑ Ⓒ Ⓓ Ⓔ	59. Ⓐ Ⓑ Ⓒ Ⓓ Ⓔ
20. Ⓐ Ⓑ Ⓒ Ⓓ Ⓔ	60. Ⓐ Ⓑ Ⓒ Ⓓ Ⓔ
21. Ⓐ Ⓑ Ⓒ Ⓓ Ⓔ	61. Ⓐ Ⓑ Ⓒ Ⓓ Ⓔ
22. Ⓐ Ⓑ Ⓒ Ⓓ Ⓔ	62. Ⓐ Ⓑ Ⓒ Ⓓ Ⓔ
23. Ⓐ Ⓑ Ⓒ Ⓓ Ⓔ	63. Ⓐ Ⓑ Ⓒ Ⓓ Ⓔ
24. Ⓐ Ⓑ Ⓒ Ⓓ Ⓔ	64. Ⓐ Ⓑ Ⓒ Ⓓ Ⓔ
25. Ⓐ Ⓑ Ⓒ Ⓓ Ⓔ	65. Ⓐ Ⓑ Ⓒ Ⓓ Ⓔ
26. Ⓐ Ⓑ Ⓒ Ⓓ Ⓔ	66. Ⓐ Ⓑ Ⓒ Ⓓ Ⓔ
27. Ⓐ Ⓑ Ⓒ Ⓓ Ⓔ	67. Ⓐ Ⓑ Ⓒ Ⓓ Ⓔ
28. Ⓐ Ⓑ Ⓒ Ⓓ Ⓔ	68. Ⓐ Ⓑ Ⓒ Ⓓ Ⓔ
29. Ⓐ Ⓑ Ⓒ Ⓓ Ⓔ	69. Ⓐ Ⓑ Ⓒ Ⓓ Ⓔ
30. Ⓐ Ⓑ Ⓒ Ⓓ Ⓔ	70. Ⓐ Ⓑ Ⓒ Ⓓ Ⓔ
31. Ⓐ Ⓑ Ⓒ Ⓓ Ⓔ	71. Ⓐ Ⓑ Ⓒ Ⓓ Ⓔ
32. Ⓐ Ⓑ Ⓒ Ⓓ Ⓔ	72. Ⓐ Ⓑ Ⓒ Ⓓ Ⓔ
33. Ⓐ Ⓑ Ⓒ Ⓓ Ⓔ	73. Ⓐ Ⓑ Ⓒ Ⓓ Ⓔ
34. Ⓐ Ⓑ Ⓒ Ⓓ Ⓔ	74. Ⓐ Ⓑ Ⓒ Ⓓ Ⓔ
35. Ⓐ Ⓑ Ⓒ Ⓓ Ⓔ	75. Ⓐ Ⓑ Ⓒ Ⓓ Ⓔ
36. Ⓐ Ⓑ Ⓒ Ⓓ Ⓔ	76. Ⓐ Ⓑ Ⓒ Ⓓ Ⓔ
37. Ⓐ Ⓑ Ⓒ Ⓓ Ⓔ	77. Ⓐ Ⓑ Ⓒ Ⓓ Ⓔ
38. Ⓐ Ⓑ Ⓒ Ⓓ Ⓔ	78. Ⓐ Ⓑ Ⓒ Ⓓ Ⓔ
39. Ⓐ Ⓑ Ⓒ Ⓓ Ⓔ	79. Ⓐ Ⓑ Ⓒ Ⓓ Ⓔ
40. Ⓐ Ⓑ Ⓒ Ⓓ Ⓔ	80. Ⓐ Ⓑ Ⓒ Ⓓ Ⓔ

Answer Sheet for Essays

For Section II, use the following blank pages to write your essays.

Chapter 22

Practice Test 1: Acing the Early Names and Dates

• •

*T*ime has come today to find out what you know. Don't worry; a little fake pain now saves potential real pain on the day of the Big Exam. The practice test in this chapter covers the period from American Indian days to the Civil War.

Just like when it's for real, allow yourself 55 minutes to answer the 80 multiple-choice questions on the first part of this test. Keep track of the time: Set an alarm for 55 minutes and go for it. The time limit breaks down to just 40 seconds per question, so mark and pass any question you're not sure of. (See Chapter 4 for more on timing strategies.) Just think about this section as an isolated multiple-direction point hunt. Don't even think about the rest of the test until you have the Section 1 multiple-choice challenge out of the way.

- ✔ **Multiple-Choice:** 80 questions, 55 minutes
- ✔ **Document-Based Question:** 1 essay, 60 minutes
- ✔ **Regular Essays:** 2 essays, 70 minutes

To make it easy to spot time periods in which you may be weak, I keep most of the multiple-choice questions on the two practice tests in chronological order, with the questions about the earliest time period at the beginning. Remember — the actual AP U.S. History exam will have the time periods of the questions all scrambled. Although the practice tests mostly stay in chronological order, I've done a little scrambling so you know what it feels like to be chronologically challenged.

The 80-questions-in-55-minutes thing on the multiple-choice section means you need a personal check in. At 30 minutes, you should be passing about question 40; this pace ensures that you have enough time to go back and shore up any weak spots. Practice tests are as much about figuring out timing as remembering answers.

For best results, don't just *say* the answers to the questions you know. *Mark* the answer sheet just like you will when the big test goes live. That way, you get in the rhythm of the real thing. If you don't want to mess up your beautiful *For Dummies* book, just copy the answer sheet.

Do *not* flip to the answer chapter (Chapter 23) when you run into a tough question to see whether you're guessing right; you'll find out soon enough when the test is done. You're not going to be flipping around on test day, and that's what you're preparing for here.

After you spend 55 fun-filled minutes answering the 80 multiple-choice questions, you'll take a mandatory 15-minute preparation period to consider your fate on the Document-Based Question (DBQ). You'll then have 45 minutes to write the best DBQ you can dredge up from your mind and associated imagination. Pause, take a deep breath, and then go on to the regular essay questions. Pick the question that seems the least threatening from Part B. Take 5 big minutes to plan your response and 30 minutes to write the essay. Then do the same thing with Part C.

Section 1: Multiple Choice

Time: 55 minutes

80 Questions

1. American natives were originally called *Indians* because

   (A) they came from India across a land bridge

   (B) Columbus thought he'd reached a land called Indiana

   (C) the Spanish Padres felt they were born *in Dios* or in God

   (D) Columbus believed he'd sailed all the way to the East Indies

   (E) that's what they called themselves

2. *Mesoamerica* in early American history means

   (A) people of the maize or corn

   (B) middle of the New World, around south Mexico and Central America

   (C) the mesas upon which many early people lived

   (D) the Midwest of the United States, where all the farms are

   (E) home of the Incas in the middle of the mountains

3. An early union of American Indian tribes in what is now New York and the surrounding area was

   (A) the Cherokee States

   (B) the land of the Sioux

   (C) the Iroquois Confederation

   (D) the Mesoamerican Empire

   (E) the Norseman Union

4. Place the major New World Indian empires in the same order as their homelands: 1) Mexico City, 2) north of Panama, and 3) from Columbia to Chile

   (A) Mayan, Aztec, Inca

   (B) Aztec, Meso, Inca

   (C) Inca, Mayan, Aztec

   (D) Meso, Inca, Mayan

   (E) Aztec, Mayan, Inca

5. What was an important food that Europeans learned to eat from the New World Indians?

   (A) corn

   (B) potatoes

   (C) tomatoes

   (D) chocolate

   (E) all of the above

6. The first explorer who sailed his boat all the way around the world was

   (A) Vasco Balboa

   (B) Ponce de Leon

   (C) Ferdinand Magellan

   (D) Francisco Coronado

   (E) Francisco Pizarro

7. The *encomienda* system

   (A) was a system of housing accommodations for Spanish padres

   (B) showed the Spanish how to cook Mexican food

   (C) governed relationships between the colonies

   (D) laid out royal land grants

   (E) assigned American Indians to colonists

Go on to next page

8. The break that allowed England more power to colonize the New World came with the

   (A) defeat of the Spanish Armada

   (B) coronation of King George

   (C) wealth of King James

   (D) Henry Hudson's fur discovery

   (E) the War of the Roses

9. Popé's Rebellion (1680) was

   (A) an intrigue in which the pope divided up the New World

   (B) an American Indian rebellion against the Spanish

   (C) the revolt of Protestant settlers against Catholic rules

   (D) a brief fight for power in the Holy See

   (E) an insurrection over the right to make whiskey

10. The main goal for the founding of the British colony of Jamestown was

    (A) to establish religious freedom

    (B) to Christianize the American Indians

    (C) to raise crops and export tobacco

    (D) to find gold

    (E) to explore the natural world of North America

11. The first African slaves came to Virginia

    (A) just a few years before the Civil War

    (B) kidnapped in American Indian canoes years before the white men came

    (C) when America started growing cotton in the years just before the Revolution

    (D) almost 400 years ago, before the Pilgrims even landed

    (E) to fight in the French and Indian War

12. When the first wave of English settlers left for the New World in the mid 1600s, most of them headed for

    (A) Virginia

    (B) New England

    (C) New York

    (D) The West Indies

    (E) Cuba

13. Which English settlers in North America were the Separatists who wanted to split completely from the Church of England?

    (A) the Pilgrims

    (B) the Puritans

    (C) the Marylanders

    (D) the Jamestown farmers

    (E) the Carolina plantation workers

14. Anne Hutchinson (1638) was a

    (A) leader of the conservative family movement

    (B) the feminist wife of Captain John Smith

    (C) the English name for Pocahontas

    (D) a freethinking Puritan expelled for her beliefs

    (E) an early witch trial victim

15. Who founded the city that would become New York?

    (A) the Duke of York

    (B) Spanish conquistadores

    (C) the Dutch

    (D) Henry Hudson, exploring on behalf of King George

    (E) The Puritans

16. If you were an American Indian looking for fair treatment in early colonial America, in which colony would you have wanted to live?

    (A) Puritan New England

    (B) plantation Carolina

    (C) newly growing Georgia

    (D) Quaker Pennsylvania

    (E) booming New Jersey

17. King Philip's War caused

    (A) Philip to assume the crown of Portugal

    (B) American Indians to destroy 12 New England towns

    (C) the English and Spanish to fight a naval battle

    (D) raids on the Southern colonies of Georgia and South Carolina

    (E) the end of troubles for the American Indians

Go on to next page

18. The *Dominion of New England* (1643) was

    (A) a local Puritan kingdom

    (B) a zone for controlling the American Indians

    (C) an area in which New England voters had complete control

    (D) an attempt by the King to control New England with a royal governor

    (E) an attempt by the New England colonies to get free for the direct control of the king

19. Which of these statements is true of slavery in the colonies before the Revolution?

    (A) the mainland British colonies got only a tiny minority of slaves taken from Africa to the New World

    (B) before 1700, most indentured servants were white

    (C) slave rebellions killed both blacks and whites

    (D) all of the above

    (E) none of the above

20. This courtroom scene from late 1600s New England shows

    (A) the Case of the Stolen Bride

    (B) the community deciding who owns Magee's Farm

    (C) the Salem Witch Trails

    (D) girls reunited with their long-lost grandfather

    (E) the power of the church to save sinners

Go on to next page

21. A high point of power for the American Indians in colonial America during the 1600s was

    (A) when they showed the Pilgrims how to have Thanksgiving

    (B) when Pocahontas got to marry a colonist

    (C) the founding of the first American Indian church school

    (D) when they besieged Plymouth and burned Jamestown

    (E) when settlers showed American Indians how to grow corn

22. The largest non-English speaking group in the British colonies before the Revolution was the

    (A) Germans

    (B) Spanish

    (C) French

    (D) Dutch

    (E) Irish

23. What was the approximate population of the American colonies in 1750, before the Revolution?

    (A) 10 million

    (B) 100,000

    (C) 100 million

    (D) 1 million

    (E) Nobody has any idea because there was no census.

24. The Scotch-Irish inhabitants in America before the Revolution

    (A) were peaceful, shy settlers

    (B) brought major investment money to the New World

    (C) settled on small farms on the frontier

    (D) made up much of the urban police force

    (E) were an important part of the Catholic church

25. Peaceful American Indians attacked by whites in Pennsylvania before the Revolution were defended by

    (A) the British Army

    (B) the Paxton Boys

    (C) Samuel Adams

    (D) Benjamin Franklin

    (E) the Indian Army

26. The colonies before the Revolution were made up of

    (A) 95 percent English settlers

    (B) a mixture of mostly English, Italian, and Spanish

    (C) almost no black people

    (D) a majority of non-English settlers in New England

    (E) the most multicultural population in the world at that time

27. The economic system in which colonies were supposed to send raw material to their mother country and buy manufactured products from only that country is

    (A) wage slavery

    (B) capitalism

    (C) mercantilism

    (D) syndication

    (E) distribution

28. The leading export crop for Virginia and Maryland before the Revolution was

    (A) tobacco

    (B) cotton

    (C) wheat

    (D) slaves

    (E) fish

Go on to next page

29. The *Navigation Acts* passed beginning in 1650 were meant to

   (A) help ships avoid dangerous reefs

   (B) provide mapping assistance to explorers

   (C) increase New England ship production

   (D) block colonial trade with countries other than England

   (E) increase colonial trade with countries other than England

30. Economically, the colonies before the Revolution were

   (A) so equal in income that everybody had the same resources

   (B) one of the poorest places in the English-speaking world

   (C) one of the richest places in the English-speaking world

   (D) the home of large manufacturing plants

   (E) entirely self-sufficient

31. Early universities like Harvard, Yale, Princeton, and Brown originated to train

   (A) doctors

   (B) lawyers

   (C) ministers

   (D) scientific farmers

   (E) politicians

32. The *First Great Awakening* of the 1730s spread

   (A) a quiet, contemplative religious feeling

   (B) the idea that the colonies were getting the short end of the stick

   (C) feelings of sectionalism separating the colonies

   (D) *New light* emotional ministers

   (E) *Old light* rational believers

Go on to next page

33. This portrait by Charles Willson Peale
    shows an American

    (A) around the time of the Revolution

    (B) just before the Civil War

    (C) in the time of Wilson Democracy

    (D) in the earliest colonial days

    (E) living in the time of Greece

Go on to next page

34. The *Three-Fifths Compromise* in the U.S. Constitution

    (A) allowed just over half of the states to block a new law

    (B) required ⅔ of Congress to approve any compromise

    (C) allowed ⅗ of the new states to forbid slavery

    (D) counted slaves as ⅗ of a person when deciding representation

    (E) mandated that three out of five voters must agree before any territory could become a state

35. The trial of *Peter Zenger* (1734) helped to further

    (A) the rights of the Dutch to equal treatment

    (B) freedom of the seas

    (C) freedom of the press

    (D) freedom of worship

    (E) access to law school

36. Which of the following conflicts was NOT a European war that included fighting in the colonies?

    (A) King William's War

    (B) Queen Anne's War

    (C) the War of Jenkins' Ear

    (D) the Opium War

    (E) the French and Indian War

37. The *Albany Congress* (1754) convened to

    (A) establish Albany as the capital of New York

    (B) win the support of the American Indians

    (C) begin a tax system for the colonies

    (D) negotiate an end to Queen Anne's War

    (E) begin planning for the Erie Canal

38. Put these British laws that angered the colonies in the right date order from earliest to latest:

    (A) Navigation Laws, Stamp Act, Intolerable Acts

    (B) Stamp Act, Navigation Laws, Intolerable Acts

    (C) Intolerable Acts, Stamp Act, Navigation Laws

    (D) Navigation Laws, Intolerable Acts, Stamp Act

    (E) Intolerable Acts, Navigation Laws, Stamp Act

39. During the American Revolution, the ⅙ of the colonists who sided with Britain were

    (A) Royalists

    (B) Loyalists

    (C) Patriots

    (D) Blue Coats

    (E) Monarchists

40. The Declaration of Independence and Tom Paine's *Common Sense* are examples of what kind of thinking?

    (A) Existential

    (B) Aristotelian

    (C) Epicurean

    (D) Machiavellian

    (E) Enlightenment

41. "I have a dream that one day this nation will rise up and live out the true meaning of its creed." These words are from a speech by

    (A) John F. Kennedy

    (B) Ronald Reagan

    (C) Martin Luther King Jr.

    (D) Harry S Truman

    (E) Abraham Lincoln

Go on to next page

42. A major problem for the patriots in the Revolutionary War was

    (A) bad field position

    (B) lack of proper training

    (C) shortage of doctors

    (D) second rate generals

    (E) lack of supplies from Congress

43. The idea of *republican motherhood* (1780) elevated the role of women by

    (A) admitting women to the Republican Party

    (B) allowing anyone who was a mother to claim government support

    (C) viewing mothers as the most important source of democratic ideas for their children

    (D) giving women full voting rights

    (E) supporting the establishment of day care facilities throughout the new republic

44. The *Land Ordinance* of 1785 and *the Northwest Ordinance* of 1787

    (A) established the new state of Tennessee in northwest Georgia

    (B) set up what would become the Midwestern states of Ohio, Indiana, Michigan, Illinois, and Wisconsin

    (C) gave free land beyond the Appalachian Mountains to veterans of the Revolutionary war

    (D) oversaw relationships with American Indian tribes on the frontier

    (E) worked on an alliance with Canada

45. The *Articles of Confederation* (1777)

    (A) left most of the power in the hands of the states

    (B) never took effect because of the Revolution

    (C) are still the basis of all government in the United States

    (D) helped to start the Confederacy in the Civil War

    (E) were passed after a vote by the people

46. One of the important pieces of legislation passed under the Articles of Confederation was the

    (A) Bill of Rights

    (B) Louisiana Purchase

    (C) Northwest Ordinance

    (D) Declaration of Independence

    (E) none of the above

47. When elder statesman Ben Franklin was leaving the Constitutional Convention, a woman asked him what form of government the United States was planning. Franklin said, "A republic, Madame, if you can keep it." What did he mean by that?

    (A) The U.S. was only going to be a republic if she could keep quiet about it.

    (B) The U.S. would be a loose confederation run by the states.

    (C) The new American government would have no judges or jails.

    (D) The U.S. was trying a real republican form of government that would require the active participation of all citizens.

    (E) The new U.S. government would choose Franklin as its leader.

48. An early government official who supported smaller government was

    (A) Thomas Jefferson

    (B) Alexander Hamilton

    (C) John Jay

    (D) John Adams

    (E) John Marshall

49. What does the First Amendment to the Constitution cover?

    (A) the right to bear arms

    (B) protection from unreasonable search and seizure

    (C) due process of law

    (D) freedom of religion, speech and press

    (E) protection from quartering troops

Go on to next page

50. What is the collective name for the first ten amendments to the Constitution?

    (A) the Charter of Freedom

    (B) the Bill of Liberty

    (C) the Bill of Rights

    (D) the Indomitable Agreement

    (E) the Founding Fathers

51. What was the most important belief of a Federalist at the time of the writing of the Constitution?

    (A) A strong central government was ideal.

    (B) The U.S. should federalize the frontier into three states.

    (C) The U.S. should have an express service for delivering mail.

    (D) Only people who had served in the federal army should be in Congress.

    (E) The government should be a confederation with most power reserved to the states.

52. Under the *Alien and Sedition Acts* of 1798, it was a crime to

    (A) criticize the president

    (B) house aliens without consent

    (C) cause sedition by failing to become a citizen

    (D) pay taxes to a foreign government

    (E) travel to Canada or Mexico without permission

53. John Marshall was

    (A) the third president

    (B) founder of the Marshall Plan

    (C) an influential Supreme Court Chief Justice

    (D) the famous inventor of the steam engine

    (E) the reason people often call sheriffs *marshals*

54. Jefferson's *Louisiana Purchase*

    (A) added 10 percent to the size of the United States

    (B) was in keeping with Jefferson's policy of a strong central government with broad policy-making power

    (C) was a good way of getting Texas into the Union

    (D) was actually contrary to Jefferson's policy of a weak central government with most power left to the states

    (E) wasn't explored for twenty years

55. The *Embargo Acts* (1807) were

    (A) designed to stop the Whiskey Rebellion

    (B) a way of putting a lid on smuggling whiskey from Canada

    (C) meant to limit trade and avoid war

    (D) the first legal attempt to stop the selling of guns to the American Indians

    (E) a way to encourage trade and growth

56. Sectionalism was an issue in the War of 1812 because

    (A) New England strongly supported the war

    (B) the South favored immediate negotiations

    (C) the Star-Spangled Banner wasn't yet the national flag

    (D) New England strongly opposed the war

    (E) the South wanted slaves to fight

57. Tecumseh was a great American Indian leader who

    (A) helped the Pilgrims survive

    (B) worked to save the life of Captain John Smith

    (C) put together an American Indian alliance and fought to save his land

    (D) signed a treaty turning over Louisiana

    (E) lead Lewis and Clark on their expedition

Go on to next page

58. Free blacks fought for U.S. victories in

    (A) the Old Ironsides fight

    (B) the Battle of New Orleans

    (C) American Indian wars on the frontier

    (D) the Civil War

    (E) all of the above

59. The Era of Good Feelings was

    (A) a time of peace after the Civil War

    (B) another name for the hippie rock-and-roll era of the 1960s

    (C) several years of cooperation after the War of 1812

    (D) a time when the colonies had plenty of food before the Revolution

    (E) a time of peace between the U.S. and Canada declared in 1820

60. In the case of *Marbury v. Madison* (1803), the Supreme Court decided that

    (A) the Court can review all laws for their constitutionality.

    (B) President Madison had to repay Marbury, thus establishing the role of executive privilege

    (C) only the federal government can collect tariffs

    (D) gun control is left to the states

    (E) Marbury could run steam boats on the Mississippi

61. This picture represents

    (A) female soldiers drafted into the U.S. Army

    (B) target practice for the Women's Artillery

    (C) the Molly Pitcher spirit of women in the Revolutionary War

    (D) the fact that women often manned cannons

    (E) the role of women in the Civil War

Go on to next page

62. Manifest Destiny means that the United States was

    (A) bound to gain independence from England

    (B) meant to rule the world

    (C) certain to get Canada and Mexico some day

    (D) fated to win World War I

    (E) meant to spread west across the whole North American continent

63. American exceptionalism means that

    (A) the U.S. has special rights and a mission in the world

    (B) Manifest Destiny is wrong

    (C) the U.S. is just like every other country

    (D) Americans should be careful of foreign powers

    (E) the U.S. may not be as sharp as other countries

64. The implied powers decision of the Supreme Court in *McCulloch v. Maryland* means that

    (A) the president can do anything he wants in times of national emergency

    (B) Congress can pass laws to carry out powers in the Constitution even though those acts aren't specifically mentioned

    (C) the Army has the power to destroy as well as protect if it's in the national interest

    (D) the Supreme Court can award titles to elected officials to carry out the Constitution

    (E) states have the implied power to nullify federal laws

65. The appeals decision of the Supreme Court in *Cohens v. Virginia* means that

    (A) defendants in a criminal case can appeal their conviction to the Supreme Court

    (B) the Supreme Court automatically decides which side has the greater appeal

    (C) the president has the right to appeal any law he doesn't agree with

    (D) Congress can appeal directly to the people over a presidential veto

    (E) an appeal signed by two thirds of the states is enough to get any law overturned

66. The Missouri Compromise

    (A) made sure Missouri was divided equally between slave and free sections

    (B) divided the power between the president and Congress in a historic meeting in old Missouri

    (C) drew the Mason-Dixon line between North and South

    (D) allowed American Indians to remain in southern Missouri

    (E) settled the tax issue along the lines proposed by Missouri

67. The Monroe Doctrine said that

    (A) President Monroe had the power to raise taxes

    (B) slavery would be confined to the South

    (C) new states could decide whether they were slave or free

    (D) foreign powers had to stay out of the United States

    (E) foreign powers had to stay out of the New World

Go on to next page

68. Along the *Trail of Tears,*

    (A) civilized American Indians were forced to leave their Southern homes

    (B) blacks marched to slavery

    (C) Irish Americans fled their starving land

    (D) dust bowl settlers moved west looking for jobs

    (E) Revolutionary War widows looked for their husbands after battle

69. The biggest voting change in *Jacksonian Democracy* was that

    (A) women could vote

    (B) all men could vote

    (C) Congress no longer elected the president

    (D) all white men could vote

    (E) the voters directly elected the Senate

70. The *spoils system* meant that

    (A) the government disposed of spoiled food

    (B) political winners gave out government jobs

    (C) Army troops were entitled to keep any captured spoils on the campaigns

    (D) corruption in politics spoiled the election process

    (E) Congress established that laws had to be reconsidered every thirty years before they spoiled

71. When early presidents worried about *nullification*, they were concerned that

    (A) states would try to revoke federal laws

    (B) Congress would overturn the powers of the president

    (C) the Supreme Court would strike down sections of the Constitution

    (D) presidential rights to the spoils system would end

    (E) the British would declare American independence null and void

72. Railroads took over from canals as the main form of transportation in the United States

    (A) before the Revolution

    (B) before the Civil War

    (C) after the Civil War

    (D) during the Andrew Jackson administration

    (E) during the Thomas Jefferson administration

73. What is the most important aspect about the John Deere Company of Rock Island?

    (A) It produced the first steel plow, used to farm American land.

    (B) It's still in business.

    (C) Rock Island eventually became a railroad town.

    (D) It's the inventor of the tractor.

    (E) It proved that a manufacturer can sell both wholesale and retail.

74. In the *cult of domesticity* (1850),

    (A) men were supposed to help with the housework

    (B) women got the right to vote and demonstrate

    (C) everyone was urged to buy domestic products

    (D) women were thought to have weaker brains

    (E) the role of women as moral leader of the household was enshrined

75. The fact that Charles Finney, a Second Great Awakening preacher, was also president of Oberlin College most importantly shows

    (A) that ministers are smart enough to run colleges

    (B) the connection between religious revival and social action

    (C) the connection between Awakening and being president

    (D) that Oberlin was a conservative school

    (E) that Awakening preachers traveled the country

Go on to next page

76. The Shakers, Brook Farm, New Harmony, and Oneida were all

    (A) early organic food brands
    (B) furniture manufacturers whose designs have lasted
    (C) farm leaders
    (D) utopian communities
    (E) Midwestern political movements

77. The *Seneca Falls Convention* (1848) was

    (A) the first important women's rights meeting in the U.S.
    (B) the first important environmental meeting in the U.S.
    (C) the labor meeting that passed the Seneca resolution
    (D) an American Indian rights convention
    (E) a religious service that was part of the Great Awakening

78. Ralph Waldo Emerson was a

    (A) Transcendentalist author
    (B) abolitionist leader
    (C) railroad organizer
    (D) textile manufacturer
    (E) leader of factory workers

79. The clauses on slavery in the Northwest Ordinance (1787) and on the future of the slave trade in the U.S. Constitution show

    (A) early opposition to slavery
    (B) early support for slavery
    (C) the value of slaves in the South
    (D) the spread of slaves to the North
    (E) the reason the U.S. was founded

80. The "peculiar institution" was

    (A) marriage
    (B) funerals
    (C) special schools
    (D) slavery
    (E) the Electoral College

STOP DO NOT TURN THE PAGE UNTIL TOLD TO DO SO. DO NOT RETURN TO A PREVIOUS TEST.

Section II: Free-Response Questions

In this section, test takers confront first the Document-Based Question (DBQ) in Part A and then the two regular essays in Parts B and C.

Part A: Document-Based Question

Planning Time: 15 minutes

Suggested Writing Time: 45 minutes

Percent of Section II score: 45

1. Discuss the changing nature of slavery and indentured servitude from the founding of the British North American colonies until the Civil War. What factors fostered the change from indentured servitude to slavery and influenced the evolution of slavery from the Revolution to the Civil War? Discuss the role of crops such as tobacco, cotton, and sugar. Use the documents and your knowledge of the time period in writing your response.

Document A

Source: Letter written by Christopher Columbus to his sponsors, the King and Queen of Spain, on his first voyage, 1493.

. . . their Highnesses may see that I shall give them all the gold they require, if they will give me but a very little assistance, spices also, and cotton, as much as their Highnesses shall command to be shipped; and mastic, hitherto found only in Greece, [and]. . . slaves, as many of these idolaters as their Highnesses shall command to be shipped.

Document B

Source: Grubb, Farley. "The Incidence of Servitude in Trans-Atlantic Migration, 1771–1804." *Explorations in Economic History* 22 (1985b): 316–39

English Emigration to the American Colonies, by Destination and Type, 1773–76

Location	Number of Immigrants	Percent Indentured Servants
New England	54	1.85
Middle Colonies	1,162	61.27
New York	303	11.55
Pennsylvania	859	78.81
Chesapeake	2,984	96.28
Maryland	2,217	98.33
Virginia	767	90.35
Lower South	307	19.54
Carolinas	106	23.58
Georgia	196	17.86

Go on to next page

Document C

> Source: Report on Indentured Servants, 1783
>
> Those who can pay for their passage arrive in America free to take any engagement that suits them. Those who cannot pay are carried at the expense of the ship-owner, who in order to recoup his money, advertises on arrival that he has imported artisans, laborers and domestic servants and that he has agreed with them on his own account to hire their services for a period normally of three, four, or five years for men and women and 6 or 7 years for children.

Document D

> Source: Black appeal to the Governor of Massachusetts, 1773
>
> We have no Property. We have no Wives. No Children. We have no City. No Country. But we have a Father in Heaven. . . .

Document E

> Source: Letter from Mississippi, 1836
>
> . . .these were all merchants, who without much Capital went to speculating in Cotton. It is in truth the only country I ever read or heard of, where a poor man could in 2 or 3 years without any aid, become wealthy. . . . More than 6,000 Negroes and 10,000 horses and mules have been sold in Yazoo County alone.

Document F

> Source: A Northern merchant threatens an abolitionist, 1835
>
> There are millions upon millions of dollars due from Southerners to the merchants and mechanics of this city alone, the payment of which would be jeopardized by any rupture between the North and the South. We cannot afford, sir, to let you and your associates succeed in your endeavor to overthrow slavery. It is not a matter of principle with us. It is a matter of business necessity.

Go on to next page

Document G

Source: Symbol of the Anti-Slavery Society

Document H

Source: Report of a slave girl, 1813

If a slave resisted being whipped, the bloodhounds were unpacked, and set upon him, to tear his flesh from his bones. The master who did these things was highly educated, and styled a perfect gentleman. He also boasted the name and standing of a Christian, though Satan never had a truer follower.

Go on to next page

Document I

Source: Census data, Antebellum Economics

In 1860 the twelve wealthiest counties in the United States were all in the cotton growing South. Per capita income in the white South was higher by 1860 than in the North. With an economy based on slavery, the South was different from any other section of Europe or the United States.

Many Southerners initially opposed slavery; hundreds freed their slaves following the Revolution. With the invention of the cotton gin after the Revolution, cotton began to make huge amounts of money. As late as the 1830s, a bill in the Virginia legislature to abolish slavery came within a few votes of passing. After that, as the profits continued to rise from slavery based cotton, Southerners made the white fluffy fiber their "king" and became addicted to black slavery.

Part B and Part C

Total Suggested Planning and Writing Time: 70 minutes

Percent of Section II score: 55

Part B

Choose ONE question from this part.

2. In what ways did the cultural background of early settlers influence the development of the pre-Revolutionary colonies? Discuss the New England, Middle, and Southern colonies with regard for TWO of the following:

   National origins

   Religious beliefs

   Ethnic background

   Reasons for coming to America

3. Some historians say that Americans bought their freedom with slave labor. Explain how this charge relates to the development of the country before and after the Revolution in at least TWO of the following areas:

   Economic development

   Political power

   Social beliefs

   Behavioral changes

Part C

Choose ONE question from this part.

4. How did the federal government change during the Jacksonian Era? Assess these changes in light of at least TWO of the following topics:

   Voting behavior

   Policy regarding American Indians

   States' rights

   Federal power

5. How did relationships between the North and the South change in the time between the Revolution and the Civil War with regard to at least TWO of the following developments:

   Missouri Compromise of 1820

   Compromise of 1850

   Kansas-Nebraska Act

   Dred Scott Decision

Chapter 23

The Answers to Practice Test 1

Only after you complete your essays in the practice test (see Chapter 22) do you peek at the answers in this chapter! You may even want to have your teacher (or another student who's roughly as smart as your teacher) read your essay efforts to independently evaluate how you sound. The essay points in this chapter are just one way to handle the topic. Your clear ideas and the political, economic, and social evidence you bring forward to support your ideas are what matter most. For any question that really stumps you, go back and review the history in this book and in your school textbook. Taking sample tests gives you an early warning so you can tune up for super success on the big AP.

For general tips about scoring and how to handle questions, see Chapters 4, 5, and 6.

Section 1: Multiple-Choice

1. **(D).** Columbus set sail for the East Indies, so the inhabitants at his destination would logically be "Indians."

2. **(B).** Remember, *meso* means middle.

3. **(C).** The Iroquois Confederation actually gave the early colonies ideas about the power of united action.

4. **(E).** *Meso* means middle, not an Indian tribe. Here's a mnemonic device: "I'm not forgetting the order of the Big Three tribes, **AM I**?" From north to south, the geographic order is **A**ztec, **M**aya, **I**nca.

5. **(E).** All four were important foods the settlers picked up from the American Indians. If you know for sure that at least two of the choices are correct, you know that (E) has to be the answer by default.

6. **(C).** Only Magellan has a GPS system named after him. The others were more local explorers.

7. **(E).** Even if you don't remember that the *encomienda* system gave Spanish colonists legal power over Indians, you can still throw out the smart-aleck answers about housing and cooking as being not worth an AP question. At worst, that gets you down to a three-choice guess, statistically worth the risk.

8. **(A).** With the Armada gone, Britain got set to rule the waves.

9. **(B).** Popé's Rebellion in the Spanish West and King Philip's War in New England were wars with the American Indians that happened at about the same time in the late 1600s. You can remember the difference if you think of the Indian leader who just happened to be called Popé as associated with the pope-following Catholic Spanish colonists.

10. **(D).** Settlers didn't find any gold, but not because they didn't try.

11. **(D).** Slavery happened early in the New World.

12. **(D).** The real money was in growing sugar in the West Indies.

13. **(A).** The Pil*grims* grimly wanted to get completely out of the Church of England; the *Puri*tans simply wanted to *puri*fy it.

14. **(D).** The *Puri*tans thought they were too *pure* to allow radical self expression, especially coming from a woman (like Anne Hutchinson).

15. **(C).** The Dutch founded New Amsterdam on the tip of Manhattan.

16. **(D).** The Quakers in Pennsylvania actually believed in treating the American Indians like human beings.

17. **(B).** Like Popé's Rebellion, King Philip's War was a battle with American Indians, so you can rule out any answer choice that doesn't include them.

18. **(D).** In the *Dominion* of New England, the King tried to *dominate*.

19. **(D).** Most slaves went to the West Indies and South America, white indentured servants did most of the hard work before 1700, and slaves rebelled when they could.

20. **(C).** The late-1600s clothes, stern judges, and multiple girls making accusations identify this picture as the Salem Witch Trials.

21. **(D).** At the height of their power and fury, the Indians came pretty close to wiping out the original colonial sites. And if you read the question carefully, you see that, although the other answer choices may be nice American Indian images, they're not about power. Regardless of the details, (D) is the only answer that satisfies the topic.

22. **(A).** The Germans were an important part of the population from the early days, complete with sausage and beer.

23. **(D).** The population of the colonies in 1750 was around 1 million; by the Revolution, it was over 2 million. The patriots fought the Revolution with fewer people than now live in the Sacramento area.

24. **(C).** The Scotch-Irish were poor-but-tough Protestant backwoods farmers.

25. **(D).** Ben Franklin called out the militia to defend peaceful American Indians *against* the bloodthirsty Paxton Boys.

26. **(D).** Outside the aptly named New England, a majority of the population wasn't technically English. Although they shared a government (often unwillingly), Scotland, Ireland, and Wales weren't part of England.

27. **(C).** *Mercantilism* means colonies send raw materials that get turned into *merchandise*. Colonies were expected to buy this *merchandise* at a nice profit to the mother country.

28. **(A).** Cotton was small-time before the cotton gin, but lots of people wanted to smoke.

29. **(D).** The Navigation Acts were mercantilism under sail: They were meant to block trade with anybody but England.

30. **(C).** The colonies were doing very well financially, thank you. See Chapter 9.

31. **(C).** Early universities were all about religion.

32. **(D).** *New light* ministers put emotion into the First Great Awakening.

33. **(A).** By the clothes and classical pose, this is the picture of a Revolutionary Enlightenment man. The other answers are wrong by generations.

34. **(D).** The *Three-Fifths Compromise* gave slaveholding states ⅗ voting credit for every slave, even though they didn't give the slaves much credit as human beings.

35. **(C).** The Peter Zenger trial helped establish freedom of the press. Notice the repeat of the word *freedom* in three of the five choices for this question. The correct answer is usually one that's part of the pattern.

36. **(D).** With sugar, tobacco, and slaves, America had its share of bad habits, but opium wasn't one of them.

37. **(B).** The Albany Congress was an American-Indian-and-settlers meeting.

38. **(A).** Remember the order of the laws goes from general to worst: first Navigation, then Stamp, and finally Intolerable.

39. **(B).** Loyalists viewed themselves as the real patriots — to England.

40. **(E).** The Revolution and its writings were pure Enlightenment. See Chapter 10.

41. **(C).** This excerpt is from Martin Luther King's famous "I have a dream" speech. Be ready for out-of-chronological-order questions: The real AP test will be full of them.

42. **(E).** Marching is difficult if you don't have shoes.

43. **(C).** This is the only answer that even fits the time period; you can throw out all the other answer choices as being too late.

44. **(B).** The ordinances set up what was then the Northwest of the new United States. In this case, you can get a clue by going with the most important answer: the AP isn't going to bother you with questions about small happenings.

45. **(A).** State power goes with the idea of a loose confederation.

46. **(C).** The Confederation's biggest legislation was the Northwest law.

47. **(D).** Look closely at the longest answers. Because test writers don't want arguments, they usually phrase the right answer carefully. In this case, (D) is the most specific, precisely worded choice (and one of only two that deal with the concept of a republic at all).

48. **(A).** Thomas Jefferson was one of the most prominent supporters of small government (although he did add a lot of territory to be governed with the Louisiana Purchase).

49. **(D).** Freedom starts in your mind with religion, speech, and press.

50. **(C).** Notice that a couple of answers contain the word *bill;* after you pick that pattern out, the Bill of Rights is hopefully ringing some bells. You can definitely get rid of (E), the Founding Fathers, as a smart-aleck answer.

51. **(A).** *Federalists* wanted a strong *federal* government. You can chuck (C) as a smart-aleck choice.

52. **(A).** The first thing a repressive government moves to protect is itself. The other answers aren't sedition.

53. **(B).** John Marshall made the Supreme Court into a powerful third branch of the federal government.

54. **(D).** Of the choices, (B) and (D) present the most important concepts. If you remember that Jefferson was for small government, you can eliminate answer (B) right away and recognize (D) as the most likely possibility.

55. **(C).** Because *embargo* means to stop trade, (E) doesn't make sense. (C) is the most important remaining choice and the correct answer.

56. **(D).** You can eliminate (C), about the Star-Spangled Banner, as a smart-aleck throwaway. Even if you don't know history, if you can eliminate one choice it's statistically best to guess.

57. **(C).** With the AP's emphasis on social struggle, people in questions will tend to be those who fought back, not just folks who went along with powerful interests. In this case, that points to (C) as the most likely answer.

58. **(E).** If you know blacks fought in more than one of these battles, you know it has to be all of them, choice (E).

59. **(C).** The Era of Good Feelings was a victory lap for the new United States, which hasn't experienced an oversupply of political good feelings since.

60. **(A).** "Review all laws for constitutionality" is the most important answer choice and the right one for this question.

61. **(C).** This picture represents the real, in spirit at least, Molly Pitcher. The other choices aren't even in the right time period; the three-cornered hats give away the time.

62. **(E).** Manifest Destiny was the idea that God intended for the U.S. to push westward to the Pacific.

63. **(A).** If you remember that American exceptionalism is the philosophy behind Manifest Destiny, you can eliminate (B) right away and zero in on (A), the choice that best corresponds to the idea of Manifest Destiny (which you've already associated with American exceptionalism).

64. **(B).** (B) is the most precise answer, which is a pretty decent indicator.

65. **(A).** Unless you're going to be a lawyer, your mind can go blank when you see Cohens v. Virginia. Carefully checking out the choices can turn the light back on.

66. **(C).** The U.S. wasn't in the business of compromising with the American Indians, so you can rule out (D). (B) and (E) don't make much sense, either; of the two choices remaining, the Mason-Dixon line is the most significant. In this case, it's not the longest answer, but it's the best one.

67. **(E).** Europe wasn't welcome to grab any more New World land.

68. **(A).** The Trail of Tears was ethnic cleansing for American Indians.

69. **(D).** The big voting news in Jacksonian democracy was that non-property-owning white men finally got to vote, so (D) is your answer.

70. **(B).** The spoils system was campaign financing before big money — in return for a little pre-election back-scratching, winning politicians gave their friends and influential supporters cushy government jobs. Answer (B) is your best choice.

71. **(A).** *Nullification* was when a state would try to make a federal law *null* and void (not applicable) within the nullifying state.

72. **(B).** Railroads started to be practical before the Civil War. In Andy Jackson's time, canals were still the happening thing.

73. **(A).** The humble steel plow changed American prairie grassland into one of the richest agricultural areas in the world.

74. **(E).** Women began to get power just by running their own households. You can eliminate (B) as being too early for women's suffrage.

75. **(B).** Pay attention to the wording of the question: it asks for the most important answer, which is that religion and social action were connected.

76. **(D).** (B) and (C) don't seem terribly important. Of the choices left, "utopian communities" seems to better describe groups with names like Brook Farm and New Harmony, and (D) is the correct answer.

77. **(A).** Women begin to stand up as a group at the Seneca Falls Convention in 1848. The date helps supply the clue.

78. **(A).** Ralph Waldo Emerson was Mr. Transcendentalism: the pivot point for separating personal spirituality from religious dogma.

79. **(A).** The United States had intended to get rid of slavery much sooner than they did — the documents in question provide for the phasing out of slavery, so you can rule out (B) and home in on (A).

80. **(D).** Even slavery's supporters called it peculiar; guilty conscience, anyone?

Section 11: Free-Response Questions

The following essay points show sample information that you can organize for your practice essays. Chapter 5 contains detailed guidance on how to write the DBQ response, and Chapter 6 gives you the lowdown on tackling the regular essays.

Part A: Document-Based Question

The DBQ asks you to discuss the changing nature of slavery and indentured servitude in relation to their evolution, economics, and crops. Here are some general PES facts on the subject of servitude you may want to pull in to your essay:

✔ Before 1700, white indentured servants outnumbered black slaves.

✔ In the Chesapeake Bay area, indentured servants grew enough tobacco to increase highly profitable exports of the smoking leaf from 1 million pounds in the 1630s to 40 million pounds in 1700.

✔ Three out of four English immigrants to this region in the 1700s were servants indentured for around five years of service to pay for their passage.

✔ The *headright* system allowed anyone bringing in a laborer to get 50 acres of land per imported worker — instant wealth.

✔ Almost half of the white indentured servants died before they finished their term of service.

✔ After 1700, more jobs in England made for fewer indentured servants.

✔ Plantation owners without indentured servants substituted black African slaves who lived longer and worked until they died.

✔ At the time of the American Revolution, the U.S. was home to fewer than 1 million slaves, mostly in the South.

✔ After the Revolution, Southern owners freed thousands of slaves, and all Northern states ended slavery. The U.S. banned the importation of slaves in 1808.

✔ The cotton gin, invented in the late 1790s, made slavery hugely profitable. One slave with a gin could do the work of 50 without; American cotton brought high prices from newly mechanized cotton mills in the U.S. and Britain.

✔ Slaves cleared new land, and cotton land spread over much of the South, as did sugar in Louisiana.

✔ By the time of the Civil War in 1860, the South was prosperous, with more than 4 million slaves.

Material from at least some of the provided documents (like the points in the following list) should appear with document letters in brackets in your DBQ essay.

✔ **A:** Shows slavery from the very first voyage of Columbus

✔ **B:** Shows that a majority of immigrants to the Middle South in the years just before the Revolution were indentured English servants

✔ **C:** Demonstrates indentured arrangements

✔ **D:** Shows the agony of slavery for Africans at the time of the Revolution

✔ **E:** Letter relating wealth from cotton and reporting Negro sales alongside horses and mules

✔ **F:** Reveals the complicity of Northern merchants in Southern slavery

✔ **G:** The often-reproduced symbol of the antislavery societies

✔ **H:** First-person report of slave driver cruelty

✔ **I:** Details the economics of slavery

✔ **J:** Emancipation of slaves, as imagined during the Civil War, with horrors of slavery behind and benefits of freedom ahead

Part B and Part C

In this section, I provide you with an overview of some points you may want to include on each of the essay choices in Parts B and C. You don't have to have all of these points, but you should have reasonable PES proof to support your thesis and analysis. See Chapter 6 for more on regular essays.

2. Cultural background of colonies

National origins: The concentration of the English in New England, the majority non-English (but still mostly English-speaking) population in central and Southern colonies, and national origin differences can be overplayed: Both rock-ribbed New England farmers and Southern planters were English. German farmers did well in the central states, and Dutch planters added farming experience to central New York.

Religious beliefs: Protestants in New England, Catholics in Maryland and Rhode Island, Church of England in the South. Quakers in Pennsylvania created a safe haven for American Indians and other religions. German Lutherans and Scotch-Irish Presbyterians added religious diversity.

Ethnic background: Most early colonists were of northern European stock with African slaves (and free Africans) accounting for almost 18 percent of the U.S. population by the time of the Revolution. Within the European background of settlers, the Scotch-Irish folks tended to be independent small farmers in mountainous regions, and German Americans often owned productive farms in the central states.

Reasons for coming to America: New England reflected the reform and separatist beliefs of the Puritans and Pilgrims who came to the colonies to found a pure society. Indentured servants in the middle South came from desperate economic necessity and, when they survived, often demanded better treatment from colonial rulers. Scotch-Irish settlers had faced oppression in Northern Ireland; they didn't put up with being pushed around in the New World. Together, the colonists, with visions of freedom and chips on their shoulders, made a formidable constituency for independence.

3. Charge that America bought freedom with slave labor before and after the Revolution

Economic development: The wealth of the South and some business profits of the North depended on slavery by the time of the Civil War. However, the growth of the colonies up to 1700 centered mostly on individual and indentured English labor. The South managed to recover and grow without slavery after the Civil War. At the time of the Revolution, 82 percent of the population wasn't in slavery. That free percentage actually increased as the Civil War approached, and the growth of the country outstripped the growth of slavery. Initial Revolutionary activity occurred in New England, which had few if any slaves. The U.S. would have achieved freedom even without slaves.

Political power: Slavery both retarded and advanced the political power of the United States. The rich Southern slave-owning economy added to the wealth of the nation. On the other hand, the escalating fight over slavery drained political resources. The South managed to control much of the political life of the country due to the ⅗ rule that gave them partial representation for all their nonvoting slaves.

Social beliefs: The unity of national purpose that began in the Second Great Awakening of the 1830s quickly dissipated as religious congregations split over slavery. Southerners had no interest in labor issues or women's rights and a complete hostility to the abolitionist movement. Due to the fragmented, almost-feudal nature of Southern society, public education failed to develop before the Civil War.

Behavioral changes: Although the North moved West, the South moved no further than the Mississippi River bottom land where it could grow cotton and sugar cane with slave labor. The Northern population soon greatly exceeded that of the South, and almost all industrial development took place in the North. Even with the wealth from cotton, the South and slavery were quickly losing ground to freedom. The U.S. got a financial boost from slavery, but it became free despite slavery's moral burden, not because of slave work's extra profits.

4. How the federal government changed in the Jacksonian Era

Voting behavior: With the beginning of universal white male suffrage, voting and electioneering became national preoccupations. This shift attracted more involvement in government policy and in polarizing issues like the Bank of the U.S. It also made American democracy more real and less of the Enlightenment experiment that had frozen in the polite-but-sterile confines of the Era of Good Feelings.

Policy regarding American Indians: Democracy is often less than idealistic when the economic interests of the voters conflict with the rights of a minority. That's what happened to the American Indians under old fighter Andy Jackson. Jackson refused to follow a Supreme Court decision favoring American Indian landowners, and he eventually set up their deportation to the West, opening up rich land for Southern settlers and slave owners.

States' rights: Although Jackson's American Indian policy helped the South, his insistence on federal rule stopped in its tracks an early attempt at nullification by South Carolina (see Chapter 11). Greater male voting led to polarization in states'-rights issues.

Federal power: Jackson increased federal power by fighting nullification and opposing the independent economic clout of the Bank of the U.S. His was the first *imperial presidency,* and although voting democracy increased, so did the power of the federal government.

5. North and South relationship changes

Missouri Compromise: Also known as the Compromise of 1820, the agreement admitted Missouri as a slave state, balanced by Maine's entrance as a free state. More importantly, the compromise drew the Mason-Dixon line between slave and free states at the 36th parallel. The agreement bought 30 years of peace between the states, but an aging Thomas Jefferson wrote that the line would eventually tear the Union apart. He was right; attempts to extend and modify the line between slave and free states led to disagreements and bloodshed that led in turn to the Civil War.

Compromise of 1850: This compromise divided land taken from Mexico, admitted California as a free state, allowed New Mexico, Utah, and Arizona to choose to be slave or free, and established the Fugitive Slave law, which made all Americans legally obligated to help catch runaway slaves even if the slaves escaped to free states. The Fugitive Slave law upset the free states, and the uneconomical prospect of slaves on dry western land did nothing to help the South. This compromise lasted only four years; its replacement (the Kansas-Nebraska Act) was an even worse deal for the North.

Kansas-Nebraska Act: The 1854 legislation allowed both Kansas and Nebraska to decide whether they wanted to be slave or free. Because Kansas and Nebraska were north of the Mason-Dixon line, the Kansas-Nebraska Act effectively repealed the Missouri Compromise, which would've designated the two new states as free. Throwing Kansas up in the air led to armed competition between slave and free forces for control of the new state constitution. Now the sides were killing each other on the field of attempted compromise. The Union's relationship was coming apart.

Dred Scott decision: The South had lost control of the Congress, but they still controlled the Supreme Court. In this decision, the South sent freed slave Dred Scott back to slavery and declared that no ruling body could make slavery illegal anywhere in the United States. The Dred Scott decision invalidated all previous carefully-crafted compromises. The North had gone beyond having a simple moral objection to slavery; with the Fugitive Slave law, the battle over Kansas, and now the Dred Scott decision, many in the North felt that the South was out to extend slavery all over the United States. The North suspected that what it called the *slave power* would send slaves to take their jobs. What had started as a gentlemanly compromise in 1820 was degenerating into a street fight.

Answer Sheet for Multiple Choice

Use this bubble sheet to mark your answers for Section I of the exam.

1. Ⓐ Ⓑ Ⓒ Ⓓ Ⓔ	41. Ⓐ Ⓑ Ⓒ Ⓓ Ⓔ
2. Ⓐ Ⓑ Ⓒ Ⓓ Ⓔ	42. Ⓐ Ⓑ Ⓒ Ⓓ Ⓔ
3. Ⓐ Ⓑ Ⓒ Ⓓ Ⓔ	43. Ⓐ Ⓑ Ⓒ Ⓓ Ⓔ
4. Ⓐ Ⓑ Ⓒ Ⓓ Ⓔ	44. Ⓐ Ⓑ Ⓒ Ⓓ Ⓔ
5. Ⓐ Ⓑ Ⓒ Ⓓ Ⓔ	45. Ⓐ Ⓑ Ⓒ Ⓓ Ⓔ
6. Ⓐ Ⓑ Ⓒ Ⓓ Ⓔ	46. Ⓐ Ⓑ Ⓒ Ⓓ Ⓔ
7. Ⓐ Ⓑ Ⓒ Ⓓ Ⓔ	47. Ⓐ Ⓑ Ⓒ Ⓓ Ⓔ
8. Ⓐ Ⓑ Ⓒ Ⓓ Ⓔ	48. Ⓐ Ⓑ Ⓒ Ⓓ Ⓔ
9. Ⓐ Ⓑ Ⓒ Ⓓ Ⓔ	49. Ⓐ Ⓑ Ⓒ Ⓓ Ⓔ
10. Ⓐ Ⓑ Ⓒ Ⓓ Ⓔ	50. Ⓐ Ⓑ Ⓒ Ⓓ Ⓔ
11. Ⓐ Ⓑ Ⓒ Ⓓ Ⓔ	51. Ⓐ Ⓑ Ⓒ Ⓓ Ⓔ
12. Ⓐ Ⓑ Ⓒ Ⓓ Ⓔ	52. Ⓐ Ⓑ Ⓒ Ⓓ Ⓔ
13. Ⓐ Ⓑ Ⓒ Ⓓ Ⓔ	53. Ⓐ Ⓑ Ⓒ Ⓓ Ⓔ
14. Ⓐ Ⓑ Ⓒ Ⓓ Ⓔ	54. Ⓐ Ⓑ Ⓒ Ⓓ Ⓔ
15. Ⓐ Ⓑ Ⓒ Ⓓ Ⓔ	55. Ⓐ Ⓑ Ⓒ Ⓓ Ⓔ
16. Ⓐ Ⓑ Ⓒ Ⓓ Ⓔ	56. Ⓐ Ⓑ Ⓒ Ⓓ Ⓔ
17. Ⓐ Ⓑ Ⓒ Ⓓ Ⓔ	57. Ⓐ Ⓑ Ⓒ Ⓓ Ⓔ
18. Ⓐ Ⓑ Ⓒ Ⓓ Ⓔ	58. Ⓐ Ⓑ Ⓒ Ⓓ Ⓔ
19. Ⓐ Ⓑ Ⓒ Ⓓ Ⓔ	59. Ⓐ Ⓑ Ⓒ Ⓓ Ⓔ
20. Ⓐ Ⓑ Ⓒ Ⓓ Ⓔ	60. Ⓐ Ⓑ Ⓒ Ⓓ Ⓔ
21. Ⓐ Ⓑ Ⓒ Ⓓ Ⓔ	61. Ⓐ Ⓑ Ⓒ Ⓓ Ⓔ
22. Ⓐ Ⓑ Ⓒ Ⓓ Ⓔ	62. Ⓐ Ⓑ Ⓒ Ⓓ Ⓔ
23. Ⓐ Ⓑ Ⓒ Ⓓ Ⓔ	63. Ⓐ Ⓑ Ⓒ Ⓓ Ⓔ
24. Ⓐ Ⓑ Ⓒ Ⓓ Ⓔ	64. Ⓐ Ⓑ Ⓒ Ⓓ Ⓔ
25. Ⓐ Ⓑ Ⓒ Ⓓ Ⓔ	65. Ⓐ Ⓑ Ⓒ Ⓓ Ⓔ
26. Ⓐ Ⓑ Ⓒ Ⓓ Ⓔ	66. Ⓐ Ⓑ Ⓒ Ⓓ Ⓔ
27. Ⓐ Ⓑ Ⓒ Ⓓ Ⓔ	67. Ⓐ Ⓑ Ⓒ Ⓓ Ⓔ
28. Ⓐ Ⓑ Ⓒ Ⓓ Ⓔ	68. Ⓐ Ⓑ Ⓒ Ⓓ Ⓔ
29. Ⓐ Ⓑ Ⓒ Ⓓ Ⓔ	69. Ⓐ Ⓑ Ⓒ Ⓓ Ⓔ
30. Ⓐ Ⓑ Ⓒ Ⓓ Ⓔ	70. Ⓐ Ⓑ Ⓒ Ⓓ Ⓔ
31. Ⓐ Ⓑ Ⓒ Ⓓ Ⓔ	71. Ⓐ Ⓑ Ⓒ Ⓓ Ⓔ
32. Ⓐ Ⓑ Ⓒ Ⓓ Ⓔ	72. Ⓐ Ⓑ Ⓒ Ⓓ Ⓔ
33. Ⓐ Ⓑ Ⓒ Ⓓ Ⓔ	73. Ⓐ Ⓑ Ⓒ Ⓓ Ⓔ
34. Ⓐ Ⓑ Ⓒ Ⓓ Ⓔ	74. Ⓐ Ⓑ Ⓒ Ⓓ Ⓔ
35. Ⓐ Ⓑ Ⓒ Ⓓ Ⓔ	75. Ⓐ Ⓑ Ⓒ Ⓓ Ⓔ
36. Ⓐ Ⓑ Ⓒ Ⓓ Ⓔ	76. Ⓐ Ⓑ Ⓒ Ⓓ Ⓔ
37. Ⓐ Ⓑ Ⓒ Ⓓ Ⓔ	77. Ⓐ Ⓑ Ⓒ Ⓓ Ⓔ
38. Ⓐ Ⓑ Ⓒ Ⓓ Ⓔ	78. Ⓐ Ⓑ Ⓒ Ⓓ Ⓔ
39. Ⓐ Ⓑ Ⓒ Ⓓ Ⓔ	79. Ⓐ Ⓑ Ⓒ Ⓓ Ⓔ
40. Ⓐ Ⓑ Ⓒ Ⓓ Ⓔ	80. Ⓐ Ⓑ Ⓒ Ⓓ Ⓔ

Answer Sheet for Essays

For Section II, use the following blank pages to write your essays.

Chapter 24

Practice Test 2: Cruising the Big AP toward Modern Times

● ●

*N*ow it's time for Practice Test 2, moving on up from the Civil War until the day before right now. Although the big AP will be light on questions about stuff that just happened yesterday, at least half the test will cover events from the Civil War on. Try it out with this chapter and see how you do. The multiple-choice section is first, followed by the essay questions.

>   ✔ **Multiple Choice:** 80 questions, 55 minutes
>
>   ✔ **Document-Based Question:** 1 essay, 60 minutes
>
>   ✔ **Regular Essays:** 2 essays, 70 minutes

Although wanting to use a computer to type out your essays on this practice test is perfectly normal, try handwriting them if you really want a lock on how the big AP will feel. You won't get computers, PDAs, or other electronic buddies on AP U.S. History game day.

Don't take the practice test with your MP3 player on while your honey steers to the drive-through. Recreate actual combat conditions: sit up at a desk, pencil in hand, where the loudest sound is the clock. Turn off your phone and computer. Any friend meltdowns can wait while you work on your future success.

Section 1: Multiple Choice

Time: 55 minutes
80 Questions

1. Southerners thought England would have to support them in the Civil War because England needed

    (A) slaves
    (B) Southern cotton
    (C) Southern steel
    (D) a friend in America
    (E) Southern mint juleps

2. Most families in the pre-Civil War South

    (A) owned about ten slaves
    (B) owned no slaves
    (C) secretly supported abolition
    (D) worked for a Republican victory
    (E) were opposed to slavery

3. Northern businessmen before the Civil War

    (A) often profited from slavery
    (B) always opposed slavery
    (C) never lent money to the South
    (D) often secretly held slaves
    (E) thought the South was sure to win

4. Which statement is true of American slavery?

    (A) Slaves were generally happy.
    (B) Slaves staged several revolts.
    (C) All blacks in the U.S. were slaves.
    (D) Importation of new African slaves continued right up to the Civil War.
    (E) The value of slavery declined until it ended.

5. *Uncle Tom's Cabin* was

    (A) the first stop on the Underground Railroad
    (B) a play about a jolly frontiersman
    (C) the most important novel of the 1800s
    (D) a favorite song of the South
    (E) the name of the first national maple syrup brand

6. Gold was discovered in California

    (A) by early Spanish missionaries
    (B) on unclaimed land days before California joined the U.S.
    (C) after years of prospecting
    (D) on land that belonged to the president
    (E) on land that belonged to rich investors

7. The policy of *popular sovereignty* meant that

    (A) whoever was most popular got to be president
    (B) the people elected whomever they wanted
    (C) new states could choose whether to be slave or free
    (D) new states could decide their own capital cities
    (E) people were responsible for their own budgets

8. The big Southern win in the Compromise of 1850 was

    (A) Arizona's slave-state status
    (B) the railroad through Atlanta
    (C) the Force Act
    (D) the Fugitive Slave Act
    (E) the Kansas-Nebraska Act

9. John Brown acted before the Civil War as a

    (A) militant abolitionist
    (B) Southern compromiser
    (C) Northern factory leader
    (D) Southern slaveholder
    (E) Northern diplomat

Go on to next page

10. In the Dred Scott case

    (A) the North won a victory for freedom

    (B) the South won a legal battle but stirred up Northern opposition

    (C) the North won a legal battle but stirred up Southern opposition

    (D) slavery became illegal

    (E) John Brown saved Kansas

11. James Buchanan was

    (A) the last president before the Civil War

    (B) the leader of the abolitionists

    (C) one of the founders of the Underground Railroad

    (D) opposed to the Dred Scott decision

    (E) a tough leader with lots of children

12. In his first election, Lincoln got

    (A) 60 percent of the vote

    (B) support from only two Southern states

    (C) less than 40 percent of the vote

    (D) respect even from those who opposed him

    (E) the majority vote in a two-party election

13. The *Monitor* and the *Merrimack* were

    (A) musicals that helped start the Civil War

    (B) two trains that raced between the North and the South

    (C) two early forms of television

    (D) the ships in the first battle between ironclads

    (E) the planes in the first battle between airplanes

14. Lincoln's Emancipation Proclamation

    (A) freed all the slaves

    (B) was in planning before Lincoln's election

    (C) followed the Battle of Gettysburg

    (D) showed the North was fighting against slavery

    (E) was politically unpopular in Europe

15. The Battle of Gettysburg

    (A) stopped the South in the Civil War

    (B) saved George Washington in the Revolution

    (C) began the American advance in the Mexican War

    (D) stopped the British in the War of 1812

    (E) was the only U.S. defeat in World War I

16. The U.S. Civil War saw

    (A) over 600,000 men die

    (B) slaves made free and economically equal

    (C) cotton die out as a crop

    (D) massive killing by angry slaves

    (E) a completely white Northern army free the slaves

17. One leader in the 1880s said that his opponents were "laying the foundation for their colossal fortunes on the bodies and souls of living men." He was probably a

    (A) labor leader

    (B) religious leader

    (C) conservative Republican

    (D) business leader

    (E) inventor

18. The main goal of Reconstruction was

    (A) building new governments and social help for the South

    (B) obtaining war reparations to repay Northern losses

    (C) rebuilding New Orleans following a hurricane

    (D) curing economic ills following the Great Depression

    (E) promoting home ownership through low-interest construction mortgages

19. The first states to give women the right to vote were predominately in the

    (A) North

    (B) South

    (C) East

    (D) Midwest

    (E) West

Go on to next page

20. The Ulysses S. Grant administration was marked by

    (A) great economic progress by freed slaves

    (B) opposition from war veterans

    (C) landslide victories by the Republicans

    (D) honest government by all parties

    (E) corruption by Grant appointees but not Grant

21. The Republicans won the Hayes election of 1872 by agreeing to

    (A) help the ex-slaves in the South

    (B) keep the tariffs low

    (C) expand the Homestead Act to the whole West

    (D) withdraw federal troops from the South

    (E) let the Democrats control the Senate

22. Frederick Douglass said, "Peace with the old master class has been war to the Negro. As one has risen, the other has fallen. The reaction has been sudden, marked, and violent." He was talking about

    (A) slavery before the Civil War

    (B) federal troops right after the Civil War

    (C) Sherman's march to the sea during the Civil War

    (D) the end of Reconstruction after the Civil War

    (E) the Spanish-American War

23. Unions in the late 1800s almost all fought for this change in the workplace, which didn't become standard until the 1900s.

    (A) equal rights for women

    (B) fair treatment of minorities

    (C) one-hour lunch breaks

    (D) the eight-hour workday

    (E) equal pay for blacks

24. Charles Darwin's theory of evolution was

    (A) immediately opposed by all major Christian churches

    (B) a challenge to everything most Americans believed

    (C) opposed by the government

    (D) endorsed by the old Confederacy

    (E) accepted by most scientists and many religious leaders

25. Most settlers in the West

    (A) got land for free from the government

    (B) bought their land from private companies or states

    (C) made plenty of money ranching

    (D) opposed the introduction of barbed wire

    (E) had enough water to grow almost anything

26. The national program that helped stop the bank panic during the Great Depression was the

    (A) Civilian Conservation Corps

    (B) Emergency Relief Administration

    (C) Twenty-first Amendment

    (D) Federal Deposit Insurance Corporation

    (E) Federal Housing Administration

27. The purpose of Jim Crow laws was to

    (A) help blacks get ahead

    (B) keep blacks in their place

    (C) allow the South to expand industry

    (D) force Crows opposed to the railroad to cooperate

    (E) honor the memory of a great American

28. The Pendleton Act of 1883

    (A) fought government corruption

    (B) allowed hiring of more government employees

    (C) regulated wool production

    (D) ended big money involvement in politics

    (E) helped farmers recover from the recession

29. The Populist Party

    (A) supported Grover Cleveland

    (B) elected only two presidents

    (C) saw many of its proposals enacted eventually

    (D) was against the eight-hour workday

    (E) campaigned in only one election

Go on to next page

30. The 30 years following the Civil War saw the U.S.

    (A) suffering from the Great Recession

    (B) going from destruction to being the manufacturing leader of the world

    (C) banning most people from immigrating

    (D) steadily helping blacks to prosper

    (E) fighting constant wars

31. Booker T. Washington, George Washington Carver, and W.E.B. Du Bois were

    (A) political leaders

    (B) union leaders

    (C) Civil War generals

    (D) black leaders

    (E) early recording artists

32. Which one of the following was an important leader in the women's movement?

    (A) Judith Ben-Hur

    (B) Emily Dickinson

    (C) Daisy Miller

    (D) Susan B. Anthony

    (E) Belle Starr

33. A leader said "the antelope have gone; the buffalo wallows are empty. . . .We are like birds with a broken wing." He was probably

    (A) an American Indian leader in 1700

    (B) an American Indian leader in 1800

    (C) a trapper in the 1820s

    (D) a frontiersman in the 1850s

    (E) an American Indian in the 1890s

34. When did historian Frederick Turner say that the American Western frontier was closed?

    (A) in 1790

    (B) in 1820

    (C) by 1850

    (D) after 1920

    (E) around 1890

35. *The Washington Post* editorialized that "The taste of Empire is in the mouth of the people even as the taste of blood is in the jungle." What period in American history was the *Post* describing?

    (A) the U.S. after World War II

    (B) the national mood during the Revolution

    (C) the North after the Civil War

    (D) the country before the Spanish American War

    (E) American opinion during World War I

36. The U.S. got Hawaii because

    (A) the Hawaiians didn't want it

    (B) sugar cane business interests grabbed the government

    (C) Hawaiian Queen Liliuokalani loved America

    (D) the British ceded it to the U.S. in return for Cuba

    (E) the U.S. defeated Hawaii in the Pacific War

37. The expansion of the United States to overseas territories like Puerto Rico and the Philippines was

    (A) supported by all Americans

    (B) opposed by radicals in the labor unions

    (C) supported by only a few conservatives

    (D) opposed by leaders like Mark Twain, Andrew Carnegie, and the presidents of Harvard and Stanford

    (E) so controversial that it led to a new government

38. Hippies, civil rights, Vietnam, and student demonstrations all became national movements in the

    (A) Roaring '20s

    (B) 1950s

    (C) 1960s

    (D) 1970s

    (E) 1980s

Go on to next page

39. Teddy Roosevelt was

    (A) the father of Franklin Roosevelt

    (B) a champion of conservation and business reform

    (C) a conservative Republican

    (D) a liberal Democrat

    (E) a hero of World War I

40. The Roosevelt Corollary to the Monroe Doctrine meant that

    (A) the U.S. would partner with any European intervention

    (B) the U.S. would intervene to fix South American problems instead of letting European powers in

    (C) the U.S. also protected Canada and Asia

    (D) The American Navy patrol would no longer exist

    (E) South American countries could do what they wanted

41. When women and working people didn't win their crusades for rights in the 1880s, they

    (A) mostly turned to violence

    (B) gave up for a while in the face of opposition

    (C) kept working so they would win someday

    (D) made a deal with big business and sold out

    (E) depended on politicians to get them some help

42. Early investigative reporters who publicized needed reforms were

    (A) spy-tellers

    (B) national enquirers

    (C) scandalrakers

    (D) muckrakers

    (E) troublemongers

43. The only president ever to resign from office was

    (A) Richard Nixon

    (B) Lyndon Johnson

    (C) Andrew Jackson

    (D) James Monroe

    (E) Jimmy Carter

44. Progressives who changed American politics in the early 1900s were

    (A) radical reformers

    (B) liberal Democrats

    (C) labor union leaders

    (D) middle class reformers

    (E) Republican conservatives

45. The first president to set aside large areas of land for national parks was

    (A) William Howard Taft

    (B) Abraham Lincoln

    (C) Franklin Roosevelt

    (D) Teddy Roosevelt

    (E) Ulysses S. Grant

46. In the 1800s, high tariffs were usually supported by

    (A) Republican businessmen

    (B) Democrats

    (C) Labor unions

    (D) British manufacturers

    (E) Farmers and ranchers

47. The Federal Reserve Act

    (A) created a national banking system without a national bank for the United States

    (B) gave the U.S. one government owned bank to run everything with central control of loans

    (C) reserved federal land for parks

    (D) saved valuable oil for time of war

    (E) reserved financial deposits to buy U.S. Bonds

Go on to next page

48. President Wilson's early policy toward World War I was to

    (A) try to get the U.S. involved early to help Britain

    (B) wait until Japan attacked the U.S. at Pearl Harbor

    (C) sell supplies to the Allies but not to Germany

    (D) help Germany until they caused a problem

    (E) try to stay out of the fight

49. During World War I, the goal of open treaties, freedom of the seas, national self-determination, and an international peace-keeping organization were all part of

    (A) Wilson's 14 Points

    (B) Britain's Royal War Aims

    (C) Germany's Imperial Policy

    (D) the Peace Proposals of France

    (E) the Republican legislative program

50. Which of these gave women the right to vote all over the United States?

    (A) the Nineteenth Amendment of 1920

    (B) the Twentieth Amendment of 1910

    (C) the Thirteenth Amendment of 1900

    (D) the Women's Suffrage Act of 1931

    (E) the Equal Rights Act of 1940

51. Who most strongly supported the Treaty of Versailles?

    (A) Germany

    (B) Russia

    (C) U.S. Republicans

    (D) isolationists

    (E) Woodrow Wilson

52. The movie *The Birth of a Nation* helped to popularize

    (A) the Ku Klux Klan

    (B) the Boy Scouts

    (C) fair treatment of blacks

    (D) immigration reform

    (E) the American Revolution

53. America's Roaring '20s were a time of

    (A) limited drinking

    (B) liberal government

    (C) fair treatment of immigrants

    (D) conservative presidents

    (E) prosperity for everybody

54. Who said that "the only thing we have to fear is fear itself — nameless, unreasoning, unjustified terror which paralyzes needed efforts to convert retreat into advance"?

    (A) Teddy Roosevelt

    (B) Woodrow Wilson

    (C) Franklin Roosevelt

    (D) Ronald Reagan

    (E) John F. Kennedy

55. The Scopes Monkey Trial concerned

    (A) the treatment of zoo animals

    (B) jungle exploration rights

    (C) the establishment of rights in hunting

    (D) teaching evolution

    (E) teaching radical politics

56. Republican President Hoover's response to the Great Depression was

    (A) a massive public relief program

    (B) to increase the size of the Army in an attempt to create jobs

    (C) to give money to businesses so that it would trickle down to the poor

    (D) to lower tariffs to make more jobs

    (E) to support veterans who marched on Washington

57. Franklin Roosevelt's program of relief, recovery, and reform was

    (A) the New Deal

    (B) the New Society

    (C) the Monroe Doctrine

    (D) the War on Poverty

    (E) America First

Go on to next page

58. The Federal Housing Administration (FHA) started under President

    (A) Lyndon Johnson

    (B) Andrew Johnson

    (C) Franklin Roosevelt

    (D) Herbert Hoover

    (E) George H.W. Bush

59. John Steinbeck's most famous book was

    (A) *Gone With the Wind*

    (B) *Little Women*

    (C) *The Grapes of Wrath*

    (D) *Uncle Tom's Cabin*

    (E) *Moby Dick*

60. The New Deal program that guaranteed small pensions for the elderly and the handicapped was the

    (A) Tennessee Valley Authority

    (B) National Recovery Administration

    (C) Emergency Relief Administration

    (D) Public Works Administration

    (E) Social Security Act

61. The Congress of Industrial Organizations (CIO) was a union dedicated to organizing

    (A) Congress

    (B) skilled workers

    (C) industry office workers

    (D) the part of an organization that had assembly line workers

    (E) whole industries including unskilled workers

62. What was the purpose of the Lend-Lease Bill?

    (A) to lend the leases on foreclosed houses to banks

    (B) to help the Allies in World War I

    (C) to make as much money as possible during war

    (D) to get supplies to the Allies in World War II

    (E) to ensure American neutrality

63. The Allies of the United States in World War II were

    (A) Britain and Russia

    (B) Britain and Japan

    (C) Japan and Germany

    (D) France and Italy

    (E) Russia and Italy

64. The last war the U.S. Army fought in which white troops were segregated from black troops was

    (A) World War I

    (B) the Civil War

    (C) World War II

    (D) the Korean War

    (E) the Spanish-American War

65. Up until 1944, almost all of the ground fighting against the Germans in Europe was done by the

    (A) British

    (B) Italians

    (C) Americans

    (D) Russians

    (E) French

66. The form of government in shortest supply in the world before World War II was

    (A) democracy

    (B) dictatorship

    (C) monarchy

    (D) colonialism

    (E) military control

67. The popular name for the legislation passed during World War II to help returning servicemen was the

    (A) Adjustment Act

    (B) Soldier's Pension

    (C) GI Bill

    (D) Bonus March

    (E) Victory Bond

Go on to next page

68. The name that Russia and its associated countries went by during their Communist period was

(A) Mother Russia

(B) the Union of Soviet Socialist Republics (U.S.S.R.)

(C) the People's Republic of Soviet Eurasia

(D) Bolshevik Workers Republic

(E) Russian Confederation of States

69. The United Nations and the International Monetary Fund started at the end of

(A) the Korean War

(B) the War between the States

(C) World War I

(D) World War II

(E) the Cold War

70. The financial assistance that helped Europe recover after World War II was the

(A) Truman Doctrine

(B) Marshall Plan

(C) Lend-Lease Bill

(D) Ford Foundation

(E) Nuremberg Federation

71. The Supreme Court decision in Brown v. Board of Education helped

(A) fund women's athletics

(B) provide college loans to poor people

(C) end segregation in education

(D) soldiers get a college education

(E) expand schools in the West

72. The United States fought Communist troops in

(A) Korea and Vietnam

(B) Vietnam and Japan

(C) Korea and Europe

(D) Vietnam and the Middle East

(E) the first Gulf War

73. The president who said he was against government but spent enough money to triple the national debt was

(A) John F. Kennedy

(B) Woodrow Wilson

(C) Ronald Reagan

(D) Bill Clinton

(E) Dwight Eisenhower

74. The president who tried to start the Great Society and sent hundreds of thousands of troops into Vietnam was

(A) Andrew Johnson

(B) Lyndon Johnson

(C) John F. Kennedy

(D) Jimmy Carter

(E) Dwight Eisenhower

75. "Ask not what your country can do for you; ask what you can do for your country." These words are from a speech by

(A) John F. Kennedy

(B) George W. Bush

(C) Bill Clinton

(D) Grover Cleveland

(E) Lyndon Johnson

76. A standoff between the Soviet Union and the United States in 1962 that could have led to nuclear war was

(A) the Panama Canal Showdown

(B) the Congo War

(C) the Berlin Airlift

(D) the Italian Bomber Crisis

(E) the Cuban Missile Crisis

77. What were the Southern Christian Leadership Conference and the Student Nonviolent Coordinating Committee?

(A) Great Awakening congregations

(B) peace movements in the 1970s

(C) teaching commissions for ministers

(D) civil rights organizations

(E) women's rights organizations

Go on to next page

78. Gerald Ford became president after

    (A) Richard Nixon resigned over the Watergate scandal

    (B) John F. Kennedy was shot

    (C) William Van Burien died in office

    (D) William Howard Taft chose him as vice president

    (E) a hard-fought election with Jimmy Carter

79. The Supreme Court case of Engel v. Vitale said that

    (A) abortion is legal in the U.S.

    (B) officials can't require prayers in school

    (C) officers must read arrested suspects their rights

    (D) Federal law supersedes state law

    (E) women must be granted Title IX rights

80. The World Trade Organization has worked to

    (A) lower tariffs

    (B) promote products

    (C) raise tariffs to protect developing nations

    (D) trade the United Nations for another world organization

    (E) restrict trade to healthy products

STOP

DO NOT TURN THE PAGE UNTIL TOLD TO DO SO.
DO NOT RETURN TO A PREVIOUS TEST.

Section II: Free-Response Questions

In this section, you'll take on the DBQ in Part A and then keep rolling through two regular essays in Parts B and C.

Part A: Document-Based Question

Planning Time: 15 minutes

Suggested Writing Time: 45 minutes

Percent of Section II score: 45

1. How did World War II change the lives of men and women in the United States? Discuss the role of social and economic trends as well as the changing nature of the U.S. political situation. Use the documents and your knowledge of the time period in writing your response.

Document A

Source: Jerome B. Cohen, *Japan's Economy in War and Reconstruction* (1949) p 354

Real Value Consumer Spending

	1937	1939	1940	1941	1942	1943	1944	1945
Japan	100	107	109	111	108	99	93	78
Germany	100	108	117	108	105	95	94	85
USA	100	96	103	108	116	115	118	122

Document B

Source: Letter home from a U.S. soldier, 1945

I think I'm well qualified to report that the Yank, 1943 version, is doing a good job in upholding the traditions of his father and his grandfather and all who came before him. His few weaknesses are a source of pride rather than otherwise. He occasionally gets drunk, but that's because he loves his home and family and is terrifically lonely for both. He's slow to anger, but when he does get mad, he fights like hell. He's quick to forgive — the picture of him giving his candy ration to Italian kids is not a publicity gag. Sometimes he gets cheated, but it's because he has a deep faith in human nature. I think he's the best there is.

We could have done very nicely without this war, but I do think it has given us a new sense of values which will go a long way in canceling any future wars.

Go on to next page

Document C

Source: Letter from the front

First is the absolute futility of war. Seen at close range, it becomes so brutal and stupid that we have to rub our eyes to believe the world is capable of it.

A second impression is the fundamental similarity of the peoples of the United Nations. I've lived and worked with British, French, Australian, South African, New Zealand, Polish, and Belgian soldiers to name a few. I'm convinced that we all seek the same general sort of life. We criticize one another for our little individual eccentricities; each of us thinks his is the best nation; but fundamentally we differ little. When this war is won, we must remember only the fundamentals and get together in a big way.

A third impression is that of America's own capabilities. London, Algiers, Paris, Rome, Florence, Marseilles, and every other city and town in every liberated country teeming with American traffic. Huge depots of American supplies, throngs of American men everywhere. If we can put forth one half the effort for peace that we've extended in this war, because it was necessary, there should never be need for another war. We must realize that peace, now, is just as necessary as the war has been.

I'm now living in a half-wrecked miner's house. There's snow and there's cold....

Document D

Source: War Bonds, U.S. Treasury Department, 1942

Go on to next page

Document E

Source: Map of Japanese Internment Camps

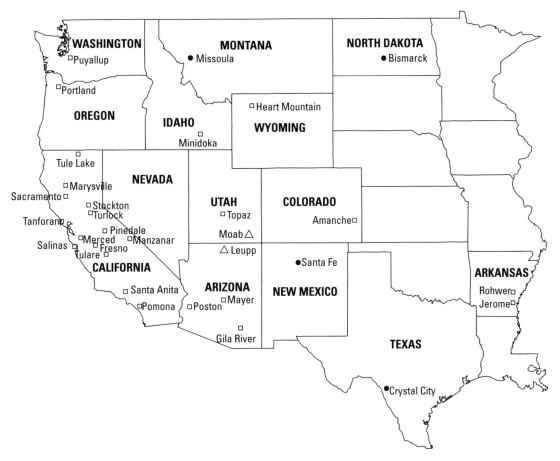

Document F

Source: World War II Experiences of a Child

I wrote letters to servicemen on tissue-thin V-mail paper that folded into a self envelope. My friends and I saved tinfoil from packages and crimped it around growing balls of foil to turn in to help the war effort. Every week at school we purchased a ten-cent War Savings Stamp and glued it into our war stamp book until we had enough to purchase an $18 War Bond which matured years later for $25. Meat and gasoline were rationed and eggs were difficult to obtain. No matter how much money you had you could only purchase the amounts for which you had unused ration stamps. People walked, took public transportation, and car-pooled. During air raid drills at elementary school we sat on the floor in the halls and sang patriotic songs

Go on to next page

Document G

Source: U.S. Office of War Information, 1943

Document H

Source: *World War II News*

Food worst problem; costs up, but pay up more

There may not be the abundance of food at home today that there was a year ago, but there is plenty to go around and although prices have risen wages have gone ahead of them. Machinery already is in motion, both governmental and private, to see that men get jobs as soon as they take off their uniforms.

People are eating differently, that's all: less meat and more of other items. Restaurants have introduced meatless days; the Waldorf in New York, for instance, has three a week. Except for shoes — which are limited to three pairs a year for each person — clothes rationing is not in sight. Candy is still plentiful, and the guy with a thirst still can slake it with all the beer he wants.

Whatever complaints are heard are directed mostly at the lack of gasoline. With one car to every four and a half people, Americans had all but forgotten how to walk. Now they're obliged to learn all over again. The Government is strict about the ban on pleasure driving. Agents check the race tracks and baseball stadiums for cars, and even the vicinity of movie houses. The only large-scale chiseling evident has been the black market in food, which the Government is taking drastic steps to wipe out.

Go on to next page

Document I

Source: GI Bill Statistics

To be eligible for GI Bill education benefits, a World War II veteran had to serve 90 days or more after September 16, 1940.

In the peak year of 1947, veterans accounted for 49 percent of college enrollment. Mortgages for GI's could cover all costs. Out of a veteran population of 15,440,000, some 7.8 million were trained, including:

- 2,230,000 in college (⅛ of all returning veterans entered college)

- 3,480,000 in other schools

- 1,400,000 in on-job training

- 690,000 in farm training

- College enrollment in millions: 1939 = 1.5, 1949 = 2.6, 1969 = 8.0, 1989 = 13.5, 2005 = 18.5 million

- Number of Americans who owned their own homes: pre-War = 1 in 3, post-War = 2 in 3.

Part B and Part C

Total Planning and Writing Time: 70 minutes

Percent of Section II score: 55

Part B

Choose ONE question from this part.

2. In what manner did the political climate of the U.S. change from the 1890s to the 1910s? Discuss these changes with regard to TWO of the following:

    Public opinion

    Business

    Environment

    International policy

3. Explain the participation of the United States in World War I and its consequences. In your explanation, include TWO of the following topics:

    Military outcomes

    Impact on the United States

    Impact on other countries

    International trade

Part C

Choose ONE question from this part.

4. Outline the causes and effects of the Great Depression in TWO of the following periods:

    1924–1929

    1930–1934

    1935–1939

    1940–1945

5. Conservative presidents sometimes take progressive steps. Discuss the contributions of TWO of the following presidents to the modern United States:

    Dwight D. Eisenhower (1952–1960)

    Richard M. Nixon (1969–1974)

    Ronald Reagan (1980–1988)

    George H. W. Bush (1988–1992)

Chapter 25

The Answers to Practice Test 2

*J*ust like with Practice Test 1 (Chapters 22 and 23), when you get through with the multiple-choice questions in the first half of Practice Test 2, don't come running for the answer sheet in this chapter. No peeking until the whole practice test is done! If you haven't finished Practice Test 2, stop reading this chapter *right now* and go back to Chapter 24! Keep moving on through the DBQ and regular essays, just like the test was the real thing. Pretty soon, it *will* be.

For general tips about scoring and how to handle questions, see Chapters 4, 5, and 6.

Section 1: Multiple-Choice

1. **(B).** It's the cotton. But, as it turned out, Britain was willing to go without a few shirts to avoid helping slavery.

2. **(B).** They were fighting for their Southern white pride against the Yankees.

3. **(A).** Hatred and fear of the slave power overcame the profit motive.

4. **(B).** Slaves sometimes fought against an overwhelmingly brutal system.

5. **(C).** If you don't know about *Uncle Tom's Cabin,* maybe you haven't been paying close enough attention. The other answers are smart-aleck choices.

6. **(B).** The Spanish were all about finding gold, but they never looked along the American River in their former possession of California.

7. **(C).** *Popular sovereignty* actually means that the people rule, but the most important issue folks were arguing about before the Civil War was to keep or free slaves.

8. **(D).** With the Fugitive Slave Act, the North had to help the South recapture slaves, something most of the North hated.

9. **(A).** John Brown was an extremely militant abolitionist, certainly no compromiser or diplomat.

10. **(B).** This is an example of a *wrong trend* question. In wrong trend questions, all of the answers except the correct one follow one pattern. Because only one answer can be right, if you can find one choice that shows a different trend, it's often correct. Of course, you have to know something about history to spot a wrong trend.

11. **(A).** Buchanan may have done better not to show up at all.

12. **(C).** Lincoln barely slipped into office.

13. **(D).** This is an example of a question you can *logic out.* Toss out the unimportant choices: musicals, train races, TV. That leaves airplanes and ships, which gives you a pretty good shot at guessing correctly even if you don't remember the *Monitor* and the *Merrimack.*

14. **(D).** Sometimes it's important to stand for principle.

15. **(A).** Gettysburg is one of the most famous battles in the Civil War, largely because the North's victory was a huge turning point in the conflict.

16. **(A).** It took a lot of deaths to free the slaves.

17. **(A).** A labor leader opposes fortunes that rob workers.

18. **(A).** Answers (C), (D), and (E) are from the wrong time period, and the North never asked that the South pay it back. That leaves (A).

19. **(E).** Tough cowboys were nice to women.

20. **(E).** Borderline-smart-aleck wrong answers: the freed slaves never made great economic progress, no one had landslide victories in the late 1800s, and completely honest government was rare.

21. **(D).** Withdrawing the federal troops that were protecting the blacks was the deal the Republicans made to hang on to power.

22. **(D).** When occupying troops withdraw, the people they've been protecting suffer.

23. **(D).** If you like the eight-hour workday, thank the unions.

24. **(E).** Most scientists, religious organizations, and Christians accepted Darwin's theory as just another way God may work in the world. A minority became upset and believed Darwin's theory threatened their faith.

25. **(B).** Land in the West wasn't cheap or easy to work.

26. **(D).** The Federal Deposit Insurance Corporation (FDIC) insured individual deposits and gave people the confidence to leave their money in the bank.

27. **(B).** Jim Crow was the name of a popular minstrel character. The Jim Crow laws restricted the rights of black people.

28. **(A).** The Pendleton Act cleaned up most corruption in government hiring, leaving only fundraising as a form of shady influence.

29. **(C).** The Populists never won a battle, but they eventually won the war.

30. **(B).** The industrial states were doing very well financially, thank you.

31. **(D).** You need to know basic background information about minorities.

32. **(D).** You also need to know the high points of the women's rights movement.

33. **(E).** It took 400 years from the landing of Columbus until the last American Indians lost their right to roam a natural world.

34. **(E).** The Americans finished settling the West around 1890.

35. **(D).** The U.S. saw how much fun England was having and wanted some of the world for itself. The Spanish-American War was America's attempt to build a small empire and "save" Spanish colonies by taking them over.

36. **(B).** It was a business agreement that the Hawaiians didn't fight.

37. **(D).** Like lots of people, these leaders thought loving freedom and building empires didn't work together.

38. **(C).** These struggles and a lot more started in the 1960s. Note that this question is out of chronological order; the real AP will have the multiple-choice time periods completely scrambled.

39. **(B).** Teddy Roosevelt was a Progressive Republican.

40. **(B).** Teddy said that the U.S. would keep Latin America tidy — no Europeans allowed.

41. **(C).** Women and working people never gave up.

42. **(D).** They raked up the muck of scandal so everyone could live in a cleaner barnyard.

43. **(A).** It was "Tricky Dick" Nixon. This is another out-of-time-order question to keep your mind flexible.

44. **(D).** The Progressives were as middle class as a mortgage payment.

45. **(D).** Teddy Roosevelt started the magnificent legacy of national parks.

46. **(A).** Republicans were in favor of the kind of government that helped them make money.

47. **(A).** The Fed doesn't have cute checks or credit cards, but it moves the money behind them. The last three answer choices are _red herrings_ designed to draw you off the path.

48. **(E).** Wilson was more evenhanded before World War I than Roosevelt was before World War II. Wilson really thought the U.S. could stay neutral; Roosevelt in his time didn't believe that.

49. **(A).** Wilson had a dream of peace called the 14 Points.

50. **(A).** Women got the right to vote nationally after World War I.

51. **(E).** Wilson got what he could in the treaty, but the world wasn't ready to police international peace.

52. **(A).** This good entertainment brought back a bad nightmare.

53. **(D).** The Republican presidents of the 1920s did as little as possible.

54. **(C).** FDR's big line couldn't have come at a better time.

55. **(D).** You have to know about evolution. All the other answer choices are red herrings.

56. **(C).** Hoover never met a business he didn't like.

57. **(A).** FDR was the real deal, and that meant a New Deal.

58. **(C).** If an agency has as an acronym, chances are fair it started with FDR.

59. **(C).** You don't need to be a culture vulture, but you should know the literary milestones.

60. **(E).** Despite early Republican efforts to kill it, Social Security is still very much part of the plans of most elderly people.

61. **(E).** The CIO formed to represent whole industries, including often-overlooked unskilled and minority workers.

62. **(D).** Beware the red herrings. If you know the historical background, you know the answer is supplies in World War II.

63. **(A).** Every other answer choice contains at least one enemy.

64. **(C).** After World War II, the U.S. woke up to the fact that freedom means integration.

65. **(D).** Russia did the vast majority of the European ground fighting in World War II.

66. **(A).** Before World War II, you could count the real democracies of the world on one hand.

67. **(C).** The bill helped change life in America.

68. **(B).** Maybe you've heard the shortened version of that name — the Soviet Union. Or maybe you've heard the Beatles' song "Back in the U.S.S.R."

69. **(D).** After World War II, the world started to go international with organizations like the United Nations and the IMF. Nobody wanted to see World War III.

70. **(B).** The Marshall Plan _marshaled_ the forces of good to help battered Europe.

71. **(C).** Brown v. Board said separate isn't equal.

72. **(A).** The U.S. jumped into the middle of two civil wars because one side was Communist.

73. **(C).** Reagan's the one.

74. **(B).** LBJ all the way.

75. **(A).** Idealism from John F. Kennedy.

76. **(E).** Some of the other answer choices are fake; the ones that did happen weren't close to 1962.

77. **(D).** Know your social movements.

78. **(A).** Ford had a bad act to follow.

79. **(B).** The First Amendment means officials can't require prayer in schools.

80. **(A).** The WTO is all about getting the world to trade, trade, trade, which is what lower tariffs promote.

Section 11: Free-Response Questions

The following sections give you sample information that you can utilize for your practice essays. Chapter 5 contains detailed guidance on how to write the DBQ response, and Chapter 6 gives you the lowdown on tackling the regular essays.

Part A: Document-Based Question

The DBQ asks you to discuss how WWII changed American life socially, economically, and politically. The following list gives you some sample PES facts you may want to include in your essay:

- When World War II started, civilian industry changed to wartime production.
- Standardization of wartime production led to more job opportunities for less-skilled workers.
- With more work available, consumer spending went up 20 percent even though production was down.
- People had to have ration coupons *and* money to buy most commodities. Gas limits were three gallons per week.
- War production was half of the economy. The U.S. outproduced all of its enemies put together.
- By the end of the war, everybody was paying federal income tax. Before the war, only 10 percent of the people paid the tax.
- Mexican workers replaced farmers off to war. Women replaced men on the assembly lines.
- Pay went up; unions organized but mostly didn't strike. The CIO fought racism and sexism in union ranks.
- World War II ended the Depression, and almost everybody had a job
- Women worked as Rosie the Riveter in wartime industry and as *government girls* in federal agencies.
- A baby boom started right after the war; births went up by 30 percent.
- The federal Fair Employment Practices Committee was the most important aid up to that time for fair treatment of blacks and women on the job.

✔ Over 120,000 Japanese Americans were interned in camps.

✔ Celebrities from Humphrey Bogart to Donald Duck supported the war effort.

✔ The United States was really united to fight the good war.

Material (such as the following points) from at least some of the provided documents should show up in your DBQ essay, with the document letters in brackets.

✔ **A:** Starting at an equalized norm, the chart shows how the war benefited un-bombed U.S. consumers but hurt their enemies.

✔ **B:** This document shows new internationalism.

✔ **C:** Internationalism and the U.S. were in the world to stay.

✔ **D:** This poster shows the threat to U.S. families from the Nazis. The solution to this threat was to buy War Bonds to help finance the war effort.

✔ **E:** Japanese internment camps were all over the West, showing lingering suspicion of foreigners.

✔ **F:** Careful living on the home front meant the whole country was working together to support the armed forces in the field.

✔ **G:** This poster shows the allies working together as a powerful cannon blasting the enemy.

✔ **H:** This document shows home front sacrifices but also optimism that problems are solvable.

✔ **I:** Wounds would slowly heal, and opportunities grew with victory.

✔ **J:** The GI Bill and changes in the economy in general were a tremendous boost for getting ahead in the new postwar United States.

Part B and Part C

In this section, I outline some points you may want to include in your essays over the prompts in Parts B and C. You don't have to use all of these specific points, but make sure you have reasonable PES proof to support your thesis and analysis.

2. Changes from the 1890s to the 1910s

Public opinion: Literacy improved, and for the first time the public started to have informed opinions based on widespread reading. Newspapers and magazines in the 1900s started to feature muckraker exposés of scandals in housing, government, and food manufacturing.

Business: Teddy Roosevelt and the presidents who followed him broke up big businesses that used their corporate power to cheat consumers. Businesses continued to expand on the strength of product innovation rather than pure power. Some big businessmen like Andrew Carnegie and John D. Rockefeller gave money for the public good.

Environment: With the frontier closed, Teddy Roosevelt began the creation of a national system of public parks that became the model for the U.S. and the world.

International policy: The U.S. asserted itself more in world affairs as the 1890s drew to a close, with the Spanish-American War and increased U.S. interests in Asia.

3. U.S. participation in World War I

Military outcomes: The U.S. got to France just in time to keep the Germans from winning. Although only small numbers of U.S. troops got into the fighting, they encouraged the Allies and discouraged the Germans into surrendering. Because no international policing organization existed, the Germans rearmed for World War II.

Impact on the United States: Despite President Wilson's idealistic 14 Points program for world peace, the U.S. withdrew into its isolationist shell after the war. Politicians refused to support Wilson's plan for the League of Nations. The U.S. had been a hero, but came away more determined than ever to stick to its own business.

Impact on other countries: Britain and France were so worn out that they were willing to sell out most of Europe to Germany to avoid another war. Russia's defeat in World War I paved the way for a Communist government. Hitler rose to save an impoverished Germany, which thought it had been stabbed in the back by giving up in World War I just when it had almost won. World War II was really World War I with a recess.

International trade: The U.S. never got paid for supplies sent to the Allies in World War I. When the U.S. economy collapsed at the end of the 1920s, the country slapped a record-high tariff on trade, which shut off any chance of working together with other nations to solve world economic problems.

4. Causes and effects of the Great Depression

1924 through 1929: Conservative Republican presidents let business do what it wanted. The stock market boomed; no one could see an end in sight for the new U.S. economy, which was based on consumer debt and high consumer spending. Republicans raised the tariff, making products more expensive. When the stock market crashed on Black Tuesday in 1929, it was the end of a long, profitable ride.

1930 through 1934: Republican President Hoover's response to the crash was the Smoot-Hawley Tariff, the highest peacetime import taxes in U.S. history. Unemployment went from 9 percent in 1930 to 16 percent in 1931 and 25 percent in 1933. Following Republican trickle-down theory, Hoover started the Reconstruction Finance Corporation, which opponents called the *millionaires' welfare*. Democratic President Franklin Roosevelt took over in 1933 and started passing New Deal programs to help ordinary people.

1935 through 1939: New Deal programs like the Federal Deposit Insurance Corporation, the Civilian Conservation Corps, the Federal Emergency Relief Administration, and the Works Administrations started to create jobs and restore hope. Other federal initiatives included TVA, FHA, SEC, NRA, and AAA. The greatest benefit for elderly people was the passage of Social Security in 1935.

1940 through 1945: New Deal programs cut unemployment in half from 25 percent to 12 percent. World War II took care of the rest of the Great Depression — by 1943, unemployment was almost nonexistent. Due in part to the economic safety net built by the Roosevelt administration, the U.S. came out of the War ready for further growth.

5. Conservative presidents take Progressive steps

Dwight Eisenhower: Eisenhower reluctantly used federal troops to enforce the school integration called for by Brown v. Board of Education. He set up a Civil Rights Commission to investigate discrimination. Eisenhower started the nationwide interstate highway system. Upon leaving office, he warned against the growing power of the military-industrial complex.

Richard Nixon: Nixon expanded welfare, Medicaid for the poor, and food stamps for the hungry. He created a new Supplemental Security Income program (SSI) for the disabled. Nixon started the Environmental Protection Agency, the Clean Air Act, and the Endangered Species Act.

Ronald Reagan: Reagan helped end the Cold War by continuing the long-established policies of opposition to Communist expansion that had been popular with both Democratic and Republican presidents before him. Reagan's tax cuts benefited the rich and didn't help the economy. He appointed the first woman to the Supreme Court and remained sunny and optimistic in troubled times.

George H. W. Bush: The elder Bush was president when the Berlin Wall fell, signaling the end of Communism as a major movement. He signed the START II treaty to limit nuclear weapons. Bush successfully kicked the invading Iraqis out of neighboring Kuwait but left Saddam Hussein in power. He also signed the Americans with Disabilities Act, which prohibited discrimination against the disabled.

Part VI

The Part of Tens

The 5th Wave   By Rich Tennant

THE JUSTICES RULE ON
PAPER vs SCISSORS vs STONE

© RICHTENNANT

In this part...

Kick back, but not too far. These Part of Tens chapters contain fun information, but they can actually help you on the Big Test. The AP U.S. History exam is going to have questions on political, economic, and social events, so remember your PES dispenser. The following chapters contain the back story on the big-time happenings and unstoppable trends that still shape U.S. history. Enjoy, and may they serve you well on your road to test success!

Chapter 26

Ten Monster Events the AP Wants You to Know

In This Chapter

▶ Checking out the background of the big happenings

▶ Seeing the social and economic factors behind the key political events

▶ Taking in the big picture around landmark times

*O*bviously, the AP Test Inquisitors want you to know the grand picture of U.S. history, but every history picture consists of little pixels usually known as facts. Trends are important, but events are the proof that trends have arrived, the champagne-cork pop after years of social and economic ferment. Chapters 7 through 21 give you all the gory details that may crop up on the test, but here I give you a quick rundown and reminder of all the *main events* that contain those details.

Obviously you don't want to go confusing Andrew Jackson with Michael Jackson. Beyond that, you'd be wise to have the big events in order, complete with a few fun facts to drop into essays and use as a shield to avoid picking a bonehead multiple choice. Refer to this chapter often if you need to brush-up on which event happened when.

Next Stop, America: Setting Up the Colonies

It wasn't just "let's get a bunch of immigrants together and play house." Putting together the American colonies took time, effort, and some often-desperate action. The time from Columbus to the Revolution is almost 100 years longer than the time that has passed from the Revolution until now. Here's the sequence of events you need to remember from this period:

✔ The American Indians were doing just fine, thank you, without all that European culture for 10,000 years before Columbus. You get a pass on most of those 10,000 years because the New World Indians were too busy inventing the Aztec, Mayan, and Incan empires in Mesoamerica to write much down.

✔ The Spanish jaunted around Mexico and south looking for treasure and setting up colonies in the 1500s.

✔ By 1607, the British got around to founding Jamestown; the Pilgrims got blown off course and started New England a few years later. It was no party; half the colonists at both Jamestown and Plymouth died in the first six months.

✔ The colonists got early help from the American Indians:

- The Pilgrims were greeted by Tisquantum, an American Indian they called Squanto, who incredibly enough had already been to Europe twice with passing explorers and spoke fluent English. *Tisquantum* (1621) taught the Pilgrims how to catch fish and build warmer houses.

- In Jamestown, the settlers had the help of Pocahontas, who not only brought food but also actually married Englishman John Rolfe. The wives of Presidents Woodrow Wilson and Ronald Reagan were her descendents.

- The American Indians shared gold, silver, potatoes, tomatoes, corn, squash, and tobacco — products that helped Europe become rich and powerful after their discovery of the New World.

✔ When the American Indians realized that the Europeans were more like hungry wolves than friendly dogs, they fought back in the mid-1600s. Too late; the colonists managed to hang on through *King Philip's War* (1675) in New England and similar battles in Virginia and New York.

Colonizing for Fun and Profit

Having an understandably short sense of humor about having their land taken away, the American Indians kept fighting when they could against increasingly overwhelming odds for another 200 years. With native attacks on the back burner during the late 1600s, colonies started popping up all along the Atlantic coast. You need to know details about the earliest (not all 13) colonies:

✔ Massachusetts was home to the Pilgrims and Puritans who came for religious freedom for themselves, but kicked out spirit-filled freethinkers like Roger Williams and Anne Hutchinson.

✔ Roger Williams then went on to found the tolerant, freethinking colony of Rhode Island.

✔ Maryland was a haven for Catholics, but Protestants were welcome too. Maybe too welcome, because Protestants in some Maryland towns burned Catholic churches. It took years, but toleration made a comeback.

✔ William Penn founded Pennsylvania on freedom for everybody and fair treatment of the American Indians. Modest William was a little embarrassed that the king named the whole woodland or *silvania* for Penn, but that didn't stop him from founding the city of Philadelphia (brotherly love) or proposing a uniting of the colonial states and even a European union. Outside of New England, most colonists came from places other than England like Scotland, Germany, and Wales.

✔ Meanwhile, Virginia prospered with slaves and tobacco. Pocahontas' husband John Rolfe got the business rolling by growing good leaf at Jamestown, and despite a warning from King James himself that smoking was "dangerous to the Lungs," tobacco proved to be an addictive money-maker. Big tobacco bucks got the Southern colonies addicted to slavery.

By 1700, the American colonies held about 300,000 people; 25,000 of them were slaves. The first Great Awakening of the 1730s and 1740s lead to more religious devotion and communication between settlements. Talk turned toward freedom, covered in the next section.

Getting Ready for a Revolution

By the 1760s, the 13 colonies were almost 2 million people strong and feeling like big dudes. They'd helped the regular army from back home in Britain kick some French and American Indian butt in the war by that same name that ended in 1763. Now it seemed time for some nice new land over the mountains.

Oh, wait a minute; the British Parliament had just declared that land closed to settlement in the Proclamation of 1763. Well, at least they could play cards. Oops, no again: Parliament had put the Stamp Act of 1765 on cards, documents, and even newspapers. How about some tea? Nope, Parliament was messing with the tea prices to favor their own investors. America may have put up with King George's bad wigs and wacky behavior, but in this dark time before coffee shops on every corner, they weren't going to put up with no tea. Who did these Parliament guys think they were?

The Boston Tea Party was a fun answer to British lawmaking without Colonial representation. Colonists thinly disguised as American Indians boarded three British ships and efficiently dumped 45 tons of tea overboard, turning Boston harbor into the world's biggest teapot. They didn't damage the ships, but tea washed up on shore for weeks. That gave Parliament something to think about. Even better, another tea ship ran aground at Provincetown. The tea was quickly liberated and reached Boston tea cups within days. What could be better than boycotting tea and getting to drink it anyway?

Parliament then passed the Intolerable Acts in 1774 to punish the citizens of Boston by closing down their vital harbor. The British surged in a lot more troops and push came to shove at Lexington and Concord. Colonial minutemen responded to what the British called an antiterrorist sweep by shooting up British regulars. Because everybody was fighting anyway, the young and determined Congress had 33-year-old Thomas Jefferson write the Declaration of Independence in 1776. After the battle of Saratoga proved that the backwoods Americans could beat the British army, the French happily piled on to fight their traditional British foes.

 George Washington never won a major battle, but he stayed in the field for six long years, usually without proper supplies or political support and with a desertion rate of 20 percent per year.

Finally the British decided to take a break from the conflict near the lovely seashore in Yorktown under the protective guns of their mighty navy. Surprise, the British navy wasn't there, and the French and Americans got the British cornered. Washington finally got the big win he deserved, and it was time for peace and independence.

U.S. Lite: The Confederation Leads to a Keeper Constitution

The United States complained and revolted against British rule, but what to do about their own government? The first try was the Articles of Confederation in 1777 (not to be confused with the Robert E. Lee-type Confederacy — that came along 84 years later with the Civil War). The Articles called for more voluntary cooperation than most people can muster. The federal government had to politely ask the states for money because it had no power to tax on its own. Each state got one vote in Congress, and it took 9 of the 13 votes to pass any laws. With this weak government, the organization of the territory from Ohio north and west under the Northwest Ordinance of 1787 is amazing.

In the same year, with much wrangling and a few drinks, Congress produced the U.S. Constitution, under which the nation is still governed. Drinking didn't get in the way of political progress. At that time, the average U.S. male had about 600 drinks a year — the first thing most of the Congressmen did after they passed the Constitution was to adjourn to the nearest tavern. A few years later, President Washington and Alexander Hamilton personally led a large army into Pennsylvania to put down the Whiskey Rebellion — not to get rid of whiskey, but to try to enforce a tax on this popular form of booze. Somehow, the nation sobered up enough to get organized.

The addition of the Bill of Rights (the first ten amendments to the Constitution) in 1791 strengthened the Constitution even further. Since then, the U.S. has made only 17 additional Amendment changes in more than 200 years. It took years of tough debate and friendly drinking to finish the original Constitution, but the results have lasted longer than any barroom promise in history.

Andy Jackson, Democracy, and Manifest Destiny

Although plenty of drinking and tobacco-chewing went on in the early 1800s, politics was more of a gentlemen's game. The nation had been through an early attack on civil liberties in the Alien and Sedition Acts of 1798 and was settling down to enjoy its freedom.

European powers provided pesky challenges that resulted in the War of 1812, but for the most part the new United States was an increasingly prosperous one-party country. The time from 1815 to 1824 was even called the Era of Good Feelings.

Early 1800s U.S. democracy had one little catch: Only white males who owned a house or a farm could vote. Even people who could vote didn't always bother; many figured the system would take care of itself.

All that changed with the contested election of John Quincy Adams in 1824. This was the first election in which all white males in most states got to vote whether they owned property or not. In a four-way race, war hero Andrew Jackson got the most votes, but John Quincy Adams got to be President because he made a deal with the other losers. That ticked off Jackson and his many followers, and they came back in force for the next election.

Jackson was president for eight years, and the several of the subsequent presidents — Martin Van Buren, John Tyler, and James Polk — were all Jackson followers.

Jacksonian democracy meant the end of rich guys controlling a central Bank of the United States. It also meant moving the American Indians out to make way for Manifest Destiny and westward expansion. Jackson invited ordinary people to be part of government, rewarding his friends with government jobs (through the spoils system) and pushing for full democracy for everyone (as long as they were white males). Jackson kept the government out of business because he thought that most of the time the government just ended up helping rich people.

My Rules or I'm Leaving: The Long Prequel to the Civil War

The amazing thing wasn't that the United States eventually became temporarily disunited by the Civil War; it was that the slavery time bomb took so long to blow up. The U.S. abolished the importation of slaves in 1808, only a few months after Britain's moral conversion, which was portrayed in the film *Amazing Grace*. All northern U.S. states and a surprising number of southern plantation owners freed their slaves after the Revolution.

However, the invention of the cotton gin made slavery so profitable that it spread throughout the South in the first half of the 1800s, despite the intention of many of the Revolutionary Founding Fathers to bring it to an early end. North and South then started a long stretch of legal wrangling over slavery:

- The first major bills passed under the early Confederation outlawed slavery in the new Northwest Ordinance of 1787.

- The Missouri Compromise, also known as the Compromise of 1820, drew the Mason-Dixon line between slave and free states; the Compromise of 1850 later extended the Mason-Dixon line out west.

- The Kansas-Nebraska Act of 1854 weakened the earlier compromises, and the 1857 Dred Scott decision by the Southern-controlled Supreme Court blew all the compromises away.

While the South got rich from slavery, the years of compromise had given the North time to get industrialized and relatively united in opposition to slavery. With the election of Abe Lincoln in 1860, it was showdown time.

If you'd been dropped into a random house in the United States in 1860, you'd have had about a 1 in 12 chance of being in a slave owning family. Of course, all the slave holding families were down South; if you had dropped into a random life in the South, you'd have had a one in three chance of being a slave. Slaves never got paid, worked from dawn to dusk, and could be whipped, sexually exploited, or even killed at the whim of their owners.

Eventually, people who weren't making money off the work of slaves (and even a few people who were) couldn't stand to see the evil system continue. The United States fought through the most horrible war in its history to get honest with the proposition that "all men are created equal."

America Fighting Itself: Civil War Basics

When the compromises fell apart in the late 1850s, the South struck with the Dred Scott decision, essentially allowing slavery anywhere in the United States. The North had been reading *Uncle Tom's Cabin* and for the first time had a pretty good picture of just how medieval Southern slavery could be.

Plus, the North was all uptight that the South may just march north with a factory's worth of slaves and take the North's paid jobs away. The South was worried that John Brown's botched raid on Harpers Ferry was the beginning of a North-sponsored slave rebellion.

Neither of these situations would have happened, but a little paranoia about the other side is a traditional prelude to wars.

When Lincoln was elected, he had to sneak into Washington to become president. The train bringing him from his home in Illinois went through Maryland, a hotbed of Southern sympathy. The fear that someone would assassinate him before he ever took the oath of office was real.

The Southern states said "we're leaving" and took over most of the federal forts in the South, but Lincoln wouldn't give up Fort Sumter, so the South started shooting. Lincoln was in a tight spot — Southern troops were nearing Washington, and all he had to defend him were a few ceremonial units including the Army band. Lincoln paced the top of Washington's hastily erected fortifications hoping to see reinforcements coming from the north. He even went to the Library of Congress and took out books on how to fight a war.

When the North got an army together, it didn't do them much good at first. The South won most of the battles, fighting on their own territory with good generals. The North barely managed to turn back two Southern invasions, first at the Battle of Antietam and then at the Battle of Gettysburg. That was enough.

Even though the North was fighting for principle (one of the only times in history when an army has fought to free somebody else) while the South was fighting for its own land and slave property (usually worth three to one in fighting morale), the North's determination through four long years of war won the day.

The United States Becomes a Big Dog

With the close of the Civil War in 1865, the U.S. was minus the free help of 4 million slaves but plus a determination to expand all across the continent and beyond. For the rest of the 1800s, mostly Republican presidents rode out economic downturns and political scandals while the U.S. economy steadily caught up with the world's only international superpower: Great Britain.

The U.S. got some technological breaks by inventing most of the useful gadgets in the late 1800s: the electric light, telephone, and mechanical harvester, to name a few. Not held back by the need to support a large military or defend an empire, the U.S. poured all its capital into growth.

Because slavery was no longer an issue, new states got created as soon as they had the population to support a government. San Francisco was well established as the Queen of the Pacific, supported by both California gold and Nevada silver. Railroads spanned the continent, the longest creation of mankind since the Great Wall of China. Ironically, much of the western railroad was built by imported Chinese labor.

By the time the 1900s neared, the U.S. was starting to cast a hungry eye overseas for more territory. The country had bought Alaska from the Russians, stolen the Southwest from Mexico, and settled out the Northwest with the British. The Hawaiian Islands fell like an unguarded flower into Yankee hands. In 1898, the U.S. fought the weak colonial power of Spain to take away Cuba and the far-off Philippines. President Teddy Roosevelt sent the fleet parading around the world. The United States had the glory; coming up next would be the burden of being a world power.

The Reluctant Dragon: U.S. as World Power

The U.S. entered the 1900s with an empire, sort of, and enough military power to scare away other nations from attacking the New World. Most of the United States wanted to mind its own business, but other nations were building up fleets and armies and trolling for empire.

When World War I broke out in Europe in 1914, the United States stayed neutral. That was hard to do, because the British had been mother country to the U.S., and the French had helped the U.S. free itself. They were fighting together against Germany and clearly needed help. Even worse, ships carrying Americans kept getting sunk by German submarines, and the Germans even hatched a crazy plot to take over Mexico. After three years of neutrality, the U.S. finally pitched in the war on the side of the Allies.

It didn't really take much fighting, but the U.S. tipped the balance, and the Allies defeated Germany in what turned out to be Round One of a two-round world war; Round Two (World War II) came later.

U.S. President Wilson had great plans for making a fair peace guaranteed by an international League of Nations that could keep future wars from developing. Oops, Congressional Republicans wouldn't go along with letting the United States help guard the peace. So, after what amounted to a 21-year truce to make more weapons, the major nations (including the United States) plunged into an even more destructive World War II.

This time the reluctant dragon U.S. sat behind its oceans for two years before being awakened by a punch in the nose from Japan. Although the U.S. lost only 2 percent of the people that Russia did fighting World War II, it was enough to convince the country to stay active in world affairs and try to preserve the peace in the future.

U.S. Government as Guardian of the People

Although the U.S. got into the social welfare game after many European countries, the nation has been steadily developing services for its people for over 100 years. Public education grew rapidly after the Civil War. At the end of that conflict, the U.S. had fewer than 100 high schools in the whole country.

By the end of World War I, most towns in the U.S. had schools, and almost all children had at least some high-school education. College was for only a small minority of the elite before World War II. After that time, the GI Bill and the growth of state colleges and universities meant that by the 2000s, most U.S. citizens had the opportunity to get at least some college education.

The watershed for social programs was the Great Depression of the 1930s. As the Depression got worse and people stood in line for bread to feed their children, Republican President Hoover actually said that although the people helped the government, the government shouldn't help the people. The people soon voted him out of office, and Franklin Delano Roosevelt (FDR) took over for the longest presidency in U.S. history.

FDR started a lot of social programs that are still active today, including Social Security, the Federal Deposit Insurance Corporation, the Securities and Exchange Commission, and the Federal Housing Authority.

President Johnson added Medicare and Medicaid in the 1960s and President Nixon supported disability insurance in the 1970s. President Clinton expanded aid to education in the 1990s and President George W. Bush added a prescription drug benefit to Medicare in the 2000s.

With its history of rugged individualism and free enterprise, the U.S. was slower to adopt social programs than many other countries, but eventually the nation began to recognize that services like police, education, and fire protection were more efficient if they were bought "in bulk" by the whole community.

Chapter 27

Ten Important Social and Economic Issues in U.S. History

In This Chapter

▶ Picking up on the big trends in U.S. history

▶ Understanding how social and economic forces provide stability

▶ Seeing how change infiltrates the established social structure

*T*he AP test pays special attention to social and economic trends. These trends both keep society the same and allow room for change.

If you don't think social and economic issues matter, take a look at your friends. Most of them probably come from the same basic social and economic background you do. The United States is the largest, most diverse multiethnic and multiracial society in history, but every one of the U.S. presidents up to 2008 have been a white male, and all but one have been white male Protestants. Economic and social structures tend to keep society the same.

Despite established structures, change happens. In the 1800s, people usually worked 10, 12, or even 14 hours a day. Today, if your boss forced you to work more than eight hours a day without special pay, he'd be breaking the law. In 1950, most Southern restaurants, hotels, and movie theaters didn't allow blacks to even come in the door. Now this behavior would get them in serious trouble and insult all their customers. In 1916, how much a woman cared about politics was irrelevant; in most of the United States, she couldn't even vote. Now women are in office everywhere. Trends show how society changes.

Economic and social trends are an important part of the big AP test. Here are ten of the most important.

Establishing U.S. Diversity

The United States is the most diverse country in the world today, but it was already that way at the time of the Revolution. Diversity helped to build understanding and bring new ideas to the U.S. Every major country in the world has contributed citizens to the United States. The Germans, Irish, Chinese, Polish, Japanese, and Africans have all taken turns being discriminated against and finally celebrated as part of the American experience.

Ethnic discrimination isn't quite over in the United States, but it raises its ugly head less in this country than in any place else on earth. The U.S. actually maintains a diversity visa, which provides a worldwide lottery for 50,000 people from countries that haven't sent many new citizens to the U.S. The people who win the drawing get to live in the United States. More than 7 million hopeful immigrants apply every year.

Defining the American Identity

What does it mean to be an American, a full citizen of the United States?

Along with diversity, the meaning of American Identity has changed through the years. Right after the Revolution, the Naturalization Act increased the time an immigrant had to wait to become a citizen from 5 to 14 long years in an attempt to limit American citizenship to only those who were born in the country. This long wait ended soon after Jefferson became president when the *Alien and Sedition Acts* were largely repealed in 1802.

The *Know-Nothing Party* (1855) briefly elected mayors in Boston, Philadelphia, and San Francisco on a platform of allowing only native-born Protestants to hold office. They had to say they knew nothing when asked because their movement was something of a guilty secret. The platform of the Know-Nothings quickly faded, and most of them joined the Republican Party and fought against slavery.

The 1950s saw an anti-Communist scare that tried to define *real Americans* as those who supported repression of certain political opinions. This behavior was so out of line with the beliefs on which the U.S. was founded that, after a few years without a Communist invasion, even rabid anti-Communists were ashamed of these tactics.

American identity has grown with the country and increasingly represents a bridge anyone can walk across if they believe in freedom.

Creating American Culture

Culture sounds like fat ladies at the opera, but it's really the sum total of all the stories, songs, and ways of living that are important to people in any given time and place. Americans have made culture, and it has also made them. In the colonial period, religious notions of creating the perfect home for a particular religion inspired some settlers to come to America. Movements like the *First Great Awakening* showed people from different denominations and settlements that they shared a common emotional response to God. Culture brings people together by helping them get a broader picture of their place in the world.

Reaction to pressure from the French and the American Indians as well as British authorities built up the idea in American culture of the rough-and-ready frontiersman shown in *The Last of the Mohicans* and in the image of the Minuteman with his rifle and plow. During the Revolution, patriots made it a point of honor to sing "Yankee Doodle Dandy," a song originally intended to mock their backwoods pretensions to civilization:

> *Yankee Doodle went to town, a-riding on a pony,*
>
> *stuck a feather in his cap, and called it macaroni.*

Yankee Doodle was a derogatory name the British used to describe what they believed to be the silly, rustic colonists who thought going to town was the most exciting event of the year. *A-riding* is Scotch-Irish slang and also probably used derogatorily; the fact that Yankee Doodle rides a pony probably implies that he can't afford an actual horse. Similarly, he can't afford a fancy European hat, so he sticks a feather in his old three-cornered hat and calls it macaroni in hopes of associating it with high French and Italian fashion.

American culture may not have been fancy, but it was effective. *Uncle Tom's Cabin* helped ignite the Civil War. Books like *The Jungle,* written by *muckrakers* trying to prevent corruption from being swept under the rug, built support for progressive reform. Women's clubs helped get the vote for females and contributed to the freedom of blacks and the spread of public education. The image of *Uncle Sam* updated the backwoods *Yankee Doodle Dandy* to a kindly uncle — dressed in the American flag — who knew the right (patriotic) thing to do.

Demographics

The United States at the time of the Revolution was a country of young people. Without a hereditary aristocracy, the 2.5 million scattered settlers, mostly farmers, who made up the country at the time of the Revolution, relied on whoever had the energy to get the job done. Jefferson was only 33 when he wrote the Declaration of Independence, and Washington was 43 when he took command of the Continental Army. The 56 delegates to the Continental Congress weren't the richest men in America; those people mostly stayed loyal to the King. The early Congressmen in 1775 showed how mobile people in America already were — more than a quarter of them had lived in two or more states.

At the time of the Revolution, about 60 percent of the Americans were from England with the next biggest groups being African slaves at 15 percent, the Scotch-Irish at 8 percent, and Germans at 7 percent. The California Gold Rush of 1849 populated the West Coast almost overnight with the first 100,000 Americans settlers. The average American lived longer at the time of the Revolution than they did during early heavy industrialization a hundred years later in 1890.

As the U.S. developed, the percent of residents who had been born in other countries grew from 1 percent in 1810 to almost 10 percent before the Civil War. This jump had an unsettling effect (which I discuss in Chapter 24), but it also provided manpower for the North in the conflict with the South. Bad harvests and revolutionary unrest drove people out of Europe, and family ties with earlier immigrants pulled them in to the U.S.

Economics

The U.S. moved from being a prosperous-but-small farming nation at the time of the Revolution to the dominant international economic power with a quarter of the world's money in the early 2000s. Early colonies didn't work out as investments for absentee British investors, who subsequently turned them over to the people who lived there. Colonists learned to support themselves quite well; by the time of the Revolution, average American living standards were better than the ones in England. That gave them something to fight for.

Between 1920 and 1985, the U.S. lived through three depressions and six recessions lasting a total of 12 years during that 65-year period. With minor recessions, the U.S. economy was growing about 75 percent of the time and in decline about 25 percent of the time in the 1900s. The Great Depression of the 1930s was by far the worst, lasting almost six years with a downturn continuing until World War II.

Although the United States has experienced bad economic times, its general growth has been consistently good through the end of slavery, the Industrial Revolution, and the postindustrial information society.

Women's Rights

Even though they made up more than half of the population of the colonies at the time of the Revolution, women exercised just about zero percent of the direct political power. They did have social and economic influence, which are evident in the letter in which Abigail Adams asks her Founding-Father husband, future second President John Adams, to "remember the ladies" when proposing rights for the new nation.

Women got their first higher education in the 1830s and began to get together at gatherings of the *Second Great Awakening*. The *Seneca Falls Conference* of 1848 started the women's movement. Women put their own cause on hold to campaign for the abolition of slavery before the Civil War. In the late 1800s and early 1900s, feminist organization grew until the passage of the *Nineteenth Amendment* in 1920 gave women the right to vote. Women joined the work force temporarily during World War II and permanently starting in the 1960s. By the 1990s, they were a regular part of the armed forces, and by the early 2000s, 75 Congresswomen were in the Capitol.

Racial Equality

Blacks, almost all of them slaves, made up 15 percent of the U.S. population at the time of the Revolution. The next largest minority from a non-English-speaking area was the German Americans at 7 percent of the population. As the United States grew, other significant minorities were the Irish, Hispanics, Polish, Jewish, Chinese, and Japanese. Each of these groups has been subject to discrimination that was in part proportional to their self-identification as a special group within America. As groups have mixed in American society, prejudice has declined.

Blacks gained freedom from slavery after the Civil War but were still subject to Jim Crow laws until the 1960s. The Chinese and Japanese were excluded from immigration in the late 1800s and early 1900s, but have since become an affluent part of the country. In the early 2000s, 10 percent of the largest counties in the United States were *majority minority,* meaning that no one race or ethnic group formed a majority of their population. During the same time, four whole states were minority majority: California, Hawaii, Texas, and New Mexico. Culture, population centers, group membership, and even families began to blend across ethnic groups in the early 2000s.

Reform

The United States was the most democratic country in the world at the time of its founding. Britain had a parliament, but its members were elected by a small minority of the population and tended to represent the interests of the rich landowners. The U.S. achieved universal white male voting without regard to property ownership in 1824, universal male voting in 1870, universal voting for men and women in 1920, and actual universal voting (including blacks) in 1964.

Major reforms included an end to the Alien and Sedition Acts (1802), more voter participation in elections (1824), the beginning of public education (1850), the abolition of slavery (1865), industrial regulation (1900), pure food (1908), the 10-hour workday (1910), election reform with direct election of the Senate (1914), no child labor (1920), the eight-hour workday and union rights (1935), Social Security (1936), the expansion of higher education (1950), civil rights (1964), Medicare and Medicaid (1966), and the beginning of environmental protection (1970).

U.S. Relations with the World

The United States had an international population even during its colonial period, but the early colonies had few resources to trade with the rest of the world. Tobacco proved a best seller, and merchants joined the international slave trade in the triangular exchange of slaves, sugar, rum, and guns.

After the Revolution, the new U.S. backpedaled hard to stay out of foreign wars until the nation fought the War of 1812 over trade rights. The country expanded west thanks to France's going-out-of-business sale of the Louisiana Purchase to the U.S. in 1803. The U.S. limited international involvement in central North America by taking half of Mexico's territory and getting Britain to agree to a compromise border with Canada. Real internationalism by the U.S. started with the Spanish-American War in 1898.

The U.S. tried to stay neutral but was drawn into World War I in Europe. Going back to splendid isolation behind the oceans, the U.S. paid for not helping keep the peace by having to fight World War II against both Germany and Japan. After World War II, the U.S. stepped up to the plate to be a world leader. In the early 2000s, the country began to accept responsibility to work with the rest of the world to limit damage to the earth's environment.

Spirituality

Spirituality is a human's relationship with the higher power it feels shapes and binds the universe together. This relationship can be expressed as a deep personal love of justice, such as that of Thomas Jefferson and Abraham Lincoln. It can also come from active participation in a religious organization, such as those supported by Jimmy Carter and George W. Bush.

The U.S. has been a leader in both forms of the expression of spirituality. Early New England was a haven for the specific religious sects of Puritans and Pilgrims; they drove out and even killed people who disagreed with their religions. Freethinkers like William Penn, Jefferson, Thoreau, and Emerson kept the United States open to personal spirituality even though they themselves didn't go to church. The U.S. has always declined to declare any particular official religion; the very first Amendment to the Constitution separated church and state.

Spiritual revival has played a major role in American history. The *First Great Awakening* (1740) connected people who would later protect the colonies in the French and Indian War and led the new U.S. to freedom in the Revolution. The *Second Great Awakening* (1830) laid the groundwork for the women's movement and for opposition to slavery. Spirituality is a fountain that refreshes committed people.

Chapter 28

The Supreme Court: Ten Greatest Hits

- -

In This Chapter

▶ Understanding the best Court decisions

▶ Following legal opinions as they developed

▶ Seeing how the Supreme Court changed history

- -

*A*s the final touch in your review of the United States' past, here are the ten most important Supreme Court decisions. The Supreme Court is the last word on the law of the land in the United States, and these ten cases are part of its claim to fame.

Being able to reference Supreme Court decisions is impressive evidence of your mastery of U.S. History on the AP exam. Because you can't make much money teaching history, who knows — you may want to be a lawyer.

Marbury versus Madison (1803)

In this early decision, the Supreme Court super Chief Justice John Marshall found that the Supremes have the final word on whether any law is constitutional. The Court refused to order that Marbury be awarded a federal legal job because the law he was using wasn't covered by the Constitution.

McCulloch versus Maryland (1819)

This case established that federal law trumps state law. Maryland wanted to slap a state tax on the National Bank established by the federal government. John Marshall found that the feds had the power to set up a bank under the *Necessary and Proper Clause* of the Constitution and that states could no more tax the federal bank than they could tax the army.

Gibbons versus Ogden (1824)

This decision states that only the feds can regulate business between the states. New York tried to set steamboat guru Robert Fulton as the only guy who could run power boats between New York and New Jersey (or license others, like Ogden, to do so). Not fair, said the court; anything that runs between states is the business of the feds. When they got around to it 140 years later, this principle allowed Congress to require civil rights in planes, trains, hotels, and restaurants.

West Coast Hotel Co. versus Parrish (1937)

This decision during the heart of the Great Depression allowed the federal government to set minimum wages for work in private industry, something the Court had previously prohibited. Parrish was a poor chambermaid whose hotel refused to pay her the minimum wage.

Brown versus Board of Education (1954)

Separate and not equal was the unspoken rule of the land before this decision came along. It set off the Civil Rights movement by declaring that segregated schools for different races had to go. Brown, an African American railroad worker, had a third-grade daughter who had been forced to travel miles to a segregated black school when a white-only public school was right in her neighborhood.

Gideon versus Wainwright (1963)

Gideon was a poor prisoner who was barely literate. In a touching, handwritten appeal, he asked the Supreme Court for help. The Supremes found that states have a duty to supply a lawyer for people who can't afford one. Gideon got a new trial and was found innocent.

Griswold versus Connecticut (1965)

This case established the *right to privacy* that kept the states from regulating personal sexual behavior that hurts no one. Griswold had been fined by Connecticut for running a birth-control clinic.

Miranda versus Arizona (1966)

Miranda was a Mexican American with little education who confessed under police questioning without being read his now-famous rights to remain silent and to have an attorney. Even people being arrested in totalitarian countries now sometimes demand police read their Miranda rights like they saw on TV. They don't know that because they're not from the U.S., they don't necessarily have these rights.

Roe versus Wade (1973)

The Court held that women have a privacy right to decide whether to have an abortion; states can't prohibit this birth-control procedure. Although many women favor the right to choose, conservative religious groups oppose abortion. The Court has been a battleground ever since.

United States versus Nixon (1974)

President Nixon had to turn over tape recordings as ordered by a federal court. The Court found that even the president has to follow the law; he can't hide behind *executive privilege.* Nixon, supported by a few of his Republican allies, had tried to argue that he didn't have to turn over evidence of his own wrongdoing to Congress because as president he had special rights. The Supreme Court held that the president is not above the law. Shortly after this ruling, Nixon resigned to avoid impeachment.

Index

Japanese Americans, 238

Jay's Treaty (1794), British-U.S. treaty, 130

Jazz Age, 219–220

Jefferson, Thomas
3rd U.S. president (1801-1808), 131–133
Declaration of Independence, 119–120, 353
first Cabinet member, 128
Kentucky and Virginia Resolutions (1798), 131
opposition to slavery, 107
slavery position, 157
strict-constructionist, 129
Virginia Statute for Religious Freedom (1786), 123

Jehovah's Witnesses, 243

jeremiad, Puritan sermons, 101

Jews, Holocaust atrocities, 243

Jim Crow laws (1890), 187–188

Job Corps (1965), 266

Johns Hopkins University, 182

Johnson, Andrew, 171, 176–179

Johnson, Lyndon B., 262–263, 265–266, 358

Joint Chiefs of Staff, 250

journalism, colonies, 108

juku, Japanese cram schools, 35

The Jungle (1906) (Sinclair) 191, 206

• K •

Kaine, Tim, Gabriel's pardon, 158

Kansas, 165, 231

Kansas-Nebraska Act (1854), 162, 165, 355

KDKA, commercial radio, 221

Kellogg-Briand Pact (1928), 225

Kelly, Florence, 189

Kennan, George, 249

Kennedy, John F., 258–263

Kennedy, Robert, 268

Kent State University, 269

Kentucky and Virginia Resolutions, 131

key concepts, 44

key terms, 16

key words, 70, 71

kinesthetic movement, study, 33

King Henry VIII (1533), 94

King Philip's War, 98–99, 352

King William's War (1690), 112

King, Martin Luther Jr, 256–257, 264–265

Kitchen Cabinet, Andrew Jackson, 142

kiva (ceremonial chamber), 90

Knights of Labor, 181, 195

Know-Nothing Party, 130, 360

Knox, Henry, 128

Korea, 251–252

Korean War (1952), 251–252

Korematsu v. United States, 238

Kosciusko, Thaddeus, 124

Ku Klux Klan (KKK), 178, 218–219, 264

Kuwait, 277

Kyoto Protocol, 281

• L •

La Follette Seamen's Act, 210

La Salle (1682), 105

labor unions
1840, 152
AFL (American Federation of Labor), 195
blue collar workers, 246
Chicago's Haymarket Square, 195
closed shops, 246
Congress of Industrial Organizations (CIO), 230
Coxey's Army (1894), 195
Eugene V. Debs, 195
Greenback Labor Party, 196
growth period, 195
Knights of Labor, 181
National Labor Relations Board (NLRB), 230
National Labor Union, 181
Norris-La Guardia Anti-Injunction Act (1932), 226
Pullman strike (1894), 195
Smith-Connally Anti-Strike Act (1934), 239
Taft-Hartley Act (1947), 246
union shops, 246

Lancaster Turnpike, 151

Land Ordinance of 1785, 125

land-grant colleges, 182

Lane Theological Seminary, 159

Laos, 261–262

Latin America, 227, 234, 262

Latinos, 284

Lawson, Thomas
Frenzied Finance (1905), 205

League of Nations, 214–215, 357

League of Peace and Power. *See* Iroquois Confederacy

LEAST troll, multiple-choice questions, 47

Leaves of Grass (1855) (Whitman), 155

Lebanon, U.S., 274, 276

Lecompton Constitution (1857) Kansas, 165

Lee, Mother Ann, Shaker, 152

Lee, Robert E, 168–170

legislative bodies, colonies, 110

Leisler, Jacob, 99–100

Lend-Lease Bill (1941), 236–237

Lewis and Clark expedition, 132

Lewis, Meriwether (1804), 132

Lewis, Sinclair, 223

Lexington and Concord battles, 117

The Liberator (1831), William Lloyd Garrison, 24, 159

Liberty Loan drives, 213

libraries, American colonies, 108

life spans, 100, 283–284

Lincoln, Abraham, 165, 167–171, 356

Lindbergh, Charles, 221, 236

linotype (1885), newspaper, 190

literacy, Gilded Age, 182

literature
19th century, 190–191
American colonies, 108
muckraking, 205

Little Rock Nine (1957), 257

Little Women (1868) (Alcott), 155

London Economic Conference (1933), 233–234

London, Jack
The Call of the Wild (1903), 191

The Lonely Crowd (Riesman), 254

Long Drive, 184–185

Long, Huey P. (1934), 231

Longfellow, Henry Wadsworth (1850), 155

lotteries, *Cohens v. Virginia* (1821), 139–140

Louisiana, 113

Louisiana Purchase, 132

Lowell, Massachusetts, Lowell girls (1813), 144

Lower Counties of Pennsylvania, Delaware, 97

Loyalist colonists, 120–121

Loyalty Review Board (1947), 250–251

Luck and Pluck (1869) (Alger), 182

lumberjack battles, 159

Lusitania, British liner, 211

Luther, Martin (1517), 93

Lutheran religion, 104–105

Lyrics of Lowly Life (1896) (Dunbar), 188

• M •

MacArthur, Douglas, 227, 241, 251–252

Macon's Bill No. 2 (1810), 133

Madison, James, 127–128, 131, 133

Magellan, Ferdinand, 89

Main Street (1920) (Lewis), 223

Maine, 140, 152, 159

maize, early corn variant, 81

Malcolm X, 264

Malinche, La, 89–90

Depression causes, 225–226
Dixiecrat Party (1948), 256
Electoral College, 280
family legacies, 277
Free Soil Party, 161, 196
Green Party, 280
Greenback Labor Party (1878), 196
initiative system, 206
Moral Majority (1980), 274
neo-conservatives (1985), 274
Operation Wetback, 255
political parties formed, 130
Populist Party, 192, 196–197
Progressives (1910), 206
Radical Republicans, 176
Redeemer groups, 177
Southern Democratic Party,
   196–197
spoils system, 142
Tammany Hall scandal, 180
Whig Party-Know-Nothing Party
   coalition (1856), 196
politics and citizenship, AP Test
   theme, 24
politics and economics at the end
   of the 20th century, 27
Polk, James, President, 160
Pontiac, Ottawa Indian, 114
Poor Richard's Almanack
   (Franklin), 108
Pope's Rebellion (Pueblo Revolt) of
   1680, 90
popular sovereignty, 161
Populism and Progressivism, 26
Populist Party, 192, 196–197
Port Royal, Caribbean piracy, 90
Portugal, 88
potato famine (1845), 149
poverty, colonies, 106–107
Powderly, Terence, 189, 195
practice tests, study strategies, 30
pre-Columbian era – 1789, 22
Pre-Columbian Societies, 25
Presbyterian religion, 104
Presley, Elvis, 253
preventative intervention,
   Theodore Roosevelt, 204
Princeton, New Light school, 109
prisons, 284
private colleges, 10–11
private enterprise, antitrust, 194
Proclamation of 1763, 114, 353
progressive relaxation, pretest
   anxiety, 36
Progressives (1910), 206
Prohibition, Volstead Act, 220
prompts, essay questions, 66, 70
proofreading, PAT method
   element, 58
Protestant Reformation, 93
PSAT, College Board test, 10
public university, 10–11

Public Works Administration
   (PWA), 229
Pueblo Revolt (Pope's Rebellion)
   of 1680, 90
Puerto Rico, 200
Pullman strike (1894), 195
Pullman, railroad cars, 184
Pure Food and Drug Act (1906), 205
Puritans, 94–95, 101, 109

• **Q** •

Quakers, 96–97, 109
Quartering Act (1765), 115–116
Quebec Act, 117
Quebec, Canada, 91, 113
Queen Anne's War (1710), 112
Question Troll, 44–45
Quiet Ears, pretest anxiety, 37

• **R** •

racial equality, 362
Radical Republicans (1866), 176
railroads
   Adamson Act (1916), 209
   Elkins Act (1902), 207
   Esch-Cummins Transportation
      Act (1920), 225
   Hepburn Act (1906), 207
   industrial growth factor, 145
   Interstate Commerce Act
      (1887), 194
   Northern Securities Company
      (1904), 207
   Pullman strike (1894), 195
   span country, 356
   spanning continent, 183–184
   standard width rails, 184
   steel rails, 184
   stock watering scam, 184
   time zones, 188
   transportation, 151
   Wabash Cases (1886), 194
   worker uprisings, 188
Raleigh, Sir Walter, 91, 97
Ramona (Jackson), 198
Reagan, Ronald, 234, 272–276
Reconstruction, 26, 175–179
Reconstruction Finance
      Corporation (RFC) Act
      (1932), 226–227
recording industry, 283
Red Scare (1920), 217–218
Redeemer groups, 177
reform, AP Test theme, 24
reforms, 362–363
Regulators' Uprising (1764), 104
relaxation, pretest anxiety, 36
religion
   Act of Toleration (1694), 97
   American colonies, 109–110

AP Test theme, 24
Congregationalist, 123
First Great Awakening, 109
Half-Way Covenant, 109
New Light preachers, 109
Old Light ministers, 109
Reform, and Renaissance in
   Antebellum America, 25
Second Great Awakening,
   109, 153–154
theory of evolution, 182–183
Transcendentalism, 147, 155
Religious Society of Friends, 96–97
Remember-the-Ladies letter, Abigail
   Adams, 124
Remington, Frederick, 199
Republic of Liberia, 158
republican motherhood,
   124, 154, 189
Republicans, Contract with
   America (1994), 279
retirement, Social Security
   Administration (1935), 230
reviews, study strategies, 34
rewards, study strategies, 34
Reynolds v. Sims (1964), 263
Rhineland, 236
Rhode Island, 95
Richardson, Henry, 190
Riesman, David
   The Lonely Crowd, 254
Rills, Jacob
   How the Other Half Lives
      (1890), 191
Roanoke Island, 91
Roaring '20s, anything goes, 220
Robinson, Jackie, 256
rock-and-roll, 1950s music, 253
Rockefeller, John D., 193–194
Roe v. Wade (1973), 263, 366
Rolfe, John, 97, 352
Roosevelt Corollary to the Monroe
   Doctrine (1905), 204
Roosevelt, Franklin D.
   Atlantic Charter (1941), 237
   GI Bill (1944), 247
   Good Neighbor Policy
      (1933), 234
   isolationism, 233–235
   New Deal, 227–230
   preparing for war, 236–237
   President (1932), 227
   social programs, 357
Roosevelt, Theodore, 200, 202–208
Roth, Philip
   Goodbye, Columbus, 254
Rough Riders, 200
rule of reason, Supreme Court
   decision, 208
Russia, 217–218, 277. *See also*
      Soviet Union
Rutgers, New Light school, 109

• S •

Sacajawea, Lewis and Clark expedition, 132
Sacco and Vanzetti (1921), Red Scare victims, 218
"Sacred Cod," Massachusetts House of Representatives, 110
sailors, 210
Saint-Gaudens, Augustus, 191
Salem Witch Trials (1692), 101
Salinger, J. D.
  Catcher in the Rye, 254
SALT II (1979), 271
Sand Creek, massacre, 186
Sanger, Margaret (1921), 220
Santa Fe, New Mexico, 91
SAT, College Board test, 10
Savannah (1819), steamship, 144
scalawags (1870), 178
The Scarlet Letter (1850) (Hawthorne), 156
schools, 33–34, 107. *See also* education
Schrank, John, 208
Scopes Monkey Trial, 223
Scopes, John, 223
Scotch-Irish, 103–104
Scott, Dred (1857), 166–167
sculptures, Augustus Saint-Gaudens, 191
searches, AP Credit Policy, 20–21
secession, Civil War cause, 169
Second Amendment, 128
Second Bull Run (1862), 169
Second Continental Congress (1775), 119
Second Great Awakening
  religious attitudes, 109
  religious diversity, 153–154
  spirituality, 146
  women's rights, 362
Securities and Exchange Commission (SEC) (1934), 229, 357
Security Council, United Nations, 249
security, AP Test, 21–22
Sedition Act (1918), 212
self-quizzes, study strategies, 28
Seneca Falls Convention, 124, 152, 154, 362
Seneca, Iroquois Confederacy, 84
Sergeant York, World War I hero, 214
servant workers, 99
Servicemen's Readjustment Act of 1944, 247
Seven Years' War, 112–114
Seventeenth Amendment (1913), 206
Seventh Amendment, 128

Shah of Iran, Iranian hostage crisis, 271
The Shame of the Cities (1902) (Steffens), 205
shantytowns, Hoovervilles, 227
sharecropping, 178
Shawnee Indians, Tecumseh, 133
Shays' Rebellion, 126–127
Sherman Anti-Trust Act, 194
Sherman, William Tecumseh, 170
shipping, Merchant Marine Act (1920), 225
Shockley, William, Japanese invasion, 243
Sierra Club, John Muir, 207
Silent Spring (Carson), 270
Sinclair, Upton
  The Jungle (1906), 191, 206
Singer sewing machine, 150
singers, rock-and-roll, 253
single men, work force, 152
Sioux Indians, 185–186
Sister Carrie (1900) (Dreiser), 191
sit-in demonstrations, 257, 264
Six Nations. *See* Iroquois Confederacy
Sixteenth Amendment, 209
Sixth Amendment, 128
Slaughterhouse Five (Vonnegut), 254
slave rebellion (1791), Haiti, 124
slavery. *See also* slaves; freed slaves
  Compromise of 1850, 161–162, 355
  cotton factor, 145–146
  cotton gin, 355
  distribution throughout the New World, 100
  Dred Scott decision (1857), 355
  economic factors, 157
  Emancipation Proclamation (1863), 169–170
  free blacks, 157–158
  Fugitive Slave Law, 161–162
  importation abolished, 355
  Kansas-Nebraska Act of 1854, 355
  Missouri Compromise (1820), 140, 355
  Northern abolition, 158–159
  Northwest Ordinance (1787), 125, 355
  poverty conditions, 107
  religious denomination splits, 153–154
  revolts, 158
  southern states, 352
  Stono Rebellion (1739), 100, 105
  synonymous with power, 146
  Thirteenth Amendment, 175
  Wilmot Proviso (1846), 160
slavery and its legacies in North America, AP Test theme, 24

slaves. *See also* slavery; freed slaves
  American Revolution, 121
  Freedmen's Bureau (1865), 176
  importation deadline, 124
  Three-Fifths Compromise (1787), 123, 127
  Union Army enlistment, 170
Smith, John, Jamestown, Virginia, 91–92
Smith-Connally Anti-Strike Act (1934), 239
Smoot-Hawley Tariff, 226
social and economic issues, 24, 360–363
Social Darwinists (1875), 183
social history, AP Test, 13–14
social programs, 357–358
Social Security, 283–284, 357
Social Security Administration (1935), 230
society and culture, 20th century, 27
Soil Conservation and Domestic Allotment Act (1936), 229
Sons of Liberty (1765), 116
The Sound and the Fury (1929) (Faulkner), 223
sounds, auditory learners, 33
South Africa, 277
South America, Roosevelt Corollary, 204
South Carolina, 97–98, 100, 105, 143
South Dakota (1890), 197
Southern Christian Leadership Conference, 265
Southern Democratic Party, 196–197
Southern states, 176–179
Southwestern territory, 156, 160
Soviet Union. *See also* Russia
  Berlin Wall (1961), 260–261
  Cold War begins, 248–251
  collapses, 277
  Communism decline, 275–276
  containment policy, 249
  Cuban Missile Crisis, 260
  declares war on Japan, 243
  German invasion (1941), 237
  Hungary uprising (1956), 255
  MAD (Mutually Assured Destruction), 261
  Mikhail Gorbechev, 276
  Nuclear Test Ban Treaty (1963), 262
  recognized in 1933, 234
  SALT (Strategic Arms Limitation Talks), 269
  SALT II (1979), 271
  Sputnik (1957), 258
  Warsaw Pact, 250
  World War II battles, 242
space race, 258, 260

BUSINESS, CAREERS & PERSONAL FINANCE

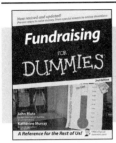

0-7645-9847-3

0-7645-2431-3

Also available:

- Business Plans Kit For Dummies
  0-7645-9794-9
- Economics For Dummies
  0-7645-5726-2
- Grant Writing For Dummies
  0-7645-8416-2
- Home Buying For Dummies
  0-7645-5331-3
- Managing For Dummies
  0-7645-1771-6
- Marketing For Dummies
  0-7645-5600-2

- Personal Finance For Dummies
  0-7645-2590-5*
- Resumes For Dummies
  0-7645-5471-9
- Selling For Dummies
  0-7645-5363-1
- Six Sigma For Dummies
  0-7645-6798-5
- Small Business Kit For Dummies
  0-7645-5984-2
- Starting an eBay Business For Dummies
  0-7645-6924-4
- Your Dream Career For Dummies
  0-7645-9795-7

HOME & BUSINESS COMPUTER BASICS

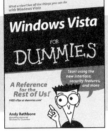

0-470-05432-8

0-471-75421-8

Also available:

- Cleaning Windows Vista For Dummies
  0-471-78293-9
- Excel 2007 For Dummies
  0-470-03737-7
- Mac OS X Tiger For Dummies
  0-7645-7675-5
- MacBook For Dummies
  0-470-04859-X
- Macs For Dummies
  0-470-04849-2
- Office 2007 For Dummies
  0-470-00923-3

- Outlook 2007 For Dummies
  0-470-03830-6
- PCs For Dummies
  0-7645-8958-X
- Salesforce.com For Dummies
  0-470-04893-X
- Upgrading & Fixing Laptops For Dummies
  0-7645-8959-8
- Word 2007 For Dummies
  0-470-03658-3
- Quicken 2007 For Dummies
  0-470-04600-7

FOOD, HOME, GARDEN, HOBBIES, MUSIC & PETS

0-7645-8404-9

0-7645-9904-6

Also available:

- Candy Making For Dummies
  0-7645-9734-5
- Card Games For Dummies
  0-7645-9910-0
- Crocheting For Dummies
  0-7645-4151-X
- Dog Training For Dummies
  0-7645-8418-9
- Healthy Carb Cookbook For Dummies
  0-7645-8476-6
- Home Maintenance For Dummies
  0-7645-5215-5

- Horses For Dummies
  0-7645-9797-3
- Jewelry Making & Beading For Dummies
  0-7645-2571-9
- Orchids For Dummies
  0-7645-6759-4
- Puppies For Dummies
  0-7645-5255-4
- Rock Guitar For Dummies
  0-7645-5356-9
- Sewing For Dummies
  0-7645-6847-7
- Singing For Dummies
  0-7645-2475-5

INTERNET & DIGITAL MEDIA

0-470-04529-9

0-470-04894-8

Also available:

- Blogging For Dummies
  0-471-77084-1
- Digital Photography For Dummies
  0-7645-9802-3
- Digital Photography All-in-One Desk Reference For Dummies
  0-470-03743-1
- Digital SLR Cameras and Photography For Dummies
  0-7645-9803-1
- eBay Business All-in-One Desk Reference For Dummies
  0-7645-8438-3
- HDTV For Dummies
  0-470-09673-X

- Home Entertainment PCs For Dummies
  0-470-05523-5
- MySpace For Dummies
  0-470-09529-6
- Search Engine Optimization For Dummies
  0-471-97998-8
- Skype For Dummies
  0-470-04891-3
- The Internet For Dummies
  0-7645-8996-2
- Wiring Your Digital Home For Dummies
  0-471-91830-X

* Separate Canadian edition also available
† Separate U.K. edition also available

Available wherever books are sold. For more information or to order direct: U.S. customers visit www.dummies.com or call 1-877-762-2974. U.K. customers visit www.wileyeurope.com or call 0800 243407. Canadian customers visit www.wiley.ca or call 1-800-567-4797.

SPORTS, FITNESS, PARENTING, RELIGION & SPIRITUALITY

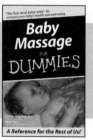

0-471-76871-5   0-7645-7841-3

Also available:

✔Catholicism For Dummies
0-7645-5391-7
✔Exercise Balls For Dummies
0-7645-5623-1
✔Fitness For Dummies
0-7645-7851-0
✔Football For Dummies
0-7645-3936-1
✔Judaism For Dummies
0-7645-5299-6
✔Potty Training For Dummies
0-7645-5417-4
✔Buddhism For Dummies
0-7645-5359-3

✔Pregnancy For Dummies
0-7645-4483-7 †
✔Ten Minute Tone-Ups For Dummies
0-7645-7207-5
✔NASCAR For Dummies
0-7645-7681-X
✔Religion For Dummies
0-7645-5264-3
✔Soccer For Dummies
0-7645-5229-5
✔Women in the Bible For Dummies
0-7645-8475-8

TRAVEL

0-7645-7749-2   0-7645-6945-7

Also available:

✔Alaska For Dummies
0-7645-7746-8
✔Cruise Vacations For Dummies
0-7645-6941-4
✔England For Dummies
0-7645-4276-1
✔Europe For Dummies
0-7645-7529-5
✔Germany For Dummies
0-7645-7823-5
✔Hawaii For Dummies
0-7645-7402-7

✔Italy For Dummies
0-7645-7386-1
✔Las Vegas For Dummies
0-7645-7382-9
✔London For Dummies
0-7645-4277-X
✔Paris For Dummies
0-7645-7630-5
✔RV Vacations For Dummies
0-7645-4442-X
✔Walt Disney World & Orlando
For Dummies
0-7645-9660-8

GRAPHICS, DESIGN & WEB DEVELOPMENT

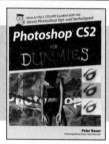

0-7645-8815-X   0-7645-9571-7

Also available:

✔3D Game Animation For Dummies
0-7645-8789-7
✔AutoCAD 2006 For Dummies
0-7645-8925-3
✔Building a Web Site For Dummies
0-7645-7144-3
✔Creating Web Pages For Dummies
0-470-08030-2
✔Creating Web Pages All-in-One Desk
Reference For Dummies
0-7645-4345-8
✔Dreamweaver 8 For Dummies
0-7645-9649-7

✔InDesign CS2 For Dummies
0-7645-9572-5
✔Macromedia Flash 8 For Dummies
0-7645-9691-8
✔Photoshop CS2 and Digital
Photography For Dummies
0-7645-9580-6
✔Photoshop Elements 4 For Dummies
0-471-77483-9
✔Syndicating Web Sites with RSS Feeds
For Dummies
0-7645-8848-6
✔Yahoo! SiteBuilder For Dummies
0-7645-9800-7

NETWORKING, SECURITY, PROGRAMMING & DATABASES

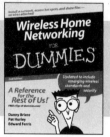

0-7645-7728-X   0-471-74940-0

Also available:

✔Access 2007 For Dummies
0-470-04612-0
✔ASP.NET 2 For Dummies
0-7645-7907-X
✔C# 2005 For Dummies
0-7645-9704-3
✔Hacking For Dummies
0-470-05235-X
✔Hacking Wireless Networks
For Dummies
0-7645-9730-2
✔Java For Dummies
0-470-08716-1

✔Microsoft SQL Server 2005 For Dummies
0-7645-7755-7
✔Networking All-in-One Desk Reference
For Dummies
0-7645-9939-9
✔Preventing Identity Theft For Dummies
0-7645-7336-5
✔Telecom For Dummies
0-471-77085-X
✔Visual Studio 2005 All-in-One Desk
Reference For Dummies
0-7645-9775-2
✔XML For Dummies
0-7645-8845-1

HEALTH & SELF-HELP

0-7645-8450-2

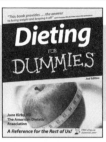

0-7645-4149-8

Also available:

Bipolar Disorder For Dummies
0-7645-8451-0

Chemotherapy and Radiation
For Dummies
0-7645-7832-4

Controlling Cholesterol For Dummies
0-7645-5440-9

Diabetes For Dummies
0-7645-6820-5* †

Divorce For Dummies
0-7645-8417-0 †

Fibromyalgia For Dummies
0-7645-5441-7

Low-Calorie Dieting For Dummies
0-7645-9905-4

Meditation For Dummies
0-471-77774-9

Osteoporosis For Dummies
0-7645-7621-6

Overcoming Anxiety For Dummies
0-7645-5447-6

Reiki For Dummies
0-7645-9907-0

Stress Management For Dummies
0-7645-5144-2

EDUCATION, HISTORY, REFERENCE & TEST PREPARATION

0-7645-8381-6

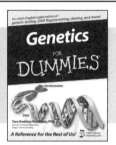

0-7645-9554-7

Also available:

The ACT For Dummies
0-7645-9652-7

Algebra For Dummies
0-7645-5325-9

Algebra Workbook For Dummies
0-7645-8467-7

Astronomy For Dummies
0-7645-8465-0

Calculus For Dummies
0-7645-2498-4

Chemistry For Dummies
0-7645-5430-1

Forensics For Dummies
0-7645-5580-4

Freemasons For Dummies
0-7645-9796-5

French For Dummies
0-7645-5193-0

Geometry For Dummies
0-7645-5324-0

Organic Chemistry I For Dummies
0-7645-6902-3

The SAT I For Dummies
0-7645-7193-1

Spanish For Dummies
0-7645-5194-9

Statistics For Dummies
0-7645-5423-9

Get smart @ dummies.com®

- **Find a full list of Dummies titles**
- **Look into loads of FREE on-site articles**
- **Sign up for FREE eTips e-mailed to you weekly**
- **See what other products carry the Dummies name**
- **Shop directly from the Dummies bookstore**
- **Enter to win new prizes every month!**

* Separate Canadian edition also available
† Separate U.K. edition also available

Available wherever books are sold. For more information or to order direct: U.S. customers visit www.dummies.com or call 1-877-762-2974.
U.K. customers visit www.wileyeurope.com or call 0800 243407. Canadian customers visit www.wiley.ca or call 1-800-567-4797.